web
Design

Concepts and Best Practices

Information Superhighway

EMCParadigm
PUBLISHING

Carolee Cameron

Senior Editor	Christine Hurney
Editorial Assistant	Susan Capecchi
Production Team	Jim Patterson, Desiree Faulkner
Copy Editor	Julie A. McNamee
Cover and Text Designer	Jennifer Wreisner
Desktop Production Specialist	Jennifer Wreisner
Illustrator	Colin Hayes Illustration
Indexer	Larry Harrison

Photo Credits: page 4, Courtesy of A/P Wide World Photos; page 54, © Jose Luis Pelaez, Inc./CORBIS.

Publishing Management Team
George Provol, Publisher; Janice Johnson, Director of Product Development; Tony Galvin, Acquisitions Editor; Lori Landwer, Marketing Manager; Shelley Clubb, Electronic Design and Production Manager

Library of Congress Cataloging-in-Publication Data

Cameron, Carolee.
    Web design : concepts and best practices / by Carolee Cameron.
        p. cm.
    Includes index.
    ISBN 0-7638-1654-X
    1. Web sites--Design. I. Title.

TK5105.888 C353 2004
005.7'2--dc21   2002040842

Text ISBN: 0-7638-1654-X
Order Number: 01582

© 2004 by Paradigm Publishing Inc.
    Published by **EMC**Paradigm
    875 Montreal Way
    St. Paul, MN 55102

    (800) 535-6865
    E-mail: educate@emcp.com
    Web site: www.emcp.com

Contents

Preface

No other professional career has come close to matching the precipitous rise of Web design—from the humblest of beginnings in the mid-1990s to remarkable levels of sophistication and artistry today. The diverse individuals, from a surprising range of backgrounds, who have flocked to Web design and development or added Web design to their skills have pushed the profession from producing the most rudimentary of Web sites in the early days to currently developing sites that accomplish impressive levels of interpersonal engagement.

Web technology has progressed rapidly, with new software, new programming models, and new hardware constantly appearing and changing the possibilities for Web designers. Because of the new tools, merely writing an HTML file and uploading it to a Web-hosting service is no longer a measure of Web design competence. To achieve the levels of sophistication now required for effective Web sites, new students will benefit from first learning the fundamentals of design by studying *Web Design: Concepts and Best Practices*.

The basic questions of Web design include:

- What does a good Web site do?
- What objectives should a Web site have?
- How can a Web site meet these objectives?
- What are the best practices for achieving these objectives?

Unfortunately, these questions are often overlooked in the first courses that design students take. Without a solid understanding of the fundamentals of Web design, new designers are doomed to the pitfalls that more experienced developers have learned to avoid. In the process of learning in this way, the sites can lack professionalism and, worse, frustrate their users and disappoint their owners. Web design can be compared to a musical performance: without grounding in the fundamentals of music and musical expression, no instrumentalist can expect to play musically, even if all of the notes are played "correctly." Likewise, without grounding in the fundamentals of good Web design, no Web designer can produce sites that take advantage of the best aspects of this revolutionary medium.

Web Design: Concepts and Best Practices introduces a broad range of essential concepts and practices that form the bedrock of professional Web design. These concepts and practices aim primarily to encourage independent, critical thinking on the part of designers. This book does not specify prescriptions for what to do in every design situation. Rather, this text grounds students in the concepts critical to Web design: the parameters, principles, guidelines, and standards researched or adopted by some of the most influential professional organizations and designers. These guidelines are not introduced as hard-and-fast rules but are discussed to encourage students to critically evaluate the sites they visit as well as those they produce. Chapter activities require students to evaluate sites according to the parameters and guidelines introduced in the chapters. Thus, the material discussed in the chapters is reinforced with evaluative activities.

Special Features

This book discusses the historical, technical, and practical aspects of Web design, and teaches fundamental Web design concepts. The following features are included:

- **CyberVisits** Chapter-opening features that showcase the work and thinking of professional Web designers.
- **Web Terms** Highlights and defines important chapter terms. These terms are reinforced with terminology exercises on this book's Internet Resource Center (IRC) at www.emcp.com/.
- **Web Links** Encourage students to investigate the Web for examples of the material being discussed in the text and to look for additional resources.
- **Input/Refresh** Essays that expand on a particular topic of relevance to the material in the chapter. With a combination of both new information and previously discussed information in a new context, these deepen the learner's perspective.
- **Do You Know?** A boxed feature in question-and-answer format that discusses a historical topic of relevance to the chapter or that clarifies a particular point in the discussion.
- **Web Activities** Require students to practice applying the concepts being taught in a particular section. These activities become slightly more challenging with each chapter, and they encourage students to use their knowledge of good Web design to solve complex design problems.
- **Topics Roundtable** Lists of questions intended to stimulate thought and discussion on the chapter topic.
- **Window to the Web** Composed of two parts: Technical Walk-Through and Design Project. The Technical Walk-Throughs introduce essential HTML skills, concepts, and step-by-step activities that allow students to practice and apply HTML skills. The Design Projects encourage students to apply design concepts as they build their own Web resource site. Each Design Project requires students to conduct research; the research reports form the foundation of their Window to the Web resource sites. The Window to the Web resource sites serve as a demonstration of student expertise to show to prospective employers and will become a resource for work in the Web design profession. The Window to the Web resource sites will include:
  - Information about free host sites, including a comparison of features
  - Sources of graphic resources (copyright free), including clip art, backgrounds, animations, and buttons
  - Sources of Web site tools such as counters, guestbooks, and dynamic scripts
  - Information on good Web page design
  - Favorites lists with links
  - Instructors can suggest additional topics and ideas for expanding these projects. These Design Projects provide students with the opportunity to demonstrate their skills and creativity.

Chapter Topics

This book covers historical, technical, theoretical, and practical issues of the Web design profession:

- Chapter 1 discusses the technical breakthroughs that led to the development of the World Wide Web and claims that, in addition to technological change, the human desire for communication and exchange with others is a force that has shaped the Web into its present form.
- Chapter 2 surveys what the Web designer does and discusses the types of talents that Web design requires.
- Chapter 3 introduces the parameters by which Web sites can be judged and the principles that support them. The chapter also discusses the concept of Web generations as benchmarks by which Web sites can be evaluated.
- Chapter 4 highlights two major issues in Web design—usability and accessibility— and provides commentary on two existing sets of guidelines that can help designers decide how to build sites that qualify as usable and accessible.
- Chapter 5 begins discussion of the Web design process, focusing on the preliminary stage, in which designers gather information, conduct research, create their first design ideas, and organize their work.
- Chapter 6 continues coverage of the Web design process, concentrating on planning information architecture, preparing material for a Web site, and creating the first working versions of a site.
- Chapter 7 finishes the discussion of the Web design process, covering the launching and testing phases especially and also discussing plans that need to be made for maintenance and periodic review. The final section discusses professional obligations—copyright and security, for instance—that should be of concern to all designers throughout the design process.

Student Resources

Besides providing terminology exercises for each chapter, this text's Internet Resource Center (IRC) at www.emcp.com/ provides additional projects, review exercises, resource links, and chapter pretests. In addition, the IRC contains Web-based career descriptions.

Instructor Resources

The password-protected instructor side of this book's IRC provides chapter tests and a final exam as well as suggested syllabi, grading plans, course-level teaching strategies, chapter-level teaching hints, and model answers for chapter activities.

About the Author

Carolee Walton Cameron is a curriculum designer, specializing in how to apply instructional theory to ensure learning success. She was the project leader for the start-up of Greenville Technical College's college-online.com, and now is the course designer and instructor for the college-online Web Design Certificate program. Her degrees and certificates include a BA in Psychology (Duke University), and MA in Instruction Systems Design (UNC, Chapel Hill), a Certificate in Expert Systems (Georgia Tech), and an EdD in Instruction Technology and Distance Education (Nova Southeastern University).

Acknowledgements

My deep appreciation goes first to my sons, Ken and Brian Lane, for taking on writing tasks to make the book come together as it did, when it did. They supported this project with encouragement, perspective, high spirits, contagious enthusiasm, and, at the point when these were most needed, words. Thank you, too, to my father, Dr. Wesley W. Walton, who listened endlessly to the latest accounts of progress, and miraculously remained enthralled with every detail and challenge of the project until the very end. Thanks to Jan Johnson of EMCParadigm, in whom I found a kindred spirit, a fellow instructional designer who understood all that I had hoped to accomplish with this book. Thanks to Christine Hurney of EMCParadigm, who took the book to a level beyond my initial vision of what it could be. And thanks to David Severtson and John Baker for their insight and diligence in improving the readability and usability of this text, making it accessible for all learners. These were the players who made this book come into being, and to whom I am and will remain grateful. But most importantly, thanks to my online students, particularly those who have taken the course for which this book was written. They are my inspiration. Their hopes and plans are what make a daunting undertaking such as this worth every bit of the effort.

CHAPTER 1

The Vision of the Web

cyber visit

NICK FINCK
Web Designer, Writer

Design Viewpoint

"I became a Web designer out of necessity and passion. The Web is my cross-roads. I was into film and video. . . . I also did a lot of animation and conventional art . . . my writing skill was just starting to evolve. I saw all these skills converging in one place. For the first time I was able to take all my talents and pull them into a single medium: the Web." Be sure to read Finck's ideas at www.digital-web.com/profiles/nick_finck.shtml.

Resume

Presently Web Designer/Creative Director, Senior Technician, and Editor in Chief for *Digital Web Magazine*. Worked with tools such as Photoshop, ImageReady, PageMaker, Acrobat, Homesite, TopStyle, Fireworks, Intersolv PVCS, and Visio. Skilled in HTML, XHTML, CSS, advanced JavaScript, DOM (DHTML), and some JSP.

Clients

Intel B2B clients, IBM, Adobe, CitiBank, Norm Thompson, Intel, Microsoft, King Estate, Hewlett Packard, Cisco, Caylx & Corolla, OrCad, and Blue Cross/Blue Shield of Boston and Benova.

Designer's Home Page

www.nickfinck.com/

Insights

"Simplification and transparency are the keys to any good design. A design is only done when you can't take anything more away from it without losing the goal. The best design is the design that the user does not see. It is transparent because it is so natural to use."

"I am a minimalist in a true sense of the word. I don't fill my designs with unnecessary elements. Design is the art of solving a problem. . . . I recognize the problem and find the simplest and most direct solution to that problem."

Nick Finck's home page (www.nickfinck.com).

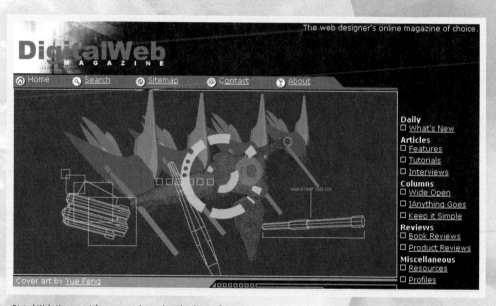

Digital Web Magazine's home page (www.digital-web.com/).

➤ Define the 10 main functions of the current World Wide Web.

➤ Identify five technological breakthroughs in the history of the Internet and the Web.

➤ Outline the history of the Web as a tool making business and interpersonal exchange possible.

➤ Describe the Web's impact on users' expectations for work, education, business, services, and human interconnectedness.

➤ Identify non-technical professions that contribute to Web design.

➤ Reflect on where the Web is now and where it is headed.

What qualities should a Web designer have? Until recently, answers to this question often emphasized technical skills. But now more people are realizing the contributions made by individuals with other talents—talents that help unleash the Web's potential. By concentrating on the main concepts and the basic process that leads to well-designed sites, this book teaches Web design from the larger perspective of the Web; that is, as a means to interconnect all people of the world and thereby help them achieve new levels of knowledge, collaboration, mutual respect, appreciation, and understanding. This book challenges you—a future Web developer—to see from a wider view what the Web is, who needs it and why, what talents and backgrounds come together to create online sites and communities that accomplish valuable purposes, and how good ideas for presenting information on the Web come from non-technical as well as technical fields. These perspectives and challenges will help prepare you to be a well-rounded, highly capable Web developer and design leader.

THE WEB: A CHANGING MEDIUM

In 1989, when Tim Berners-Lee proposed a hypertext system for the Internet, there were no Web designers, no **browsers**, no online colleges, and no travelocitys or amazon.coms. Berners-Lee, a software designer with a degree in physics, had worked briefly at the Particle Physics Lab at CERN (*Conseil Europeen pour la Recherche Nucleaire*, or European Council for Nuclear Research), the nuclear research lab in Switzerland. His assignment was to design systems to network the CERN computers. To help him connect the confus-

Tim Berners-Lee

browser
Software that allows your computer to find and read files from other computers connected to the Internet. The browser retrieves files; decodes them; displays text, images, and links; and activates the links to make use of their hypertext capability.

ing, international "web" of CERN researchers and projects, he created a non-linear, "web-like" program. This was the beginning of his vision of a decentralized, organic, interconnected "world" of information, accessible from anywhere by anyone. Berners-Lee's solution of creating electronic links, initially within CERN, allowed the diverse types of computers of the researchers, dispersed among all the countries and universities or agencies at which they worked, actively to share documents and collaborate on projects. His vision became reality in 1991. In just over a decade, these humble beginnings have led to the World Wide Web of today, an electronic community that allows users to shop, learn, communicate, and be entertained, far surpassing Berners-Lee's original vision.

At first the Web was the "darling" of government and research institutions, which sponsored and developed the Web in its early days. Using the Web required significant technical know-how at that time. Since then, however, the Web has grown into a rich communications medium that more and more people use regularly. The Web is a sophisticated technical tool, but creating a Web site now requires designers with more than technical skills. Artists, businesspeople, teachers, and social scientists bring expertise that is just as important to the success of Web sites. In fact, their contributions are critical if the Web is to fulfill its promise.

A Transformative Technology

The Web has changed the world so much that it is deemed a "transformative technology"; that is, a technology that produces a level of change expressed in terms of a factor of 10 or greater. A transformative technology must increase speed, distance, productivity, or some relevant, measurable quality at least tenfold (times 10). The automobile and the airplane were transformative changes in terms of time and distance. People could travel about 30 miles a day by horse. The automobile increased this figure by a factor of 10 (to 300 or more miles), and the airplane produced an increase of an additional factor of 10, to more than 3,000 miles. These inventions transformed the way people think about distance and travel.

In a similar way, the computer has transformed how people think about work—how work is accomplished and even the nature of the work itself. The use of computers has increased the speed at which work is done and the range of what is accomplished and expected. Business accounting, data management, inventory control, and patient monitoring are just some of the areas in which the computer has had significant impact. Business records that once were updated biweekly are kept up-to-the-minute and can provide not only summary reports but also "real-time" support for critical decisions through testing the numbers and their projections against various "what if" scenarios. Data that once were organized in alphabetized card files are reordered instantly, making it possible to track trends, select items or individuals by particular characteristics, and follow up appropriately. Inventory that previously was accounted for only periodically can be tracked immediately, allowing for "just-in-time" replacement of items as they are used.

The Web is bound to have a similar effect on how people live and work. As a transformative technology, the Web yields major benefits to businesses as well as individuals by providing a "gigantic information marketplace where individuals and organizations buy, sell, and freely exchange information and information services among one another," as Michael Dertouzos writes. The Web's varied access to information, immediate collaboration processing, frequent exchange of critical communications, fast turnaround times for business transactions, and other profound and significant contributions has made it an important part of public and private life. The Web has created unanticipated benefits and is finding its way into unexpected places.

THE WEB AND E-COMMERCE The Web was not designed as a place for commerce, but businesses soon realized its potential value. By the end of 2002, more than 600 million people worldwide will have access to the Web, and they will spend more than $1 trillion shopping online, according to a study by the IDC research firm. E-commerce grew to $500 billion in 2001, a 68% increase over 2000, according to IDC. Carol Glasheen, program vice president of IDC's Global Research Organization, told the *E-Commerce Times*:

> Once people get over the security and privacy hiccups, as well as other problems that are not directly related to e-commerce, and have access to wider product offerings, e-commerce will become as widespread as offline commerce

Much of the increase in e-commerce is due to skyrocketing international business-to-business (B2B) sales. Industry surveys conducted by the U.S. Census Bureau reported that merchant wholesale e-commerce reached $213 billion and manufacturing reached $777 billion in the year 2000. A survey of selected services yielded a 2000 total of $37 billion. Retail e-commerce sales totaled $29 billion in 2000 and $36 billion in 2001. As shown in Figure 1.1, by the end of the second quarter of 2001, total retail e-commerce had already surpassed the level reached by the end of the third quarter in 2000 (over $20 billion), suggesting a conservative estimate that by year end, totals would surpass $40 billion.

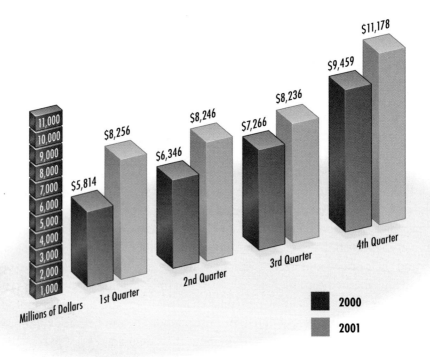

FIGURE 1.1 Growth of E-Commerce, 2000-2001

E-commerce retail sales have risen from just under $6 billion in the first quarter of 2000 to over $11 billion in the fourth quarter of 2001.

Source: U.S. Census Bureau, <www.census.gov/eos/www/ebusiness614.htm>.

The Web has been used to streamline methods of work and production and to make work easier for individuals. For example:

- **Employee Recruitment** Companies can allow candidates and job hunters to post their resumes on the company Web site. Recruiters can quickly locate qualified candidates for current and future positions. In addition, dozens of sites (such as flipdog.com) post job openings from numerous companies and help individuals manage their job searches by allowing them to post resumes and be notified when jobs that meet specified criteria are posted.

- **Marketing** Specific potential consumers can be reached by "co-branding"—placing ads on sites visited by those likely to be interested in particular goods and services. LatPro, a small company that offers career services for Spanish- and Portuguese-speaking professionals, generated 8,500 new registrations with co-branding strategies at a cost of $1,000 per month, compared to $8,000–$10,000 per month using traditional advertising.

- **Sourcing** Using the Internet to find sources of needed materials more efficiently has cut industry cycle times (time lapse between a purchase need and receipt of the goods) by 25–30%.

- **Telecommuting** According to the International Telework Association and Council (ITAC), by allowing some of their workers to work from their homes (9.6 million reported telecommuters in 2001), businesses have reduced turnover by 20%, increased productivity by up to 22%, and cut absenteeism by 60%. Telecommuting opened up employer access to an available workforce of approximately 10 million (or more) people with disabilities who want to work (www.disabledperson.com/) and made it easier for businesses to adhere to the Americans with Disabilities Act, the Family and Medical Leave Act, and the Clean Air Act.

Root Link www.flipdog.com/
Direct Link www.flipdog.com/js/loc.html
Why Go? Use the FlipDog Web site to find jobs offered in your area.

Companies also have been able to cut costs significantly by using the Web efficiently:

- Training and education budgets have been cut by as much as 20%.
- The cost of essential goods has been cut by 5–20%.
- Corporate legal services have been cut by 30%.
- U.S. businesses saved more than $4 billion in 2000 through online booking systems for travel.

For individuals, the Web provides increased opportunities for training and education, reduced prices for goods and services, savings on travel expenses, online job hunting and linking with potential future employers, and telecommuting as an employment benefit and opportunity.

Root Link www.travelocity.com/
Direct Link www.travelocity.com/Vacations/
Why Go? Search for a flight, a hotel, or an entire vacation.

THE WEB AND THE FOURTH LEVEL OF CHANGE The examples in the previous section illustrate the kinds of change Web technology is capable of creating. Some of these changes reach as far as the fourth level on Steven Gilbert's taxonomy of the four levels of change set in motion by technology (see Figure 1.2):

1. Technology is used to do things that are already being done—same things, different means.
2. Things already being done are done more efficiently through technology—same things, done better or faster.
3. Things that could not have been done before are now possible—an expanded version of things that were done before, enabled by what is newly possible because of the technology.
4. Things that are done are themselves changed—different things, different possibilities, different content, different scope. At this level, the methods and limitations of the past are left behind.

The nature and use of the Web have reached this fourth level in the lives of tens of millions of individuals, businesses, associations, and agencies actively using and contributing to its "virtual" world.

FIGURE 1.2 Four Levels of Change Caused by Technology
Steven Gilbert's taxonomy illustrates the scope of change produced by different types of technology, from making certain tasks easier to perform to changing how people think about the tasks they normally do.
Source: Adapted from Steve W. Gilbert, "Teaching, Learning, and Technology: The Need for Campuswide Planning and Faculty Support Services." *Change.* (March/April 1995).

From first to fourth level in less than a decade, these changes have profoundly affected who uses the Web, who designs for it, and how these designers view and accomplish their work. The phenomenal emergence of the Web is a demonstration of the human desire to be part of an interconnected world, with access to knowledge, resources, and each other, as well as to businesses, institutions, research agencies, and other potentially valuable interconnections. As a means for interconnection, the Web has changed the world; similarly, as the demand for interconnection has escalated, the world has changed the Web.

A Medium for Connection

The Web does more than increase business efficiency and profitability; it also enhances everyday life by enabling connection, communication, and the acquisition of knowledge. At first, Web sites did little more than allow you to view stored documents. Now the Web shows how things are changing right now—in real time. Among other things, the Web enables users to:

- Find up-to-the-minute news and weather reports about any place around the globe.
- Check traffic on a route to take to work or an appointment.
- Track a shipment while it is being delivered.
- Watch real-time events in space travel (such as at NASA's Web site).

At the Pacific Stock Exchange, floor traders execute trades with the help of wireless devices, which send buy and sell orders, thus helping prevent the misinterpretation of instructions shouted or scribbled by other traders. Cellular phones and other "Internet appliances" allow access to the Web, providing instant information for anyone from almost anywhere.

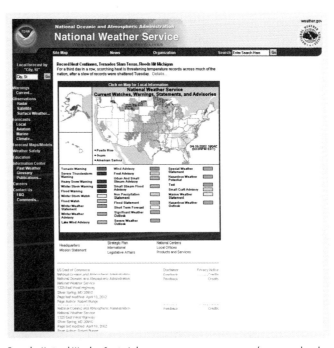

From the National Weather Service's home page at www.nws.noaa.gov/, you can select the city for which you would like current weather information, including temperature, precipitation, warnings and advisories, and forecasts.

Root Link www.spaceflight.nasa.gov/
Direct Link www.spaceflight.nasa.gov/realdata/tracking/index.html/
Why Go? To see the location of the Space Station orbiting above Earth.

The immediacy of the Web is illustrated by a story of one New Jersey family that found a cat stowed away inside the engine compartment of their car when they stopped at a rest area on Connecticut's Merritt Parkway. They posted a picture and information on a Web site, and the cat's owner, who lived in Boston, recognized her pet on the site; pet and owner were reunited.

Given that today's Web is able, and expected, to do all these things—to increase the efficiency and profitability of business and to satisfy the human desire for interconnection—designing Web sites calls upon more than just the talents of programmers and graphic designers. Web developers need to bring to their work a thorough understanding of the Web's capabilities, the types of audiences using the Web, and how the Web is perceived.

The Web's main functions are to inform, entertain, and enable interaction and exchange among its users. Some individuals might use the Web for one primary purpose, but designers must be aware of all the Web can offer and how those features are delivered to its users.

Like the elephant described by the four blind men, who described only what they touched, the Web could be described differently by different users, but they would describe one or more of ten main functions (see Figure 1.3)

- **Telecommunications Technology** The Web is a communications network of modems, cables, phone lines, and satellites that connects millions of computers used by hundreds of millions of individuals and organizations around the world.

- **Medium for Collaboration** The Web is a place where people with similar interests and needs are able to interact with each other, work together, study and learn collectively, and communicate about shared interests.

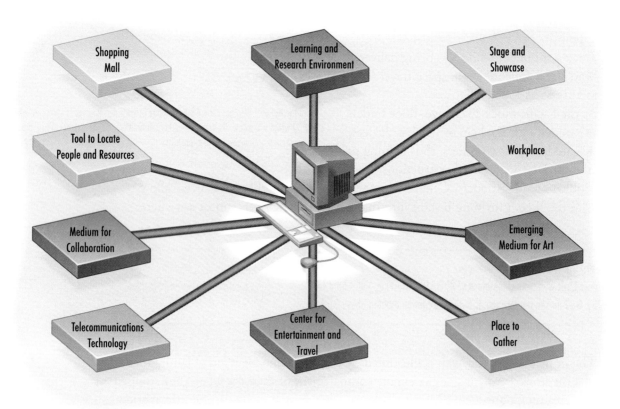

FIGURE 1.3 The Main Functions of the World Wide Web

- **Tool to Locate People and Resources** Individuals can look for jobs, employers can find qualified candidates, homeowners can find services they need, and friends and family members can locate each other and make contact.
- **Shopping Mall** Clothes, furniture, books, music, software, airline tickets, hotel rooms, rental cars, and thousands of other items are readily available for purchase on the Web, often at a discount. Customers often can get more information about their purchase from the Web and find the shopping experience more efficient and personalized.
- **Learning and Research Environment** Virtually any topic, question, or area of interest can be explored on the Web. A wide assortment of classes is offered online. Research can be conducted by visiting the online catalogs of public, university, and government libraries, and the entire texts of published articles can be downloaded from publishers' sites.
- **Stage and Showcase** Visual artists, animators, graphic designers, musicians, movie makers, writers, and other artists exhibit their work in a variety of performance and art media. These online portfolios demonstrate the artists' abilities to prospective clients and employers.
- **Workplace** A growing proportion of those now actively employed perform their work "virtually," from home-based offices and specialized services shops, using the Web to connect with employers and clients. This trend reflects the growing interest among businesses and individuals in obtaining and providing the best possible resources and values without limitations of time and place.
- **Emerging Medium for Art** The Web enlists creative talents in entirely new venues for publication, presentation, and display using a new toolset that includes logo art, still and animated graphics, "movies" and video clips, sounds and music, and 3-D virtual-reality experiential "worlds."
- **Place to Gather** Families and friends can stay in touch more immediately than they can by regular mail and less expensively than by phone. Individuals can set up continuous interpersonal access to each other whenever they are online by using instant messaging, chat rooms, and e-mail utilities to create a sense of togetherness.
- **Center for Entertainment and Travel** An increasing variety of engaging games, sport and movie highlights, music performances, and "virtual" travel experiences are available from all parts of the globe.

web **1.1 activity**   THE WEB FROM MULTIPLE VIEWS

The purpose of this activity is to allow you to explore the Web from multiple viewpoints and then present your findings. Using your Web browser, go to www.ceoexpress.com/. This is a metasite, a site that links to other sites. Print the home page, which contains the full set of categories and links. Review these categories and highlight ones that you want to visit.

Select a site from three of the following views of the Web to explore. Note that due to the evolving nature of Web sites, these headings may change. If they do not match the following list, locate others with similar meanings. (Your browser can locate the following headings quickly by pressing Ctrl+F in both Internet Explorer (to use the Find tool) and Netscape (to use the Search tool).

- **Telecommunications Technology** Explore links from "Cutting Edge" or "Tech Magazines and News."
- **Tool to Locate People and Resources** Explore links from "Personal Finance," "Small Business," or "Directory Search."
- **Shopping Mall** Explore links from "Autos" or "Shopping."
- **Learning and Research Environment** Explore links from "Health" or "Reference."
- **Center for Entertainment and Travel** Explore links from "Unwind," "Sports," or "Travel."

Prepare a report to share your findings and discoveries. Include a brief description (one to two pages) of the sites you visited, including information about what they have to offer. Compare the sites by answering the following questions about each site.

1. Which designs did you prefer and why? From the sites you visited, show examples of well designed pages and poorly designed pages. Explain the design strengths and weaknesses of the pages.
2. Which sites were the most usable and easy to navigate? Explain the reason for your answer.
3. Did the sites you visited provide current and reliable information? What criteria did you use to assess this?

Also include one or two screen captures from the selected sites to illustrate and exemplify points you have made. (To copy a screen that is showing in the browser window on a PC, hold down the Alt key and press Print Screen. Then use Paste to insert the screen capture in your Word document. On a MAC, hold down the Command and Shift keys and press 3 to create a copy; then use Paste to insert.)

BREAKTHROUGHS: A HISTORY OF THE WEB

The World Wide Web did not suddenly appear with all its capabilities intact. The Web's history includes dramatic change spurred by the human desire to connect with others and by technical breakthroughs of the past several decades. These breakthroughs, summarized in Figure 1.4, are an important part of the history of the medium.

Interconnected Computers

Connecting distant computers to allow data exchange now seems such a common practice that it is hard to imagine the struggle to achieve it. In fact, some computer scientists were initially skeptical that such interconnection was even possible.

EARLY NETWORKS The first breakthrough occurred when scientists in California and Utah succeeded in sending a message between two computers in 1969. A great deal of work preceded this accomplishment.

In the late 1950s and early 1960s, the U.S. Department of Defense was concerned about nuclear attack by the Soviet Union, which in 1957 became the first country to send a satellite—Sputnik—into orbit. The Soviet achievement rattled U.S. leaders. If a

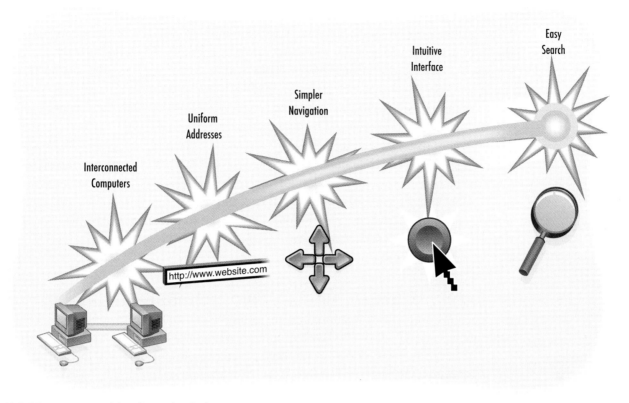

FIGURE 1.4 Breakthroughs in Web Technology

The history of the World Wide Web has been marked by five significant technological breakthroughs that have made it more widely available and easier to use.

nuclear attack occurred, interconnected computers would assure that the country could maintain control of its computerized defense system.

The defense department also saw networking as a way to obtain greater access to powerful computers, which were expensive and therefore scarce. Because many of the department's research projects required high-powered computers, which the department did not possess, this scarcity would delay progress toward defense against nuclear war. The department thus set up the Advanced Research Projects Agency (ARPA) to develop a network of computers that could exchange information among them. ARPA, later renamed Defense Advanced Research Projects Agency (DARPA), managed the creation of this network by funding development efforts at various research institutions.

Networking powerful computers would help overcome one of the biggest disadvantages of research computers at the time—computing resources were extremely limited compared to demands and needs. Computers during these years performed calculations at slow rates—compared even to the speed of today's desktop computers. And, because these computers were scarce, scientists had to sign up for computer time. Networking would allow institutions to share computers, which meant that researchers would not have to wait as long to analyze data; if their institution's computer was unavailable, researchers could use another computer on the network.

ARPA's initial network relied on phone lines that already existed and used telephone-style "circuit switching" to connect and transmit data between computers. This was inefficient, however, because unlike a telephone conversation, in which voice data flows continuously, computer data flows discontinuously. Large amounts of information are sent in short periods of time, followed by long periods of silence. Devoting one phone circuit to a connection between two computers was wasteful because for most of the connection time, no data would be flowing.

Donald Davies, at the National Physical Laboratory (NPL), began considering other means of sending messages such as "message switching," the method used to send telegrams. However, this method had problems with delays. As each message reached a "node" or connection on its way to its destination, it had to wait in the queue while previous messages awaited their turns to be sent on. So Davis came up with the idea of breaking the message into pieces that could be transmitted quickly and then reassembled. These short pieces of messages are called "packets" and the transmission method is called **packet switching**. Using this technique, data is broken down into small electronic packets that are sent separately, with embedded instructions about how the packets are to be reassembled on the other end. In 1969, this method was tested in an experiment that involved transmitting data between two distant computers, one at the University of California, Los Angeles, and the other at the University of Utah. It worked. ARPANET, as the network was named, was off and running.

AN EXPANDING SYSTEM Although the goal of ARPANET was to provide alternative locations from which weapons systems could be controlled, interconnecting the computers produced escalating levels of interest within academic and research communities, where such interconnection was seen to have important potential for sharing research findings. When Ray Tomlinson, an ARPANET researcher, developed the initial program through which messages could be sent and received over the network in 1972, e-mail was introduced, and it took off precipitously. By 1973, transatlantic cables had been laid that made an international network possible.

Throughout the 1980s there was increasing interest in computer networks and this had important effects as other U.S. agencies and institutions developed their own networks. By 1981, ARPANET was a growing network that had expanded to include over 200 smaller networks. Soon, heavy traffic on the system led the Department of Defense to split the network into two parts: ARPANET, for handling advanced research activities, and MILNET (for Military Network), to be dedicated to military use. Also in 1981, the National Science Foundation (NSF) funded Computer Science Network (CSNET) for use by educational and research institutions that did not have access to ARPANET.

Institutions that used the UNIX operating system were able to connect to the growing network when two **protocols**—rules for handling and routing data packets—called Transmission Control Protocol and Internet Protocol (TCP/IP) made these connections workable. The City University of New York started BITNET ("Because It's Time" Network) by interconnecting university IBM mainframes. In 1986, with funding provided by NSF, NASA, and the Department of Education, CSNET became the National Science Foundation Network (NSFNET), offering e-mail and connections to the supercomputers at Princeton, the University of California, University of San Diego, and Cornell. Also in the early 1980s, large companies began adding their own networks.

Funding for early networks had come from the federal budget. Tax dollars helped pay for these early efforts to establish a nationwide computer-networking system. But with exponential increases in network use, the defense department and the NSF recognized that the networks had moved beyond their military and scientific purposes. Both agencies saw that further possibilities could become reality only if other groups were involved in development. Plenty of groups were intensely interested in becoming involved. Because commercial traffic was prohibited on NSFNET, commercial e-mail enterprises saw an opportunity to provide services to meet the needs of businesses.

packet switching—
A method of efficiently distributing messages among networked computers that involves breaking a message into sections, called packets, that are independently transmitted from computer to computer to computer until all packets reach their final destination. There, the packets are reassembled into the original message. Web pages are transmitted in packets, each one numbered and marked with a destination address.

protocols
For the Internet, a set of rules for converting data that is sent and received by computers connected to the Internet. Protocols tell a computer how to turn computer code into the pictures and words shown on the computer screen. HyperText Transfer Protocol (HTTP) is the set of rules for converting HTML code into the text and images drawn on browser software.

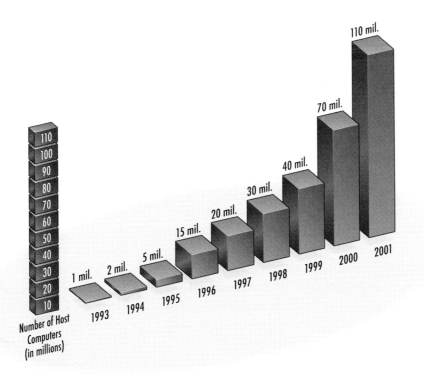

FIGURE 1.5 Increase in the Number of Host Computers, 1993–2001
Source: Internet Software Consortium, <www.isc.org/>.

In 1989, NSF allowed two commercial e-mail services to connect to the network (MCI and CompuServe), setting loose the phenomenal growth and development of the global enterprise side of the Web. Gradually, the government-funded network became a commercially sponsored venture. For a while, the NSF co-managed the network with a private company. Soon the name of the network changed, this time to the Internet, and businesses, schools, and government agencies began hooking up.

With each increase in capacity came heavier use, which led to overload on resources, which led to congestion, which led to additional increases in funding to pay for increased capacity. This continuous cycle of growth and overload became the familiar pattern of the Web. By March 1993, after the World Wide Web had become a reality, Web traffic on NSFNET measured 0.1% of the total traffic on this network. By September 1993, that figure had escalated to 1%, an increase of a full order of magnitude (10 times). Eventually, the defense department closed down ARPANET, and NSF moved forward to turn over the Internet to others in order to return its attention, energies, and funds to other initiatives. The Internet was moving forward in its current privatized version.

By 1994, private companies known as Internet Service Providers (ISPs) began maintaining the backbone that connected the nation's computers. Demand took off exponentially, escalating from 1 million host computers in 1993 to 110 million by 2001 (see Figure 1.5).

Uniform Addresses

Such rapid growth could not have happened if the network's addressing system were not organized uniformly. To enable user access to all interconnected computers, a uniform addressing system was essential. The necessity for such a system was recognized by the end of 1982, "when the experimental Internet had done its job, and the Internet bandwagon was ready to roll," according to James Gillies and Robert Cailliau.

Craig Partridge of BBN (Bolt, Baranek, and Newman), Jon Postel, and Paul Mockapetris of the University of Southern California worked out details for what they called a **Domain Name System** (DNS). This system uses addresses that, when read from right to left, move from broad to specific. So when read from right to left, the computer address "jrice.it.santefecc.fl.us" indicates an address in the United States; then an address in Florida; then an address at Santa Fe Community College; then an address in the Information Technology department; and finally, the computer name of the individual the address belongs to.

By 1985, when the number of host computers linked to the Internet approached the 2,000 mark, DARPA was able to convince the burgeoning Internet community to adopt this uniform system for addressing. "The logical, straightforward, DNS way of addressing was one of the things that later fed into the World Wide Web," write Gillies and Cailliau.

As additional elements of this worldwide addressing system were designed and adopted, attention to uniformity was firmly upheld. Conventions for addressing on the Web, which started after the DNS was developed, followed additional universal naming standards for **domain names**, such as the conventions for domain suffixes and URL (Uniform Resource Locator) extensions. Table 1.1 lists the established extensions (and some new ones just starting to be used).

TABLE 1.1 Domain Suffixes and Web Extensions

Suffix	Type of Site	Examples
.gov	government	www.statelocal.gov/ www.senate.gov/ www.house.gov/
.net	network-related	www.hypermart.net/
.mil	military	www.dscc.dla.mil/
.com	commercial	www.amazon.com/ www.dell.com/ www.yahoo.com/
.edu	educational	www.duke.edu/ www.harvard.edu/ www.umn.edu/
.org	non-profit	www.goodwill.org/ www.redcross.org/ www.un.org/
.aero	airlines	www.dublin.airport.aero/ www.londoncityairport.aero/
.biz	business	www.legaltimes.biz/
.coop	business cooperative	www.osg.coop/
.info	unrestricted, general	www.bmw.info/
.name	individuals	www.peter.morgan.name/

Simpler Navigation

At this point (that is, around 1985 to 1990), the Internet was still primarily for the technically literate. To offer something to everyone, the Internet had to become easier to use, which meant creating a usable "interface" to the network. An **interface** is a way of allowing a user to relate to and interact with a computer. A television's knobs or buttons are its interface; likewise, a computer interface enables users to exercise control over its actions. The early Internet required users to have considerable knowledge about computer systems because browsers did not exist. Interacting with computers was done via a keyboard, not a mouse. Computers that accessed the Internet ran on UNIX, an operating system that performed tasks based on commands the user typed on an otherwise blank monitor screen.

Commands were specific codes that you couldn't guess at, spell incorrectly, or even look up quickly. When accessing a UNIX-based computer from a DOS-based work station, DOS know-how was an additional necessity. The following is an example of UNIX code typical of the strings of text that were input on UNIX computer systems.

```
$ mount Saturn/usr/loca/bin usr/local/bin
$ mount -a -v -t nfs -o noexec -r
```

This code instructs a computer to load a file from a computer named Saturn and to give certain privileges to the person requesting the file. When point-and-click access became possible with Web browsers, such arcane UNIX code became unnecessary for most computer users.

In addition to facing the challenge of DOS and UNIX, early Internet users needed to supply the addressing information that permitted their computers to retrieve documents from a remote computer, which could be located thousands of miles away or in the next room. Like the commands required to run a UNIX machine, computer addresses could be long and foreign looking. There was no room for even the slightest mistake. Users often were also required to have login IDs and passwords to access another computer's documents, and finding those documents in the filing system on the remote computer sometimes proved difficult.

The barrier facing most people as they began using the Internet was the amount of training required to learn the right commands to accomplish a specific task. But a breakthrough occurred with the development of easier methods for "navigating" the Internet—for getting where you needed to go with less knowledge and effort than before. Navigational aids came in different forms: hypertext links (selected from a list) could be used to move among pages, and navigational software (or utilities) reduced cruising Internet to a task of making choices from a list the software provided.

In 1989, Tim Berners-Lee at CERN proposed an information-sharing system with the following goals:

- Allow universal access, regardless of what type of computer was being used.
- Use a consistent user interface that would look and behave similarly on all computers.
- Allow links between documents, allowing distribution of text, graphics, video, and audio.

To help reach these goals, Berners-Lee and a colleague introduced a hypertext coding method called **HTML** (Hypertext Markup Language). Hypertext (based on the hypercard system that was introduced earlier and used on Apple computers) is any electronic text file that contains links to sections within itself or to related documents located on other computers.

interface
The point at which a computer interacts with its user—typically a human being, but also can be another computer or electronic device. Includes the navigation buttons and links, input boxes, and search, and other tools that enable users to interact with the site, moving within it as suits their needs and interests, and making use of what is available there that is of value to them.

HTML
Hypertext Markup Language. An international standard to represent text in an electronic form for exchanging documents. Defines the structure of documents (titles, headings, paragraphs, quotations, and other elements) and governs the display of text (font size, for instance).

The primary feature of hypertext is the ease with which it allows individuals to retrieve a document from another computer that is connected to the Internet. To permit this to happen (and make it easier for people to use), hypertext links "point" to the **URL** address of a target computer. These links often point directly to the document the user is requesting. But the user does not have to type in the URL. Instead, the individual writing the code for the Web page must make sure the link uses the correct address.

By selecting a hypertext link, or **hyperlink**, the user instructs a computer to connect to another location, whether on the same computer or a remote computer, and retrieve the requested information, which then appears on the screen. In essence, hyperlinks save the user from entering the long address that specifies a document's location, making the Internet accessible to users from non-technical as well as technical backgrounds.

HTML also enables documents to be viewed on different computers (Macs, IBM PCs, PC-compatibles, UNIX-based, and others) with small changes in appearance but without change to the actual content. HTML tags mark a document's structural elements—headings, paragraph text, block quotations, and others—and the retrieving computer displays each element according to established standards. For the most part, the document you see on your screen matches the one the creator intended. The creation of HTML made the World Wide Web possible.

The Web still needed more features to make it easy to use. Hyperlinks could help a user move from one document to another, but how could users access documents for which no one had provided hyperlinks? When the Web was in its infancy, users often memorized addresses for such sites or sometimes used massive directories to find them. Web directories, printed in small type on thin pages, were common, and they could weigh as much as the phone book of a large city.

Text-based menu utilities, such as Gopher, provided some measure of help. To use Gopher, the user would type "gopher" at the DOS prompt. The screen then presented a menu of choices that would help steer the user to a desired location. Each choice presented the user with a narrower category of choices, a hierarchical type of organization. Using Gopher, a user would start with the most general location or choice, and then would follow a sequence, making increasingly more specific selections until reaching the desired information, making the following sequence of selections:
- continent
- country
- state

Once at this point, a user might select a path such as:
- university
- department within the university
- office within that department
- information resource within that office

Locating desired information was not always so straightforward, however. If a user were interested in looking up an academic organization in the University of California system but did not know on which campus it was located, such a search could require navigating large portions of the hierarchical menus on each of the nine UC campuses.

The logical organization of Web sites within the Gopher system made it easier, but not simple, to find an Internet document. As long as a user guessed correctly where a site was located, navigating a Gopher hierarchy was efficient. But it was easy to get lost, and backing up to begin a new path was a common frustration.

```
Directory  UCCSN System Computing Services (Las Vegas, Nevada)
Directory  UFONet - UFO and Alien information
Directory  UIUC College of Education
Directory  UJA University Programs Department
Directory  UNC-Educational Computing Service (ECS)
Directory  US Bureau of Labor Statistics (LABSTAT)
Directory  US Geological Survey (USGS)
Directory  US Institute of Peace
Directory  US Internet Gopher
Directory  US Military Academy, West Point, NY
Directory  USGS Atlantic Marine Geology
Directory  USGS Geographic Names Service at the Yale Peabody Museum
Directory  USiS Internet Services
Directory  UT Austin General Libraries  Gopher
Directory  UT Austin, Grad School of Library & Info Science
Directory  UT-Austin Mathematics
Directory  UToledo Biology
Directory  UToledo Physics & Astronomy Gopher
Directory  UW Publications Services Gopher Server
Directory  UW-Green Bay Gopher
Directory  UW-Platteville Client Support Center
Directory  Unicom Systems Development Gopher (Austin, Tx)
Directory  Unidata Program Center, Boulder, Colorado
Directory  Union College (Schenectady, New York)
Directory  United Lithographers
Directory  United States Bureau of Mines Gopher
Directory  United States Bureau of the Census
Directory  United States Department of Agriculture, Economics and Statistics Gopher
Directory  United States House of Representatives
Directory  United States Naval Academy
Directory  United States Senate Gopher server
Directory  United States Sports Academy
Directory  Univ of Tennessee Dept of Geological Sciences
Directory  Univ. of Oklahoma, Health Sciences Center
Directory  Universities Space Research Association
Directory  University Corporation for Atmospheric Research (UCAR)
Directory  University Extension - Missouri Gopher
Directory  University Library Gopher, New Mexico State University, Las Cruces NM
```

A sample screen of selections using Gopher.

This menu-driven interface divided an unwieldy number of choices into logical categories, but navigating the menus was laborious. If users reached a dead end, they had to retrace their steps through earlier screens to go another direction. And—perhaps the most severe limitation—users had to know in which category to look to find the information they needed. Still, because it eliminated the need for the user to know a site's address before accessing it, Gopher significantly altered the Internet user's ability to obtain significant resources and connections, and it was a welcome, even amazing, improvement.

Intuitive Interface

This early stage of navigating the Internet by using text-based utilities such as Gopher and making choices from long lists, went through a major breakthrough when graphical user interface software (**GUI**—pronounced "gooey") was introduced. A GUI has a Macintosh- or Windows-style look, rich with graphics that make using a computer more intuitive. At this point, the World Wide Web was born.

Early in 1993, at the University of Illinois at Urbana-Champaign, an undergraduate Marc Andreessen developed Mosaic software that offered a graphical interface to sites that were accessible via the Internet. Now text and graphics could be combined to create Web pages. Offering point-and-click access to Web documents, Mosaic was so easy to use that in 1994, Jim Clark, chair of Silicon Graphics, teamed with Andreessen to introduce Netscape, the commercial version of Mosaic. Netscape's intuitive design opened the window to the Internet for a greater variety of users. Netscape was the first widely available Web browser; later, Microsoft introduced its own competing browser, Internet Explorer, which started the now-famous "browser wars."

GUI
Pronounced "gooey." A graphical user interface is an interactive, graphics-based computer screen that allows the user to give commands to the computer using visual elements that represent available actions and data.

With these GUIs, Web navigation became a simple process of "clicking" the mouse button to select from a number of visual choices. Visitors to a Web site can navigate from one page to another using hyperlinks to "go" to other pages within the site or even to other Web sites—immediately. Behind the scenes, while the user surfs the Web, the browser retrieves files of information from computers at different locations throughout the world. For the user the experience is like taking a drive in the country. Even for first-time and novice users, the experience is empowering.

Easy Searching

Another barrier that kept the Web from being user-friendly was the difficulty of finding information. The Web could not fulfill its potential because users were required to know the exact URLs of the sites they needed to visit. To transform the process of finding information on the Web, search engines entered the picture, creating an efficient process for locating resources based on users' particular needs. This technical breakthrough allowed today's Web to become the significant, empowering, interconnected force it is today.

With search engines, the computer network does much of the work of finding the resources. Users no longer have to know where to look for information or resources. Instead, these resources can be accessed using the capacity of computers to store millions of pieces of information and match pieces of information with a specified pattern. Search engines identify documents that contain words that match the search list a user provides. Searches can be broad, locating all Web pages that contain at least one of the words the user provides. Searches can be narrowed to find only those Web pages containing an exact phrase. Thus, search engines allow users to focus on a specific question or need. For instance, a user might wonder, "What is congestive heart failure? What are all the options for treatment?" and then conduct a search for sites that contain both the phrase *congestive heart failure* and the term *treatment*.

Search engines differ from directories. To construct directories involves various strategies to analyze as many Web documents as possible and catalog the sites that possess content relevant to particular topics. Web sites are selected for inclusion based on criteria such as the reliability of the site's information or the reputation of the organization. These selected sites are then grouped according to topic, and a user can search this directory for particular needs. However, directories do not catalog every Web page in existence. That is why searching a directory provides surprisingly rapid results: directories limit the amount of searchable information to those sites the directory provider deems appropriate.

Root Link www.altavista.com/
Direct Link www.doc.altavista.com/help/search/search_cheat.html (then click on Search)
Why Go? To learn how the AltaVista search engine works so you can plan efficient searches that yield the types of results you need.

On the other hand, search engines can check every document available on the Web. Using a "Web crawler" to create rough indexes of topics in advance, the engine searches across the Web for a term or combination of terms, considering a Web site to be relevant if it matches any part of the user's search request. Table 1.2 provides a list and descriptions of some of the major search engines.

Search utilities and the strategies they use for searching are based on Boolean logic. This involves combining search terms—words that describe the topic you are researching—with the Boolean operators AND, OR, and NOT (and others) to limit the search results to

TABLE 1.2 Major Search Engines

FAST Search	www.alltheweb.com/	A collaboration between Dell and AlltheWeb, launched in 1999, which introduced a tool that behaves like a search engine but is able to "deliver a subsecond search response time" through an advanced cataloging strategy. The current catalog includes over 600 million full-text documents, with plans to handle many billions of documents.
HotBot	www.hotbot.com/	An early search engine, launched in 1996 as Wired Digital's entry. Results come from the Teoma service, with secondary results coming from Inktomi, and directory information from Open Directory.
Inktomi	www.inktomi.com/	Search engine created at UC Berkeley, and then formed into its own company. The Inktomi index powers several other services such as HotBot and iWon. No way to query the Inktomi index directly.
AltaVista	www.altavista.com/	One of the oldest "crawler-based" search engines. Offers a large index of Web pages and a powerful set of advanced search commands. Launched in 1995 and was owned by Digital; then run by Compaq; now run by a spin-off of Compaq, CMGI.
Ask Jeeves	www.askjeeves.com/	An intuitive, "intelligent" Web-interaction engine that allows users to ask "Jeeves" a question using natural language. Jeeves then answers, using language-parsing, data mining, and knowledge-base creation tools in combination with the "cognitive strengths and capabilities" of human editors. The goal of this engine is to "deliver a humanized online experience."
Teoma	www.teoma.com/	A "popularity engine": takes into account what choices people make, given a list of search results. Ranks top choices higher on future lists. Owned by Ask Jeeves.
LookSmart	www.looksmart.com/	Human-compiled directory of Web sites. Can be used as a stand-alone but also supplies results to MSN Search, Excite, and others. Inktomi provides LookSmart with search results when a search fails otherwise to find matches. Independently launched in 1996, backed by Reader's Digest for a year, then bought back by company executives.
Google	www.google.com/	A top choice for Web searchers. Offers the largest collection of Web pages of any "crawler-based" search engine. Uses link analysis as a primary way to rank search result pages.
Northern Light	www.northernlight.com/	A favorite search engine among researchers. Features a large index of the Web and the ability to cluster documents by topic. Includes a large collection of documents not generally accessible to search engines including newswires, magazines, and databases.
Yahoo!	www.yahoo.com/	The Web's most popular search service and the largest human-compiled guide to the Web. A reputation for helping people find information easily. Employs about 150 editors. Lists over one million sites.

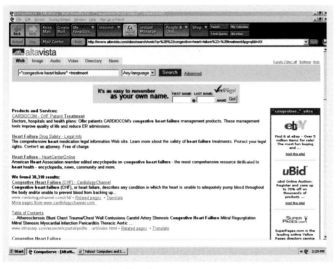

FIGURE 1.6 Results of an AltaVista Search Strategy
The results of a search will vary as new Web pages that match the search terms are added or removed from sites around the world.

what would be most useful. Combining two words with the Boolean operator AND, for instance, instructs the search engine to look for Web sites on which both words appear. Operator OR looks for Web sites that contain either word; NOT returns sites that contain the first word but not the second word.

To search the Web for information on the treatment of congestive heart failure, for example, the following search strategy was used on the AltaVista search engine:

+"congestive heart failure" +treatment

The plus signs make the terms that follow them "required." The quotation marks around "congestive heart failure" limits the search to sites where this phrase appears in this exact combination and word order. This search produces thousands of results, providing annotated links to sites that might have useful information on this topic, sorted in terms of potential value (see Figure 1.6). Results from the search include reliable resources that could be valuable to a person seeking essential information about congestive heart failure treatments. For more information on conducting a successful Web search, see the Input/Refresh box in this chapter.

The Web Now

With the help of search engines, the ability to get valuable and reliable information quickly and without having to know exactly where to look made the Web's resources so accessible that it changed the way the Web was used from that point forward. Once a medium for a few, the Web became a medium for many. This vast web of information could be accessed quickly and used to answer specific needs and questions, a development that altered forever the way Web users approached information, knowledge, and expertise. Now individuals could conduct personal research to guide them in various areas of their lives.

And so, with each technological breakthrough of the past several decades, another barrier separating people from a world of resources has been eliminated. The Internet and the World Wide Web have become useful tools that permit immediate exchange and communication. With these changes to the Web and the changes produced by it, creating a Web site, reserving and registering a URL domain, locating a "host" (or server) to house the site, and maintaining the site are attainable goals for large and small businesses and individuals. Having a Web "presence" has become important to anyone needing to interconnect with others and has become critical for most businesses.

input*refresh*

SUCCESSFUL WEB SEARCHING

Given that the Web is vast and filled with potential value, it is essential to develop excellent search skills and strategies. Many novice Web users know to go to a search engine such as AltaVista, or a directory such as Yahoo!, to find Web sites on a given topic or to answer a particular question. However, users equipped with advanced search strategies and an understanding of the available tools will more likely find what they are looking for.

Strategic searching is more than typing in a keyword using a search tool; instead, it is a process of moving repeatedly through a systematic four-step cycle:
1. Define and clarify the question.
2. Design a search expression.
3. Obtain and evaluate results.
4. Refine the question and strategy.

In addition, strategic searching includes choosing the appropriate search tool.

DEFINE AND CLARIFY QUESTION The more clearly a question is stated, the more strategic the search can be. Some questions are specific, yielding one sort of search strategy. Others are general, requiring more of an exploratory approach before zeroing in on specifics.

There is a difference, for example, between wanting to learn about travel in India; temperatures in India in January; the religions of India; the culture of India; and the history, location, and design of the Taj Mahal. A search for "India" is too broad to find information specific to each of these topics. When defining the question, it is critical to add specific terms to the general term to narrow the search properly without ending up at dead ends or on unrelated side trips.

DESIGN SEARCH EXPRESSION Designing a search expression means coming up with a particular combination of terms that likely will yield the desired results. This generally involves planning Boolean combinations of terms, using AND when multiple terms are required, OR when several options are allowable, and NOT when something is to be excluded. An additional convention for most

search engines is that words that are contained within quotes must appear together, in that exact order, for there to be a match.

Some search engines, such as Ask Jeeves, allow the formation of questions in natural language, meaning that questions can be written the way a user would actually ask them. These search engines then "parse" the question and convert it to a search expression.

Designing good search expressions takes thought and a problem-solving approach. The first strategy might or might not yield the desired results. The initial search expression is primarily to determine what types of results it produces in order to continuously improve strategies until the desired results are achieved.

For example, depending on the search engine, a search for *gifts AND baskets* might yield sites in which both these words appear within the text, no matter where or in what combination or order they appear. Or, it might yield only sites in which both these words were included in the <head> tag of the HTML code, as part of the title, or as part of the "description" or "keywords" META tags. A search for "*gift baskets*" would yield only sites in which these two words appear together and in that order. Depending on the question, the second search expression might yield a more useful list of results. Narrowing the search based on the question is necessary to close in on the sites that are useful. For example, if the question is "Where may I purchase gift baskets online and have them delivered to a friend in California?," additional terms such as *purchase* and *deliver* can be added to the initial search to narrow search results further.

OBTAIN AND EVALUATE RESULTS The results must be examined to determine how appropriate they are to the question and its underlying need. Useless results make it immediately apparent that the strategy needs to be changed. Sometimes, users must click over to the second or third page (or beyond) of results while scanning the list to determine whether the "hits" are potentially useful. Often, one or two useful results can be used to guide changes in the search expression to get more hits of that type. Other times, it becomes immediately clear that another search engine is necessary for this particular search.

To make best use of a results list and to learn better strategies for searching, users should consider the first several lists as explorations to provide feedback and guidance for obtaining more useful results.

REFINE QUESTION AND STRATEGY Refining the question and strategy is key to effective searching. A Web search is not a one-shot proposition; instead, it is essential to continue to improve upon the search strategy until the results yield sites that answer the search question. This is the only way to ensure useful results, and develop and improve search strategies and skills.

The following are ways to refine the question and strategy:

- Look at patterns in the results to see what is and is not working in the current strategy.
- Read (or reread) the advanced search strategies "Help" section for the search engine or engines.
- Use a site that is an example of the type of results desired as a model to refine the search strategy. One technique is to right-click, choose View Source, and look at the title, description, and keywords used for the site. This model might provide clues about which words to use when searching for additional sites of the same type.

TYPES OF SEARCH TOOLS Understanding the logic of search tools, the differences among them, and the various strategies they use to locate and organize information will help determine the best search tool for a particular search. Four types of search tools are available: search engines, directories, hybrid combinations of these two, and meta-search engines.

Search engines operate by looking for matches between the terms entered for the search and words that actually are included on the billions of pages on the Web. These words from Web pages are organized in advance into databases that are built automatically using Web robots (also called bots, spiders, or crawlers). These bots use various predetermined methods for building these databases.

Some bots collect only information from certain key areas of the HTML code for the page. These key areas are in the <head> section of the code, namely the title (the text that comes between the <title> open tag and the </title> close tag), and the description and keywords (entered as two types of META tags, <meta name="description"> and <meta name="keywords">). The following is a sample of the section of the HTML code used by these Web robots.

```
<head>
<title>Web Search
Strategies</title>
<meta name= "description"
content= "A discussion of
strategies for planning and
conducting effective and
efficient Web searches using
search engines, directories,
hybrid combinations of the two,
and meta-search engines." />
<meta name="keywords"
content= "search, web search,
web search strategies, search
engines, web directories, meta-
search engines, meta-search,
strategic web searching" />
</head>
```

Many search engines allow sites to "register" so that data from the pages of the site will be more intentionally gathered by the Web robots. Sites that are registered often are reviewed to ensure that no violations appear in the descriptions and keywords used, and no page redundancies exist (redundancies are sometimes used to manipulate future search outcomes).

Some search engines use "full text indexing," taking into their prepared-in-advance databases every word on the site, or every word before some defined point within the site. Depending on the strategy used by the search engine Web robot, different results (called "hits") are listed in response to any given set of search terms. If the terms you use in your search are not in the search engine's pre-prepared database for a particular site, there will be no match, and that site will not be included on the results list.

Directories are built differently than search engines. To create directories, humans analyze sites and classify them into logical categories according to the sense of what the site includes. These categories are then offered as options, allowing Web users to move down a hierarchy, from category to subcategory, in search of the section of results that will be of most use.

Hybrid combinations of search engines and directories generally provide both directory categories that are pre-indexed by humans and a search tool that goes beyond these indexes to include results from databases built by Web robots.

Meta-search engines perform searches across multiple search engines, each of which has used Web robots to gather database information. This allows Web users to view results for a given search expression from a number of different search engines at the same time. This can be illuminating and useful for determining which engine will yield the best results for a particular search need.

The prevalence of the Web can be demonstrated in the number of domain names registered in just over a decade. Network Solutions, a leading agency that provides InterNIC domain name registration, registered the first two .com business domains to Symbolics Technology in March 1985 and BBN (Bolt, Beranek and Newman—a learning design company located in Boston) in April 1985. Both were large and well-funded enterprises. Twelve years later, the one millionth business registered a domain. This domain, bonnyview.com, went to a small enterprise, Bonny View Cottage Furniture, on Traverse Bay in Petoskey, Michigan, that makes handcrafted, vintage-styled furniture. Like Bonny View Cottage

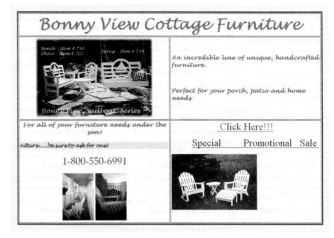

The one-millionth business domain to be registered was bonnyview.com/.

Furniture, organizations large and small have made the move to establish a Web presence.

According to a monthly survey by Netcraft, the number of sites approached 4 million in 1998, 10 million by 1999, 26 million by 2000, and over 36 million by 2001. In 2002, there was a small drop in sites, attributed to a decrease in the incentive for domain name speculators to buy and hold names in order to sell them later at a profit. The total number of sites, however, according to Netcraft's October 2002 survey, remains over 35 million.

web 1.2 activity

BIRTH OF THE WEB TIME LINE

Search the Web for particular types of information that you need to create a Birth of the Web Time Line. Begin this quest by using several of the leads provided and then find additional information by using several search engines.

Construct a six-year time line of significant events in the emergence of the World Wide Web from 1989 through 1995. Show key events, people, agencies, challenges, and breakthroughs in a well-designed time line. Combine histories, pictures, charts and graphs, and quotations. Prepare the time line for presentation to your class.

Start your research at "A Little History of the World Wide Web," located at www.w3.org/History.html. Follow links to the various specifics, including background from the 1940s, 1960s, and 1980s, and more detailed sequences of the events for 1989-1995. Then, follow these instructions to find a list of resources about Internet history using HotBot indices.

1. Go to www.hotbot.com/.
2. Click the Computers & Internet link.
3. In the list that appears, click the Internet link.
4. In the list that appears, click the History link.
5. Look at two or three of the "Site Recommendations" and select the best one to use for your project.

Continue your search for key players in the Web story by using search engines such as HotBot, Google, and Yahoo!. Try search terms such as "Web history" and "early Web." Another good search strategy is to use the names of some of the key people and agencies involved in the early Web, such as Tim Berners-Lee and CERN.

THE FUTURE OF THE WEB: STORIES AND PARADIGMS

With more than one million domain names registered, and more being registered every day, the Web is becoming indispensable to the conduct of business and interpersonal exchange. The many directions in which the Web has developed—beyond the initial concepts and visions of its founders—have given birth to new markets, opened new careers, and changed the way people conduct business, accomplish work, gain information, attend school, and interconnect and collaborate with others. Careers that are entirely unique to the Web have joined earlier, more traditional lists of job titles. Web designer, Web marketing editor, Web content manager, chat room moderator, Web publisher, Web content editor, Web marketing producer, Web technologist, interface designer, Web graphics designer, technical producer, and product development manager are among the many emerging job titles that create new possibilities for employment and new challenges within this burgeoning global resource and medium of exchange.

Problems to Overcome

Yet, beginning in 1999, a new reality set in. Internet companies started closing as investors became jittery about the inflated promises made by the dot coms, the Web-based businesses that believed business could be done in entirely new ways. Web visionaries, excited about using the Web to bring buyers directly to sellers, thus freeing the market and driving prices down, were right about the Internet opening new markets and freeing up exchange within old ones. However, business leaders now recognize that the Internet is not a business model, merely a channel. As with any business, Web businesses need to deliver value to customers, make more money than they spend, and build a loyal client base. As business sense replaced initial high hopes, key trends about Internet business have become clearer.

ACCESSIBILITY Accessibility refers to designing Web sites that are capable of being used or seen by users. Accessible Web sites are appealing and helpful, with clear instructions for users and information that can be readily located. More specifically, accessibility refers to making Web sites usable for people with disabilities. For example, if sound—music and recorded speech, for instance—is to play an important role on a site, designers must think of ways in which hearing-impaired users can be provided the same information.

Root Link www.awarecenter.org/
Direct Link www.awarecenter.org/tips/
Why Go? A "must read" for issues related to Web page accessibility.

Anyone who has surfed the Web has visited a site whose information is not accessible because the site is extremely frustrating to use. Information is difficult to find, links to other pages or to different Web sites do not work, or page elements load slowly and seem to have no purpose. When a user visits a Web site, the site must be available as quickly as possible. Delays are tolerable only if the site experience is significantly better than a faster-loading site's experience.

SECURITY For the Web to be a medium that encourages interpersonal and business connections, Web sites must ensure that privacy is preserved. Viruses, worms, and Trojan horses—computer programs that can destroy information on your computer, clog networks by flooding the Internet with computer-generated e-mails, or do other types of damage—can pass through the Internet before their activity is detected. The Internet also has been used to commit crimes such as stealing personal information (credit card, drivers license, or social security numbers, for instance) or personal harassment. Each of these areas can and must be addressed as part of the Web site design process. Virus protection software and firewalls are necessary to protect against viruses. Encryption technologies keep private information private. Authentication strategies protect against identity theft. These issues will be discussed in greater detail in Chapter 7.

Skills Needed on the Web

Web sites have evolved to new levels of design and sophistication, featuring interactive components that inform users of new features or that ask questions and then provide information or features tailored to their individual interests. But even if interactive features are easy to use, they do not by themselves eliminate the need for good design. As expectations for the Web increase—that is, as users expect the Web to provide more services and information or to satisfy more of their desires, good Web site design becomes more complex. The number of skills required to build good Web sites has increased. Updated technical skills are only the beginning. The following lists other skills that have become essential, broadening the range of backgrounds and talents that can lead to valuable contributions to the profession of Web design.

- **Writing** Writers bring models and standards of excellent writing.
- **Visual Arts** Graphic artists, professional photographers, and video designers bring models and standards of professionally rendered original art.
- **Information Science** Librarians and information designers bring research skills, resources, and knowledge of how people seeking information formulate their questions.
- **Business** Managers, finance experts, CEOs, and other business leaders bring knowledge of how to attract customers, organize commercial enterprises, and tailor a business or organization to the needs of specific regions of a country or the globe.
- **Technology** Programmers and other technology experts bring an appreciation of structure, standards, and modularization, pressing for the essential benefits of well-designed, non-redundant code.
- **Social Sciences** Counselors and human resource professionals bring better ways of interacting with Web site visitors, including an ability to design effective questions and surveys to obtain accurate user feedback.
- **Teaching and Learning** Teachers and professors understand what is necessary for people to learn. They bring essential knowledge about the process of drawing out performance in others and supporting their growth and development.

- **Dramatic and Performing Arts** Actors, musicians, and other performing artists know best what produces excitement and memorable experiences.

The World Wide Web Consortium (W3C) home page at www.w3.org/ is an essential bookmark for Web designers. It provides information about current and emerging guidelines and standards.

The design of information is especially critical. Web sites for large companies must make information available to customers without making it difficult to find. Knowing how to arrange information so customers can quickly locate what they need is a skill and an art. The emerging field of information architecture is devoting attention to this subject. Those who enter this field will be drawn largely from careers that already deal with the organization of information: library science and business analysis, for example.

Educators design Web sites to bring enriched learning experiences, including immersion activities, to students and others. They design and teach online classes. They set up classroom-to-classroom collaborations across the world, joining students together for learning activities that would have been impossible before the Web—e-mail exchanges between American students and the children of Chernobyl; satellite watches from all over the globe to track progress; discussions between schoolchildren and scientists; advanced science and language classes offered to collections of students from across the country to bring the advantages of a broader scope of classes to even remote locations with small student populations. They network with other educators, sharing lesson plans and lively instructional content across their Web sites.

On sites that are not school related, learning professionals design the instructional content of the site so visitors can gain information. They teach their students to design Web sites and set up and manage school and class sites. Instruction design is a major part of business sites, particularly when there are things visitors need to learn (about the technologies being sold on the site, for example, including how they differ and what the significance of those differences are) to make use of what the site makes available to them.

W3C

World Wide Web Consortium (the 3 means WWW). An international group of experts who work to standardize the ways that images, data, and interactivity are delivered through the Internet. The W3C is committed to helping to provide vision and standards for the future growth of the Internet.

Standards for the Future

With developments occurring in so many aspects of Web technology and use, the Web could become a chaotic world in which Internet companies introduce incompatible technologies that make universal access impossible. Realizing this, in 1995 Tim Berners-Lee, the man who set the Web loose, established the World Wide Web Consortium (**W3C**), an organization whose goal is to develop standards and guide research on all aspects of the World Wide Web. W3C's home page lists all of its current projects.

The following examples illustrate the W3C's interest in developing a Web that is accessible, easy to use, and of greatest service to all its users.

- **Web Accessibility Initiative (WAI)** W3C's commitment to lead the Web "to its full potential includes promoting a high degree of usability for people with disabilities," as its Web site says. One technology that will help make this happen is VoiceXML, a version of XML that enables a Web page to make use of voice-activated commands.

- **Device Independence** A coordinated effort to make wireless and other devices, such as TV sets, able to access the same Web that desktop computers access. The goal is to avoid "fragmentation of the Web space" and the need to design a completely separate Web site for each kind of device.

- **Semantic Web** An effort to put machine-understandable data on the Web. As the W3C's Web site puts it, tomorrow's programs "must be able to share and process data even when these programs have been designed totally independently." The goal is to have computerized devices handle as much of the routine tasks as possible without human intervention—for instance, automatically scheduling appointments by linking personal calendar programs on handheld devices with other computerized calendars.

These three programs certainly call for updated technical skills. The Semantic Web, for instance, will require database programmers to add new techniques to their skill sets.

Another technical development that promises to make information more available to Web users is the shift to XHTML as a standard with stricter requirements than HTML for structure, modularity, and uniformity. This emerging standard incorporates into Web coding some of the benefits of XML, a language that defines the structure of a document and the structure of the data itself, making it possible to exchange and use information from different types of databases. The shift to XHTML standards contributes to critical developments in accessibility and is increasingly important because of the proliferation of wireless devices in the marketplace.

As technological developments continue to revolutionize the way people use the Web, work, and live, those with technical skills will have considerable opportunity to develop specialties. That specialization should be pursued with full awareness of the goals of the technology and the W3C's goals that address human needs. Technical skills will be called upon to support the work of designing useful, responsive Web sites.

The Web as a Paradigm Shift

A paradigm governs people's perception of the world—what is of value, what to expect, how to accomplish goals and tasks. When the ways in which people perceive the world and accomplish their goals shift to a fundamentally different plane, there has been a "paradigm shift." Consider the following stories that illustrate the paradigm shift the Web has produced. Many things that were once impossible are now done with ease. Time, distance, and disability—factors that constrain work and play—have lost much of their power. Now, with the Web, people can connect any time, to any place, to any person, at any pace. Students are not limited to learning in schools that are located where they live. Committed professionals can continue to contribute even if disabilities prevent them from leaving home. Intercultural learning can occur through direct personal experience with people living halfway around the world.

The following stories, and many more like them, define an entirely different range of possibilities, each requiring thinking beyond the constraints of the past. Now, many of the constraints on Web designers come from the lag between an idea and the specific means to achieve it. Web developers will have many opportunities to devise the means by which the world and its people will connect, work, and live. They will find many occasions for innovation and plenty of times that require adapting existing tools to new situations. This is what Web designers do.

SCENARIO 1: MARIE MAXWELL

Marie Maxwell is a technology director for a large school district in Connecticut. She loves her work and is unable and unwilling to leave it to pursue her doctorate. However, there is much she wants to learn, and she has always aspired to earning a doctorate at some point in her career.

She enters a three-year doctoral program in Instruction Technology and Distance Education (ITDE) with Nova Southeastern, a university noted for its innovations and excellence in distance education. Instructors for the program are selected because they are recognized experts in their fields. They teach online from their various locations in North and South America and Canada. Visiting professors are also engaged from England, India, and Vancouver, among other locations.

Because Marie is able to attend this program at a distance, all research, projects, and even her dissertation have practical applications within her current professional responsibilities. For group projects, she participates on teams that gather online from their scattered locations in Georgia, North Carolina, Florida, and California to complete major design plans, research evaluation projects, and collaborative papers. She travels three times a year to Florida for face-to-face meetings with the other 24 students in the program.

This rich mix of learning opportunities provides her with challenges and highly meaningful experiences. She successfully completes her doctorate within the three-year timeframe, and moves forward in her career as Dr. Maxwell.

SCENARIO 2: VINCENTE CHAMARRO

Shortly after sunrise, Vincente Chamarro boards the high-speed train that will take him to his biweekly staff meeting at InterMed. The company designs and manufactures pacemakers and other medical devices that can be monitored over the Internet. Vincente is a product manager for InterMed's Cardiac Devices division. For more than three years, he has worked from his mountain home and communicated with the InterMed office by computer and telephone (telecommuting), but meets face-to-face with the marketing team every two weeks to maintain personal contact and resolve any issues that cannot be handled well through remote communication.

Arriving in the city at 7:30 a.m., Vincente gets off the train and heads for the company headquarters two blocks away. As he walks to work, he pulls a cell phone from his pocket and says a Web address, "www.ananova.com," into the mouthpiece. In a few seconds the face of a virtual newsreader named Ananova appears on the high-resolution screen of the cell phone. Vincente says, "News," and Ananova begins reading the latest headlines from around the world.

As he walks into his office on the ninth floor of the InterMed building, Vincente remembers that he needs to check his bank balance. He issues a command to his computer with the words, "Turn on and go to the Web site for Fidelity National Bank." He continues with, "This is Vincente Chamarro. What's the balance in my checking account?" The bank's automated teller system recognizes his voice and promptly reports that he has $1,956 in his account. "Good," he thinks, "no need to transfer any funds from savings."

The marketing team will meet to discuss plans for exhibiting at the upcoming international trade show for cardiac surgeons to be held in Zurich, Switzerland. Reflecting on his communication needs for the show, Vincente decides to buy a new handheld that will let him track all the materials his company ships to Zurich. A handheld would also provide access to current cultural events and street locations for Zurich and other European cities.

Vincente accesses a Web site where he can purchase the most powerful handheld on the market. A Web cam enabled with advanced pattern recognition software captures his image and quickly compares it with others in a database of images. "Hello Vincente," says a human-sounding voice, "Would you like to place an order?" Vincente tells the automated ordering system what he wants. The order is repeated for confirmation, and the purchase is deducted from his bank account. He can expect to receive his new "toy" in two days.

Vicente's meeting with his marketing manager and team members proceeds without a hitch. They approve his plan to use the company's Ananova-like synthetic character, Jillian, to pitch their new devices over computer monitors at the international trade show. Vincente has outlined a script for Jillian and now he just needs to write it. Vincente stays late to finish a rough draft, dictating to his computer until 8 p.m. As soon as he finishes the script, he directs the computer to send copies to team members and leaves to catch the 8:50 train home.

Vincente Chamarro's job is made easier through advances in speech recognition, natural-language processing, and artificial intelligence technologies. Those same developments are poised to bring a whole new level of customer care and individualization to computer users worldwide. Driving these changes is an intricate interaction among computer hardware manufacturers, scientists, and software developers.

SCENARIO 3: MARK GARCIA Late for his doctor's appointment, Mark Garcia walks briskly down the hallway on the 10th floor of the Metropolitan Medical Center. He had received four last-minute calls as he left the office, and traffic was heavy heading into downtown Seattle. "The doctor is always late anyway, so there should be no problem," he thinks as he walks into the clinic. Mark checks in at the front desk and is told to take a chair, that he will be called in turn. "Good," Mark says under his breath. "This will give me time to catch up on a few items."

Mark rotates his left arm a few degrees to view the screen on his wrist computer. The device, slightly larger than a wristwatch, contains a small screen, a keyboard, a pen-like stylus, a small clock, and a tiny microphone and speaker. Small buttons adorn its perimeter. With stylus in hand, Mark touches the *Internet* icon and utters the Web address of his favorite florist. At the site he orders a dozen red roses to be sent to his sister in Boca Raton, Florida. He charges them to his Visa account and is assured they will be delivered in time for her birthday luncheon at noon tomorrow.

Next, Mark states the URL of his bank into the computer microphone. A screen appears showing a menu of online banking activities. In the appropriate space, Mark types a brief message requesting the bank to transfer $250 from his savings account to his checking account. Within seconds, the message "Transaction completed" confirms that his request has been processed.

He carefully states the address of MyCiti.com. With the site's home page on his screen, Mark follows the familiar routine of indicating he wants to pay his regular monthly expenses, including the home mortgage payment, the telephone bill, the electricity bill, and the recyling charges. The transactions proceed smoothly. The final item on his mental agenda is to make a business-class reservation for a quick trip to San Antonio, Texas, the next afternoon. This task, too, is handled quickly at MyCiti.com, and Mark completes the payment details just as he hears his name being called.

Until a few years ago, who would have imagined that at the beginning of the twenty-first century, people would be able to buy flowers, groceries, clothes, and cars, as well as pay their bills, with just a few clicks on a computer? Yet today, as Mark does in this scenario, people around the world use the Internet daily to manage their personal and business affairs and to locate and purchase a variety of products and services—a modern phenomenon called *electronic commerce (e-commerce)*. Although some of the technologies Mark used are not yet widely available, they will become part of everyday life soon.

SCENARIO 4: JANELLE ANDERSON Janelle Anderson pulls into the supermarket parking lot and parks near the entrance. As she prepares to leave her car, she realizes that she forgot to bring her shopping list. Mulling over her options, she shrugs, takes her cell phone out of her purse, and walks into the store.

Janelle activates her phone as she heads down the aisle with her shopping cart. The phone immediately links her to the Web through a wireless connection. She taps an icon on the screen, and a Web browser appears. Janelle ignores the blinking e-mail alert and goes straight to her home Web site. The house Web server recognizes her password and she is in. Tapping through the menus to the KITCHEN section, she opens up the automated page for the refrigerator. She notes that the temperature in the unit is within normal limits.

Janelle then selects a live video feed, and from miles away a Web cam begins transmitting images of the refrigerator contents. She smiles, recalling the day she purchased the refrigerator with all its ultramodern connectivity features. Janelle remembers telling her husband that the options were great, but that she could not picture herself ever using them. But here she is, viewing a full-color display of the inside of her refrigerator. Janelle examines what is in the fridge, and sees that she needs to buy chicken, milk, and some more fruit. Scrolling back to the menu, she chooses PANTRY to check the supply of cereal and bread. With a satisfied smile, she snaps the phone shut and pushes her cart down the aisle to begin selecting the items she needs.

Live video on a cell phone might seem like science fiction, but an early version of this technology was already available in October 2001. Announcing its service as the world's first third-generation (3G) wireless phone system, Japan's NTT DoCoMo manufactured a trial run of 4,000 devices and sold them all in one day. Within a few years of its debut, the new 3G wireless technology is expected to make a similarly huge impact the world over, both in cell phones and in handheld computers. With an Internet connection speed 40 times faster than rates available in 2001, the new devices symbolize the direction of Internet development—continually faster wireless connections that are available 24 hours a day.

web 1.3 activity   TOUR A VIRTUAL MUSEUM

The purpose of this activity is to experience a virtual field trip and explore a learning space that gives you control of what you want to learn about. To accomplish this, visit and explore Xpedition Hall on the National Geographic site at www.nationalgeographic.com/xpeditions/hall/index.html.

1. Go to the site and look around.
2. Proceed to the Places and Regions area (click on Area II on the map). Locate and experiment with the Satellite Spyglass (click on the picture of a spyglass). Experiment with the spyglass, using it to zoom in on your own area of the country, and then Europe, Asia, Australia, Africa, and South America.
3. Explore other areas of the hall, including: I. World in Spatial Terms; II. Places and Regions; III. Physical Systems; IV. Human Systems; V. Environment and Society; or VI. The Uses of Geography.

Xpedition Hall at www.nationalgeographic.com/xpeditions/hall/index.html

Spend 30 minutes learning and experiencing the site. When you have completed your explorations, describe your experience by addressing these questions:

1. What made the exploration of the site interesting?
2. What observations can you make about the way you moved around the site, controlling your learning experiences?
3. In which areas did you spend the most time? The least time? Why?
4. Were there areas where you wanted to have more information or options? Describe these.
5. As you explored, did you think of additional questions that were not answered on the site? What were these questions?

apply & practice

Online Quiz

As a review of the key concepts in this chapter, define the terms in the following list:

browser
domain name
Domain Name System (DNS)
GUI
HTML
hyperlink
interface
packet switching
protocol
URL
W3C

After you are confident that you understand this chapter's content, go to this book's Internet Resource Center (IRC) at www.emcp.com/ and take the self-test online quiz for this chapter. Review any questions you answered incorrectly, and then study the related chapter material again. Retake the online quiz as many times as you need to reach full mastery (90–100%).

Topics Roundtable

1. What were the key events, technologies, individuals, trends, and needs that led to the level of acceptance and widespread use the Web is experiencing today?

2. What personal experiences can you share from your own encounters with the Web?

3. What are your thoughts about how things could have gone differently as the Web emerged? (For example, what if one of the breakthroughs had not happened when it did? What if there had not been a single addressing system?)

4. What does the Web change in your life now? Give three examples from your own experience in which the Web changed an end result. Discuss how the results would have been different without the Web and its resources.

5. What do you consider the positive and negative factors with "telework" (working online without having to report to a physical workplace)?

6. What are the possibilities and challenges of online learning? How does this option change your views about learning as a lifelong pursuit?

window to the web

➤ Use a text editor to write HTML code.
➤ Use your browser to open and view HTML files.
➤ Describe how HTML works.
➤ Demonstrate an understanding of the basic HTML rules and the basic HTML tags necessary for any Web page.
➤ Create an HTML shell and practice basic HTML coding.
➤ Create a report on free host sites and format that material in HTML.
➤ Begin planning the look and structure of your Window to the Web resource site.

technical walk-through

A Web page is an electronic creature made up of a collection of text and image files that are stored separately on a host computer. These files are sent to the computer of the user who has requested the page, and then are reassembled by that computer's browser. This means that a single Web page can require dozens of files, each with a name that uniquely identifies it. But for all the complexity, the effect is simple: When a visitor arrives at a Web page, the browser retrieves the various files, puts them together to construct the page, and then displays the page on the screen. This assembly happens invisibly to the visitor.

The programming language that makes all this possible is called **HyperText Markup Language (HTML)**. HTML specifies where each element of a Web page goes, how much space it can use, what it looks like, and much more. HTML is often referred to as **code**, and writing HTML is called **coding**.

The HTML that you will be learning in these Technical Walk-Throughs is in the process of being replaced by the higher standard of **XHTML (Extensible Hypertext Markup Language)**. XHTML was developed by a working group of the **World Wide Web Consortium (W3C)**, the Web's standards body. Existing Web sites are being updated to meet the XHTML standard. This updating process is time consuming, which is a good reason to try to comply with the new standard as much as possible now to make the eventual transition easier.

The latest version of HTML is HTML 4.01. In HTML 4.01, some of the tags allowed in former versions of HTML are deprecated (their use is being phased out), or not allowed. HTML 4.01 exists in three variations: strict, transitional, and frameset. You will be using transitional HTML in the Technical Walk-Throughs.

HTML 4.01 encourages the use of **Cascading Style Sheets (CSS)**. A single **style sheet** can be used to indicate all of the formatting for any number of Web pages, all of which can be linked to a single style sheet located in a separate file. Styles also can be "embedded" in a Web page, or even located within a single HTML element. Using styles is a much more efficient method of controlling Web page formatting when compared to the traditional method of entering formatting tags throughout an HTML file. By using a single linked style sheet, multiple changes can be made to multiple pages simply by changing the tags in the style sheet. For example, to change the background color without a style sheet you would edit each Web page, locating the background color tags and changing them. Using a style sheet, the change is made once, and then applied to all pages the style sheet is linked to.

Unfortunately, browser support for CSS is uneven, with different browsers supporting CSS to different degrees. Although in principle CSS is not complicated, its use today requires some level of skill to address the difference in support by browsers. For that reason, CSS is not covered in these lessons. Instead, the aim of the Window to the Web lessons is to build your proficiency in transitional HTML. After you have mastered HTML, you can begin learning about CSS and adapting your coding to meet its requirements. If you want to learn more about CSS, the W3C has a CSS home page containing the information you need at www.w3.org/Style/CSS/.

How HTML Works

HTML documents are written in text, using HTML **tags** (see Figure 1.7). Tags tell browsers (such as Internet Explorer or Netscape) how to display the material in an HTML file. Tags are usually paired. A **start tag** tells a browser where to begin carrying out an instruction, and an **end tag** follows, telling the browser when to stop following the instruction. For example, the body start tag (<body>) instructs a browser that the material following the tag is part of the main body of a Web page, and the end tag (</body>) lets the browser know where the main body ends. Note that start and end tags are identical except for the slash (/) contained in end tags, and that tags are always contained within angle brackets (< >).

A set of HTML instructions is known as an **element**, and text located between paired tags is known as **element content**. For example, **<title>This Is a Title</title>** is an example of an HTML element that lets a browser know that the text contained between the tags is the page title. The TITLE element is displayed at the top of the browser window.

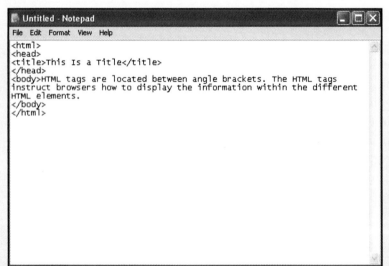

FIGURE 1.7
HTML tags are located within angle brackets (< >). The text in between the tags is element content, and the set of tags and element content compose an HTML element.

HTML Tag Functions

The main HTML tags are used to:
- Control how text looks on the page.
- Insert and control graphics, play music, or show video files.
- Provide links to pages within the site and to URLs at other sites.
- Create tables for the layout of text and graphics.
- Assist search engines in locating and cataloging Web pages so Web users can find items of interest to them.

Other types of HTML tags are used with less frequency and are not reviewed here. Others work only on certain browsers. For example, the audioscope tag (<audioscope>) works only on WebTV. Thus, when building a Web site, developers think regularly about **browser compatibility**—that is, whether their ideas can work on all browsers and whether they need to include code tailored for a specific browser. In addition, not all tags work on every **platform**, or type of computer or access device being used. Most application programs have had to be written to run on a particular platform, once for a Windows computer and then again for a Macintosh. Some technologies (such as Java) allow programs to run on different machines without being completely rewritten for each platform.

In general, the code in a simple HTML file is interpreted sequentially, from the top of the file to the bottom. The browser starts with the first line of code and works its way down the file one line at a time, executing the commands associated with each tag, and finishes with the last line in the file. For a simple HTML file, there are no exceptions to this rule. With HTML files that include other programming languages, the sequence gets more complex as the logic of the code is followed.

To learn how to use HTML, you must know how to use a **text-editing program** to create HTML code, and how to view these files through your browser after they have been created. After you have learned these skills, you can practice coding in HTML by following the step-by-step instructions throughout the Technical Walk-Through sections of this book.

Text-Editing Programs and Browsers

To enter your HTML code, you need to use a text-editing program such as Notepad (Windows) or Simple Text (Macintosh). These programs do not automatically insert formatting or HTML tags. Avoid programs such as Word or FrontPage that add their own formatting. In order to see exactly how a Web page goes together, it is best to avoid the added confusion of the tags and styles that are inserted by some editing packages. This will ensure that your code is "clean," simple, and under your control. Later, when you use editing packages that automatically create code, sometimes you will need to troubleshoot, and understanding HTML will help you repair any problems. Also, code created by FrontPage and some other Web-page editors is generally not well structured and not always compliant with XHTML standards. The best way to fully understand what is going on is to get "under the hood" to examine the inner workings, and to anticipate some of the problems that can occur. This requires direct experience with HTML code.

Before creating a file with a text editor, set up a file structure to hold the Web files you will create. Be sure to pay close attention to where files are saved because you will need to locate them again. By creating a file structure that makes logical sense, you will be able to locate project files later to make changes and to upload them to the Web. When you upload files, you will be using the "browse" function to locate the files, moving through folders and subfolders to the exact spot where each file was saved. If you are creating files for a Web site, all of the files for the site should be stored under a single folder, or **root directory** for the site. For a larger site, you can create subfolders within the site's root directory folder to hold the various types of files that you will be using (see Figure 1.8).

Before you begin, you should know that the HTML files you will be creating need the .html (or .htm) extension so browsers can recognize them. The .html extension is more current, so use it for all of your HTML files, although .htm will work. When saving a file Windows might automatically add a .txt extension even if you key the .html or .htm extension, and this extension might be hidden from view. Although Internet

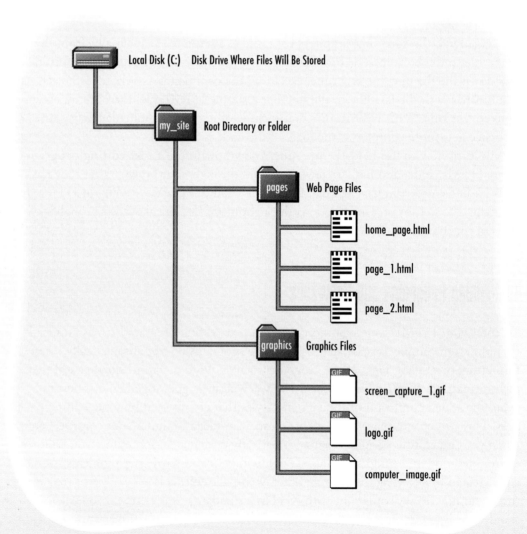

FIGURE 1.8
A Web site root directory or folder, with subfolders containing the different types of files composing the Web site.

Explorer will still be able to read the document, other browsers might not be able to, so the file name will need to be changed using the Rename function.

VIEW FILE EXTENSIONS

To view file extensions, you need to have the appropriate settings selected. For example, in Windows Explorer, select the settings to view file extensions by following these steps:

1. Double-click the *My Computer* icon on your desktop.
2. Click Tools on the Menu bar.
3. Click Folder Options on the drop-down menu.
4. Click the View tab in the Folder Options dialog box that appears.
5. Scroll down the check box list that appears until you find Hide extensions for known file types. The box to the left should not have a check mark in it. If it does, click to remove the check mark.
6. To finish, click Apply and then click OK.
7. Look at documents in Windows Explorer to see that your files all show their file extensions.

By default, Notepad displays only text files (.txt). If you cannot find an .html file that you know exists, make sure you have opted to view All Files (*.*) from the Files of type list.

CREATE A WEB PAGE FILE

To prepare to write HTML code, create an .html file in your text editor by following these steps:

1. Open your text editor.
2. Click File and then Save As and name your file "shell.html" (or another name of your choice, as long as all file-naming rules are followed). File names cannot contain spaces and generally should be in lowercase letters. If you want to separate words in a file name, use an underscore (_). Remember to give your file an .html or .htm extension (see Figure 1.9). If you forget to indicate the extension, your browser will not be able to read the file.

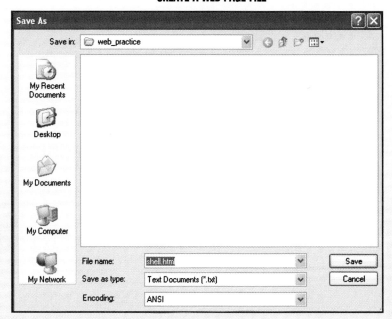

FIGURE 1.9
Creating a file in a text editor (Notepad).

3. Indicate where you want the file to be saved. For Windows, create a new folder named "MyWebs" within the MyDocuments folder. For Mac, place the new MyWebs folder where it will be most readily found. Within MyWebs, create a new folder named "web_practice". Save all files created in the Technical Walk-Through sections in this folder. You can create a different file structure if you like, as long as you design it logically and create folder names you will remember later.

4. Click Save when you are finished.

Now that you have created an HTML file, you need to see how it will look when viewed through a browser, such as Internet Explorer or Netscape. You do not have to be online to do this. Internet Explorer users can click on the Work Offline button if the Connect To dialog box appears. With Netscape, if the Connect To dialog box appears, click Cancel, and click OK when the Alert dialog box appears.

The shell.html file you just created does not contain any HTML coding, so when it is viewed on your browser, the screen will appear blank. To see how HTML works when viewed on your browser, you need to enter some HTML tags and some text. This forms an HTML element that a browser can interpret and display.

VIEW HTML

View the HTML source code for a Web page by following these steps:
1. Use your text editor to open the shell.html file.
2. Key a body start tag **<body>** and then key the following text: **This is a demonstration of how HTML tags work and how HTML looks when viewed through a browser.**
3. Key a body end tag **</body>**.
4. The HTML element you just created should look like this:

```
<body>This is a demonstration of how HTML tags work and how
HTML looks when viewed through a browser.</body>
```

5. Save the file. Now you are ready to see what the HTML code you just entered looks like when viewed through your browser.
6. Open your browser window.
7. Click File and then click Open from the drop-down menu that appears.
8. Browse to locate the file you just created. (This is when it is essential to know the file name and where the file is located on the system. Since you will be using files with .html or .htm extensions, they will not show on the file list if it automatically defaults to *.txt, as only text files will appear. If this happens, change the file list to show all files by selecting *.* from the drop-down box for Files of type.)
9. After you have located your file, click Open in the dialog box, and then click OK to display your file. You should see the text you entered between the body tags on your browser screen (see Figure 1.10).
10. After viewing the text, switch back to your text editor, delete the code entered in Step 2, and save the file.

The text you entered between the body tags appears on your browser screen.

When entering HTML code, you should periodically check the results by viewing your file in the browser, especially during your first attempts at coding. To do this, you will need to save the file in your text editor and then click Refresh in your browser to see the updated result. If a problem exists, it should be easy to determine which small section of code caused it. When numerous coding changes are made at the same time, it becomes more difficult to track down which change is causing a problem.

How to View Source Code

Source code is the term for the HTML code behind any Web page viewed by a browser (see Figure 1.11). The easiest way to view the source code for any Web page is to right-click on the page and then click View Source (Internet Explorer) or View Page Source (Netscape). This capability is useful because it allows you easily to troubleshoot HTML code that you have written. If you notice errors when viewing a file you have written, you can quickly look at your file (the source code) to track down the cause of the error. You can then edit your work and resave it. Clicking the

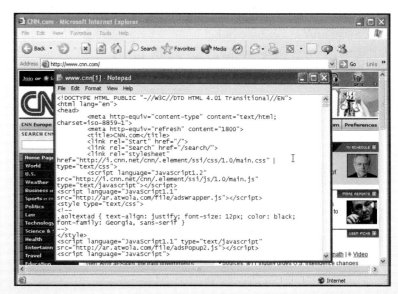

FIGURE 1.11
Using a browser to view source code for www.cnn.com/.

Refresh button on your browser (Internet Explorer) or the Reload current page button (Netscape) forces the browser to bring in the latest version of the file, enabling you to see whether the changes you made were successful.

Editing code viewed by Internet Explorer and Netscape works slightly differently. When you click View Source in Internet Explorer, the Microsoft text editing program (Notepad) automatically opens up displaying the HTML code of the page that was open on the browser. You can then edit and save the source code document just as you did when creating your shell.html document. Netscape works differently because it uses its own Web page editor called Composer. Many versions of Composer allow users to specify an external text editor such as Notepad, but the latest versions do not.

With Netscape, you can see the source code by clicking View on the Menu bar, and then clicking Page Source from the drop-down menu that appears. You can view the source code, but you cannot edit it. To edit the source code, you have to click File from the Menu bar, and then choose Edit Page from the drop-down menu that appears. This opens up the Netscape Composer with a blank screen. To see the source code again, click the <HTML Source> tab at the bottom of the screen. You then can edit and save the source code. You can preview how any changes to the code will look in the browser by clicking on the Preview tab at the bottom of the screen.

Viewing source code is also a useful learning tool. You can learn more about how HTML works by viewing the code behind Web pages created by others. Sometimes the code for these other pages appears complicated because the pages were created using HTML-editing programs such as FrontPage. As you gain experience, however, you will quickly begin to recognize what you are seeing.

EDIT SOURCE CODE

Use the code from a real Web page to practice editing source code by switching back and forth from your text editor to your browser. You should get used to this because you will be doing it frequently when you create Web pages.

1. Connect to the Internet and then open the CNN home page at www.cnn.com/.
2. Find and open a news article. Write down the headline at the top of the article and the title bar title that appears at the top of your browser window.
3. View the source code for the article you selected by right-clicking and selecting View Source (Internet Explorer), or View Page Source (Netscape).
4. Click Edit and then Find. To locate the headline and the title that you wrote down, key it in the Find box and press Enter. The same text might appear between the title tags (<title></title>) at the beginning of the page, and between another set of tags. The headline text might not appear using Find, because headlines on Web pages often are inserted as their own separate graphic files. Do not worry about all the code you see; some of it may not even be HTML. The purpose of this exercise is to familiarize you with using your text editor and browser to enter, check, and change code.
5. When you locate the headline, change it to something else. Change the title bar title also. You will not be changing anything on the CNN Web site. To do that, you would have to save the page on the CNN server. Because you are saving the changes on your own computer, only you will see the changes you have made.
6. Save the file using Save As, remembering to use the .html extension, and use your browser to open and view it. Click the Refresh button to force the browser to bring in the current version of the Web page. You should see the new headline

and title you entered (see Figure 1.12). If you do not see it, view the source code again to see if you entered it in the wrong place. Try changing other sections of the page to see what happens.

FIGURE 1.12
You can change the headline and title bar title or text of a news article on a Web page.

Now that you know how to create, view and edit Web files, you are ready to begin working with HTML.

A Basic HTML Shell

You will begin writing code in HTML by creating a basic **HTML shell** containing four paired sets of basic HTML tags (the HTML, HEAD, TITLE, and BODY elements). The shell can be used as a template for creating any Web page. Whenever you are coding, key both sets of any paired tags right away to avoid the possibility of forgetting an end tag, a common mistake made by beginners. After you have keyed in both tags, move your cursor between them to key any text or elements that you want to place there.

To comply with HTML 4.01 requirements, all HTML files should include HTML version information (also called the doctype) at the top of the file. This is to let browsers know what kind of HTML 4.01 is being used (strict HTML 4.01, transitional HTML 4.01, or frameset HTML 4.01). This information follows a prescribed format and does not need to be modified. For transitional HTML, the information is:

```
<!DOCTYPE HTML PUBLIC "-//W3C//DTD HTML 4.01 Transitional//EN"
"http://www.w3.org/TR/html4/loose.dtd">
```

The HTML tag (<html>) follows the Document Type tag (<doctype>) to tell the browser that the file it is reading is an HTML document—that is, the file contains content marked with HTML codes. Like most HTML codes, the HTML tags come in pairs, a start tag (<html>), which appears at the top of the HTML file, and an end tag (</html>), which is placed on the last line of the file.

The head tags (<head></head>) define an area that contains identifying information for the sake of the user, the browser, and search engines. Much of this information is not displayed on a Web page, but search engines use it to catalog Web sites and to match sites to the terms users might employ in a Web search. One of the header section's only pieces of information to display on the Web page is the title, which appears in the title bar at the top of the Web page window. Like the HTML tags, the head tags come as a pair: the start tag (<head>) to start the header and the end tag (</head>) to end the header.

Located between the head tags are the starting and ending title tags. The title you place between these tags shows at the top of the browser window when the page is on the screen. Netscape browsers use the words between these tags for the default text of a "bookmark" and Internet Explorer uses the same for the default text of a "favorite," so choose your title with care.

Search engines read titles and display their contents in listings, so it is a good idea to put additional information relevant to the page in with the title. For example, if you want to make sure that search engines know your Web page deals with some of your personal interests, you could list those interests as part of the title of your page:

```
<title>My Home Page: Web Development, Web Design, History,
Music, Travel</title>
```

There is no limit to the amount of information you can place in a title, but you should be aware that search engines only display or index a portion of any Web page title.

The body tags enclose the material that displays in the main area of the browser. All the textual and graphic content a designer intends to display on a page is placed after a body start tag (<body>). Following the text and other content, the body end tag (</body>) finishes the body section.

Finally, the HTML end tag (</html>) indicates the end of the HTML file.

USE HTML TO CREATE AN HTML SHELL

Create an HTML shell that you can use as a starting point when creating future Web pages by following these steps:
1. Use your text editor to open the shell.html file.
2. Delete the material you entered earlier for the step-by-step procedure on viewing HTML files with a browser.
3. Key the HTML version information for a transitional HTML document:

```
<!DOCTYPE HTML PUBLIC "-//W3C//DTD HTML 4.01 Transitional//EN"
"http://www.w3.org/TR/html4/loose.dtd">
```

4. Press enter, key **<html>**, and then press Enter again. (Pressing Enter is not actually required, but it makes the code easier to read.)

5. Key **<head>** and then press Enter. This defines the start of the head section.
6. Key **<title></title>** and then press Enter.
7. Key **</head>** to end the head section of your Web page and then press Enter.
8. Key **<body>**, and then press Enter. This defines the start of the body section.
9. Key **</body>** to end the body section of your page.
10. Key **</html>**. Your file should look like Figure 1.13. Save the file when you are finished.

FIGURE 1.13
An HTML shell.

When entering HTML code, you should use only lowercase letters. Although HTML is case-insensitive, which means it does not matter whether tags are in uppercase or lowercase, using capital letters is a bad habit to develop because it violates the stricter rules of XHTML. Given that XHTML standards require all tags to use lowercase letters to be valid, it is best to start developing this habit now.

You should also note that file browsers ignore any spacing, tabs, or hard returns in an HTML document. Special tags are required to make browsers recognize those commands. Thus you can use spacing, tabs, or hard returns freely to separate elements of your code to make it easier to follow if you need to troubleshoot or revise it later.

USE AN HTML SHELL TO CREATE A WEB PAGE

Create a Web page using an HTML shell by following these steps:

1. Use your text editor to open the shell.html file. Use the Save As command to save the file as **home_page.html**. Using the Save As command prevents you from writing over the shell file, and allows you to use it over and over again to create new Web pages.
2. Insert the following text (indicated in magenta) between the title tags (<title> </title>) and after the body tag (<body>). You can change this and any other text later if you want to.

```
<html>
<head>
<title>Home Page</title>
</head>
<body>Welcome to my home page.
</body>
</html>
```

3. Save the file and then open home_page.html in your browser. The text you placed between the title tags should now appear at the top of the browser window, and the text you placed between the body tags should appear on your browser screen (see Figure 1.14).

FIGURE 1.14
This is how your home_page.html file should appear in your browser.

If it seems that HTML code must be followed as precisely as a "secret" code, this is a fitting observation. The "magic" of the Web is possible only when all the elements follow the rules exactly.

Heading and Paragraph Tags

The **paragraph tag** (<p>) is used to force breaks to the next line and to add space between paragraphs. Paragraph tags are an example of tags that can include additional instructions to the browser beyond the tag itself. These additional instructions are called **attributes**, and define the characteristics of the element content. Each attribute has a **value**, meaning a specific choice for that attribute. Some tags can have more than one attribute, such as size and color. The order of the attributes is not important, but all the attributes must be contained within the tag.

The ALIGN attribute can be added to the paragraph tag with one of four possible values: left, center, right, and justify. For example, coding **<p align="center">
Insert Paragraph Text Here</p>** results in a paragraph centered on a browser's screen. The default value for paragraph tags is left alignment, so you do not need to enter an attribute and value for left-aligned paragraph tags. Some browsers do not support the justify value, so if you use this value you should check to see how your file displays on the most popular browsers.

Heading tags (<h1> . . . <h6>) can be used to provide a heading to a paragraph or to a section of a Web page. HTML has six levels of headings: <h1>, the largest, through <h6>, the smallest. These tags are paired, so each heading must be enclosed within heading start and end tags. Usually only <h1> through <h4> headings are used, because <h5> and <h6> tags result in text that is smaller than the default text size of most Web pages.

action

CREATE HEADINGS AND PARAGRAPHS

Add a heading and two paragraphs to your home_page.html file by following these steps:

1. Return to your text editor to view home_page.html.
2. Press Enter after the start body tag and code Welcome to my home page. as a level 1 heading.

```
</head>
<body>
<h1>Welcome to my home page.</h1>
```

3. Add two paragraphs to your home page.

```
<body>
<h1>Welcome to my home page.</h1>
<p>This is the opening paragraph of my home page.</p>
<p>This is the second paragraph of my home page.</p>
</body>
```

4. Save the file and refresh your browser. The screen should look like Figure 1.15.

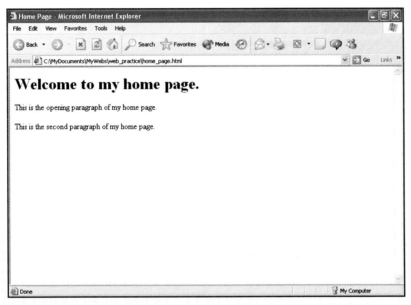

FIGURE 1.15

This is how the heading and paragraphs you created should appear in your browser.

action

ADD AN ATTRIBUTE TO A PARAGRAPH

Add an alignment attribute to the paragraph tags to center paragraphs on your page by following these steps:

1. Return to your text editor and center the first paragraph.

```
<p align="center">This is the opening paragraph of my home
page.</p>
<p>This is the second paragraph of my home page.</p>
```

2. Save your file and then refresh your browser. Your first paragraph should be centered.

How to Add Comments

Comment tags allow programmers to enter comments or information into HTML documents. Anything enclosed by the starting and ending comment tags will not be displayed by browsers. Comment tags are similar to Post-It® Notes for HTML. You can use them to place reminders, to explain why something was done in a certain way, or to indicate future plans for Web pages. A comment starts with a `<!--` and ends with a `-->`. These codes signal to the browser that the information between the codes should not be displayed. For example, if you plan to insert an image onto a Web page but do not have the image available when you are coding the page, you can insert a comment such as `<!-- Insert Graphic Here -->`. That way you will know exactly where you want to paste the image when it is available. Comments explaining why things were done in a certain way also can assist others who might have to work on your code. Comments can be seen by anyone who views the source code for the page. If you do not want others to see your comments, you must remove them before you upload your pages to a server.

ADD COMMENTS

Practice adding comments to your home page by following these steps:
1. Return to your text editor to view the home_page.html file.
2. Key the following comment just before the body start tag:

```
<!-- Expand on this section with an introduction to my Web site. -->
<body>
```

3. Save the file and view it in your browser. Do you see what you just keyed?

The Copy and Paste Function

You can use the copy and paste functions of your text editor to speed up the coding process and make troubleshooting much easier. After a set of code is correct, copying and pasting also prevents errors from being introduced. Never key code that is already available. Take care to select only the code you want, and all of the code you want. Missing just one tag or even a portion of a tag during copying will result in code that does not work. You should also be careful that you do not paste over code that is already in a file.

Practice using the copy and paste function in the following steps:

1. Return to your text editor to view the home_page.html file.

2. Use your cursor to select and highlight all of the code in home_page.html. You can copy the code using your text editor's menu commands, or you can use keyboard commands. For Windows, use Ctrl+C to copy to the Clipboard. On a Mac, use Open Apple+C.

3. Now open a new file and then paste the code you just copied into it. You can use the menu commands Ctrl+V (Windows) or Open Apple+V (Mac).

4. Replace the text located between the body start tag and end tag with the following text:

```
<body>
<h1>Welcome to my home page.</h1>
<p align="center">This is the opening paragraph of my home
page.</p>
<p>This is the second paragraph of my home page.</p>
Using copy and paste saves a lot of time and can help avoid
coding errors.
</body>
```

5. Use Save As and give the file a new name so it will not overwrite your earlier file.

6. Open the file on your browser. You should see the new text you entered on your browser's screen.

design
project

For this project, you will create the first part of a Window to the Web resource site that you will add to in the next chapters. The final site will include at least the following information, developed over the course of this and subsequent chapters:

- Information about free host sites, including a comparison of features
- Sources of graphic resources (copyright free), including clip art, backgrounds, animations, and buttons
- Sources of Web site tools such as counters, guestbooks, and dynamic scripts
- Information on good Web page design
- Favorites lists with links

1. Use a search engine to gather information about at least six free host sites. The information you gather will later be incorporated into your Web site, and will also be useful when you are ready to upload your pages and place your site online. Make sure to gather notes that include any reference material that will be needed later, such as URLs, publishers, author, and so on. You will be comparing and rating features of these free host sites in your Web site, so be sure to gather this information as well. You should also search for sites that rate free hosts. Feel free

to conduct any additional research you think is beneficial. Bookmark the sites so you can easily locate them again. Write a report summarizing your findings.

2. Create a folder for the files that will make up your Window to the Web resource site. Name this folder design_project, and save it under the MyWebs folder you created earlier. Be sure to save any files that will make up your Design Project in this folder. Remember to type file names in lowercase, and do not include spaces or symbols in file or folder names. You can use the underscore symbol to separate words in the file name, such as home_page.html.

3. Use your shell.html file to create a start for the first page of your site, a page that includes information about Web hosts. Reuse your shell.html template file to create blank Web pages for each of the additional pages of your full site, including one page for each of the following topics:
   • graphic resources
   • sources of tools
   • page design information
   • favorite links

   Remember to use Save As to rename each page while keeping your shell.html file intact. You can name these additional files as you like, but be sure to give them names that make sense and will help you identify their contents when you are browsing for them in the future. Save a copy of the home_page.html file that you created in the Technical Walk-Through section of this chapter in the design_project folder. Use comment tags to insert your ideas and plans as notes for your future reference.

4. Use the Web host information page you created to present the report you created for the Research Assignment. Use copy and paste to place the text where you want it to appear within the body of the page's code. Create headings and paragraphs. Experiment with different heading sizes and paragraph alignments.

CHAPTER

2

Web Design: Profession and Purpose

cyber
visit

ROBIN WILLIAMS

Author, Instructor

Design Viewpoint

"There are two aspects of Web design that will determine what league you're in as a designer. One is visual aspect: making the site look appealing, compelling, or entertaining; creating sophisticated graphics and intuitive navigation; and using good visual judgment in the presentation of content. The other aspect is technological: knowing how to design and optimize pages and graphics for efficient downloads and display; knowing the basics of Web technology; and being familiar with what advanced or enhanced technologies should be recommended and implemented. . . . The phrase 'Web design' is a short way of saying 'design, programming, technology awareness, and information architecture, not to mention expertise in Web software applications and human relations.'"

Resume

Has taught both traditional and digital design, typography, desktop publishing, and Web design. Books published in 16 different languages. Co-founded the Santa Fe Mac Users Group and the New Mexico Internet Professionals Association. Has participated in workshops and seminars all across North America. For more information, visit www.readsouthwest.com/rwilliams.html.

Clients

Santa Fe User's Group, Peachpit Press, Center for Creative Imaging, Stanford Alumni Communications, ComputerLand, International Typeface Corporation, and Boston Computer Society Magazine.

Designer's Home Page

www.peachpit.com/home-sweet-home/

You Found It!

Bookmark this site because now you have a fun source for
technical tips, links to web tools, how-to tips and resources,

downloadable goodies, and various surprises and treats
from
Robin Williams and her entourage of digital specialists.
Be it ever so humble, there's no place like your own web site.

Robin Williams

Select which version of the site you wish to view:

No-nonsense version   Enhanced version
(reduced bells and   (requires Netscape 3.0 or
whistles)   later and QuickTime)

Insights

"Two of the most important factors in good Web design are repetition (consistency) and clarity. A visitor should never have to figure out how to use your navigation system, where they are in the site, or whether they are still in your Web site or have jumped somewhere else."

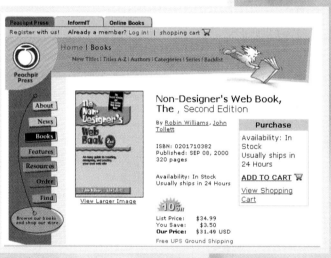

To view this page, go to www.peachpit.com/books/catalog/68859.html and search for *The Non-Designer's Web Book*.

"Just remember the rule, especially when you find yourself seduced by a busy background pattern: if it looks hard to read, it is!"

"I think the info-highway (for lack of a better term) is going to be bigger and more powerful than we have yet to imagine. It will affect all of our lives in a major way."

"I am a minimalist in a true sense of the word. I don't fill my designs with unnecessary elements. Design is the art of solving a problem. . . . I recognize the problem and find the simplest and most direct solution to that problem."

Objectives

➤ Outline the main tasks in the Web design process.
➤ Identify five paths for entry into the profession.
➤ Identify the potential hazards of defining the Web design profession too narrowly.
➤ Assess your own learning needs and set goals to increase your skills in Web design.
➤ Describe the five purposes for Web sites.

Web design is a career for many types of individuals with different talents. For some people, the attraction of the Web design profession lies less in its technical aspects and more in its artistic aspects. But these two poles should not be considered the only choices open to those interested in Web design. As this chapter will show, the many purposes that Web sites serve create a demand for people whose talents lie, not only in technical or artistic fields, but in other areas that are addressed or used on the Web.

WHAT DO WEB DESIGNERS DO?

Every Web page has onstage components—those things a visitor sees, reads, hears, clicks, or fills out (such as a form asking for information). But behind these visible elements is an array of offstage components: the codes, scripts, and elements that make the page and the site work. Web designers create entire Web sites with careful consideration to both visible and invisible aspects of the site.

An Overview of a Web Designer's Tasks

On average, when a Web user arrives for the first time at a Web site, it takes about seven seconds before this casual visitor decides whether to stay or to move on. In that short amount of time, the page needs to appeal enough so the visitor begins to interact with it. What encourages visitors to stay? To engage users, a Web page needs to connect with their cognitive processes and emotional responses; it should fulfill the desires for interesting, satisfying, and appealing experiences; it should cause visitors to think and to feel joy, curiosity, excitement, a sense of belonging, and anticipation. It is no small task to design Web sites that engage users.

To engage a visitor, a Web page needs to connect with the visitor's cognitive processes as well as emotional responses.

Determining what brings (or will bring) users to a site is one of the first tasks for a designer or design team to accomplish. Clearly, for a medium as rich and useful as the Web, making this determination is more than a matter of creating valid HTML code or attractive graphics. Web designers are now required to have skills in an increasing number of disciplines. If a Web site is to serve a purpose for its owner and for its visitors, and if the site is intended to encourage human interconnection, non-technical skills are increasingly important, perhaps equally as important as the technical skills the Web initially required. Creating sites that fulfill the Web's potential requires high-level analytical skills involving perception, expertise, and experience in many areas of life, human interaction, visual and verbal communication, and business. In fact, to obtain the status of Certified Internet Webmaster (**CIW**) or Master CIW Designer requires training in many of these areas, in addition to learning the technology.

This chapter covers the process of determining the purpose of a Web site a bit later. First, however, look at the main tasks performed by Web designers in organizing, coordinating, and carrying out a Web design project. Because a Web site can include many components—graphics, text, audio and video, and interactive features—one of the most important concerns of any design team is to organize the process from beginning to end, staying in contact with each other the entire time. Individual team members usually exercise responsibility for particular aspects of the design project, but communication among all members will help the team progress toward a well-designed, useful site. Web designers are involved in three main tasks, which are listed below and then described in the following sections.

- Gather and organize content.
- Design the technical and interpersonal features.
- Test and adjust.

GATHER AND ORGANIZE CONTENT Site content, the substance on which the site will be based, includes all those things users will read, see, and hear: diagrams, visuals, logos, and images, as well as text. To accomplish the task of gathering content, Web developers often carry out a combination of interviews and other content-gathering processes. Because Web content can include visual elements as well as audio elements, a developer's job also can involve researching and developing material in these other media. To develop the content for the site, the designer evaluates the thematic suitability of the content, asking whether it communicates the essential message well, but also determines the best medium for communication: What messages need to be presented as text? What can be effectively communicated through artwork, photo, or logo? Should audio files be used for the benefit of visually impaired users or to enhance the site?

When considering thematic suitability, a Web developer asks whether the material helps to establish a **Web presence**—the identity for the site's owner, whether it is a business, an organization or enterprise, or an individual. How well does the site represent the owner's point of view? Is the site's content focused specifically at meeting the owner's needs, as well as the users' needs? Because the text, the "talking" part of the site, plays a major role in creating this presence, the designer ensures that it is high-quality, publication-ready "copy"—well written, interesting, and communicative. Another set of tasks for the designer pertains to photographs and graphics, which provide the visual interest for the site and need to work effectively toward accomplishing the goals of the site on the behalf of the owner.

CIW
Internet and Web certification program for those entering or advancing in the information technology profession. Vendor neutral, meaning it does not teach technology from just one company (such as Microsoft). Offers certificates in various job roles and skill levels. Information can be found at ciwcertified.com/.

Web presence
Fundamentally, having a page or site available on the World Wide Web. Serves as a representation of the site's owners. Can vary in scope from a site offering little more than e-mail, to a site that features visitors' contributions, to a site with hundreds or thousands of Web pages for a large business.

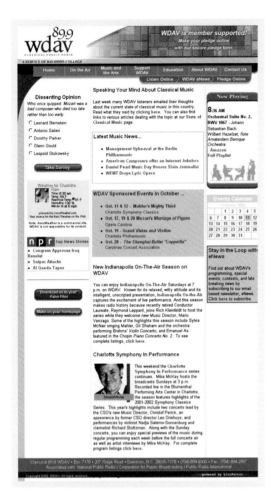

The WDAV Classical 89.9 site at wdav.org/ provides an excellent combination of visual interest with high-quality copy. The design supports the "identity" of the site's host by using the page banner to alternate announcements of upcoming performances and the Classical 89.9 logo.

Another responsibility of a Web developer is to ensure that the site's information is organized in ways that capture interest and engage the minds and emotions of users. A complex organization might have a large amount of information to share with visitors of its site. To ensure that these visitors do not suffer "information overload," a site designer needs to apply good principles of instructional design that keep visitors from feeling overwhelmed or lost. Sites should be broken into singular modules containing a unified thought or idea. These individual elements of information then need to be grouped into logical categories. Psychological research has shown that the human mind has a capacity to take in only five to nine concepts at a time (an intake limitation of 7 ± 2). If a category of information contains more than nine items, it is a candidate for further subdivision.

DESIGN TECHNICAL AND INTERPERSONAL

FEATURES As will be discussed at length in Chapters 5, *Phase I: Prepare and Plan,* and 6, *Phase II: Design and Produce*, gathering content does not necessarily come before the job of designing the look, feel, and interface of the site. Site designers often carry out this task while content is being gathered. Depending on the purpose of the site, design of the main technical and interpersonal features might even precede the accumulation of the content.

Table 2.1 provides examples of the types of features that might be included in a Web design. Even if actual content has not been gathered, design work can begin by planning these features. The table provides the types of questions a Web designer needs answers to early in the design process.

DO YOU KNOW?

Question What does a Web editor do and what types of skills are needed?

Answer A Web editor plays an important role on the Web design team. The Web editor collects, selects, writes, edits, and proofreads online content and establishes the writing style of the site. A Web editor studies and researches topics, and verifies facts, dates, and statistics, using standard reference sources. In addition, the Web editor peruses content for errors in spelling, punctuation, and syntax. This person coordinates the editing work with the design team and helps review the layout. There are several types of Web editors: associate editor, editor, senior editor, editorial assistant, managing editor, and section editor. Usually, no one editor does all of the tasks listed.

A skilled Web editor must understand how to communicate effectively on the Web. A good Web editor must have a passion for accuracy and detail, the ability to do many tasks, a distinct yet appealing writing style, and the ability to work as a team member. In addition to a broad knowledge of HTML and XHTML, experience with Dreamweaver, Photoshop, and other Web design programs can be useful.

TABLE 2.1 Possible Web Features

Technical Features	Questions
Navigation Aids	What types and how many? (Will they be image based, text based, or both?)
Text	Will there be any textual enhancement (such as a scrolling marquee) that must be coded specially?
Multimedia	Will the site use audio, video, or advanced graphics?
Database	Is a database required? Where will the database be stored? What plans are in place to ensure the database survives power failures or security breaches?
Server	How much space will be required to upload all of the site's files and programs?

Interpersonal Features	Questions
E-mail	Who will visitors be able to send e-mail to if this feature is included? Who will respond?
Audience Appeal	How can the site attract visitors and appeal to their preferences?
Multimedia	Will multimedia be used primarily to entertain, to convey information, or for some other reason?
Internal Use	Will employees of the sponsoring organization use the site to communicate with each other?
Communications	Will the site distribute the organization's press releases, or will it be used only to allow visitors to communicate with the organization?
User Feedback or Information	Will the site use input forms to collect feedback and information from visitors?

As the list of features in Table 2.1 makes clear, Web designers help establish a site's navigation system, which is the means for users to move around and control their experiences. Some of the most important features of a site's look and feel are the navigational helps, which might appear in the text, in the site's graphics, or in both. These features should be designed to make the site "intuitive" so that visitors will feel comfortable and in control and will not get lost in a maze of confusing links. Well-designed navigational aids also make the site work as a unified whole: every link clearly indicates where the user will be taken, every page is clearly linked to other parts of the site (especially the home page), and other options are always available for the user to exercise. A site diagram is a great design and navigation tool: it helps the designer to plan the site and the user to navigate it.

Other site elements that the site designer plans and prepares are forms—the primary means by which visitors interact with the site. Forms allow visitors to perform tasks, conduct research, submit information, or seek help. Although these technical features might require the assistance of a programmer, their purpose and usefulness are important design issues. Do they enhance the site's usefulness? Do they provide services or information that visitors find useful? Do they encourage users' loyalty to the site? To answer these questions, tests for usability and user responsiveness need to be carried out. Information from these tests usually results in revisions to the design.

When site designers plan the technical and interpersonal features of the site, some other types of technical questions are extremely critical. With the variety of computer configurations in the world, the best Web designers think of how a Web site will work

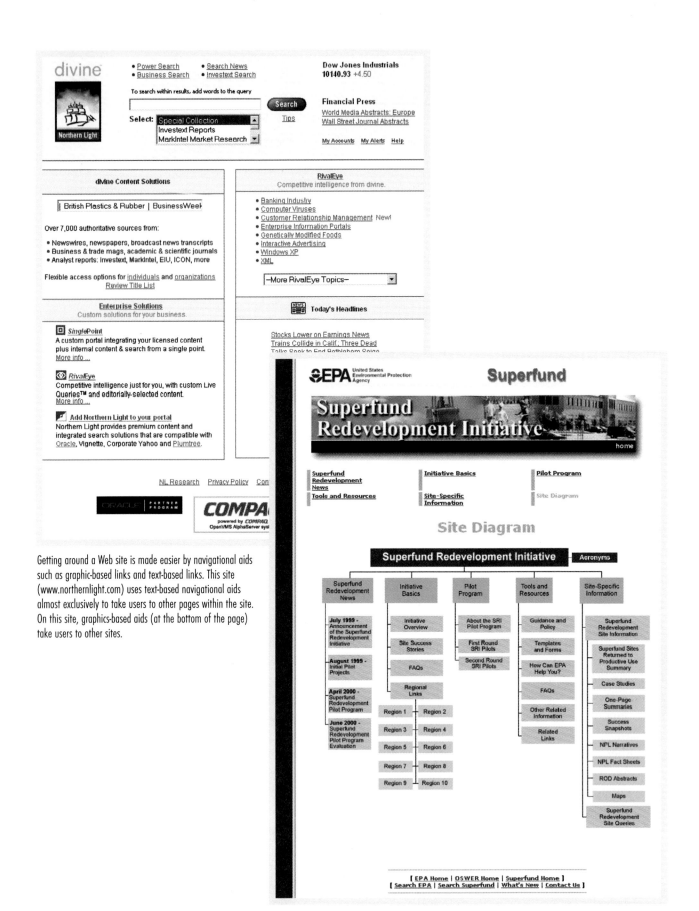

Getting around a Web site is made easier by navigational aids such as graphic-based links and text-based links. This site (www.northernlight.com) uses text-based navigational aids almost exclusively to take users to other pages within the site. On this site, graphics-based aids (at the bottom of the page) take users to other sites.

A Web site diagram can help users navigate because it indicates where in the site's organizational structure the user is at any point in time.

in different browsers, on different computer screens, and with different access speeds and operating systems. Although the Web is a community with goals of universal access, variety among computers is a fact of life (and will continue to be until technological innovation ceases). These differences must be accommodated.

Finally, Web designers are in charge of essential production and organizational matters. What software is to be used in development? What files and folders need to be set up, what file-naming conventions will be established and followed, and is everyone informed of these matters? Complex Web sites consist of numerous computer files. Misplaced files wreak havoc, but the team that organizes early and remains committed to the plan has already eliminated some major sources of potential problems. (See "Input/Refresh: Anatomy of a Uniform Resource Locator" for important information about the relationship between URLs and folder- and file-naming conventions.)

TEST AND ADJUST As a necessary part of carrying out a Web design project, Web designers perform essential project management tasks, whether they are working independently or as part of a project team. One essential part of project management is quality control, a process that includes continuous testing and revision.

The following questions are vitally important in quality control during a Web development project:

- Is the site easy to understand?
- Is it engaging and interesting?
- Does it have value for the user?
- Is it easy to navigate?
- Does it have a unified and consistent look and feel?

Seeking the answers to these questions helps a design team create a site that offers a positive experience for all of its visitors. Before a project is ready for launch, it goes through multiple cycles in which the design team seeks the approval of the client. As the client responds, the design team makes adjustments as needed, until the project is ready to be launched and used. This review and approval process is important to ensure that the site addresses the purposes and goals the client intended. But the testing process is not over. After the client has given written approval of the site, the design team tests the site with actual users and repairs any areas that might be misleading, confusing, or otherwise ineffective. This process also can require multiple cycles, but ultimately it saves time, as well as ensures that the site is positively received.

Throughout the design and testing stages, the goal for the design team is to produce a Web site with a professional look and feel. The completed site must exhibit trustworthiness and good business sense. Few Web sites can afford anything less than the level of polish that gives them credibility and enlists the trust and respect of site visitors.

Five Paths of Entry to Web Design

What careers will help train tomorrow's Web designers? What expertise will people from these careers bring to the Web-design profession? Many might think that technical training will be the most important quality for anyone entering Web design. Although the Web employs sophisticated technology—and continually looks for technical innovations—the purposes for which the Web has been put to use often go beyond technical knowhow.

input refresh

ANATOMY OF A UNIFORM RESOURCE LOCATOR

When users explore the World Wide Web of sites and pages, a clever mechanism is making sure they get the files they ask for. Basically, users send URLs and then servers send files to the users. A Uniform Resource Locator (URL) is the address of a file accessible on the Internet and is most often used to ask a server computer to send a file (such as a Web page) to a site visitor. The parts of a URL work together to tell the right computer to send the right file and render it so the visitor can view the file on-screen. Figure 2.1 illustrates the parts of a URL.

PROTOCOL In this example, http: means HyperText Transfer Protocol. Other protocols appear in the URL as ftp:, gopher:, telnet:, and news:. This part of the URL tells a browser which communication standard to use when transferring files to and from the server computer.

In this text, as well as in other sources, the http:// is assumed when Web references are provided.

DOMAIN The domain specifies which computer on the Internet contains the file a user wants sent to his or her computer. When people share Web sites, they usually provide only the domain part of a URL and let the user click deeper into the site to find details.

A domain name is looked up (by the browser) in a Domain Name System (DNS) (a phonebook-like list of domains) to find the corresponding numeric IP (Internet Protocol) address (such as 148.122.0.15). This number is used to route the request for a file to the right server computer that will respond by sending the file requested to the address of the user's computer. Often, each Web site has its own domain.

FOLDER PATH A folder is a named location for a collection of related files. When working on your computer, all of the files you create are stored in folders, often in folders within folders, or folders within folders within folders. A path is shorthand for describing a particular folder's location, as in \Fred\resume\images\. This path means look in the "images" folder inside the "resume" folder that is in the "Fred" folder. The path given in a URL specifies the exact folder location on the server computer where the browser is to look for the file that is to be displayed.

FILE NAME A file name specifies the name of the file the visitor wants to view. Many files are sent to the visitor's browser in the HTML format (top_page.html or index.htm). If the file name is left blank, the browser will display the file named index.htm.

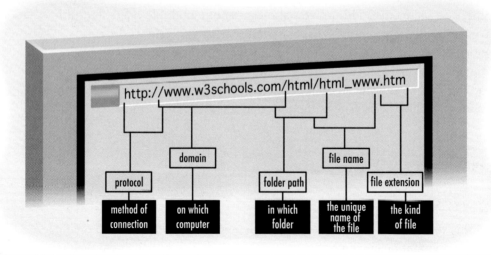

FIGURE 2.1 The Parts of a URL

FILE EXTENSION The browser handles files with special file extensions differently. For example, a file with the extension ".pdf" is viewed using the Adobe Acrobat file viewer (the user's computer must have the software installed, of course). The file extension helps the computer determine the type of file and the software to use when displaying and modifying that file. Other special extensions include .wrl for 3-D files; .wav, .mp3, and .mid for sound files; and .mov and .avi for video files.

EXAMPLES OF URLS The URL http://www.yahoo.com/ instructs the browser to retrieve and display the file index.htm from the root folder on the Yahoo! domain's server. The URL http://www.w3.org/TR/REC-html40/struct/links.html gets an HTML file called links from the folder named struct within the folder named REC-html40 within the folder named TR on the www.w3.org/ domain's server (see Figure 2.2).

The ftp://ftp.ftpplanet.com/Browsers/ URL views the list of files and folders available in the Browsers folder of the ftpplanet.com FTP site. The http://www.adbusters.org/home/ URL retrieves the index.htm file from the home folder of the adbusters.org Web site because the file to be retrieved is not specified.

TIPS

- You can learn a great deal watching the address (usually at the top edge of your browser) change as you click from page to page. When you begin to organize the files and folders of your own Web site, having looked at the structure of Web sites you like will help you with your design.
- Hover the mouse over any link on a Web page and look at the status bar at the bottom of the browser window. If this screen element is turned on, it will show the destination URL for that link.
- If a direct link from a Web search is particularly valuable, back up to the root link for the site and investigate other areas of the site. To get to the site's home page, edit the URL that appears in the address bar. Position the cursor at the end of the URL, and back over and delete the folder names until you are left with the root folder's name. In either case, after confirming the URL in the address bar, press the Enter key (or click on Go) to be taken to your new destination.

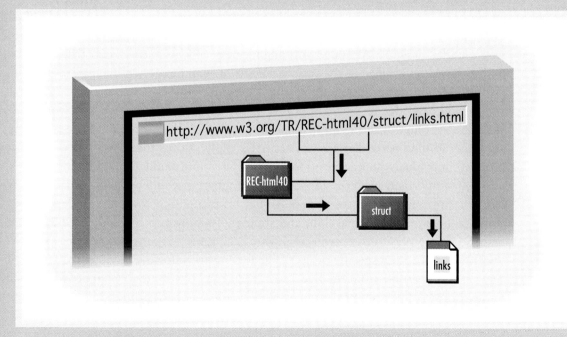

FIGURE 2.2 Folder Structure

The Web is a business tool, a marketplace, a workplace, and a gathering place. To meet the demands of a commercial enterprise, for instance, those with relevant business skills will have much to offer. In the early days of the Web, individuals needed extensive technical backgrounds to land jobs at the Internet startup companies. But many companies that survived did so because they hired people with backgrounds in marketing—people who could define the images of these new companies, people who could *sell*. Successful startups also had help from people with backgrounds in finance. A major dot-com required enough money to acquire the machines and the human resources to get the company up and running.

And so the list continues. The Web's visual richness requires designers who have experience in creating and manipulating graphics. The Web's interactive dimension, in which users and site sponsors expect to interact and form relationships, calls for designers with talent in the formation and enhancement of interpersonal connections. To continue the Web's growing importance as a place for research and learning, designers with knowledge in instructional design, teaching, and learning processes will find their place within the Web design community.

Root Link www.fortune.com/
Direct Link www.fortune.com/careers/
Why Go? To learn about the corporate world from an entrepreneurial perspective. Useful to anyone who wants to know the role technology plays in corporate strategy. Topics cover small business, investing, careers, corporate news, and stocks. Articles change regularly, but the Web and the Internet are frequent features.

Five career paths that can lead into the Web design profession are listed in Figure 2.3. Each career path brings unique types of expertise to the Web design profession. As you set out on the path toward the Web design profession, determine where your strengths lie. Identify those areas in which you already have training or experience, and note those in which you need to learn more. One of your goals should be to become a well-rounded designer. Although you might not be able to master every field of Web design, broad knowledge of the various aspects of Web design will increase your proficiency in designing and producing quality Web sites.

Broad knowledge of Web design is certainly appropriate for those who work in a Web design studio. Although teams permit work to be divided among team members according to their particular areas of expertise, design teams that consist of well-rounded individuals are in a position to cooperate more readily. Broad knowledge is especially important, however, for freelance designers and independent contractors. Web design teams can draw on the knowledge base of many individuals, but independent contractors rely on their own skills and abilities. Training and continuous education help. So does professional networking, which can assist freelancers in seeking expertise they might need for a specific project. The lists in the following sections show just some ways in which people from the five career paths can contribute to Web design, now and in the future. A full team of designers, with a variety of backgrounds and skills, might not necessarily think to make use of all its collective experience. As the Web develops into a truly human community, however, the process of developing appealing Web sites will come to include these areas of expertise and the many roles they encompass.

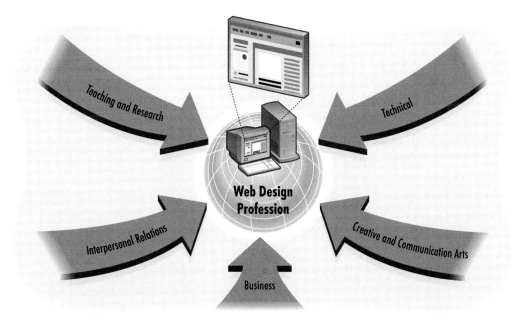

FIGURE 2.3 Five Paths to the Web Design Profession

TECHNICAL PATH Of all the careers now involved in Web design, the technical path developed earliest, because heavy technical demands were required of those who worked as designers in the early stages of the Web. At that point, all pages needed to be coded directly into HTML. Thus, programmers and others with strong backgrounds in technology were among the first to develop Web sites.

Root Link whatis.techtarget.com/
Why Go? To get more from your online experience, and to find useful answers to questions about the technological aspects of Web design, use the "what is" word database of Internet technology.

Although coding by hand is less necessary now (because of Web design software such as Dreamweaver and FrontPage), there are still heavy technical demands. Whatever software is used to develop Web sites, computer code is still the basis of the technology, and an understanding of the code helps teams design intelligently, make adjustments, and troubleshoot any difficulties. Files must be created, organized, and maintained. They must be transferred to the Web-hosting service, and site visitation data must be collected and compiled. These jobs require a solid understanding of the technology, especially when it is necessary to troubleshoot a broken link or missing graphic.

Technically trained individuals perform the following duties and meet these challenges:

- **Coding** Standards and best practices are now being established for HTML coding to increase the degree to which code will work on any browser, on any handheld device, and on all other alternate means for accessing the Web.

    The W3C (World Wide Web Consortium) is advocating that all HTML coding conform to the higher standards of **XHTML**, an "**extensible**" version of HTML. Code must be more systematically planned; be more "compliant" to coding standards; use only those HTML tags that are applicable to all major browsers;

XHTML
Extensible Hypertext Markup Language. A transitional language between HTML and XML, in which Web pages of the future are to be written.

extensible
Able to be expanded upon or added to. Designing Web and Internet protocols to be extensible makes it easier to add new features. The X in XML and XHTML stands for extensible.

be more modular (in essence, reusable); and use style sheets and other strategies to reduce the size of code files to be transmitted and processed.

- **Programming** Scripting languages, such as JavaScript and ActionScript, as well as other languages, such as Java, C++, Visual Basic, and ASP (Active Server Pages), enhance Web sites and make them more dynamic, customizable, and interpersonal. These languages will continue to play a role in Web development.

- **"Front End" Design** The front end of a Web site—the visible page that allows visitors to interact with the site—is much like the front end of any software application. Experienced applications programmers who can design functions, menus, and buttons that are "intuitive" to users and who can create interfaces that communicate clearly and are accessible to all will find their skills employed here.

- **"Back End" Design** Increasingly, Web sites are driven through a "back end"—a database of products, information, or services. Such sites produce the effect of giving customized response by providing current, applicable information to users' immediate needs—for flight information or stock quotes, for example. Those with a background that includes designing and querying databases are particularly valuable in planning and implementing these data-driven Web sites. And if database practices change, those conversant with database theory will be able to advise their teams on the best ways to proceed.

- **File Management and Transfer** Logically organized file and directory structures, clear file-naming schemes, and good habits of saving and backing up files are important to a well-functioning site with hundreds of components. These talents are critical not only in designing a site but in maintaining one as well, because site maintenance calls for the systematic updating of files. Confusion arises quickly unless site planners preserve the same directory structure online as they used in developing code for the page.

  Misplaced files or mismatched file names are often to blame when links are broken or graphics do not appear. The browser follows code to the letter, so there is no room for error. Individuals with strong technology backgrounds have an awareness of file structure and have developed systematic methods and habits for file naming and file management. These habits are highly valuable to the tasks and challenges of Web design.

BUSINESS PATH Because the Web initially leant itself to more informal uses, the critical business issues of professionalism, image, customer satisfaction, credibility, reliability, profitability, and reputation became increasingly important as this shifted. Individuals with training and experience in business will make the following types of contributions:

electronic commerce (e-commerce)

Using electronic means to support business transactions. Includes electronic transfers of funds and data as well as business-to-client and business-to-business transactions that support the buying and selling of goods and services. Allows customers to locate products and services; select and purchase them; and arrange for shipping, delivery, and support.

- **Business Mindset and Professionalism** An **electronic commerce (e-commerce)** Web site exists to attract customers, to encourage them to purchase goods or services, and to develop loyalty to the company. Every second of audio or video and every inch of text or graphic must present the company well and enlist whatever follow-up action is needed from site visitors.

  Although Web sites do not have the same costs associated with using or reusing extra words and images as do print-based projects, this is no reason to ignore the need for sharp focus and well-considered planning. The needs of the intended client must be anticipated and addressed—without wasted words or images.

Nor can any errors exist on a Web site. Professionalism is equally significant on the Web as on any other medium of business presence; spelling errors, grammatical problems, and misinformation lower visitors' overall impressions of the capability of the Web site owners.

- **Management** A Web site project becomes a management challenge, whether the project is carried out by a team of designers or by an individual designer. Initial proposals for work need to be developed with care, given that the proposal becomes the contract of work for the project. Expectations and costs; needs for client participation; time lines, tasks, and subtasks; review and approval processes; and processes for change requests all need to be clearly outlined and carefully negotiated in advance.

  Time lines for projects are often tight, with many points where interaction between designer and client needs to be orchestrated in advance so the results satisfy, and hopefully surpass, the client's expectations. As with any challenging management process, the project needs to be broken into parts and structured so that those pieces that need to move along simultaneously do so, and then come together at appropriate points, all within the projected timeframe for the project. Web designers with management skills know from experience that to avoid bottlenecks, to ensure reliable progress, and otherwise to keep the project on track, key management tasks must take place. Knowledge of these tasks, and the capacity to carry them out, are valuable skills and contributions.

- **Marketing and Sales** Most Web sites have marketing and sales requirements, whether the site sells products and services or promotes knowledge, interaction, and ideas. In the business world, the concept of "positioning" addresses a key need of all Web sites—that the site become known for something in particular and known to the particular group of people it is targeted to attract.

  When a potential customer visits a Web site, the design team hopes for particular action and responses from the visitor. People with strong marketing and sales backgrounds know that for visitor interest to result in action, the specific actions need to be clearly orchestrated, and directly requested—you need to "ask for the sale." (One technical device that increases the chances a visitor might purchase something from a Web site is a **cookie**, a small file containing information about the visitor's preferences and tastes. Each time the user visits the site, the cookie helps the server select which material to send to the user's browser.) Web designers with marketing and sales backgrounds bring important judgments and ideas about how to make the site appealing, approachable, and desirable, and how to build the visitor's confidence sufficiently for them to take action.

CREATIVE AND COMMUNICATION ARTS PATH With such importance placed on a Web site's visual and emotional appeal, individuals with strong backgrounds in art, music, drama, and other creative arts play a significant role in design. The Web of the future will make more extensive use of these arts, so these contributions will remain important:

- **Writing Publication-Quality Text** The text on a Web site is the key to the communication process and must be well written. The style of good Web site writing is direct, vibrant, and welcoming. Published Web site copy requires perfect spelling, grammar, and style.

> **cookie**
> Information that a Web site stores on a user's computer so it can distinguish that user from other users. Cookies also record information you provided the last time you visited the site (account name, the last page you visited, what you looked at most, and so on). This information can be used to direct banner ads for certain products that are presumed to appeal to individuals whose information matches the visitor's information.

- **Graphics Layout and Design** A well-designed site applies all of the key concepts of excellent graphics layout and style. Experience in graphic design contributes to a full awareness of how to use colors well, how to design for visual contrast and focus, and how best to produce Web pages that are highly readable, uncluttered, and visually appealing.
- **Music, Art, Drama** Strengths in music, art, and drama are also useful for Web site design. Many sites include musical elements to enhance the communications process. Ability in art is helpful for generating original graphics and logos. On advanced Web sites, a sense of drama is also important. The entry page can be created to produce a dramatic effect, intriguing visitors, and inviting them in.
- **Gaming and Virtual-Reality Development** Strong narrative instinct helps in designing gaming sites, where visitors expect to be drawn into a story to solve puzzles, find lost persons, or win spectacular victories. Experience in developing (or using) games and virtual-reality environments will help teams make judgments about the effectiveness and quality of such experiences.

INTERPERSONAL RELATIONS PATH Because most Web sites serve purposes that relate to forming some sort of relationship with their users, and many attempt to build community, individuals with experience in human relations, psychology, or sociology will prove valuable to the design process. Individuals who understand something about the nature of group dynamics and personal interactions will find these areas in which to make contributions:

- **Interviewing and Question Design** When Web sites aim to invite participation and provide for interaction, effective interviews and questions that stimulate user response play a major role. Individuals with skills in designing interaction and connection among people can serve a vital function in the planning stages of a Web site project because they can assist in interactions with the client.
- **Design for Engagement** Web sites employ increasingly creative and complex forms of interpersonal dynamics and interactions. Chat rooms and moderated discussion boards frequently resemble virtual versions of workshop settings in which a group engages in activities, processes the insights, and acts upon them. Web site versions of such dynamics will be effective to the degree they are grounded on the principles and methods of face-to-face encounters; however, human relations professionals also will be best qualified to suggest ways Web-based encounters could go beyond face-to-face encounters in ways made uniquely possible by the Web.
- **Creating Community and Interconnectedness** Skill and experience with facilitation—the capacity to guide the performance and involvement of others—are useful in creating a dynamic sense of community and interconnectedness for a Web site. Skill and experience with moderating the exchanges and interactions of individuals is useful when helping them to participate constructively and with consideration, to listen as well as speak, and to respond as well as initiate.

RESEARCH AND TEACHING PATH Because the Web is vast and becoming larger by the day and is increasing in resources to be tapped for any number of purposes, backgrounds in research and teaching professions become extremely valuable to the design of sites. These tasks and challenges of Web design will be among those areas where you can make these important contributions:

- **Design to Support Learning** Even on Web sites designed for sales and services, an essential part of the effectiveness of the site is determined by whether or not the visitor learns how to navigate and use what the site has to offer. Web designers with a background in education have important experience with how best to build knowledge that enables people to understand and empowers them to act with confidence.
- **Design to Support Research** People seek out Web sites with learning and research quests in mind. A background in research, familiarity with libraries and cataloging systems, an understanding of copyright and patent issues, and experience matching people with resources provide important information about how people search for what they need.
- **Design to Address Intercultural Issues** The Web is a world community, and cultural diversity is its trademark. Experience with intercultural relations is essential in helping Web sites communicate with people from diverse cultures. Because Web sites can (and likely will) be accessed from all over the world, it is important that they practice awareness and consideration of each culture's styles and meanings.

The Hazards of Defining Web Design Too Narrowly

Web design work can be defined too narrowly in two ways. One is to define too narrowly the range of essential talents necessary for expert practice of the profession. As the World Wide Web becomes a pervasive medium, just like TV, radio, film, and print, and as its influence grows beyond that of earlier media, the scope of essential designing skills for the Web continues to expand. Because today's Web involves more than HTML coding and graphic design, it is important to engage designers with a full range of skills who can develop Web sites that bring benefits to their intended users.

The second way Web design work can be defined too narrowly is when the purposes of Web sites are defined restrictively or not at all. A Web site might have one predominant purpose—knowledge, decision support, task support, interconnection, or recreation—but that does not mean the site can ignore the standards appropriate for other purposes. Each feature should be evaluated to determine whether it addresses a purpose other than the presumed purpose for the site. If so, a design team must make sure it satisfies all relevant criteria. In addition, evaluating Web sites from the perspective of every type of purpose can uncover hidden potentials for greater effectiveness.

Narrow definitions of Web design can lead to deficient sites, even to sites that alienate or offend users, confuse visitors with complicated navigational features or poorly conceived content, or frustrate users in obtaining what they need or want. Bad design obviously affects sites, but it also diminishes the overall quality of the Web itself, offering poor examples and negative experiences that can impact the reputation of the Web in terms of its present configuration and future configuration.

Narrow conceptions of Web design also have personal impact. For a medium that is marked by change, narrow specialization could make it difficult for an aspiring Web developer to find—and retain—a place in the profession. Technological, economic, and cultural change replace old assumptions often enough. Some technologies are replaced entirely and some are extended beyond the limits of their first versions, new cultural sensitivities arise as the Web extends into places previously unexposed to electronic technology, and economic conditions require greater flexibility in the workforce.

Consider the issue, too, from the perspective of the owner of a site. If everyone on the design team is a specialist, who makes sure everything fits together well? Too much specialization breaks a team into competing groups, and no one, it might seem, understands the client's full needs.

It might seem daunting to consider working in a profession that encompasses this wide diversity of needs, but you might already have many of the necessary qualifications. Formal education and real world experience form a good basis for your development as a capable designer. Seek opportunities to capitalize on your strengths and to learn the skills you need to develop. Material is available in online courses, which allow you to study manageable pieces of curriculum at a reasonable pace. By enlarging your skill set and knowledge base, you will increase your ability to analyze, create, and revise Web sites that accomplish the full range of purposes they exist to fulfill. You also will be practicing the discipline of employing all the talents the profession requires.

To help you take a conscientious look at the path you are taking toward the Web-design profession, use the worksheet in Figure 2.4 to assess your skills in the five career paths leading to Web design. As you improve skills, return to this list to note your progress and to select additional skills for you to develop.

Under these five career paths, rate your skills according to a numeric scale (1 = low level of skill, 5 = high level of skill). Pick three skills (from the 18 total) in which you rated yourself highest. Circle the asterisk (*) after each of these three skills to mark it as one of your areas of strength. Then, pick three other skills you need to learn or develop further. Place a box around the asterisk following each of these three skills. You now have a list that can serve as a guide to your entry into Web design and your continuing development of your skills.

By filling out this worksheet, you will see what skills and experience you bring to the profession of Web design—perhaps more than you might have anticipated. You also should see that you have much to learn. Use this assessment as a planning tool throughout your career as a Web designer. In addition, take the following steps and repeat them periodically:

1. Stay in touch with current job descriptions of the skills and experience wanted in Web designers currently being hired. Conduct a Web search and make notes. One good place to begin is at www.wetfeet.com/.

2. Continuously update your resume after each course you take and project you participate in. Highlight "functions" you have experienced and define clearly your current level of performance and capability.

3. Stay current on issues and possibilities of certification. For example, review the skills list for Site Designer certification through the Certified Internet Webmaster (CIW) initiative. To assure you are looking at a current list, go to the CIW and other certification Web sites (www.certification.net/ and ciwcertified.com/ are two good places to start).

Technical

1 2 3 4 5	Coding	*
1 2 3 4 5	Programming	*
1 2 3 4 5	Front-end design	*
1 2 3 4 5	Back-end design	*
1 2 3 4 5	File management and transfer	*

Business

1 2 3 4 5	Business mindset and professionalism	*
1 2 3 4 5	Management	*
1 2 3 4 5	Marketing and sales	*

Creative and Communication Arts

1 2 3 4 5	Writing publication-quality text	*
1 2 3 4 5	Graphics layout and design	*
1 2 3 4 5	Music, art, drama	*
1 2 3 4 5	Gaming and virtual reality	*

Interpersonal Relations

1 2 3 4 5	Interviewing and question design	*
1 2 3 4 5	Designs for engagement	*
1 2 3 4 5	Creating community and interconnectedness	*

Research and Teaching

1 2 3 4 5	Teaching and learning	*
1 2 3 4 5	Research	*
1 2 3 4 5	Intercultural issues and relations	*

FIGURE 2.4 Skills Assessment Worksheet

web 2.1 activity

A FUTURE DESIGN TEAM

You have decided that when you complete your education as a Web designer, you will form a Web design team that works with small businesses to create new Web sites and improve existing Web sites. Your team will consist of one or two partners in addition to yourself. After evaluating your own background and strengths, identify the additional skills the partners will need to bring to the business. Create a statement that communicates the team approach that will make your design partnership successful. Carry out this project by following this procedure:

1. Research careers, opportunities, and areas of focus within Web design. Consider the following sources and others of your choosing:
   - America's Job Bank (AJB) at www.ajb.org/ for a list of close to 1 million jobs
   - America's Career Infonet at www.aciNet.org/ for employment prospects, and state and local wages, career resource library, embedded links to AJB job listings, state profiles with population demographics, top 10 occupation lists links to state Web sites, and employer database

2. Define the skills and experience you have now and prepare a resume-style description to summarize your strengths.

3. Define the skills needed from the partners that you want to find to join your design team. Write job descriptions for yourself and each other member of your team. Use bulleted lists to create a clear picture of the various roles. For information on job descriptions and titles, explore the "Tech Jobs" area of www.zdnet.com/, especially the job listings in the categories "Web Designers" and "Web Developers." Take note of the requirements employers list in their job announcements.

4. Create a print report that communicates the information you developed for Steps 1–3.

Visit the ZDNet's Tech Job Page by navigating there from the home page, www.zdnet.com/. At www.zdnet.com/special/filters/techjobs/, register as a user and practice doing searches for jobs in Web design, Web development, Web editing, Web training, or other areas of interest. These screen shots show results of a search for "web design" and, within that, a more limited search for Dreamweaver skills.

WHAT ARE WEB SITES FOR?

Web sites, like the Web itself, exist for a purpose. Clarifying the purpose of a Web site is crucial to the success of a Web design project and to the effectiveness of the site. But the purposes for Web sites can go beyond those ever conceptualized for earlier media of communication and exchange. Thus, developing a Web site often requires stepping beyond the constraints of designing for earlier media. A capable Web designer understands this and is ready to work toward this goal with a complete understanding of what the Web in general, and a Web site in particular, attempts to accomplish.

Two Perspectives

Developing a site that accomplishes its intended purpose requires bringing together the perspectives of two entities: the site owner/sponsor and the intended visitor/user. From the perspective of the owner or sponsor, the site's purpose is based on what the owners/sponsors want to accomplish and how they want to be perceived. From the user's perspective, the site's purpose is based on the identity of the intended users and their reasons for visiting. These perspectives, which should not be at odds with each other, form the foundation of purpose that guides the project from start to finish. These perspectives should achieve balance, perhaps slightly in favor of the user, but without ignoring the goals of the sponsor (see Figure 2.5).

From the perspective of the business, organization, individual, or enterprise that owns the site, part of the purpose of the Web site has to do with what the owner wants its image—its identity or "presence"—to be. The following questions should be asked

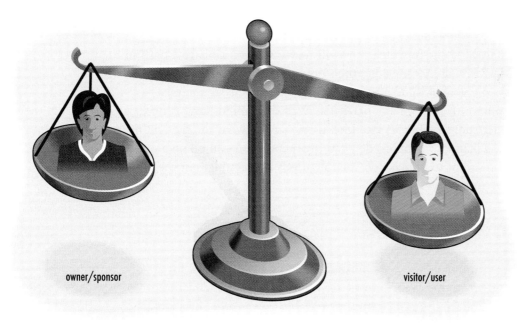

owner/sponsor   visitor/user

FIGURE 2.5 Balancing a Web Site's Purpose
A good Web site must balance the needs of the owner/sponsor and the visitor/user, but should slightly favor the latter.

early in the design process by the design team to elicit important information concerning how a Web site fits the owners' vision of relating to the intended audience.

- Why do the site sponsors want to have a Web site?
- With whom do they want to connect and why?
- What do they hope their visitors will take away after visiting their site?
- What do the sponsors hope to gain from this?
- What do they want their visitors to remember about them and about the site?
- How will they know that this hoped for "image" and "identity" has been achieved?

Owners should be encouraged to think about their general objectives, strategies, and missions and how the Web site will enhance and not interfere with their previous efforts, whether these efforts are on previous Web sites or not.

A Web site conveys the sponsor as an actual "presence"—an enterprise or individual who is "there," or present. The ideal is not just an electronic presence on the Web but a human entity that responds to users' needs and requests through the medium of the Web. To be well perceived, a sponsor's site must create the sense that visitors are welcome, that the host knows who the visitors are and what they need, and that the host is standing by, ready to address those needs.

Feeling welcome is important to users. Whatever the site represents, it is the basis upon which visitors will form conclusions about the enterprise sponsoring it. Web relationships are formed (or lost) through the briefest of encounters. Much rests on the initial impressions of a site: the level of rapport that is produced; the quality of information that is provided; the value of the learning that occurs; the degree to which essential services are offered and problems are solved, and the speed and clarity with which the site is presented. These aspects affect the level of allegiance visitors feel.

To help owners establish this rapport, design teams might consider asking the following questions to identify the potential users of a site:

- Who are the intended visitors for this site?
- Why will they come?
- Will they achieve what they came for?
- Will the experience be positive for them?
- Is this a site to which they will return when they have a need in the future?
- How will the site affect their opinions or actions, now and in the future?

The goal of these questions is to produce a needs analysis—a list of the most important features that a particular Web site should have. A needs analysis of the site's owner/sponsors and its intended users clarifies what the site will need to provide and how. Chapter 5 contains detailed instructions on compiling a needs analysis. For now, it is important to understand the role needs analysis plays in the design process.

Five Purposes of Web Sites

Determining a Web site's purpose should not be difficult for anyone with modest experience using the Web. Knowledge of Web site purposes comes from everyday experience. Still, to begin determining a Web site's purpose, first look at the URL's extension (the ".com" or ".edu" at the end of the Web address). The extension indicates the type of organization sponsoring the site. (These extensions were listed in Chapter 1.) Extensions offer fairly reliable clues about whether a site's main purpose is to encourage

TABLE 2.2 Why People Go to the Web

Motivation	Characteristic
Seek knowledge	The need to find information and useful resources in order to learn and become more knowledgeable
Make a decision or solve a problem	The need to find tools and resources that will help users solve a problem or make a decision
Accomplish a task	The desire to find tools, goods, or services that enable users to accomplish a task they need to get done
Interconnect	The desire to connect and interact with others with similar interests, useful knowledge, or some other basis of commonality
Have fun	The desire to enjoy an experience or be entertained

commerce (to sell you something or to advertise products or services for sale), to represent an educational organization, to offer access to government agencies and information, or to fulfill some other purpose.

Another way to assess the purpose of Web sites is to discuss users' motivations for visiting sites. Numerous motivations bring people to the Web. Table 2.2 characterizes the main categories.

Many, if not most, Web sites fulfill purposes that are some combination of these five motivations. These purposes are examined separately to understand the particular characteristics, challenges, and demands involved for each. The following sections also associate each type of purpose with the particular combination of Web designer backgrounds and talents that are likely to be used for a site with that purpose.

ASSIST THE SEARCH FOR KNOWLEDGE When visitors come to the Web seeking knowledge, they generally come with a question in mind. Because of the ready availability of knowledge on the Web, people have come to regard knowledge as something to be accessed and used, not buried in library archives or locked in experts' brains. In this changed relationship, knowledge is seen to be accessible and valuable—something to be sought out and applied immediately at the point at which a need or question arises. Users also expect to exercise control over the path they take through the information they find. They expect to find more specific information if they need it and to resume parts of their search when they want to. As visitors enter pages, they scan for cues that will lead them to the particular resources they seek.

Sites that provide information and resources to support the knowledge quests that visitors will engage in must do the following:

• Be extremely well structured.
• Be logically organized.
• Anticipate what users will think, ask, wonder, and need.
• Let users focus on cognitive issues rather than on how to navigate and use the site.
• Allow users to print out critical, specific chunks of information (no 20-page printouts).
• Allow users to search within the site to locate what they are looking for efficiently.

- Provide bibliographical information so the credibility of the site's information is clearly evident.
- Provide content that has substance.

Only through structure designed to facilitate research can a site deal with the extreme diversity of those who are seeking information. Web designers with backgrounds in research, teaching, information or instructional design, or in the creative and communication arts will be especially prepared to offer valuable insights to the design process for Web sites with this type of purpose.

Root Link www.invisibleweb.com/
Why Go? To get results typically not found with traditional search engines. InvisibleWeb searches archives and databases as well as other search engines. Take an InvisibleWeb tour to learn how this resource works.

SUPPORT DECISION MAKING AND PROBLEM SOLVING If the purpose of a Web site is to support decision making and problem solving, the site must anticipate the types of decisions and problems users might be dealing with. People make decisions about many things in life: health, finances, where to live, work and career options, home purchases, parenting, education, and many more. A site with this type of purpose provides access to knowledge, but it also guides users through the decision-making process. Think of this type of site as the Web's equivalent of a personal coach. It helps you think through a situation, establish goals, and see the possible results of different decisions before you have to make a decision.

What do these situations have in common to allow Web developers to be able to design a site for any of them? A site whose purpose is to support decision making and problem solving must also anticipate the tools users will need to help them arrive at a decision or solution. To support decision making and problem solving requires more than providing information. This site purpose demonstrates the need to think outside the normal constraints of designing for earlier media. Additional elements for a Web site could include tools and processes that lead users through various viable options, allowing them to see the possible results of a certain course of action, or they might require the use of **multimedia** tools that allow for virtual-reality experiences, which illustrate the results of certain decisions more vividly than descriptions in text. Features that come close to approximating real situations but also allow delays in making decisions until users have the information they need can help them choose the option they prefer with much more certainty.

Users need to work both forward and backward through the problems or decisions they are facing. Working forward, they will gather information so they can identify options. Then, working backward, they will be engaged actively in processes that help them compare options in order to make a choice.

As an example, Ken and Debra Harris are newlyweds planning to move from California to the Research Triangle Park in North Carolina. Ken is a virtual reality programmer working on independent contracts. Debra is a desktop publishing specialist and will be seeking a job after their move. They need to make a decision about where they will live to have access to job opportunities. Also, they need to decide whether to rent or to purchase a home. They expect to accomplish all of this through the Web,

multimedia

Makes use of more than one method of presentation (visual, auditory, or experiential). Often, multimedia implies text mixed with sound and/or video. A multimedia Web site might include Flash movies, MPEG video, Quicktime video, Shockwave movies, or animated GIF images. Interactive multimedia responds to the choices of the viewer.

before they travel to follow through and lock in a final plan. The actual visit to North Carolina will be for just a week—all the time they expect to need to reach closure on plans they essentially will have in place before they leave their driveway. During this single week in North Carolina, they expect to arrange the final logistics for the decisions they have come to through their use of the Web, finalizing home selection, purchase or rental arrangements, loans, renovation plans, and the move itself. Then they plan to return to California briefly, just long enough to pack up, and arrive in their new home within the month.

To support these decisions, Ken and Debra need to work forward to:

- Sift through readily accessible information about the region, including schools, transportation, community resources, and lifestyle benefits.
- Study traffic and commuting issues.
- Determine the range of areas where they might consider living, studying detailed maps to ensure access to major highways from areas that feature the quietness and trees of a less congested community.
- Locate possible homes, available for rent or purchase, to match their needs, requirements, and budget.

Then, they will work backward to:

- Compare the costs of renting a home with the costs of purchasing one (factoring in down payments, renovation costs, interest rates, and taxes).
- Identify and clarify viable options.

Next, they work forward again to:

- Obtain complete information about potential homes, both for rent and for sale.
- Review photographs of the top possibilities (perhaps even take a "virtual tour" of some homes and surrounding property).

Finally, they work backward again to locate a real-estate agent whose approach and personality fit with theirs.

Web users who seek support in a decision-making process bring a blend of information needs similar to Ken and Debra's in that the information they seek has immediate

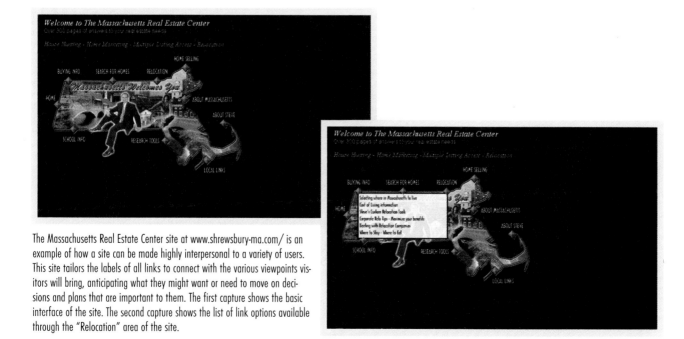

The Massachusetts Real Estate Center site at www.shrewsbury-ma.com/ is an example of how a site can be made highly interpersonal to a variety of users. This site tailors the labels of all links to connect with the various viewpoints visitors will bring, anticipating what they might want or need to move on decisions and plans that are important to them. The first capture shows the basic interface of the site. The second capture shows the list of link options available through the "Relocation" area of the site.

relevance. They want to accomplish a major task for which they need a great deal of information. The fact that the decision has immediate and possibly major significance means that users place higher demands on sites they will use to help them make decisions. So, although sites that support decision making and problem solving overlap in purpose with those that facilitate research, knowledge contributes to the decision-making process, but is not the final goal of such sites.

Root Link www.daypop.com/
Direct Link www.daypop.com/search_tips.htm
Why Go? To find out what's going on in your home town or anywhere else in the world. Focuses on current events and up-to-date news. Excellent source of news for a city, state, or region. Search Tips help get you started.

To design this type of Web site effectively, designers must anticipate fully the extent and demands of the decision-making processes that will be used when users seek out their site. For the site to support visitors in making decisions, it must:

- Offer resources and knowledge needed to support the decision process.
- Stimulate ideas and questions, providing a systematic process to assist users in thinking through their decision or problem.
- Provide necessary tools to explore "what if" scenarios and to weigh the pros and cons of the various choices and options.
- Provide reliable, credible input and experiences from, or even interaction with, experts or peers to help in the decision process.

Web designers who bring backgrounds and talents in interpersonal relationships and business will be particularly able to offer unique and valuable insights to the design process for Web sites with purposes that relate to the support of decision making and problem solving.

HELP USERS ACCOMPLISH TASKS When visitors come to sites to accomplish tasks—buy a book, track a package, find a hotel, make an airline reservation, pick out a seat for a play—the site needs to include a readily understood means for them to do this. For the seven seconds typical users will stay before deciding to stay or move on, they will scan the page to see how to accomplish what they came to do. If they find what they need and understand how to perform the task, they will stay to complete it. If the experience is a positive one, they will be back when they have a similar need. Otherwise, they will find a site that better serves their needs. Although it sounds obvious, a Web site that supports users in accomplishing tasks needs to be designed so users can succeed. Too many sites frustrate users who come to accomplish some task and are unable to.

As an example, Morgan Elliott has a silver flute, in excellent condition, which she wants to sell via the Internet. To accomplish this task she needs a Web site that enables her to:

- Look up other items similar to hers to get a sense of pricing and availability.
- Understand clearly how negotiations and follow-through will work when there is potential buyer for her flute.
- Create a listing where a potential buyer will be able to find it.
- Check to determine the level of interest that has been shown in her posting.

She locates an "electronic garage sale" site that exists for the purpose of supporting such a task. When she arrives at the site, she starts right in to post a sales notice. Her experience is not positive. The cluttered auction pages make it difficult for her to find information and to figure out what to focus on or do next. The navigation confuses her completely. It takes her over two hours to post a note about her flute because of all the "special requirements" for sellers. She finds no way to save her posting while she is working on it and actually loses all her work at one point, which requires her to start over. After posting the ad, she is unable to edit it again, which forces her to live with several typos she finds after her posting goes live.

A site that supports users who want to perform tasks requires that visitors be able to:

- Understand immediately how to accomplish the task.
- Quickly find the tools they need without thinking about where to look on the screen.
- Figure out what to do next at each point in the process.
- Save work so it is never lost.
- Be able to edit work, even after it has been posted (or be warned when they will not be able to do so).
- Perform the task in a reasonable amount of time.
- Understand instructions so they do not have to redo things.

The demands for functionality and clarity placed on these Web sites call for designers with technical and business backgrounds. These types of individuals will be particularly suited to providing leadership in the design of these sites.

PROVIDE OPPORTUNITY FOR INTERCONNECTION Sites with the purpose of establishing connections between people enter into a complex arena of how best to facilitate the level of communication necessary for a group of unacquainted visitors to find each other and interact productively. Who will these people be? With whom will they want to interact and why? What will they consider to be a valuable interaction? What will they need to know to begin? What do they hope will come of this interaction?

In the early days of the Web, **newsgroups** were one of the few ways in which Web users could connect with others. Bulletin boards are another example of the early relational possibilities of the Web. These early forms of interconnection limit users to posting and exchanging messages. Although this method of interconnection improves upon the time lag it takes to exchange letters delivered by the postal service, it does not address the desire for real-time interconnection, topic-focused discussion and exchange, information seeking, and sharing that goes beyond a user's immediate circle of family and friends.

As an example, consider JoAnn and John Kerr, a couple with a home in the mountains of North Carolina, who want to connect with families in Europe, particularly Switzerland or the Netherlands, that might have an interest in exchanging homes with them for 2–3 week vacations. By making exchanges of this sort, the Kerrs hope that they will be able to travel more, save on hotel and restaurant expenses, and experience other countries at the deeper levels generally not possible for tourists.

For the Kerrs to interconnect at a level sufficient to build trust and accomplish their purpose of finding a match, they would need to:

- Find viable options to match up with European families that might be interested in exchanging homes with them.
- Investigate the areas where the possible home trades might be arranged to determine whether this is a place they want to spend their vacation.
- Communicate with the other family, even when there are language differences.

newsgroups
Allow users to exchange messages (similar to e-mails) in a public forum for distribution via the USENET worldwide network of news discussion groups. Each newsgroup tries to focus on a particular subject and has rules, outlined in an FAQ (frequently asked questions) page, governing the behavior of participants, who must use proper "netiquette."

- Establish rapport with the other family so both families can be assured they are compatible and that an exchange between them will work out well.
- Determine travel costs to and from the exchange site and local transportation costs once there.
- Set up the schedule and logistics for the actual home exchange.

For such a process to be supported by a Web site, the site needs to provide a means and a process for people to find and relate to each other. Users need opportunities to interact with others who have similar interests and to form connections. The process must allow participants to learn about each other, to begin to trust each other, and even to befriend each other.

For intercultural exchanges to occur, translation between languages could be a concern. Web sites can be outfitted with tools that translate between certain languages, thus reducing the need for either party to understand the language of the other, although translation from one language to another can present challenges that could affect how visitors regard the site.

Another prevalent concern is how people behave on such sites. **Netiquette,** or rules of proper conduct on Web sites and the Internet, helps to make sure site users are treated respectfully and that all exchanges are conducted with integrity. Only then will users be able to discuss the possibility of forming plans together. After potentially successful matches have been set in motion and arrangements are being made, users will need help of a more practical nature as they orchestrate the actual exchanges, make travel arrangements, follow through on their plans, and later close the loop when they return home.

There are many challenges to designing Web sites with purposes that relate to forming connections. Such sites need to be designed to:
- Enable visitors to determine whether the site suits their interests, values, and lifestyle.
- Create a sense of comfort and security that communications on the site will be kept safe and appropriate.
- Facilitate a process that allows people to learn enough about each other so they can interact more specifically.
- Provide a means for individuals to discuss common interests directly without seeming to form a "clique" within the larger group.
- Moderate and resolve any issues or conflicts that come up between people in their interactions.
- Provide assistance with language and cultural differences and challenges.

Web designers who bring backgrounds and talents in interpersonal relationships and in research and teaching will be particularly able to offer unique and valuable insights to the design process for Web sites with purposes that relate to forming connections.

netiquette

Etiquette, or a code of conduct, for users of the Internet. When writing e-mail, newsgroup messages, and instant messages, users should not be negative (flaming), annoyingly repetitive (spamming), or dismissive. Cross-cultural netiquette includes intercultural sensitivities and considerations. Observing previous postings can help users catch the tone of appropriate communication.

Homelink.org Home Page at www.homelink.org/ allows users to look for homes to use as a residence in countries where they plan a long-term stay. This site connects owners of homes with potential residents, providing ways for parties to swap accommodations for vacations or temporary work assignments.

PROVIDE OPPORTUNITY FOR RECREATION Web sites with the purpose of providing experience and entertainment begin with awareness of an audience and of what it will find enjoyable. For some, enjoyment means games, puzzles, and activities that stretch the mind or provide excitement or a novel experience. Music, sports, and movies are other forms of entertainment people seek on the Web. Other sites provide an entirely different form of experience—the "immersion" experiences of virtual reality, for instance.

As an example, Kevin Walters likes to explore unusual experiences to gain a sense of what they would be like firsthand. He particularly seeks out immersion experiences in which he can explore places that would not be possible for him to experience otherwise. To have this type of experience, he needs to:

- Enter the "place," and know how to move around in it.
- See images of the place (and possibly hear sounds) that give him the sense that he is experiencing it.
- Move around the place, using his own interests to guide his movement.
- Learn about what he is seeing as he develops questions about it.

Kevin's interest is captured when he locates a site that offers a "virtual field trip" of an underground missile silo—abandoned and closed up for years and definitely off limits to the public. To provide this virtual experience, the Web site developer had gained access to the silo and taken a large collection of photographs, climbing down into the massive, dark, and eerie underground area, exploring and photographing all the various

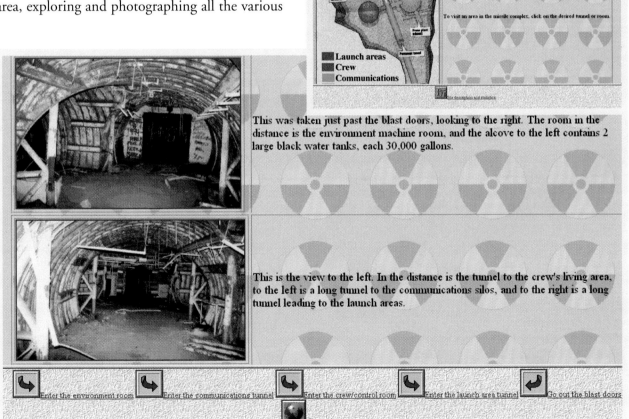

At the Atlas Missiles Tours site at triggur.org/silo/ a visitor can experience a virtual tour of an underground silo for nuclear missiles. The site consists of photos of abandoned tunnels, shafts, and living spaces. One helpful feature of the site is the map. By clicking on a portion of the map, you can navigate through the tour of the missile complex.

deserted underground rooms and equipment. Kevin accesses the site and spends several hours wandering the vast maze of corridors, studying the impressive equipment, learning about the infrastructure that was needed to support this underground "factory," and attempting to get a sense of what it would have been like to build this maze, or even to have worked there.

Experiences like these bring to life otherwise abstract concepts. To provide entertainment and experiences, the site needs to be:

- Graphically rich—with impressive images
- Sound enhanced—in cases where this would add to the experience
- Visually and cognitively engaging—combining elements to view with elements that capture interest and engage curiosity and thought
- Participative—with opportunities for the visitor to play an active role
- Stimulating—in terms of causing visitors to think, and offering compelling dynamics such as mystery, creativity, and elements of surprise

For such sites, the emphasis is often on the unusual, the dramatic, even the exotic. Visual, auditory, and narrative interest will be high on the list of requirements for sites of this nature. Designers with backgrounds in technical areas and in the creative and communication arts are particularly qualified to offer insights to the design process for Web sites with purposes that relate to recreation.

Root Link www.linkdup.com/

Why Go? To discover the hottest, most creative Web sites, check out linkdup. They are constantly updating, have a fully cross-referenced and searchable listing of categories, and weed out the less interesting sites so you don't have to.

Root Link www.webmonkey.com/

Direct Link www.hotwired.lycos.com/webmonkey/frontdoor/tour.html

hotwired.lycos.com/webmonkey/e-business/building/

Why Go? To find comprehensive Web site training and tutorials. Take a tour of the beginner, builder, and master levels of training resources and then explore what's involved in setting up your own e-business.

web **activity**   **A WEB SITE'S PURPOSE**

In this activity, visit three sites of your choice and identify the purpose of each. Then, consider two additional questions:

1. Given this purpose, to what degree does each site accomplish its purpose?
2. What, if anything, is missing in terms of the site's success at accomplishing this purpose?

Working individually or with a partner, conduct a Web search and choose three sites that are of particular interest to you. Indicate your rationale for choosing each site. Then enter each site, trying to determine which of the five purposes, singly or in combination, the site is designed to serve:

- To provide information, knowledge, and useful resources
- To support users who need to make a decision or solve a problem
- To enable users to accomplish a task
- To facilitate interconnection
- To provide entertainment or experience

Review the sites to determine the degree to which each site accomplishes its apparent purpose. Prepare a one- to two-page report on your observations, including what you have determined to be missing, addressing questions such as:

- To what degree is each site successful at serving one or more of the five purposes?
- Do any of the selected sites fulfill all of the purposes? What patterns do you see?
- What improvements might you recommend to the designers for these sites?
- What do the sites do particularly well?

a p p l y & practice

Online Quiz

As a review of the key concepts in this chapter, define the terms in the following list:
CIW
cookie
electronic commerce (e-commerce)
extensible
multimedia
netiquette
newsgroups
Web presence
XHTML

After you are confident that you understand this chapter's content, go to this book's Internet Resource Center (IRC)at www.emcp.com/ and take the self-test online quiz for this chapter. Review any questions you answered incorrectly, and then study the related chapter material again. Retake the online quiz as many times as you need to reach full mastery (90–100%).

Topics Roundtable

1. Describe your own path to Web design and how it fits in (or does not fit in) with what you have done thus far in terms of studies and career.
2. What do you consider to be your greatest challenges as a developing Web designer? What will be your greatest strengths?
3. What experiences have you had, positive and negative, using the Web in the search for knowledge? Share several actual examples.
4. Compare the processes you followed for searching for knowledge before and since you have used the Web. How has your process changed over time since you began using the Web? Describe these changes.
5. Give several examples of times when you have used the Web for decision making and problem solving or for accomplishing tasks. Share one positive and one negative experience.
6. Give examples of ways in which you use the Web as an opportunity for interconnection or as a source of recreation. What benefits have you experienced? What issues do you foresee in your own life, or in the lives of people you know, in terms of retaining a sense of balance between online and actual experiences of these types?

window to the web

CONTROLLING WEB PAGE TEXT AND BACKGROUND APPEARANCE

➤ Control text alignment and appearance using line break, block-quote, division, and preformat tags.

➤ Use character entities to replace characters with special meanings in HTML.

➤ Use horizontal line tags to section content.

➤ Emphasize text using bold and italic tags.

➤ Change font style and size.

➤ Control color by using HTML hexadecimal color codes.

➤ Change text and background colors.

➤ Create a report, formatted in HTML, on Web site tools such as counters, guestbooks, and dynamic scripts.

➤ Apply the HTML skills you have learned so far to create additional Web pages for your resource site and improve the appearance of earlier pages.

technical walk-through

By now, you have learned the basics of creating a Web page, complete with headings and paragraphs. When viewed through a browser, the pages you have created display as black text on a white background. Web pages would be boring if they were limited to those choices. Fortunately, a number of HTML tags enable you to change the appearance of the text and background in your Web pages. Using these tags allows you to make your Web pages dramatically more attractive, improving their visual appeal, and increasing the chances that viewers will stay on to view what you have created.

Line Break Tags

In your **home_page.html** file that you created in Chapter 1, you might have noticed that the use of paragraph tags (<p></p>) and heading tags (<h1></h1> through <h6></h6>) automatically inserted vertical space after each use of the paired tags. If you want to insert additional vertical space, or break a line of text, you can use the **line break tag** (<br />). Unlike paragraph and heading tags, line break tags can be stacked one on top of the other to increase the amount of vertical space beneath a paragraph or line of text. Note that the line break tag is considered an empty element and does not require a closing tag. However, XHTML standards require that elements without closing tags insert the / of the close tag within the open tag, preceded by a space, like this: **
**.

Add vertical space to Web page text using the line break tag (<br />).

1. Use your text editor to open the **shell.html** file. Save the file in the **web_practice** folder, and name it **practice.html** using the Save As command.

2. Key the tags and the element content (shown in magenta) into the HTML shell as indicated following this paragraph. (Note that you can use the cut and paste functions to enter the second and third paragraphs because they are identical to the first one).

```
<!DOCTYPE HTML PUBLIC "-//W3C//DTD HTML 4.01 Transitional//EN"
"http://www.w3.org/TR/html4/loose.dtd">
<html>
<head>
<title>This Is My Practice Page</title>
</head>
<body>
<h1>This is a level one heading.</h1>
<p>I will be experimenting with using line break tags to break
lines in the text of this Web page. Line break tags can also be
used to create vertical space.</p>
<p>I will be experimenting with using line break tags to break
lines in the text of this Web page. Line break tags can also be
used to create vertical space.</p>
<p>I will be experimenting with using line break tags to break
lines in the text of this Web page. Line break tags can also be
used to create vertical space.</p>
</body>
</html>
```

3. Save your file and then open and view it in your browser. It should appear like the document displayed in the browser screen illustrated in Figure 2.6. Notice that the heading and paragraphs are separated by vertical space equivalent to one blank line.

4. Return to your text editor. Now you will use line break tags to create more vertical space, and to break a line. Key the

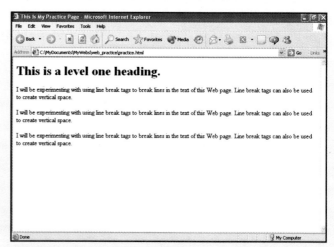

FIGURE 2.6
Browsers automatically display vertical space (blank lines) after headings and paragraphs.

line break tags as indicated in the following code:

```
<!DOCTYPE HTML PUBLIC "-//W3C//DTD HTML 4.01 Transitional//EN"
"http://www.w3.org/TR/html4/loose.dtd">
<html>
<head>
<title>This Is My Practice Page</title>
</head>
<body>
<h1>This is a level one heading.</h1>
<br />
<p>I will be experimenting with using line break tags to break
lines in the text of this Web page. Line break tags can also be
used to create vertical space.</p>
<br />
<br />
<p>I will be experimenting with using line break tags to break
lines in the text of this Web page. Line break tags can also be
used to create vertical space.</p>
<br />
<br />
<p>I will be experimenting with using line break tags to break
lines in the text of this Web page.<br /> Line break tags can
also be used to create vertical space.</p>
</body>
</html>
```

5. Save the file and refresh your browser. You should notice extra lines after the heading and between the paragraphs. The second sentence of the third paragraph should begin on a new line (see Figure 2.7).

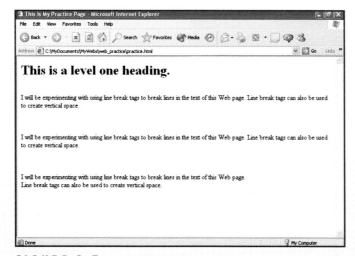

FIGURE 2.7

Line break tags have been used to create more vertical space in the displayed text and to move the second sentence of the third paragraph so that it starts on a new line.

Blockquotes

Blockquote tags (<blockquote></blockquote>) offer another method for controlling the way text appears on a Web page. Blockquote tags indent text on both the left and right margins, making them useful for setting off short passages of text, such as quotations. Blockquote tags also can be nested (contained within each other) to further indent a quotation or passage within or below a blockquoted passage.

Indent the text of your practice Web page using blockquotes.

1. Return to your text editor to view the **practice.html** file.

2. Place the cursor just after the ending paragraph tag (</p>) of the third paragraph. Press Enter to begin a new line (this will not show on the page, but will make your code easier to follow), and key the following:

```
<p>I will be experimenting with using line break tags to break
lines in the text of this Web page.<br /> Line break tags can
also be used to create vertical space.</p>
<blockquote>
Blockquote tags can be used to offset text. They are useful
particularly for lending emphasis to quotations or short
passages of text.
</blockquote>
```

3. Save the file and refresh your browser. The text located between the blockquotes should be indented on both margins.

4. Return to your text editor and then key the following:

```
<blockquote>
Blockquote tags can be used to offset text. They are useful
particularly for lending emphasis to quotations or short
passages of text.
<blockquote>
By nesting blockquotes, you can indent text even further. If the
text within the nested block quote runs to a second line, the
line will indent under the first line.
</blockquote>
</blockquote>
```

5. Save your file, and refresh the browser to view the results. The text you just entered between the second set of blockquotes should be indented even further than the first section of blockquoted text (see Figure 2.8).

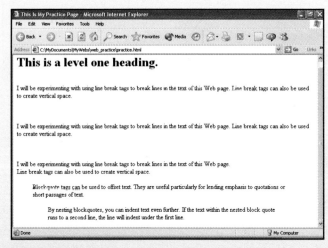

FIGURE 2.8
Blockquotes indent text on either side and can be nested to indent text even further.

Division Tag

Division tags (<div></div>) reduce the need to key an attribute and value each time you want to align HTML elements in a large section of a Web page. Instead, division tags can be used to control the alignment of all the HTML elements contained between the paired division tags. If there are any elements within the division tags that you want to align differently than the specified division value, you can key a different alignment value for that element, and it will override the division tag value. Alignment for any elements after this new instruction will revert once again to the value called for in the division value. Division tags can reduce the amount of coding within a Web page by reducing the number of times alignment attributes are repeated.

ALIGN HTML ELEMENTS

Use division tags (<div>) to reduce the number of alignment attributes and values that need to be coded in a Web page.

1. Use your text editor to open the **shell.html** file and then save it as **practice_1.html** using Save As.

2. Using the practice_1.html file, key the following:

```
<html>
<head>
<title>This Is My Practice 1 Page</title>
</head>
<body>
</body>
</html>
```

3. Add the following code between the body tags in your practice_1.html file.

```
<body>
<h1 align="center">Division Tags Can Speed Up Coding</h1>
<h3 align="center">Anyone Can Do It!</h3>
<h3 align="center">Save Lots of Time by Using This Handy Tag</h3>
<p>The division tag reduces the need to key an attribute and value
each time you want to center or right-align HTML elements in a
large section of a Web page. Instead,
division tags can be used to control
the alignment of all the HTML elements
contained between the paired division
tags.</p>
<p>If there are any elements within the
division tag that you want to align
differently than the specified division
tag value, you can key a different
alignment value for that element, and it
will override the division tag value.
Alignment for any elements after this
new instruction will revert once again
to the value called for in the division
tag value.</p>
<h2 align="center">The End</h2>
</body>
```

4. Save the file and open practice_1.html in your browser. Your browser should display the text as shown in Figure 2.9.

FIGURE 2.9

The ALIGN attribute is used to format this screen.

5. Return to your text editor and use Save As to save **practice_1.html** as **practice_2.html**.

6. On the second practice page, practice_2.html, change the title as follows:

```
<title>This Is My Practice 2 Page</title>
```

7. Remove all of the ALIGN attributes.

```
<body>
<h1 align="center">Division Tags Can Speed Up Coding</h1>
<h3 align="center">Anyone Can Do It!</h3>
<h3 align="center">Save Lots of Time by Using This Handy
Tag</h3>
<p>The division tag reduces the need to key an attribute and
value each time you want to center or right-align HTML elements
in a large section of a Web page. Instead, division tags can be
used to control the alignment of all the HTML elements contained
between the paired division tags.</p>
<p>If there are any elements within the division tag that you
want to align differently than the specified division tag value,
you can key a different alignment value for that element, and
it will override the division tag value. Alignment for any
elements after this new instruction will revert once again to
the value called for in the division tag value.</p>
<h2 align="center">The End</h2>
</body>
```

8. Save the file and open practice_2.html in your browser. All the text on the page should be left-aligned.

9. In your text editor, place your curser just to the right of the body start tag (<body>). Press Enter to create a new line, and key the following:

```
<body>
<div align="center">
```

10. Close the division tag as follows:

```
<h2>The End</h2>
</div>
</body>
```

11. Save the file and then refresh your browser. All of the text on the page should be center-aligned. With the division tag, you were able to do this by coding only one ALIGN attribute and value. Without using the division tag, you had to enter an ALIGN attribute and value for each HTML element.

12. Return to your text editor and change the code in practice_2.html so that the two paragraphs are left-aligned as was shown in Figure 2.9. Change the code as follows:

```
<p align="left">The division tag reduces the need to key an
attribute and value each time you want to center or right-align
HTML elements in a large section of a Web page. Instead,
division tags can be used to control the alignment of all the
HTML elements contained between the paired division tags.</p>
<p align="left">If there are any elements within the division
tag that you want to align differently than the specified
division tag value, you can key a different alignment value for
that element, and it will override the division tag value.
Alignment for any elements after this new instruction will
revert once again to the value called for in the division tag
value.</p>
<h2>The End</h2>
</div>
</body>
```

13. Save the file and refresh your browser. All the element content should be centered, with the exception of the two paragraphs that you left-aligned. Note that this is one of the rare cases in which you will need to use a "left" alignment value, because it is usually the default paragraph setting. In this case, the division start tag overrides the default left alignment of the paragraph tags, thus making it necessary to enter a "left" alignment value for each paragraph. Note how "The End" automatically reverts to center alignment after the left-aligned paragraphs.

Using the division tags will be useful to you later on, because they are used in styles and also can be used to align images and lists.

Preformatted Text Tags

The **preformatted text tag** (<pre></pre>) is a paired tag that preserves the text formatting of any text located between the tags. Text formatted using preformatted text tags will be displayed differently than the other text on a page. It will appear in a **non-proportional** (also known as **monospaced**) font, meaning that all letters have the same width. For example, in a non-proportional font, an "I" is the same width as a "W," whereas in a **proportional font**, the "W" is wider. Also, preformatted text does not adjust if the window or screen size of a browser is changed by a user. This means that some text might not be viewable if that happens. Despite these drawbacks, the PRE element is useful for displaying code, poems, or other material with varying margin and spacing requirements.

USE PREFORMATTED TAGS

Use preformatted text tags (<pre></pre>) to preserve the formatting of text just as you keyed it.

1. Use your text editor to open the **shell.html** file, and rename and save it as **practice_3.html**.

2. Place your cursor between the title tags (<title></title>), and key the following:

```
<title>This Is My Practice 3 Page</title>
```

3. Place your cursor just after the body start tag (<body>), press Enter to create a new line, and then key the following text, indenting the lines of text as shown.

```
<body>
<p>This practice page demonstrates the use of the PRE element.</p>
<pre>
Using
     Preformatted
                Text
                  Tags
                    Preserves Text Formatting
</pre>
</body>
```

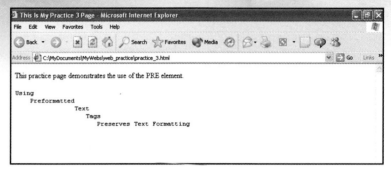

FIGURE 2.10
Preformat tags can be used to preserve text formatting that would otherwise be ignored by browsers.

4. Save the file, and open **practice_3.html** in your browser. Your browser should display the text formatted just the way you entered it into your HTML file (see Figure 2.10). Notice that the font is different from the font on the rest of the page because it is monospaced instead of proportional.

5. Return to your text editor and delete the preformatted text tags to see how the text would look without the tags.

6. Save the file and refresh the browser. Without the preformatted text tags, the browser ignores any of the spacing you entered between the text, and the text appears in-line. Notice that the text is now displayed in a proportional font similar to the text on the rest of your screen.

7. Return to your text editor, re-insert the preformatted text tags, and save the file.

You should be aware that any HTML code contained within preformatted text tags will still be handled as code, not as preformatted text. For example, if you were to place the code from an HTML shell within preformat tags, the lines of code would not be displayed on the browser screen. The browser will ignore the preformat tags and treat the shell just as it normally would, showing nothing because there is no element content in an empty HTML shell. Even if you were to enter text between the body tags of the HTML shell, only this text and not the code would appear on the browser screen, again because the browser is overriding the preformatted text tags and following the HTML instructions.

Character Entities

If you want to re-create HTML code so that it appears on your browser's screen instead of being acted upon by the browser, you must use **character entities**. Certain characters and symbols have a special meaning in HTML, such as the left and right angle brackets (< >) used in HTML tags. If you keyed **<Test>** in an HTML file, the browser would not display "<Test>". Browsers would interpret the angle brackets as enclosing an HTML tag or code that they do not recognize, and therefore ignore it as an illegal tag. If you keyed **
**, again the browser would view this as code and act upon it rather than show it on the screen.

Character entities are used to get around this problem. Character entities are combinations of text, numbers, and punctuation used to represent any characters that have special meanings in HTML. For example, the character entities for left and right angle brackets are **<** and **>**. Keying these character entities instructs a browser to display left and right angle brackets. Character entities exist in two forms. Earlier versions used numbers instead of letters or words. For example, **<** is the letter equivalent of **<**, and **>** is the letter equivalent of **>**. Character entities composed of letters and words are easier to remember, but they are not as well supported by browsers as the numerical versions.

There are hundreds of different character entities. The W3C has a Web page listing HTML-recognized character entities at www.w3.org/TR/REC-html40/sgml/entities.html#h-24.2.1, but many other sites contain information on character entities as well.

If you find that a symbol or character you enter in an HTML document does not display, or has an unintended effect, it is likely that it has a special meaning in HTML. In that case, look up the character you want the browser to display in a character entity list to find its character entity equivalent. Character entities are case-sensitive and do not include spaces, so be careful to key them exactly as they appear in the reference table.

USE CHARACTER ENTITIES

See how HTML code works when placed between preformatted text tags, and then use character entities to replace the tag angle brackets so the code will display properly.

1. Use your text editor to open the **shell.html** file.
2. Right-click and select the shell code in the file, and right-click again to copy it.
3. Close the shell.html file, and open your **practice_3.html** file.
4. Delete the text you previously entered between the preformatted text tags.
5. Paste the shell code you copied between the preformatted text tags.
6. Save the file and open it in your browser to view it. You will notice that your browser does not display any of the HTML code that you entered in the PRE element. That is because the HTML code overrides the preformatted text tags, and your browser acts on the code just like it would without the preformatted text tags.
7. Return to your text editor.
8. In the pasted code from shell.html, replace all left angle brackets (<) with the character entity **<**, and all right angle brackets (>) with the character entity **>**. You can cut and paste to speed up this process.
9. Save your file and refresh your browser. The HTML shell should now appear just as you copied it in your file (see Figure 2.11). If it does not, review your code to make sure all of the angle brackets were replaced.

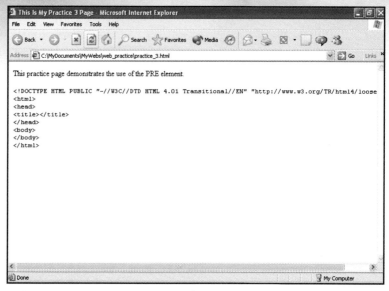

FIGURE 2.11

Replacing HTML angle brackets (< >) with character entities allows the display of HTML code on a Web page.

Horizontal Rule Tags

Visible lines, called horizontal rules, can be used to divide sections of text. The **horizontal rule tag** <hr /> is not paired and XHTML standards require that a blank space followed by / be inserted within the open tag. Unlike heading and paragraph tags, the horizontal rule's default alignment is "center." Although they have been deprecated under HTML 4.1, attributes can be added to the horizontal rule tag to control the width, size, alignment, and shading of the line. Ideally, HTML coders will use a style sheet to control these attributes, but for the time being these attributes will work with current browsers when used within the code for the page.

USE HORIZONTAL RULES

Use horizontal rules to section text and make the Web page layout more attractive.

1. Use your text editor to open the **practice_2.html** file.
2. Key a horizontal rule tag after the H1 element:

```
<h1>Division Tags Can Speed Up Coding</h1>
<hr />
```

3. Save your file, and open it in your browser. You will notice a line extending across the page just below the first heading on the page. You can further adjust the appearance of this line by using attributes and values.
4. Return to your text editor and then key the following:

```
<hr width="75%" />
```

5. Save the file and refresh your browser. The horizontal rule on your page should now appear somewhat shorter. The percentage is in relationship to the width of the page, so in this case, the line should extend across 75% of the page visible in the browser.

6. Return to your text editor and then make the following changes to change the width of the line:

```
<hr width="75%" size="10" />
```

7. Save the file and refresh your browser. The horizontal rule should now appear considerably thicker. Notice how the line is shaded.

8. Return to your text editor. To change the horizontal rule to a solid line, key the following:

```
<hr width="75%" size="10" noshade />
```

9. Save the file and refresh your browser. The horizontal rule should now appear in the same width and size as it did previously, but as a solid line instead of a shadowed one.

10. Return to your text editor. The default alignment for horizontal lines is "center," so if you want another alignment, you must enter this as an attribute in the HR element. To change the alignment of the horizontal rule, key the following:

```
<hr width="75%" size="10" noshade align="left" />
```

11. Save the file and refresh your browser. The horizontal line will now be aligned to the left side of the Web page.

12. Delete the ALIGN attribute for the horizontal rule and then save the file.

```
<hr width="75%" size="10" noshade align="left" />
```

Bold and Italic Tags

The **bold** (<b></b>) and **italic** (<i></i>) paired tags can be used to add emphasis to text. Bold and italic tags can be used together ("**nested**") to add both **bold** and *italics* to words or characters. Because these tags can be used together, it is important to know that the order in which tags are nested must follow certain requirements in the new XHTML standard.

Generally, the rule is, "First opened, last closed." When nested, either tag can come first, but the nested tags must be closed in the reverse order. The following example shows the correct and incorrect ways to nest tags calling for the enclosed text to be bold (<b>) and italicized (<i>).

Correct:
```
<b><i>Bold and Italicized</i></b>
<i><b>Bold and Italicized</b></i>
```
Incorrect:
```
<b><i>Bold and Italicized</b></i>
```

The first two examples are correct because the tags are nested symmetrically, which means that the bold tags are on the outside, and the italic tags are on the inside, or vice versa in the second example. The incorrect example shows a nesting error known as **overlapping**. The bold start tag (<b>) is on the outside, but the bold end tag (</b>) is on the inside. When reading that line, a browser might be confused because the italic start tag (<i>) is trapped alone between the pair of bold tags. Note that the head open and close tags are the exception to this rule. Because the head is a section separate from the body of the HTML document, its start and end tags appear before the body tags.

Use bold (<b>) and italic tags (</i>) to emphasize text on your Web page.

1. Format the word "division" in the first paragraph of the practice_2.html file so that it appears bold on your browser.

```
<p align="left">The <b>division</b> tag reduces the need to key
an attribute and value each time you want to center or right-
align HTML elements in a large section of a Web page. Instead,
<b>division</b> tags can be used to control the alignment of all
the HTML elements contained between the paired <b>division</b>
tags.</p>
```

2. Format the word "division" in the second paragraph so to that it appears italic in your browser.

```
<p align="left">If there are any elements within the
<i>division</i> tag that you want to align differently than the
specified <i>division</i> tag value, you can key a different
alignment value for that element, and it will override the
<i>division</i> tag value. Alignment for any elements after this
new instruction will revert once again to the value called for
in the <i>division</i> tag value.</p>
```

3. Save the file and refresh your browser. Each of the three occurrences of the word "division" in the first paragraph should appear in bold, and each of the four occurrences in the second paragraph should appear in italics (see Figure 2.12).

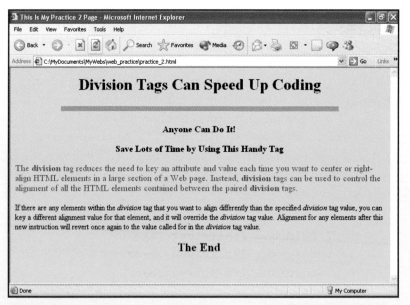

FIGURE 2.12
Bold and italic tags can be used to emphasize text.

4. Return to your text editor and practice coding with bold and italic tags, both alone and in combination, following the rule of symmetry for the order of close tags.

Font Style, Size, and Color

A **font** is a style of typeface. For example, Times New Roman and **Arial** are two commonly used fonts in printed material and on Web pages. If a font is not designated in HTML, the document will appear in a default font determined by the font resident (located) on the computer displaying the browser. **Font tags** (<font></font>) and attributes are handled by style sheets under strict HTML 4.1 and XHTML, but are still legal and in common use as inline codes in transitional HTML 4.1. Font tags are paired. Failure to key a font end tag will mean that all subsequent text will appear in the font called for in the attribute value.

The attribute for font style is called FACE. The value for the FACE attribute is the name of the font style. Because the fonts resident on any given computer differ, it is important to designate more than one font when keying a value for the FACE attribute. When a font is unavailable on a computer, the text will appear in a default text that can be very different from the one called for in the attribute value. Instead of designating a single font, HTML coders can enter a list of font styles, ordered by preference. For example:

```
<font face="Times New Roman, Arial, Helvetica">
```

A browser interpreting these instructions first looks for the Times New Roman font. If that font is available, the element content covered under the instruction is displayed in the Times New Roman font style. If the font is unavailable, the browser then looks for Arial, the next font in the list, and keeps looking until it locates a font that is available. If none of the specified fonts is available, the browser displays the element content in its default font.

When choosing font styles, you should be able to access a list of available fonts from your menu bar. If not, you can select Format, and then choose Font from the drop-down list that appears. Scroll down to see a list of available fonts. When coding, be sure to key the font name exactly as it appears in the font list on your computer.

SELECT FONT STYLE

Use the font tag (<font>) to choose the font styles you like.
1. Return to your text editor. Place your cursor just before the first paragraph tag, and press Enter to create a new line above the paragraph tag in the practice_2.html file.
2. Key a font tag (<font>), along with a face attribute and values for three different fonts of your choosing:
```
<font face="font name 1, font name 2, font name 3">
```
   Be sure to key the font names exactly as they appear in your computer's font list. Do not forget to separate the names using commas and a space.
3. Save the file and refresh your browser. The paragraphs in the practice_2.html file should now be displayed in a different font style. If not, it might be because the preferred font style you indicated was the same as the default font your browser was already using, or because one or more of the font styles you selected was

unavailable. If that is the case, return to your text editor and reorder or add new fonts to the list of font values in the face attribute. Save and refresh your browser to see whether the font you chose appears. Notice that all the text appearing after the font tag you entered displays in the same font. This is because you did not enter a font end tag (</font>).

4. Return to your text editor and key **</font>** after the first paragraph end tag.
5. Save your file and refresh your browser. The first paragraph displayed should be in the font you chose, while the second paragraph will be in the default page font.

You also can use the FONT element to indicate the size of the font by using a SIZE attribute. Seven sizes are available, but these are relative, not absolute sizes. This means the size of the font is relative and depends on factors such as the screen resolution of the computer being used to view the page and/or the computer platform. Font sizes differ from heading sizes in that the smaller the number, the smaller the size. For example, whereas **<h1>** is the heading tag for the largest heading size, **size="1"** is the value for the smallest font size. On most browsers, **size="3"** is the default font size, which is approximately equivalent to 12-point type.

Use the SIZE attribute to choose the size of the font:

1. Return to your text editor.
2. Place the cursor just after the closing quotation mark after the last font name in the FONT element and key **size="4"** as shown below:

```
<font face="font name 1, font name 2, font name 3" size="4">
```

3. Save the file and refresh your browser. The first paragraph of the Web page should now appear in a slightly larger font size than the second paragraph. If it does not, check to see that you keyed in the font end tag for the first paragraph.

The FONT element also can be used to change font color. Before learning how to do that you need to understand HTML hexadecimal color codes.

Hexadecimal Color Codes

HTML text and background color values can be specified in two different ways. The easiest way is to specify a color value by name, such as blue or red (see Table 2.3). However, the number of colors that can be specified by name is limited compared to the millions of colors that can be specified using hexadecimal (base 16) **RGB (red-green-blue)** values for color. The list shown in Table 2.3 is just a sampling of the possibilities.

TABLE 2.3

Color Names and Equivalent Hexadecimal Numbers

Aqua	"#00ffff"
Black	"#000000"
Blue	"#0000ff"
Fuchsia	"#ff00ff"
Gray	"#808080"
Green	"#008000"
Lime	"#00ff00"
Maroon	"#800000"
Navy	"#000080"
Olive	"#808000"
Purple	"#800080"
Red	"#ff0000"
Silver	"#c0c0c0"
Teal	"#008080"
White	"#ffffff"
Yellow	"#ffff00"

Hexadecimal color values are expressed using the pound sign (#), followed by six digits or letters. These color values are referred to as **hexadecimal codes**, or **hex codes**. For example, #008000 is the hex code for green. The first pair of digits or characters of the code represents the red value, the second pair represents the green value, and the last pair represents the blue value. Each color in the three-color RGB combination has 255 possibilities. The purest red, green, or blue results when the highest possible value, ff, is used for that color, and the lowest possible value, 00, is used for the other two. For example, pure blue has the value #0000ff (no red, no green, and the highest possible value for blue).

The hexadecimal system is used because it only needs two digits to represent numbers that would require three digits using the decimal system, thus shortening the number of digits needed for each color code. In the hexadecimal numbering system, the count starts with 0, but after 9 goes to a, b, c, d, e, and f (the hexadecimal equivalents of 10, 11, 12, 13, 14, and 15) before shifting to a 1 in the digit to the left (which in base 16 is the 16's place). Thus, 11 in hexadecimal would equal 17 in the decimal system ($1 \times 16 + 1 = 17$). You can see how this would save space by looking at the example of ff, the hexadecimal equivalent for 255 in the decimal system. In the hexadecimal system, the first f is multiplied by base 16, or 15×16, and the product is added to the next f, or 15. Thus ff = $15 \times 16 + 15 = 255$.

Knowing how to count in hexadecimal allows you to experiment and specify millions of colors by changing the red, green, and blue values in a hex code. However, do not despair if you do not immediately grasp how to count using the hexadecimal system. Many color palettes are available on the Internet that show colors and their hexadecimal equivalents. Two easy to use color palettes can be found on the WebMonkey site at hotwired.lycos.com/webmonkey/reference/color_codes/, or at the WebEnalysis site at www.webenalysis.com/colortable.asp. Just look at the color palette, locate the color you want, and note or copy the hex code equivalent (see Figure 2.13). If you have a good color printer, you can print these charts out for easy reference.

The use of HTML elements and attributes for specifying color has been deprecated in favor of using style sheets. However, they are still allowed in transitional HTML. Understanding how HTML color works will make the transition to style sheets easier.

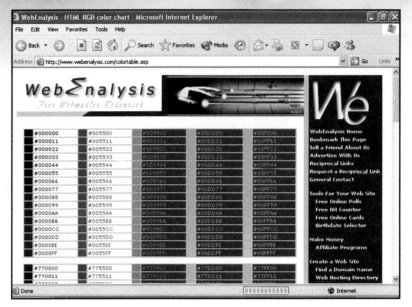

FIGURE 2.13

Color palettes such as this one at www.webenalysis.com/colortable.asp can simplify the task of specifying colors for your Web page text and background.

One concept that might be puzzling at this point is that lighter shades of color are produced when higher levels of color are specified. This is because when working with light rather than with pigments (paints, for instance), all colors in the RGB color scheme combined together create white. In the next action section you will experiment with the use of color in the practice_2.html file. This might take a lot of experimentation until you get it right.

SPECIFY TEXT COLOR

Follow these steps to specify the font color for any text appearing in your Web pages:

1. Return to your text editor.
2. Place your cursor just after the FACE attribute, press the spacebar to create a space, and then add the COLOR attribute for red:

```
<font face="font name 1, font name 2, font name 3" size="4"
color="red">
```

3. Save the file and refresh your browser. The first paragraph in the practice_2.html file should now appear in red.
4. Return to your text editor and change the COLOR attribute to the equivalent hex code:

```
<font face="font name 1, font name 2, font name 3" size="4"
color="#ff0000">
```

5. Save the file and refresh your browser. The text in the first paragraph should still be displayed in a red font because you replaced "red" with the hex code for red. Note that the "ff" in the code is in the area reserved for red in the RGB triad. The maximum value is ff, and 00 for none. Therefore, this value calls for a pure red (maximum red, no green, no blue).

6. Return to your text editor.
7. Use your knowledge of the hexadecimal counting system to change the values of red, green, and blue in the hex code to create a lighter red.
8. Save the file and refresh your browser.
9. Continue experimenting with other colors.

Change the background color of a Web page by using a different tag:
1. Return to your text editor.
2. Place your cursor inside the body start tag <body>, between the word "body" and the right angle bracket. Press the spacebar once to create a space.
3. Key **bgcolor="yellow"**. (Note that the word yellow is enclosed in quotes.)
4. Save the file and refresh your browser. The background color of your Web page should now appear in yellow (see Figure 2.14).
5. Experiment with changing the text and background color of the practice_2.html file to discover color combinations you like. Try using hexadecimal as well as word values. You will discover that certain combinations of text and background color make attractive, easy-to-read pages, while other combinations produce the opposite result. Be sure to note for future reference the hex codes for the text and background colors of combinations that look appealing and provide good contrast.

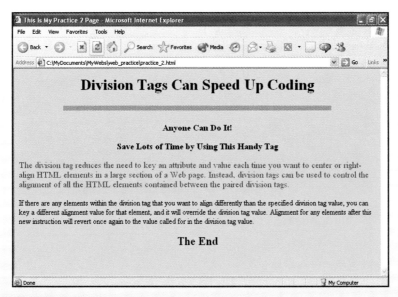

FIGURE 2.14
The BGCOLOR attribute is used to change the Web page background color.

design
project

1. Use a search engine to gather information about Web sites offering Web site tools such as counters, guestbooks, and dynamic scripts. Make sure to gather notes that include any reference material that will be needed later, such as URLs, publishers, and authors. You will be comparing and rating these resources on your Web site, so you will need this information as well. Feel free to conduct any additional research you feel may be beneficial. Bookmark the sites so you can easily locate them again. Write a report summarizing your findings.

2. Create a new Web page (or pages) and use Copy and Paste to insert the content of the report you created in Step 1 above. Use the HTML skills you have learned so far to improve the appearance of the Web pages you have created for this Design Project. Experiment until you find the combination of background color and text you want to use with your pages. Look at different font styles and decide which font style, or styles, you will use on your pages. Be sure to choose a font style that is likely to be supported by other browsers and computer platforms. Use line break, blockquote, division, and preformat tags to arrange text on the pages the way you want it to appear. At each stage of your work, seek input from other students to see whether they agree or disagree with your choices. Use comment tags to indicate any page features that you want to add later, such as tables, lists, and graphics. After you have learned those skills, you can return to the page and use the comment tags to locate those areas so that you can implement the desired improvements.

CHAPTER

3

Tools to Evaluate
Web Design

cyber visit

DAVID SIEGEL

Type Designer, Typographer, Writer, Web Site Designer, Speaker, and Consultant

Design Viewpoint

"The Web . . . is a communications medium; it's important that we take advantage of the way people like to consume information."

"If you want your company to win online, you'll have to make your customers into winners. You'll have to start thinking like a start-up and asking the right questions."

Resume

Founded Studio Verso, 1999, a high-end Web design and strategy consulting firm; published *Creating Killer Web Sites*, *Secrets of Successful Web Sites*, and *Futurize Your Enterprise;* has given more than 100 public speeches on the Internet and business; and played a key role in the evolution of design standards on the Web.

Clients

Hewlett-Packard, Cisco Systems, Sony, U.S. Government, Computer Sciences Corporation, Leisure Planet, and others.

Designer's Home Page

www.dsiegel.com/

Insights

"A good button doesn't need any extra help announcing that it's a button."

"If your browser doesn't let you change the background color, consider getting one that does. As it turns out, white is a better background for reading text than gray. . . . While not every Web page has to have a Braille version, it should be possible for people who are, say, colorblind, to reasonably override the defaults set by the page designer. There should be enough flexibility in the language that people with special needs or lower-end hardware can see what's right for them."

www.dseigel.com/

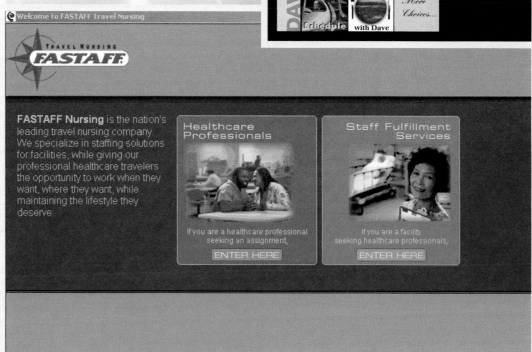

www.fastaff.com/

➤ Define 4 key parameters and the 12 enabling principles that support them.
➤ Apply qualifying questions to assess the degree to which current Web sites accomplish the 12 principles.
➤ Identify the four generations of Web sites.
➤ Evaluate Web sites using a structured process based on generations, parameters, and principles, identifying areas of strength and opportunities for improvement.

Successful Web sites require more than well-written code, interesting graphics, and the latest gadgets. Beyond the technical aspects of the code, beyond the glitz of colors and Flash movies, there are principles that govern how designers choose among various design options as they build sites.

BASIC WEB SITE PARAMETERS AND UNDERLYING PRINCIPLES

parameters
In Web design, the properties that define the fundamental characteristics and behaviors of Web sites. Also, standards by which to evaluate the general qualities of a site. In Web design, the parameters are communication, visual appeal, utility, and engagement.

Designing for the Web consists of challenges unique to itself, but practices developed for the graphic design and publishing fields that preceded the Web can and do inform good Web design.

Although Web sites and their purposes, needs, and requirements vary, four key **parameters** form the foundation of a functioning and effective Web site: communication, visual appeal, utility, and engagement. Applying the principles of the first two parameters is not exactly a cut-and-dried procedure using objective criteria in every case. Still, because the first two parameters deal with what is viewed and read on a Web page, they deal with concrete issues that are basic to designing material for public consumption. The utility and engagement parameters are slightly different. A good deal of subjective judgment is required to apply their principles, but they concern issues that call for evaluative judgments and more advanced ideas: whether a Web site is useful and whether it engages an audience.

principle
A fundamental law or guiding statement that exhibits or imparts a characteristic quality. Web design principles underlie the parameters by which the behaviors and characteristics of a Web site are established.

These key parameters describe the broad context in which successful design must proceed and provide a means for clarifying when a Web site has a successful design and when the design falls short. Thus, these parameters, along with their associated **principles**, function as criteria by which Web sites can be judged. These parameters provide the broad support at a general level for judgments about existing sites and also help the designer plan and analyze sites for the future. This section discusses each key parameter and its underlying principles.

Parameter I: Communication

Communication is the heart of the Web and Web design. Without communication, there is no Web site, regardless of how many pages exist and how visually impressive they might be. By its nature, this parameter focuses on content, whether that includes audiovisual elements or is restricted to text only. For a Web site to achieve communication, it must succeed in meeting the three enabling principles: clarity, legibility, and readability.

Jack Davis and Susan Merritt have written extensively on Web design principles and identify "three hurdles" for Web site visitors. The first hurdle is the first moments of the visit when the site must clearly communicate that it will be useful to the visitors. The second hurdle is the next 10 seconds, which is the window of time for convincing visitors that they will be able to navigate the site readily. The third hurdle is the next minute, when the site must convince visitors that the content is of real interest and value to them. Web developers should work to create Web sites that will achieve clear, legible, and readable communication within the time constraints imposed by these hurdles.

CLARITY To communicate presumes the desire to convey information, share hopes, express concern, spread joy—in other words, to connect with others. Communicating makes ideas available to others, which is only possible if the ideas are clear.

In the case of the Web, clarity—or clear communication—means "speaking" directly to the user, with an awareness of what will make the most sense. Readers will continue reading only if what they read clearly offers some benefit to them. This is unlikely to occur when the writer's thoughts are obscure. For communication to be clear and productive, the writer's ideas need to be transmitted unimpeded to the reader.

At all times, the priority in writing is to be fully aware of what readers know and need to know at each point, so they clearly understand and benefit from what is being

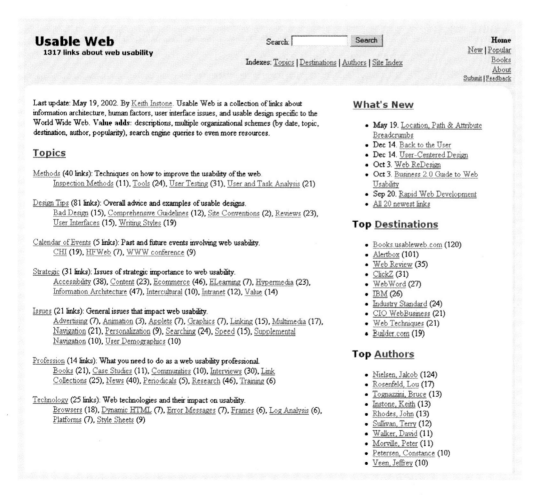

Visit www.usableweb.com for an example of a clear and appealing opening screen that is organized with a focus on the anticipated users. The purpose of the site is clearly stated, to provide "a collection of links about information architecture, human factors, user interface issues, and usable design specific to the World Wide Web."

offered. In the early stages of a visit, for instance, users scan screens and do not read in detail. This rapid reading style requires that all messages be clearly stated, without extraneous material that obscures the main message. Choose an opening that appeals directly to visitors and captures their interest.

Because building a Web site is a form of publishing, the site's material should meet high standards that apply to published writing; in other words, the material should be without error. Spelling errors and typographical mistakes should be avoided. All material should be accurate and current. Whether conclusions are supported or not can be subjective, but no site should publish unclear or unsubstantiated claims as if they are facts. Clearly outdated information also detracts from a Web site's capability to communicate. In all of this, there is a technical dimension, too. Clear communication depends upon well-constructed navigation: broken links stop the flow of information, and hard-to-use navigation obscures the message as users focus instead on how to get what they need. Errors on the initial pages are especially serious as they lower the overall impression of the site, regardless of the other admirable qualities the site demonstrates.

Linking to other sources is often appropriate, but such material also should communicate clearly. In other words, material from another source must be evaluated. Just because it is available on the Web does not mean it achieves the principle of clarity. When content from other sources is used, acknowledge the creators of that material. This meets copyright requirements but also increases the credibility and professional tone of the site. Copyright is discussed in more depth in Chapter 7.

Other technical issues affect clarity in specific ways on the Web. Because some people with visual impairments might rely on screen readers that turn text into speech, writing should make sense when read aloud. Also, alternative access devices such as personal digital assistants (PDAs) have limited screen space. Wordiness taxes the patience of visitors who have to scroll through numerous screens to understand what could be said more concisely. In other words, writing should pass the tests for accessibility and usability, concepts that are covered in more detail in Chapter 4.

Root Link www.press.uchicago.edu/
Direct Link www.press.uchicago.edu/Misc/Chicago/cmosfaq.html
Why Go? To read the University of Chicago's Manual of Style in its online edition. This reference covers writing style and matters dealing with the use of art, typefaces, and layout. The manual is intended primarily for publishers of printed material, but is useful to the Web community as well.

To determine the degree to which a Web site accomplishes the principle of clarity, ask these questions:
- Does the site communicate clearly and efficiently with logical organization?
- Does the site communicate how the user can benefit from the site?
- Does the site meet high-quality publishing standards by being error free?

LEGIBILITY Legibility means that visitors are able to see the text clearly, without impediment. To support this principle, Web pages should be designed with consideration for what visitors will see, vision challenges they might have, types of screens being used, and other issues that will impact the ease with which visitors relate to the Web site. This principle relates primarily to text, but also affects how designers should treat art, photographs, and other visual elements. The primary concern here is making sure all elements on a page are visually clear.

Density of text, for instance, affects legibility. Text that uses small type or piles up numerous long paragraphs can discourage a user from reading even the first sentence. Text that is too densely packed or too wide across the page can be difficult to see and read. Headings, bulleted lists, numbered lists, and other means that break the text into more manageable parts make the verbal portions of the Web site more graphic—more like compositional elements in a graphic design—and more readily grasped. Graphics that convey important pieces of information should have enough space around them so that they appear prominent.

The legibility of a site is also influenced by visual design variables such as color and font choices. Dark letters on a dark background or light letters on a light background are both hard to see. Some fonts are more difficult to read than others, particularly the more decorative fonts.

A Web site should contain well written and well organized text. The site contains a lot of text, but the design reinforces the organization by guiding the reader.

Behind these considerations is the fundamental notion—familiar to designers of printed media—that communication is enhanced when the eye quickly grasps how to approach a text. Hard-to-read type and poorly arranged blocks of text can lead to a sense of disorganization, which causes confusion and limits communication.

To determine the degree to which a Web site accomplishes the principle of legibility, ask these questions:

- Is the font on the site easy to read?
- Do headings, bulleted lists, numbered lists, and other textual components make the verbal content more graphic and thus easy to read and understand?
- Are text formats suitable in terms of color contrasts, fonts, and density of text?

READABILITY As legibility concerns how the text is arranged on-screen, readability refers to how the writer presents the subject matter. Legible text invites the eye, but readable text engages the ear.

To meet the principle of readability, Web sites should use writing that captures the interest of readers, enabling them to connect what they are reading to what they already know. In other words, the writing never loses touch with the familiar, even when explaining what is unfamiliar. The writing is active and personable, has a point of view, uses familiar expressions (those that are natural and not forced), and speaks with a unified voice. When crafted this way, writing makes even unfamiliar subjects more memorable, because it has appealed to contexts that the reader understands.

Writing to communicate on the Web is different from putting "words on a page." Effective Web writing uses fewer words, not more. When writing for the Web, an author should write economically and eliminate wordy or self-indulgent language to help the site communicate its message directly and vividly.

To determine the degree to which a Web site accomplishes the principle of readability, use these qualifying questions:

- Does the site provide a context for understanding the text, including familiar terms and phrases?
- Is the site's language vivid, active, and personable?
- Is the reader able to follow the concepts being presented and remember them?

web 3.1 activity

THE COMMUNICATION PARAMETER

Callahan Family Photo Album at pages.ivillage.com/fncallahan/.

Practice evaluating how well an existing site achieves the objectives of this first parameter and its underlying principles. Use the following procedure.

1. Create a check list using the qualifying questions for each of the three underlying principles (clarity, legibility, and readability) for the communication parameter. There should be a total of nine questions (three for each principle).

2. Visit the Callahan Family Photo Album site at pages.ivillage.com/fncallahan/. (If the site is no longer active, use the screen capture to determine the degree to which each of the qualifying questions is met.)

3. Answer each of the qualifying questions to determine how well this site meets each of the three communication principles. As you work through the qualifying questions, make notes about which features led you to arrive at your answers. Be able to support your judgment. Assess the degree to which each principle has been met by answering the qualifying questions provided for each principle and by using this method for arriving at a score:

a. Each qualifying question that receives a positive answer receives one point. A score of 0 indicates that the qualifying question was not met.

b. Determine which principles have been not met, partially met, mostly met, or fully met, based on total points from the qualifying questions, as follows:

Number of "Yes" Answers	Determination
0	not met
1	partially met
2	mostly met
3	fully met

c. The communication parameter has been achieved if all three associated principles are mostly or fully met (scores of 2–3 for each principle, or a total score of 8–9).

4. Write a short report explaining the results of your evaluation.

Parameter II: Visual Appeal

The second parameter, visual appeal, concerns the important aspect of drawing users into a relationship with the site. This parameter emphasizes the aesthetic appeal of the site, but deals with more than just beauty. Visual appeal strongly supports communication and demonstrates that the designer has thought through the best ways of arranging and presenting material for the benefit of the user. The aesthetic component is critical, however. A site that communicates well and looks appealing is more likely to attract and retain users than one in which chaotic visual design distracts from the site's communicative elements. Three principles that underlie this parameter are visual richness, style, and unity.

Root Link: www.digitalauthor.com/

Why Go? To visit a site devoted to the development of Web content. Includes articles on writing for Web sites, working with graphics and multimedia, and other content-related questions.

VISUAL RICHNESS A pleasing Web site uses plenty of visual cues without losing focus of its need to communicate. Although a Web site can deliver large amounts of information and experiences quickly, "that plethora of information has the potential, if not delivered well conceptually and graphically, to be just another load of visual pollution on the world's growing stockpile of excesses," say Davis and Merrit, co-authors of *The Web Design WOW Book*. Visual richness, not pollution, is critical to attracting visitors to stay and explore a site.

Keeping the screen uncluttered is one important step to reducing visual pollution. Strategies that eliminate clutter include active cursor behaviors (messages that show only when the cursor "floats" over a particular area on the screen) and tools that are visible only where and when they are needed. Screens should include only necessary tools and information.

In Web design, many times "less is more," meaning that fewer graphics can convey information better than many indiscriminately arranged graphics. Ironically, white space

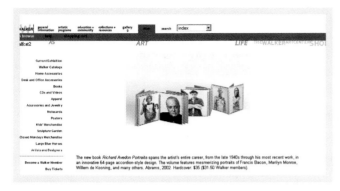

The new book *Richard Avedon Portraits* spans the artist's entire career, from the late 1940s through his most recent work, in an innovative 64-page accordion-style design. The volume features mesmerizing portraits of Francis Bacon, Marilyn Monroe, Willem de Kooning, and many others. Abrams, 2002. Hardcover: $35 ($31.50 Walker members).

This site (shop.walkerart.org/) uses less material to create more impact. Also, the Web page uses white space and the overall page is well balanced.

or large areas of a single color, when balanced against other visual elements, can establish visual richness better than an assortment of richly colored photographs. Balance is key: graphical elements should complement so-called negative space. Individual elements should be of high quality, well chosen, and well placed, but not overwhelming. Animations, if used, should be used sparingly so they do not compete with each other or confuse the visitor by moving at different rates.

Visual richness can be increased by using contrasting typefaces and colors to set off what is important. Contrast demands attention. For instance, headings set in large, bold type lend richness to a page of gray-looking text. Such contrast also calls attention to the major divisions of the material to be read: it guides the visitor's eye down the hierarchy of information, thus enabling quick scanning to help a visitor locate needed information.

Images also should be the highest-quality resolution possible without being too large to download in a reasonable amount of time. Download times depend on numerous variables, which are important to consider. Web site design should be geared toward the computer speed most likely used by potential visitors; it is seldom advisable to design for users with fast computers when your audience might not own them.

To determine the degree to which a Web site accomplishes the principle of visual richness, use these qualifying questions:

- Does the layout of the site look welcoming and interesting, combining graphic and text elements well?
- Do all the graphic elements balance well with each other rather than compete?
- Are graphics used effectively to increase the clarity and communication of the site?

STYLE The second principle that helps create visual appeal is style. Style—the look and feel of a Web site—is the overall visual identity a site conveys, the distinctive visual approach it takes to the content and its audience. Style conveys moods or tones in which the site treats its material, formal or informal, playful or serious, youthful or mature, businesslike or casual, and so on. Style should never be chosen indiscriminately; however, the site's intended users will dictate certain aspects of the style and should always be greeted in a tone they would expect.

Styles are not garnishes, or "a sauce by which a dull dish is made palatable," to quote style authorities William Strunk and E. B. White. Yet, many Web sites show a "style" being tacked on ad hoc, without regard to content—and often in competition with it. For example, background colors and images often interfere with the communicative elements that brought many visitors to the site, making the pages difficult to read, or even illegible. To quote Web design expert David Siegel, "gift wrap makes bad stationery."

There are also technical reasons for avoiding complex background images and other embellishments to a Web page. Background images take time to load, so a site that employs one sacrifices speed for a decorative feature. These images are also frequently responsible for users' inability to read the text. A photograph, for instance, shows areas

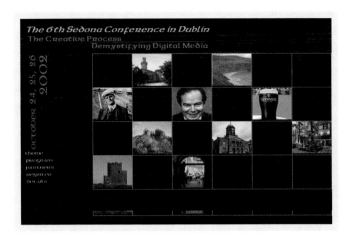

Visit www.paulelsner.com/dublin/index.html to see a good use of contrast, well-sized images, and balance between images and text. By keeping image sizes small, the designers of this site have created visual interest while ensuring that the page will load quickly. The vertical format and graphic font for the dates of the conference add to the visual interest of the site. The intense blue and green of the text creates a vivid contrast against the black background.

Visit www.cooktek.com/ to see a site that deserves "Yes" answers to all three qualifying questions about style.

of light and dark, and its colors will vary, but coding cannot instruct the type to contrast with these constantly varying hues. When a background image is used, it needs to be selected with these factors in mind. Images also should fit the screen, which means it must not only fit within the screen's boundaries, but also be sized so that it works well with the text when combined with the other content on the page. On some Web pages, images might be the most important elements, but in that case, any textual material probably will need to be considered captions, not main textual content.

To determine the degree to which a Web site accomplishes the principle of style, use these qualifying questions:

- Is the style of the page suitable for the purpose, content, and intended audience for the site?
- Do the various stylistic elements of the page seem to fit together, including color combinations, fonts, and graphic elements?
- Do the various stylistic elements create an overall effect that is attractive?

UNITY Unity contributes to visual appeal by organizing complex informational relationships and reducing unnecessary complexity. Unity can be achieved using visual elements that are treated consistently throughout the site. A consistent theme in color, navigational elements, and logos, and use of a visual **metaphor** help provide the sense that the site makes up a single whole—a "place" through which a user instinctively knows the way.

Repetition is one way to achieve a unified design. Elements can be repeated to tie together the different pages of a complete site, making each page look like part of a whole. Repetition is also effective as a visual organizer that aids in navigating a site: visitors do not need to learn their way around again on each new page if navigational aids appear in the same spot from screen to screen. When buttons, colors, format, layout, and **typography** are repeated, these elements create a sense of order.

Use a familiar metaphor that will unite the content of the site. Visitors already know how to interact with a television or a map of the United States and how to move around in a gallery or museum. Visual cues based on these familiar objects naturally suggest to users what they can expect to find when they explore certain areas of the site. For example,

metaphor
An artistic device implicitly comparing one thing to another ("Drowning in money"—an example from language, for instance). In Web design, refers to the use of one (usually visual) idea to help orient users in their visit to a site, often as a navigational aid.

typography
The art and discipline of designing, selecting, and arranging the type styles used for textual material.

At the Disney Online Site at disney.go.com, visitors see pathways that connect the various "lands" of Disney World's Magic Kingdom; they know to move along these pathways to get to the area they want to see next.

when shoppers visit a shopping mall, they know to enter it and then expect to find items they might want to buy while visiting. Similarly, Web sites should guide visitors with visual metaphors.

To achieve unity, content should be related in a visual sense. It should be immediately obvious which screen elements are related to each other: related elements should be close to each other, unrelated elements should have space separating them. For example, captions should appear close to the photos they explain; headlines or subheads should be near the text to which they refer; but a search tool should be separated from a form for verifying user information. Designers Robin Williams and John Tollett have observed that, "Often on Web pages (as well as on printed pages), many items are orphaned unnecessarily, and many other items have inappropriate relationships." This type of error creates visual confusion, which detracts from the appeal of the site and obscures communication.

A consistent alignment scheme also helps reduce visual confusion and should be used on the entire page. This does not mean that everything is aligned along the same edge but that everything on a multicolumn page has the same alignment—either all flush left, all flush right, or all centered.

Gateway's site at www.gateway.com uses consistent alignment and a clear relationship between the pictures and the text to help visitors make sense of the complex information presented.

To determine the degree to which a Web site accomplishes the principle of unity, use these qualifying questions:

- Does the design present a simplified, visually oriented way of accessing the site and its content?
- Is an appropriate, consistent visual style used throughout the site (including buttons, colors, layout, typography, and the metaphor it might employ)?
- Do visual relations and contrasts create pleasing effects that help orient visitors to the site's organization?

THE VISUAL APPEAL PARAMETER

Practice applying this set of questions to assess the visual appeal parameter in combination with those for the communications parameter.

1. Create a check list using the qualifying questions for each of the three underlying principles (visual richness, style, and unity) for the visual appeal parameter. There should be a total of nine questions (three for each principle).
2. Visit the Animation Factory Web site at www.animfactory.com/.
3. Answer each of the qualifying questions to determine how well this site meets each of the three visual appeal principles. Use the same scoring and assessment process as in Web Activity 3.1.
4. Use the check list you created for Web Activity 3.1 to assess this site's success in terms of the communication parameter.
5. Write a summary of your evaluation of this site in terms of the visual appeal and communication parameters, citing specific examples.

Parameter III: Utility

The third parameter, utility, ensures that Web sites provide users with what the Web promises—a convenient, easy way to share information, answer questions, provide entertainment, purchase goods, or serve any other purpose considered useful by the visitor. There must be something of sufficient value to visitors to encourage them to stay, make use of what the site has to offer, and return to use this site again when a similar need arises. Three principles that promote utility are intuitive interface, navigability, and value.

The Animation Factory Web Site at www.animfactory.com/.

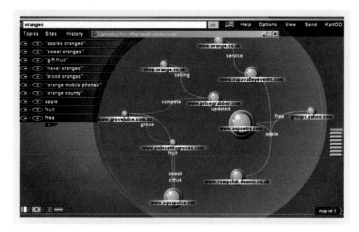

Kartoo.com presents search results that show interconnections between sites with color-coding. Also, the relative size indicates the quality of the hit. This layout is an intuitive way of showing search results.

INTUITIVE INTERFACE To "interface" means to interact with an environment; a user interface is the bridge between human users and the technology they are attempting to use, whether it is a mobile phone, an automobile, a computer, or a Web site. The user interface for a Web site is the means by which users interact with the site, locate what they need, perform functions, and accomplish tasks.

An effective user interface should be easy to use. It should be immediately clear to users how to perform tasks on the site. The standard term for this is "intuitive" (see Chapter 1 *The Vision of the Web*): an intuitive interface enables users to accomplish what they came to do and to proceed through the entire site without being distracted by the details of how this occurs and, more important, without having to learn completely different procedures on every page. As Steve Krug says in *Don't Make Me Think,* "when I look at a Web page it should be self-evident. Obvious. Self-explanatory."

Although it might seem obvious, one issue should be raised: an interface is not intuitive unless it actually works. The tendency might be to consider non-working utilities a technical matter. But from the point of view of the user, non-functioning utilities make the site difficult to learn. Persistent users might stick with a non-functioning utility long enough to conclude that the poor performance is the code's fault, but the result is the same: a user has been stymied in an attempt to use a site.

To determine the degree to which a Web site accomplishes the principle of intuitive interface, use these qualifying questions:
- Is the interface clear and predictable?
- Do users learn how to interact with the site without difficulty or frustration?
- Do users successfully accomplish what they came to do?

NAVIGABILITY To "navigate" a Web site is to move through and around it, going from page to page and feature to feature. "Navigability" refers to the ease with which the user does this. A good navigation scheme can be used easily, with clearly identified links. Visitors should be able to progress through the site without having to backtrack to the home page. At any given spot in the site, it should be clear to users where they are, where they can go next, and how to get back to where they were earlier.

At the base of a navigable Web site is an understanding of what will be important to the site's users. A well-designed site should anticipate how visitors might want to "consume their information," as David Siegel puts it. Design experts Robin Williams and John Tollett write that on a well-structured site "the purpose of the site is easily apparent from the very first page, information is easy to find, and you don't get lost in the depths of the site."

Organized material makes a navigation scheme easier to construct. It helps if the subject matter is predigested, well researched, and fully understood by the designer. To organize the information, the designer must first understand it. The logic of how the material is to be grouped and arranged for best use from the viewpoint of the user is based on the meaning of the material.

Any barriers to effortless navigation, whether real or imagined, should be removed so that visitors are able to access what the site has to offer. Barriers to entry include such frustrations as delays moving among pages of the site (e.g., from lengthy download times) and unnecessary (or transparently marketing-based) registration screens. Several variables can affect download time, which is based on the cumulative size of the combined files it uses and the access speed of the user's system (see Table 3.1). Designers should not assume that high-speed connections are the norm for users of the sites they design. Access speeds also can depend upon the amount of Internet traffic at one time or on one site.

TABLE 3.1 Connections and Access Speeds

Connection Type	Average Speed	Comments
Dial-up Modem	Up to 56 Kbps	Uses current copper telephone wire; lowest cost connection; widely available. Offers slowest connection speeds, ties up the phone line, and shares bandwidth with other users.
ISDN	128 Kbps	Uses current copper telephone wire; more widely available than DSL or cable. Offers dedicated bandwidth and choice of "always-on" or dial-up service. Costs as much as DSL and is the slowest of the broadbands. Has limited availability unless installed within three miles of the telephone company's switching area.
DSL	256 Kbps to 1.5 Mbps (dependent on price plan)	Uses current copper telephone wire. DSL is great for broadband-hungry businesses. DSL providers offer different upload/download speed packages, and guarantee steady speed with dedicated bandwidth. The line doubles as a phone line, and connection performance is unaffected by bad weather. More vulnerable to hackers with its "always-on" connection; has limited availability unless installed three miles from the telephone company's switching center; is more costly than cable; and is difficult to install.
Cable	500 Kbps to 1 Mbps	Uses cable provider's coaxial cable connection. Great for the average home user. Offers fast download speeds, lower cost, wide availability, and easy installation. Can have crowded lines, a need for firewall security because of its "always-on" and shared bandwidth nature, slower upload speeds, and performance issues due to weather and radio frequency interference.
Satellite	500 Kbps	Uses satellite dish for both upload and download. Most widely available. Expensive initial installation. Shares bandwidth with other users, has high levels of delay (making online game-play impossible, and chat sessions awkward), is monitored by the provider, and has performance issues during weather.

To determine the degree to which a Web site accomplishes the principle of navigability, use these qualifying questions:

- Is it immediately clear how users can move around the site?
- Are users able to move around the site, forward and backward, without encountering barriers, dead ends, or other frustrations?
- Are users able to make guided choices on the site, or are they forced to resort to trial and error?

VALUE Regardless of how intuitive the interface or how easy the navigational features, the value of the site determines whether visitors will remain on a site and return later. In contrast to television, the Web is an active medium in which visitors expect to do something themselves beyond standing by as an audience. The principle of value involves anticipating what will be meaningful and valuable to a visitor and providing it.

Because most people use Web sites for their own purposes, they must be able to answer two primary questions: "What's here for me?" and "How do I get to it?" These questions create tension between making numerous options available immediately so visitors do not have to dig for them (a "shallow" site) and presenting fewer options at a time but arranging them hierarchically so visitors can choose the most logical paths to what is important to them. If information is buried too far down into a hierarchy (a "deep" site), visitors might lose patience trying to find it, thus reducing the site's usefulness.

Perception of a site's value increases if the site proves valuable to returning visitors. Users who return to a site want to experience or learn something new; they want to feel rewarded for making the effort to return. That does not mean that new features must be added constantly, or that the site's content must constantly change for the sake of change. But, on the other hand, too much stasis offers visitors little incentive to return. Continuing value results from a superabundance of content—more content than anyone can absorb in one visit; it might be the product of the tools available on the site; it might result from content that changes to keep it current; or it might come from interpersonal relations available to users of the site. In whatever way the value is delivered, continuing to provide it helps ensure that users will not abandon the site in a search for greater value.

To determine the degree to which a Web site accomplishes the principle of value, use these qualifying questions:

- Are users able to accomplish tasks that are of value to them while visiting the site?
- Will users remember the site for providing something of value?
- Will users come back to the site the next time they need to accomplish a similar task?

Root Link www.amasci.com/
Direct Links www.technology.niagarac.on.ca/people/mcsele/lasers/
www.windworld.com/
www.pulse-jets.com/
Why Go? To find links to some of the most exciting and innovative science Web sites. How to build a home-made jet engine, laser, or experimental musical instrument. Also includes a link to Web design tips.

web 3.3 activity

Practice applying the questions about the three principles of the utility parameter: intuitive interface, navigability, and value.

1. Create a check list using the qualifying questions for each of the three underlying principles (intuitive interface, navigability, and value) for the utility parameter. There should be a total of nine questions (three for each principle).

2. Visit the Dr. Koop Web site at www.drkoop.com/ and attempt to use the site to accomplish a task such as finding a health care clinic, getting an insurance quote, or obtaining information on alternative medicine.

3. Use the same scoring system as before to assess this site in terms of the utility parameter.

4. Also, assess the site in terms of the communications and the visual appeal parameters.

5. Write a summary of your evaluation of this site, citing specific examples.

Parameter IV: Engagement

The fourth parameter concerns whether users for whom the site is designed will actually be engaged by it, benefit from it, enjoy visiting it, and plan to return regularly. The question goes beyond "Does it work?" to "Is it worth my time to interact with it?" This parameter broaches a tough question: Does the Web site justify its existence by providing experiences significantly different from those of earlier types of media? If a site does nothing but offer online versions of printed material that views visitors as "audience," it can hardly be considered an engaging site. On Web sites that engage, visitors participate actively—they must be the doers.

Three principles that help achieve engagement are user awareness, user-centered purpose, and interpersonal rapport.

USER AWARENESS Defining, knowing, and anticipating visitors, what they will need, and how they will be likely to find and use the site are major considerations. When evaluating anticipated users, go beyond considering visitors as a passive audience. Think instead of participants—visitors want and expect to have an active role. Sites that have multiple audience groups need to carefully define each group, what it wants to do, and what it has to contribute.

Dr. Koop's Web site at www.drkoop.com/.

Building an engaging site is like beginning a dialogue. First, to set a dialogue in motion, the initial speaker should consider the point of view of the initial receiver. In Web design, the site's purpose needs to be developed around the visitor's point of view.

Second, visitors need to feel that they are being "heard" and responded to. The more personalized and immediate this response, the greater the sense of relationship and engagement.

Individual visitors will have their own ideas about what they want to do and will want to control their own experiences, at their own pace, and in a sequence they choose. Visitors want to interact with the site in their own particular ways with the site responding to them suitably. If a site does not clearly show that it caters to, and responds to, visitors' needs, it is unlikely to be found engaging, particularly over time, by any one visitor.

To determine the degree to which a Web site accomplishes the principle of user awareness, use these qualifying questions:

- Is it clear what types of visitors this site hopes to engage?
- Would the site draw these intended visitors and succeed at engaging them in interaction?
- Would these targeted users recognize immediately that this is a site with which they would benefit from interaction?

USER-CENTERED PURPOSE Interaction with users requires that the site's purpose match the purpose users are seeking to fulfill. A site does not need to serve every purpose or attempt to meet everyone's needs. However, a visitor should be able to identify a site's main purpose immediately. User-centered purpose is shown through this focus on addressing users' needs from their point of view. Any of the types of purposes of a Web site—assisting the search for information, supporting decision making and problem solving, helping users accomplish tasks, providing an opportunity for interconnection, or providing recreation (see Chapter 2)—can be accomplished using user-centered design. A site's purpose will be assessed at a glance by visitors to the site and will be a factor in determining whether or not they feel they have come to the "right" place and whether they then become engaged and participate.

The Barbie Web site at www.barbie.com/ is designed to attract a specific type of visitor and provides opportunity for activities that these young female visitors enjoy.

User-centered purpose is shown also through how the site puts visitors in charge of their own experiences. The site should invite users in and consider the unique wants and needs of each guest. Allow users to know where to find what they want instead of making them guess or follow excessive numbers of links. Automate tasks computers do very well: place a search engine on the site so they can have their computers find what they need; offer to store passwords and user IDs so visitors are not forced to interrupt their visit to track down information they might have recorded earlier. To become engaged, users need to have the sense that they will benefit from their participation. This is especially true when a site requests information from the visitor.

To determine the degree to which a Web site accomplishes the principle of purpose, use these qualifying questions:

- Is the site purposeful from a user viewpoint (for knowledge, decision support, accomplishing tasks, interconnectedness, enjoyable experience)?
- Is the user-centered purpose of the site immediately apparent from the entry page and forward?
- Will the site invite in and engage visitors who arrive to accomplish this purpose?

Root Link www.biglion.com/index.htm
Direct Link www.biglion.com/directory/Computer/Digital_Cameras/
Why Go? For an online shopping portal to the biggest and best online stores. Helps you search for the knowledge that assists you when you need to buy.

INTERPERSONAL RAPPORT Assuming that a site's interface has created the sense of interaction and that the site's purpose encourages visitors to stay, the actual interaction—the sense of interpersonal rapport—determines the duration, nature, and value of the relationship between the visitor and the site or, through the site, its sponsor.

A virtual relationship depends on the existence of sufficient interpersonal rapport to develop feelings of comfort, trust, appreciation, understanding, warmth, and other interpersonal qualities that encourage contact and connection. To succeed at this is a challenging task that requires envisioning, or even rehearsing, the interpersonal exchanges that might actually occur on the site. An imagined dialogue can successfully capture and replicate important qualities of successful interpersonal exchange. The language, tone, pace, emotional energy, warmth, and other essential qualities of initial face-to-face contact can come out in this type of exercise. The goal is to understand the process by which constructive, valued relationships develop and to institute that process on the Web site.

To determine the degree to which a Web site accomplishes the principle of interpersonal rapport, use these qualifying questions:

- Would visitors feel sufficient comfort, trust, understanding, and warmth to be drawn to relate to the site actively?
- Would they have the sense that they are appreciated and that they have entered into a positive relationship?
- Will this sense of relationship be sufficiently engaging to bring them back?

Assess the degree to which a Web site achieves the engagement parameter by meeting the principles of user awareness, user-centered purpose, and interpersonal rapport.

1. Create a check list using the qualifying questions for each of the three underlying principles (user awareness, user-centered purpose, and interpersonal rapport) for the engagement parameter. There should be a total of nine questions (three for each principle).

2. Visit the University of Phoenix Web site at www.phoenix.edu/.

3. Evaluate this site in terms of the engagement parameter, using the scoring system identified in Web Activity 3.1. As you evaluate the site's success in engaging visitors, ask why the site designer chose the categories and entry points you see on its home page. Then, visit the site from each of three perspectives: a potential student, a faculty member, and a corporation. What is your experience of the site from each of these three perspectives? What type of relationship would you expect each type of visitor would have with this university?

4. Then assess the site in terms of the communications, the visual appeal, and the utility parameters.

The University of Phoenix Web site at www.phoenix.edu/.

4. Write a summary of your evaluation of this site in terms of all four parameters. What ideas might you suggest to make the site more engaging to one or more of its groups of users?

THE FOUR GENERATIONS OF WEB SITES

The parameters reviewed in the previous sections identify guidelines by which designers can judge existing Web sites and design sites to achieve specific goals. These parameters evolved as Web designers considered the principles that would guide their efforts to use the new technologies becoming available to them. Just having the ability to include forms on a Web page, for instance, did not mean that designers immediately understood how to make them easy to use, taking users' habits or preferences into account. Nor did they envision every use to which forms could be applied. Although some designers thought using multimedia sounded exciting, others questioned how it could be used effectively. What use of multimedia is most appropriate for a Web site? Is there a use for it that has not been considered yet?

Thus, it is not only new technology that impelled the achievement of these four parameters. As users reacted to new technologies, their expectations for what Web sites should do began to change, and these changed expectations helped shape the direction the Web took.

It is useful to look at the Web in developmental terms, tracing the major shifts, each of which led to the next stage of design. This book refers to each of these stages as a **generation** and each generation is associated with one of the four parameters just discussed:

- Generation 1: Communication
- Generation 2: Visual Appeal
- Generation 3: Utility
- Generation 4: Engagement

The differentiation among four generations becomes an important means for evaluating existing sites and for identifying how to move a particular site to the next level. Not every Web site needs to be designed as a generation 4 site (although generation 4 sites tend to have greater vibrancy). Redesigning a Web site to the next level involves a significant change, however, and knowing what that change must be makes it easier for Web designers to understand the tasks before them.

Each shift that opened the way to the next generation was made possible through technological advances that expanded users' expectations. Of the more important changes that occurred through these shifts, those regarding the **communication model** were perhaps the most far-reaching. A communication model is the fundamental idea regarding who has information, who will deliver it, and who will listen. Whereas the earliest Web sites presumed creators of sites were the ones with the knowledge to be shared, as the Web developed, users and designers began thinking along entirely different lines: that the users also, not the creators alone, had much to share.

This change in thinking did more to bring out the potential of Web sites that strived to incorporate new technologies. Web designers did not create a model first and then proceed to employ the newest gadgets. Instead, when Web sites offered new experiences to their users, hindsight shows that developers had expanded the possibilities for thinking about whom the site is for and why it exists.

The following sections explore how generations progressed through different models of communication. Each generation also compared itself (implicitly) with an existing type of publication, and the Web has evolved in its self-understanding on this issue over the generations. This historical survey has practical benefits for a student of Web design because it shows how Web design concepts grew out of the work itself.

Achieving effective design sometimes requires thinking beyond the parameters and beyond the communication model that is driving the design team. The Web has started to become a medium with its own set of qualities, with its own unique identity. The historical sequence of generations becomes useful for today's site designer as a classification system and as a design process model.

generation
A single step in the history of the development of Web sites; a type of Web site developed from an earlier type, incorporating characteristics from earlier types, and adding characteristics of its own. Born through an advance in computer and communications technology, but reaching maturity only by defining an essential design quality that fulfills part of the promise of the Web.

communication model
An understanding of the network by which information is exchanged. Here used to refer to how Web sites are built to support communication among site sponsors and users.

Generation 1 Web Sites

The earliest form of the World Wide Web was startlingly simple when compared to Web sites today. The Web's first pages consisted of text and hypertext and no more. These represent the first generation of the Web. In general, early Web sites simply reused text documents, often in essentially their original formats. Links worked like the table of contents in a book, allowing visitors to jump to the section of the document they wanted to view. This sometimes meant that an entire Web site consisted of one file that contained the entire text of the document as well as all of the HTML codes needed to display it on a browser.

These sites were primarily governed by a model of "one-to-many" communication. In this model, the audience is perceived as the recipient of knowledge dispersed by one who possesses it, a model that typifies the printed book or the lecture hall. In the early days of the Web, designers might not have known how to make these sites more compelling, but in hindsight, it is clear that they lacked, besides graphic enrichment, the interactive dimension so prevalent in today's Web sites.

Web designers can use the generation 1 criteria to guide the development of the textual component of a site before developing the other components that will eventually bring the site to a later generation level. Because a generation 1 site consists only of text, meeting this generation's criteria can help a project establish the textual component of a more advanced site.

High-quality generation 1 sites that exist on today's Web might still primarily contain textual material, but the copy is presented in a way that makes best use of the hypertext and search capabilities of the Web. For example, a designer might break text into its elemental parts and organize it into hypertextual (non-linear) sets of pages (files) interconnected by links. This redesign transforms linear, text-based information into a rich, accessible resource containing information that can be accessed to find answers to specific questions. The advantage of hypertextual organization is that it provides users with the ability to jump around rather than being forced to follow a fixed-order sequence.

Generation 1 sites continue to have value on the Web and serve a purpose, especially for organizations that distribute information frequently. Web publication of written materials provides important benefits:
- Conservation of resources spent on printing and distributing written material.
- Elimination of clutter from the workplace.
- Assurance that everyone on staff has access to (and uses) the most current version of essential documents.

Generation 1 models are also appropriate for sites on which material is archived—that is, stored for later reference but not subject to change. For such purposes, a generation 1 site might be all that is needed.

To determine whether a site is generation 1, ask questions such as these:
- Is the Web site reminiscent of a report or book?
- Does the site consist mostly of text with little, if any, graphic enhancement?
- Does it seem that the text has been transferred, essentially intact, from printed documents?
- Does the text appear to be scanned in and only minimally adjusted to the additional capabilities of the Web?
- High-quality generation 1: Is the site primarily textual but in a way that makes full use of the capabilities and advantages of the hypertext medium, supporting users in their independent and personalized use of the material?

For Web sites that depend heavily on text and hypertext, the parameter that is most closely associated is communication. Thus, effective generation 1 sites should conform to the principles under that parameter: clarity, legibility, and readability.

Generation 2 Web Sites

The shift from generation 1 to generation 2 Web sites began in the mid-1990s as it became more practical to incorporate graphics, and later other media, to increase the visual and auditory interest—the excitement—of web sites. When these sites were appropriately designed, the addition of graphic elements generally added to the quality and impact of the site. But as the Web moved to generation 2, important design challenges had to be addressed. The shift to well-designed generation 2 sites involved more than simply inserting favorite graphics or music. When graphics were incorporated into a site, "can do" was not sufficient. What was essential were "Why do?" and "Can I do it well?" Attention to the parameter of visual appeal and its associated principles was essential to avoiding the drawbacks of novelty and unrestrained enthusiasm.

The rich graphics and the sophisticated layouts of generation 2 Web sites also did not automatically improve communication. That is still the case. Lessons and insights from the early history of the Web offer important guidance today. When graphics first became possible and were all the rage, many Web sites featured graphic elements that bore little relationship to the textual content. For graphics to contribute, they must be carefully chosen to support the purpose of the site.

Visit ce.eng.usf.edu/pharos/wonders/Forgotten/tajmahal.html to experience a generation 2 site that uses graphics to support the purpose of the site.

DO YOU KNOW?

Question How did people create on-screen drawings in the early 1980s when screens could handle only text?

Answer To understand just how revolutionary and exciting it seemed in the late 1980s to display photographs and artwork on computer monitors, consider that before this, during the early 1980s, "computer art" had to be created with the textual characters available on the computer keyboard. This meant using characters and symbols such as: * - / \ _ |) ; ~

Visit www.chris.com/ascii/index.html to see a collection of ASCII artwork and pictures made entirely out of characters.

Some of these symbols are now used in e-mail and other communications to draw the "emoticons"—drawings showing facial expressions such as ;-) (winking face), :((sad face), and :O (surprised face). Another technique was "reverse blank," in which the keyboard characters were used to draw, coloring in the picture's background in green, white, or amber (the colors on the early monochrome screens), and drawing the boundaries of the object as a blank space. It was possible to draw and program a game of Donkey Kong using these techniques, which was considered amazing at the time. A gallery of computer character set art is available at www.textfiles.com/art/.

Early generation 2 sites were often notorious for trying users' patience. The initial technologies were only barely able to handle the demands of transmitting the significantly larger image files. In the mid-1990s, handling simultaneous downloads of text and graphics files required computers with power near the upper limits of what most individuals had. This often caused long delays while a page was being assembled by the browser. Visitors would lose patience and move on, eventually deciding to focus on the relevance and substance, rather than the graphic appeal of the sites they visited.

The same could be said of the additional enhancements of sound and video. Although initially they captured and held viewers' interest for their novelty value, the curiosity soon wore off. Some Web users actually opted to disable all audiovisual elements on their computers by altering the settings on their browsers. Text-only versions of sites loaded faster and gave users the information they were seeking, even if the experience was less entertaining and inspiring. This problem with graphic images is no longer the barrier it once was, although a page can still be bogged down when too many large graphic (or other multimedia) files are downloaded at once.

Thus, although new visual features became available, early efforts to use them were only the beginning. The ongoing design task became learning to use them well.

With improvements in the technologies of transmission over the past few years, however, and with greater attention to successful use of visual material, graphics are now an important and generally expected part of the design of a Web site. In addition, if a site's graphic components are integrated successfully with the text, a visitor could truly miss an important part of the experience if a browser's graphic capabilities were disabled. Not that the graphics should compromise the communication of content. Some standards discussed in Chapter 4 cover the topic of how to make a Web site communicate even when the user (for whatever reason) is not viewing the graphic components on a site. But when graphics truly enhance the content, a user's experience is much more rewarding.

As Web designers addressed the problems inherent in integrating graphics with text, they began moving beyond the metaphor of the text-heavy book. But even given the enhancements of audio and visual elements, the metaphor that came to govern the design of such sites was still that of an existing print-based model—the look and visual appeal of a glossy magazine. And, due to the lack of interactivity, generation 2 sites still had only one primary model of communication to guide them—the one-to-many speaker (or writer) to audience model. Yet, generation 2 sites still exist and serve a useful purpose for those organizations who primarily want to distribute information, including audiovisual elements, but who do not see their site as being a source of active exchange with the audience.

The principles under the parameter of visual appeal (visual richness, style, and unity) should apply to all efforts to develop a site beyond generation 1. When graphics are clearly an integrated and meaningful part of the design, Web sites accomplish new levels of appeal and professionalism. A clear difference emerges between the graphics that are poorly integrated into a Web site and those that are well integrated. Even now, it is common to find generation 2 Web sites that are overfilled with elements that do not belong. New Web designers are notorious for designs that quickly lead to visual overload—an onslaught of animated graphics, mixed fonts and colors, and distracting backgrounds—and their work is easily spotted. More advanced sites are designed in such a way that the tasks of communication are shared between text and graphics, each element enhancing the other, and together carrying the message.

To determine whether a site is generation 2, ask questions such as these:
- Are visual and/or other elements used as an integral part of the design of the site?
- Do the graphic and other multimedia enhancements increase the appeal of the site?
- Do the visual and multimedia elements load quickly enough that you are not frustrated with awaiting their arrival?
- Do the sound and music elements (also the animations) stop their "looping" before their interest and value has passed and they begin to become annoying?
- High-quality generation 2: Are the graphics consistent in theme and metaphor, improving the communications level of the site or otherwise enhancing its appeal?

Ronnie Arts Home Page

Miniatures
Miniature Series
Clocks
Clock Movements
Contact and Orders
Originals

Home | Originals | Miniatures | Miniature Series | Clocks | Clock Movements | Contact & Order

Visit www.ronnie-arts.com.au/ to see a generation 2 site in which visual appeal is integrated meaningfully, and does not cause visual overload.

A fundamental difference exists between generation 1 and generation 2 sites, on the one hand, and generation 3 and generation 4 sites on the other. The first two generations tend to focus primarily on the site owner's interests. Such sites are built to inform users of the activities of the company or organization sponsoring the site. The content provided for users is designed primarily to fulfill their needs for information. Visiting generation 1 and 2 sites is like visiting the library. These sites provide information, but to accomplish anything with this information requires going elsewhere and using tools these sites do not provide.

With generation 3 sites, the focus changes to individual users who visit these sites to get information they need and do something with it immediately. Generation 3 sites became tools for visitors, more user-centered than focused on the organizations sponsoring them. And with generation 4, Web sites started to appeal more directly to the human desire to meet, talk, and listen—to interconnect.

One of the major sources of this change came from new technologies. As Web designers gained skill and insight in their work on sites of the first two generations, additional, more powerful Web programming tools such as Java applets, CGI scripts, and JavaScript were developed to offer elements of functionality that could enhance the usefulness of Web sites, not just their visual appeal and other special effects. As design professionals learned to make use of these new possibilities, they recognized that, however vibrant or captivating, audiovisual enhancement by itself does not significantly change the communication, nor fully enlist the interconnected medium of the Web. The transition to generation 3 involved substantive change: Web sites now were incorporating functionalities that enabled visitors to put them to use.

As new tools became available, Web sites were designed to be more functional and thereby became more valuable to visitors. A generation 2 real estate site might provide photos of homes for sale and information about them. A generation 3 site went beyond this, anticipating which tools would allow visitors to act upon information, solve problems, or make decisions. The site might provide tools for searching the listings based on key characteristics (location, price, number of bedrooms), mortgage calculators, pre-qualification forms

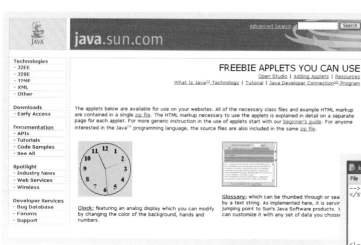

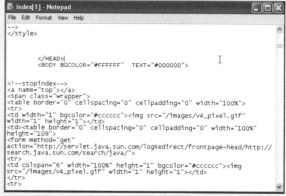

Visit java.sun.com/openstudio/index.html to see a Web site that uses typical Java applets to provide functionality. Navigate to the sample of the clock applet and right-click to choose View Source to locate where and how the applet is activated in the HTML code.

Visit www.discovery.com/ to see a Web site that offers JavaScript to provide visual dynamics for the site. Right-Click and choose View Source to locate where and how the browser knows that there will be JavaScripts included in the HTML code.

for loans, renovation planning ideas and resources, and other tools users might use to make decisions. Visitors were being viewed as doers, not just receivers—as individuals, not just an attentive mass.

As Web sites became more useful, a clear shift in designers' emphasis began to occur. Visitors and the quality of their experience now became the primary concern. If users were visiting sites to obtain information and perform worthwhile functions, developers paid attention to the tools they might need to make better use of the information the site provided—search tools that allowed them to locate information relevant to them as quickly as possible, for instance, or ways to order the services or goods they located on the site.

Generation 3 sites began to regard visitors as judges of the value of the information they obtained. Thus, generation 3 sites communicated information from the more complex basis that simulated a one-to-one communication model—tailoring functionality at the individual level. This shift of the predominant model of communication marked the major opening of possibilities associated with sites of this generation.

The design task now focused on determining how optimally to combine the benefits of sites that incorporated the best from the two past generations (searchable and accessible information, graphically enriched) with the advanced potential of the third (the ability to provide useful functionality).

Underdeveloped early generation 3 sites revealed that perhaps the developer had a limited understanding of the tasks users might want to accomplish and what information they would be seeking to accomplish them. Still, generation 3 sites were a leap forward in defining the Web's unique role in communication and exchange as a dynamic medium that could be of real use to visitors. Since the advent of generation 3, the incorporation of these complex possibilities into the design of sites has matured. On the best generation 3 sites, visitors perform most of the action and end up feeling they have accomplished something meaningful and valuable. Generation 3 sites engage visitors in activities that are tailored to their own needs. This creates an entirely new range of possibilities and an expanded potential for the value of Web sites.

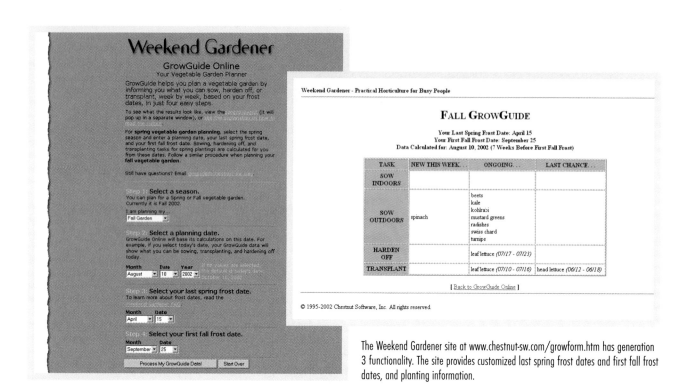

The Weekend Gardener site at www.chestnut-sw.com/growform.htm has generation 3 functionality. The site provides customized last spring frost dates and first fall frost dates, and planting information.

Visit the www.expedia.com site to try out its generation 3 functionalities such as selecting travel dates from a calendar, searching for the best flights, booking flights, and in some cases, even selecting your seat on the plane. Follow links to special deals such as European getaways. Follow up by selecting destinations, flights, and hotels.

Some early generation 3 Web sites were exemplary, offering the best of generation 1 and 2 (clearly presented information and appropriate graphics) and also the breakthrough functionality of generation 3. On today's Web, there are plentiful examples of generation 3 sites, as functionality has become a common feature. Garden sites, travel sites (which let travelers book airplane tickets, ground transportation, and lodging), mapping sites (which provide maps and aerial photos of almost any place in the world), and many other examples that exemplify the new vitality and utility brought into play by generation 3.

Root link www.terrafly.com/

Direct link Type in your own address or city.

Why go? To "fly over" aerial photos of any neighborhood in the world. Real estate agents can save time by showing their clients properties to help with their house search. Travel planners can show actual resort photos, not staged marketing materials.

Building a generation 3 site requires an ability to create meaningful activities that put the user in control. A generation 3 site calls upon developers to apply the principles of utility, the third parameter discussed earlier, and its underlying principles of intuitive interface, navigability, and value.

To determine whether a site is generation 3, ask questions such as these:
- Am I able to interact with the site?
- Am I able to complete a task or work through an idea or plan?
- Will the site be of possible value to someone whose needs and interests are aligned with its purpose?
- High-quality generation 3: Does the site succeed in enabling me to fully accomplish a task that is important to me, efficiently and without confusion or backtracking?

Generation 4 Web Sites

The next generation of sites moved beyond "activity" to "interactivity." Whereas generation 3 sites provide tools that help users personalize content to their own uses, generation 4 sites engage visitors in interaction, not only making them the doers, but also giving them a "voice" and a participatory role in the evolving value of the site.

The need to meet the human desire for interconnection and exchange was the most astounding change in thinking about the Web's role. The desire to turn the number-crunching, word-chewing machines on user's desktops into useful tools for learning, discovering, interacting, and exploring—not just through a computerized version of an encyclopedia but through the real-time, data-gathering potential of interconnected computers—formed this fourth generation.

As the complexity of communication and interaction has increased, one-to-many communication (the model for generation 1 and 2 sites) has been continuously enriched. The utility of generation 3 sites contributed the notion that information could be personalized to communicate and interact with individuals one-on-one. With

inputrefresh

LESSONS LEARNED FROM PROFITABLE INTERNET COMPANIES

Early enthusiasts of Web-based enterprise thought, unrealistically as it turns out, that it would be enough to "build it [a Web site] and they will come." Buyers would connect with sellers directly, and all would be well, so the thinking went. But many e-businesses have failed.

As with any business, there needs to be a reason. The Web can produce new forms of connection, but it is still necessary for businesses to exercise smart business planning. According to ZiffDavis' extensive surveys, conducted to identify its "Smart Business 50" list, companies that are successful online exemplify lessons such as these:

1. Make yourself a market (UPS and Fidelity).
2. Use the Internet to collaborate with other companies to expand toward more complete offerings of products and services (GE, American Express, REI, Schwab, and Lands' End).
3. Build to order (Dell Computer, Herman Miller, IBM, Bank of New York, Boeing, and Procter and Gamble).
4. Exploit content (Sigma-Aldrich, Intel, Kaiser Permanente, Army and Air Force Exchange Service, Costco, Spiegel, Fisher Scientific, Hewlett-Packard, Cisco, Viacom, Dow Jones, and CVS).
5. Learn online (General Motors, Raytheon, Avon, Burlington Northern Santa Fe, and American Airlines).
6. Your store is a Web site (Staples, Kmart, Eli Lilly, and Southwest Airlines).
7. Be patient (Capital One Bank, U.S. Mint, Barnes and Noble, Wal-Mart, W.W. Grainger, and Boise Cascade Office Products).
8. Make e-products (Carrier, Neiman Marcus, Major League baseball).

Consider these examples:

- For Lands' End, the Web has become its largest source of new customers; almost 25% of online buyers are new customers to Lands' End. Internet business for Land's End yielded $218 million in sales in 2001, a 59% increase over the previous year.
- Office Depot reported worldwide Internet sales of $982 million in 2000 and is anticipating $1.5 billion in 2001 and $2.5 billion by 2003.
- General Motors administers 1,300 courses for its 88,000 managers and professionals, taught via satellite video and Web-based e-learning.

generation 4 sites, the notion of interconnectedness has added the many-to-many exchange to the model.

Improvements that lead a site to this next level are less about appearance, or even functionality, and more about increased interpersonal dynamics. Thus, the fourth parameter, engagement, with the underlying principles of user awareness, user-centered purpose, and interpersonal rapport, governs the design of such a site. On some of the earliest generation 4 Web sites, for example, teachers were able to share lesson plans and engage in active communication with students and parents, readers to review and comment on books, travelers to share their travel tales and experiences, and students to exchange ideas across cultures about their lives, beliefs, and customs. Whatever the nature of the content, generation 4 sites allow for communication, exchange, and interconnection.

As a generation 3 site, amazon.com provided visitors with ways to quickly locate the kinds of books they had an interest in, read staff-written reviews of these books, and purchase them if they wished. With the advancement to generation 4, amazon.com enlisted visitors as participants in the value of the site by allowing them to write their own reviews of books they had read and to sell used copies of books they owned with the financial arrangements handled by Amazon.

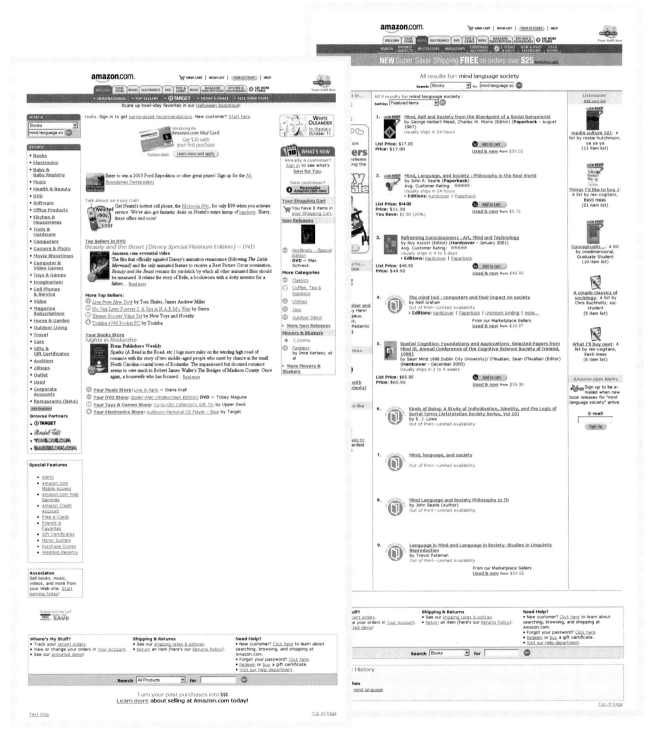

As a generation 4 Web site, amazon.com allows visitors to participate in the site by writing reviews and selling used books.

Generation 4 Web sites gain value as time goes by, not solely as a result of the efforts of the site owners and designers, but also because of what visitors contribute. Another example of a generation 4 Web site is the "Community" area of the ZDNet site (www.zdnet.com/community/). Jakob Nielsen—a renowned authority on Web site usability—publishes his AlertBox columns on Web site design, usability, accessibility, standards, coding, multimedia, and graphics on the ZDNet site. In the Community area, moderated forums allow visitors to become "members" of the community and participate in the discussions, enriching the site continuously.

To determine whether a site is generation 4, and the degree to which the generation 4 additions achieve high levels of quality and effectiveness, ask questions such as these:

- Am I able to participate meaningfully in the value and "life" of the site?
- Do others participate in ways that allow them to share and "have a voice"?
- Does the site have a dynamic "feel" to it, as though its existence is, in itself, creating an opportunity for the valuable gathering of knowledge and sharing of experience?
- High-quality generation 4: Are contributions to the site coherent and constructive? (This generally indicates that the site has a "moderator" who is responsible for judging the appropriateness of various interactions and contributions.)

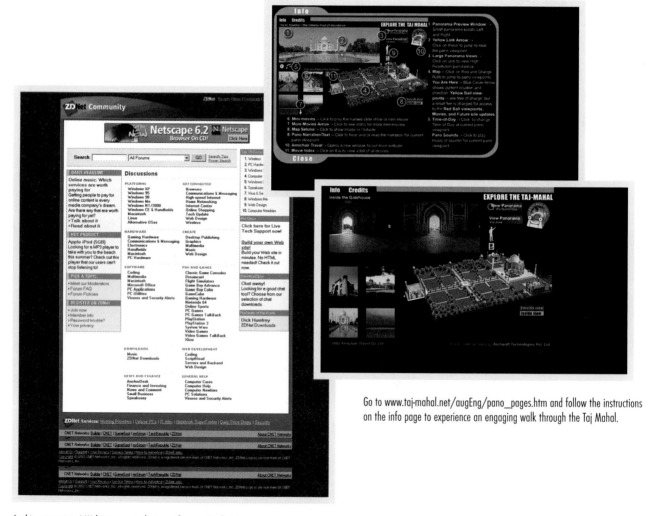

Go to www.taj-mahal.net/augEng/pano_pages.htm and follow the instructions on the info page to experience an engaging walk through the Taj Mahal.

At this generation 4 Web site, www.zdnet.com/community/, visitors can become members of the community and can participate in discussions.

Continuity and Change

Although each Web generation established its own characteristics, each carried forward the best qualities of the previous generations. The mature level of information architecture and presentation of generation 1 sites carried forward to generations 2, 3, and 4; sites must still have hypertext material organized for effective use on the Web. Since generation 2, sites must strive to incorporate the best graphic elements to support the parameter and underlying principles of visual appeal. From generation 3 forward, utility and functionality have been essential components of sites that make use of dynamic, information-driven technologies. Now, with generation 4, advanced design thinking has expanded to support interconnection. Table 3.2 provides a summary of the four Web site generations we have seen so far. Will there be a next generation?

TABLE 3.2 Characteristics of the Web Site Generations

Generation Number	Content of Site	Model of Communication	Role of Visitors	Governing Metaphor	Value to Users
1	Text provided by site owner	One-to-many	Passive audience	Book	Replaces paper, text-only documents
2	Text, graphics, and multimedia provided by site owner	One-to-many	Passive audience	Magazine, radio, and television	Replaces illustrated documents
3	Text, graphics, multimedia, and utilities provided by site owner	One-to-one	Active users	Software	Provides engaged experiences personalized to individual users
4	Text, graphics, multimedia, utilities, and other material provided by site owner and visitors	Many-to-many	Active, engaged users interacting with each other, contributing to the site's content (and sometimes its design)	World Wide Web	Provides a medium for interaction among users and for accomplishing worthwhile goals

activity

The purpose of this activity is to evaluate a Web site and to propose ways to improve it by upgrading it to the next generation level.

1. Find three Web sites that all focus on the same general content area, such as local chambers of commerce or medical information sites. (Select sites with a number of pages that you can visit in a reasonable period of time. Choose sites that allow you to evaluate every page and to finish your evaluation of each site in 5 to 10 minutes.)

2. Use the four-generation and the parameter models to evaluate each site. Write a report that describes the main features and generation level of each site, including the URLs.

3. Of the three sites, select the one that has the best potential for being upgraded. In your report for this activity, make recommendations for redesign of this site to the next generation level. Include a proposal explaining the work that must be done. Outline in detail the answers to the following questions:

    •   What is your rationale to support the need for these changes? Which specific principles (and their associated parameter) are not being fully met?

    •   What features would be added to the site?

    •   What advantages would there be in upgrading the site to the next generation?

    •   What design changes would be required?

a p p l y & practice

Online Quiz

As a review of the key concepts in this chapter, define the terms in the following list:

communication model
generation
metaphor
parameters
principle
typography

After you are confident that you understand this chapter's content, go to this book's Internet Resource Center (IRC) at www.emcp.com/ and take the self-test online quiz for this chapter. Review any questions you answered incorrectly and then study the related chapter material again. Retake the online quiz as many times as you need to achieve full mastery (90–100%).

Topics Roundtable

1. Describe a Web site of your own choosing in terms of the four key parameters—communication, visual appeal, utility, and engagement—and their underlying principles. To which generation does the Web site you chose belong? Explain the reasons for your answer.

2. Why is each of the four parameters important and what can go wrong with a site if one of them is not met? How do the four parameters interact with each other?

3. Is it possible to have a generation 4 site that fails to meet the requirements for the communication parameter? Of the visual appeal parameter? Of the other two parameters? Why or why not?

4. Describe the differences between writing a long research paper and writing material for use on a Web site. If a research paper is published on the Web, what changes might you make so the material communicates effectively?

5. How would you decide which generation level is appropriate for a Web site you are designing?

6. How do you envision the next generation of Web sites?

window to the web

CREATING TABLES FOR WEB PAGE LAYOUT

➤ Create tables.
➤ Modify table size, borders, background, line color, and so on.
➤ Use the non-breaking character entity to prevent empty cell collapse.
➤ Insert text into tables.
➤ Stack and nest tables.
➤ Create a report on resources for good Web page design, formatting that material in HTML.
➤ Use tables for data and layout control in your Web pages.

technical walk-through

Tables can be used to display data on Web pages, but they are more commonly used to control the layout of text and graphics. Tables control layout by creating a grid in which various page elements can be placed. Most of the Web pages you view every day use tables for layout control, but because these tables usually have invisible borders, you cannot see them.

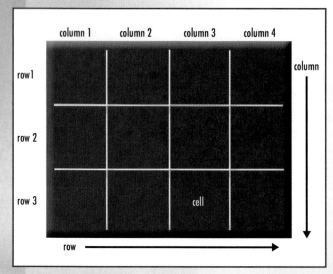

FIGURE 3.1
Tables are composed of columns, rows, and cells.

Basic Table Tags

A **table** is a grid formed of columns and rows. **Columns** span pages vertically (from top to bottom), while **rows** span pages horizontally (from side to side). The intersection of a column and a row is called a **cell**. Cells can be filled with HTML elements such as text, other tables, lists, and graphics. To help identify the location of a column, they are numbered from left to right, while rows are numbered from top to bottom (see Figure 3.1).

Three basic HTML tags are necessary to create any table. **Table tags** (<table></table>) are used to start and end tables. The TABLE element's table start tag (<table>) instructs a browser that the instructions that follow will be used to create a table. The table end tag (</table>) informs a browser that there are no more table instructions. **Table row tags** (<tr></tr>) are contained between the table tags, and are used to instruct a browser to create rows. Each row in an HTML table must be indicated by a table row start tag (<tr>) and a table row end tag (</tr>). Each pair of table row tags must contain at least one pair of **table data tags** (<td></td>) to make up the cells. Each pair of table data tags instructs a browser to create a single cell in the row in which the table data tags are located. Each table data start tag (<td>) must be closed by a table data end tag (</td>). A typical table will have a number of paired table data tags in each row. Between the table data start tag and the table data end tag goes the content ("data") for the cell. Each cell in a row forms part of a column when the rows are stacked one on top of the other. All of these basic table tags can include attributes and values to specify their size, width, height, spacing, color, and so on.

When coding tables, the Tab key and Enter key can be used to indent the table cell elements. The Enter key enters line breaks between each table row (see Figure 3.2), and the Tab key indents the table cells. This does not affect the table's appearance, but makes it easier to sort out where each row starts and ends when troubleshooting or updating code.

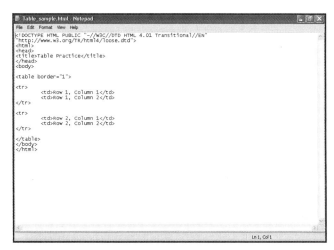

FIGURE 3.2

Using the Tab key and Enter key when coding makes it easier to identify the different table elements.

action

CREATE A TABLE WITH BASIC TABLE TAGS

Use the basic table tags to create a table:

1. Use a text editor to open the **shell.html** file.
2. Save the file as **table_practice_1.html** using the Save As command.
3. Key the following title:

```
<!DOCTYPE HTML PUBLIC "-//W3C//DTD HTML 4.01 Transitional//EN"
"http://www.w3.org/TR/html4/loose.dtd">
<html>
<head>
<title>This Is My Practice Page</title>
</head>
<body>
</body>
</html>
```

4. Key the basic table tags and key the cell content between the body tags of the HTML shell as indicated below:

```
<body>
<table>
<tr>
<td>Row 1, Column 1</td>
</tr>
</table>
</body>
```

5. Save the file and use your browser to open and view table_practice_1.html. You should see the words, "Row 1, Column 1" in the upper-left corner of your screen. These words are contained in the single table cell that you created, but you cannot see the table because your browser has not been instructed to create a visible border.

6. Return to your text editor to view the source code of your table_practice_1.html file.

7. Border sizes are indicated in pixels, with "1" being the smallest size. Key the following BORDER attribute and value inside the table tag:

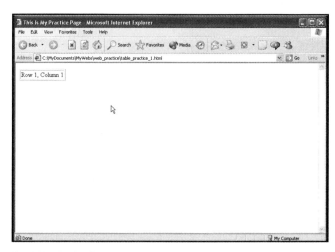

```
</head>
<body>
<table border="1">
<tr>
<td>Row 1, Column 1</td>
</tr>
</table>
```

8. Save the file and refresh your browser to view the changes you have made. The single-cell table you created now has a narrow border (see Figure 3.3).

FIGURE 3.3

Using table tags to code a single table row and table cell produces a table with one cell. The cell borders are visible because a border attribute and value have been entered in the table tag.

9. Experiment by entering different pixel sizes to see the effect on the border.

10. Return to your text editor to view the source code of your table_practice_1.html file.

11. Select and copy the table cell code indicated in magenta to create an additional column for the table:

```
<table border="1">
<tr>
<td>Row 1, Column 1</td>
</tr>
</table>
```

12. Paste the table cell code that you just copied below the table cell code you copied it from (see the following):

```
<table border="1">
<tr>
<td>Row 1, Column 1</td>
<td>Row 1, Column 1</td>
</tr>
</table>
```

13. Change the column number in the text content for the table cell code you just pasted, as indicated here:

```
<td>Row 1, Column 2</td>
```

14. Save the file and refresh your browser to view the changes you have made. You have just increased the number of columns in the table from one to two.

15. Return to your text editor.

16. Select and copy the table row code as indicated in magenta to create additional rows:

```
<table border="1">
<tr>
<td>Row 1, Column 1</td>
<td>Row 1, Column 2</td>
</tr>
</table>
```

17. Paste the table row code you copied just below the table row code you copied it from, as shown here:

```
<table border="1">
<tr>
<td>Row 1, Column 1</td>
<td>Row 1, Column 2</td>
</tr>
<tr>
<td>Row 1, Column 1</td>
<td>Row 1, Column 2</td>
</tr>
</table>
```

18. Change the row numbers in the text content of these new rows to read as indicated here:

```
<td>Row 2, Column 1</td>
<td>Row 2, Column 2</td>
```

19. Save the file and refresh your browser to view the changes you have made. Your table now has two rows and two columns (see Figure 3.4).

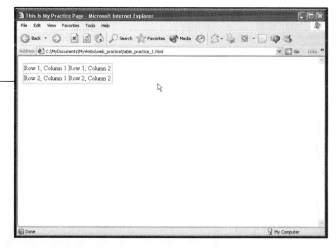

FIGURE 3.4

A simple table consisting of two rows and two columns. Because a width attribute and value were not specified, the browser has sized this table to fit the contents of the table cells.

The WIDTH Attribute

The width of any table can be controlled using the WIDTH attribute, which is contained within the table start tag (<table>). The value for this attribute can be indicated either in pixels, or as a percentage of the screen page the table occupies. Using a percentage value is the preferred method for controlling table width because of the variation in computer platforms and browsers. If you do use a pixel value, "585" is the maximum recommended width. It is possible to go higher than this, but the width might not be supported by some browsers. If no width is indicated, a browser sizes the width of a table to fit the cell contents.

You also can indicate the width of the cells in the table by entering a WIDTH attribute and value inside a table data tag (<td>). All of the cells located in the same column as the table cell with the WIDTH attribute will have the same width, while the width of the columns to the right and/or left will shrink or enlarge. This is because entering a WIDTH attribute and value in a table cell does not change the width of the table. Table cells must adjust to any change in size of an adjacent cell, because the combined width of the cells in any one row cannot exceed the width of the table.

It is possible to use a HEIGHT attribute to set the height of the table, but this use is deprecated under HTML 4.1. The HEIGHT attribute works in exactly the same way as the WIDTH attribute. The height of a cell is normally sized according to its content, or the content of its neighboring cells if any of them are larger. You can use other methods to increase cell height; for example, you can use the ROWSPAN attribute to combine two or more cells. You will learn about the ROWSPAN attribute later in this Technical Walk-Through.

Use the WIDTH attribute and corresponding value to increase the width of your table and its columns:

1. Return to your text editor to view the source code of your **table_practice_1.html** file.
2. Key a WIDTH attribute and value:

```
<table border="1" width="75%">
```

    Note that the values are enclosed in quotation marks.

3. Save the file and refresh your browser. The table should now span approximately 75% of the screen (see Figure 3.5).

FIGURE 3.5

Keying a WIDTH attribute and value of 75% in the table tag causes a browser to display the table across 75% of its screen.

4. Return to your text editor.
5. Key a WIDTH attribute of 75% in the first table cell of the first table row:

```
<tr>
<td width="75%">Row 1, Column 1</td>
<td>Row 1, Column 2</td>
</tr>
```

6. Save the file and refresh your browser. The first column of your table now occupies 75% of the table width (see Figure 3.6). Notice that the second column has shrunk because it must occupy the remaining table width.
7. Return to your text editor. Delete the two WIDTH attributes that you added in Steps 2 and 5.

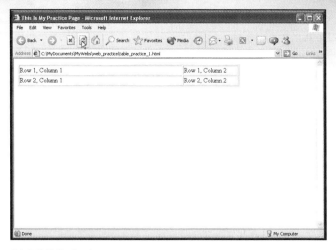

FIGURE 3.6

Keying a WIDTH attribute and value of 75% in a table cell causes that cell, and all the other cells in that cell's column, to stretch across 75% of the table.

Table Alignment

Your table is left-aligned on the browser screen by default. Tables can be aligned by using a division tag (<div>), or by entering an ALIGN attribute and value in the table tag (<table>).

ALIGN A TABLE

Center-align your table using an ALIGN attribute (align=) and value, just as you learned to do with the paragraph tag (<p>):

1. Return to your text editor to view the source code of your **table_practice_1.html** file.
2. Key the following inside the table tag:

```
<table border="1" align="center">
```

3. Save your file and use your browser to view it. Your table will now be centered on the browser screen.

COLSPAN and ROWSPAN Attributes

The COLSPAN (colspan=) and ROWSPAN (rowspan=) attributes are used to span columns and rows. "Spanning" means that a cell is merged with one or more cells so that together they create a cell that spans (crosses) more than one column or row. A common error made by beginners is to forget to delete cells in the area to be spanned. For example, if you indicate a COLSPAN attribute value of "4" in the first table row of a four-column table, you must delete the remaining three table cells for that row. If you don't delete the remaining three cells in that row, the browser will create a cell spanning four columns, and then three more cells after that. The result will be a first row, which has a negative effect on the layout of the entire table (see Figure 3.7). To avoid this problem, make sure that the total number of cells you are creating with a COLSPAN or ROWSPAN attribute does not exceed the number of columns or rows in the table.

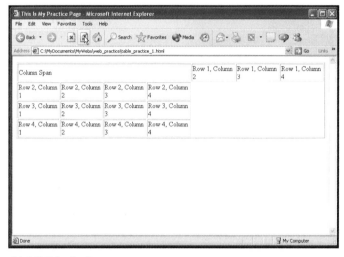

FIGURE 3.7

Make sure you do not forget to delete cells in rows or columns to be spanned, or you will end up with a table that looks something like this one.

USE THE COLSPAN ATTRIBUTE

Use the COLSPAN attribute to span columns in your table.

1. Use what you have learned so far to re-create the table pictured in Figure 3.8. Use the two-row table in your **table_practice_1.html** file to create a larger table by using the Copy and Paste feature of your text editor to create the cells and table rows as necessary. Remember to renumber the row and column numbers within the cells because their locations within the table will be changing.

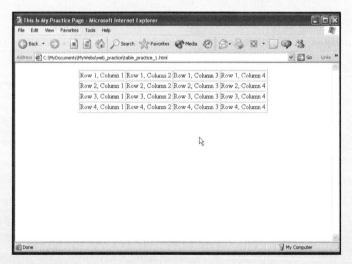

FIGURE 3.8

Re-create this table using the HTML table tags and attributes that you have learned so far.

2. When you are finished, return to your text editor to view the source code of your expanded table.

3. Locate the first table data tag (<td>) in the first row of your table. Key the COLSPAN attribute and value as indicated below to create a cell that spans all four columns of your table.

```
<tr>
<td colspan="4">Row 1, Column 1</td>
<td>Row 1, Column 2</td>
<td>Row 1, Column 3</td>
<td>Row 1, Column 4</td>
</tr>
```

4. Change the "Row 1, Column 1" text in the cell code you just modified to read "Column Span" as follows:

```
<td colspan="4">Row 1, Column 1Column Span</td>
```

5. Save the file and refresh your browser. The first row of your table will now span four columns. However, the table will now appear somewhat jumbled, with three more short cells crammed to the right of the long cell you just created, and a large empty space located just below these three extra cells (see Figure 3.7). Correct the problem with your table in the following steps.

6. Return to your text editor.

7. Delete the three table cells in the first row that follow the cell with the COLSPAN attribute and value.

```
<tr>
<td colspan="4">Column Span</td>
<td>Row 1, Column 2</td>
<td>Row 1, Column 3</td>
<td>Row 1, Column 4</td>
</tr>
```

8. Save your file, and refresh your browser. The first row of your table should now span all four columns, and the remaining rows should appear as they did before you entered the COLSPAN attribute (see Figure 3.9).

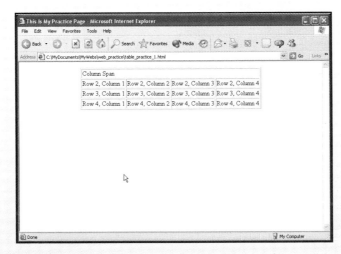

FIGURE 3.9
The COLSPAN attribute has been used to create a cell that spans all four columns of the first row in this table.

USE THE ROWSPAN ATTRIBUTE

The ROWSPAN attribute works in the same way as the COLSPAN attribute, so use the ROWSPAN attribute to span rows in the table:

1. Return to your text editor to view the source code of your **table_practice_1.html** file.

2. Find the table data tag (<td>) for the first cell in the second row of your table. Key the ROWSPAN value and attribute inside the tag as shown here:

```
<table border="1" align="center">
<tr>
<td colspan="4">Column Span</td>
</tr>
<tr>
<td rowspan="3">Row 2, Column 1</td>
<td>Row 2, Column 2</td>
<td>Row 2, Column 3</td>
<td>Row 2, Column 4</td>
</tr>
```

3. Change the "Row 2, Column 1" text in the cell you just modified as shown below:

```
<td rowspan="3">Row 2, Column 1Row Span</td>
```

4. To avoid a jumbled table, delete the cells located in the rows to be spanned:

```
<td colspan="4">Column Span</td>
</tr>
<tr>
<td rowspan="3">Row Span</td>
<td>Row 2, Column 2</td>
<td>Row 2, Column 3</td>
<td>Row 2, Column 4</td>
</tr>
<tr>
<td>Row 3, Column 1</td>
<td>Row 3, Column 2</td>
<td>Row 3, Column 3</td>
<td>Row 3, Column 4</td>
</tr>
<tr>
<td>Row 4, Column 1</td>
<td>Row 4, Column 2</td>
<td>Row 4, Column 3</td>
<td>Row 4, Column 4</td>
```

5. Save the file and refresh your browser. Your table now features a cell spanning three rows, located just below the first row spanning four columns (see Figure 3.10). Using the COLSPAN and ROWSPAN attributes might take some practice. Because this is an important skill, experiment with these two attributes until you thoroughly understand how they work.

FIGURE 3.10

The ROWSPAN attribute has been used to create a cell spanning three rows in this table.

Non-Breaking Character Entities

One important characteristic of tables you should know about is that a cell without any content will disappear. This phenomenon is also referred to as a "collapsed cell." If you need to have empty cells in a table, you can avoid collapsed cells when you do so by using the character entity for a non-breakable space, ** **. Inserting this character entity will prevent the cell from collapsing even though it is empty.

PREVENT CELL COLLAPSE

First, experiment by removing the contents from one of the cells in your table to see what a collapsed cell looks like. Then, insert a non-breakable space character entity to keep the cell from collapsing:

1. Return to your text editor to view the source code of your **table_practice_1.html** file.

2. Locate the content in the second cell of the second row (Row 2, Column 2) and delete it:

```
<table border="1" align="center">
<tr>
<td colspan="4">Column Span</td>
</tr>
<tr>
<td rowspan="3">Row Span</td>
<td>Row 2, Column 2</td>
<td>Row 2, Column 3</td>
<td>Row 2, Column 4</td>
</tr>
```

3. Save your file and refresh your browser. You should now see that the second cell of row 2 has collapsed (see Figure 3.11).

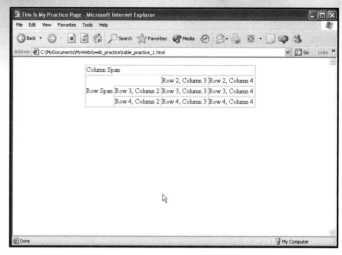

FIGURE 3.11
A table cell without any element content will collapse (disappear).

4. To restore the empty cell so that it is visible, return to your text editor.
5. Key a non-breakable space entity in the content area of the empty cell:

`<td> </td>`

6. Save your file and refresh your browser. The cell that had disappeared should now reappear as an empty cell (see Figure 3.12).

FIGURE 3.12
Using a non-breakable space character entity ( ) prevents an empty cell from collapsing.

The CELLPADDING Attribute

The CELLPADDING attribute (cellpadding=) is used to add white space between the contents of a cell and the cell's border. This makes tables easier to read and more professional looking. The CELLPADDING attribute and value are located inside the table start tag (<table>). Cellpadding values are indicated using pixels.

Use the CELLPADDING attribute (cellpadding=) to add white space inside the cells of your table:

1. Right-click to view the source code of your **table_practice_1.html** file.
2. Key a CELLPADDING attribute and value inside the table start tag:

```
<table border="1" align="center" cellpadding="15">
```

3. Save the file and refresh your browser. Your browser will now display more white space between the cell contents and borders (see Figure 3.13).

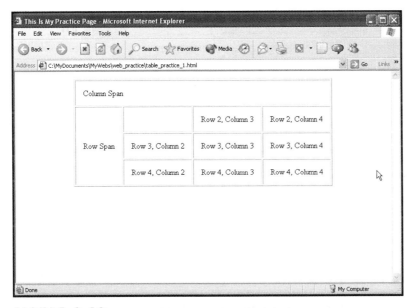

FIGURE 3.13
The CELLPADDING attribute can be used to increase the amount of white space between a cell's content and its borders.

The CELLSPACING Attribute

The CELLSPACING attribute (cellspacing=) works just like the CELLPADDING attribute, except that its function is to increase the amount of white space between the table cells.

Use the CELLSPACING attribute (cellspacing=) to add white space between the cells of your table:

1. Return to your text editor to view the source code of your **table_practice_1.html** file.
2. Key a CELLSPACING attribute and value inside the table start tag:

```
<table border="1" align="center" cellpadding="15"
cellspacing="10">
```

3. Save the file and refresh your browser to open and view it. You should now notice a border of white space between the cells in the table (see Figure 3.14).

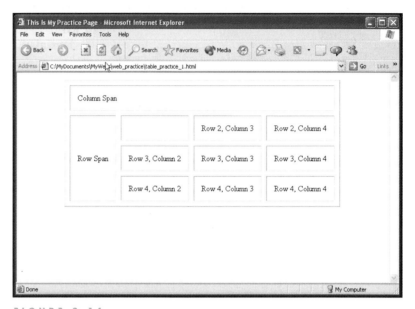

The VALIGN Attribute

The VALIGN attribute (valign=) is used to vertically align the content located within a cell. The values for the VALIGN attribute are "top", "middle", "bottom", and "baseline". The top alignment places the cell contents near the top of the cell, the middle alignment places them in the middle, and the bottom alignment places them on the bottom. The baseline alignment aligns the contents of all the cells in a row to a common baseline, so that they are all vertically aligned. The VALIGN attribute is placed inside the table data start tags <td>. You should be aware that unless a table HEIGHT attribute has been indicated, vertical cell content alignment using the VALIGN attribute might not work because in a normal table cell, there is little or no space for the text to move vertically. If you are using a CELLPADDING attribute, it might appear that there is ample space, but the cell content will be constrained by the invisible borders of the cell padding. If you have used the ROWSPAN attribute, the resulting cells will be large enough for the cell content to move vertically within the cell.

Use the VALIGN attribute (valign=) and value to vertically align the cell content of your table:

1. Right-click to view the source code of your **table_practice_1.html** file.
2. Locate the table row containing the ROWSPAN attribute. Key vertical alignment values inside the table data tags <td>:

```
<tr>
<td rowspan="3" valign="bottom">Row Span</td>
<td> </td>
<td valign="top">Row 2, Column 3</td>
<td>Row 2, Column 4</td>
</tr>
```

3. Save the file and refresh your browser. The "Row Span" text should now be located in the bottom of its cell. However, the text in the cell where you entered a "top" alignment has not changed (see Figure 3.15) because there is no vertical space for the text to move in.

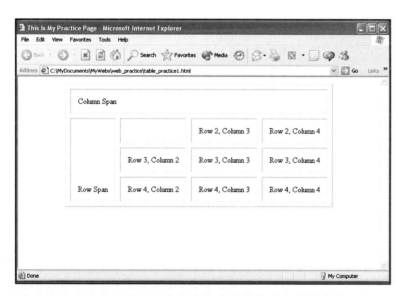

If there is sufficient vertical space within a cell, the VALIGN attribute can be used to vertically align the element content within a cell.

The ALIGN Attribute

The same ALIGN attribute (align=) used with paragraph and table tags also can be used to align the content of a cell along a horizontal axis. An ALIGN attribute and value must be placed inside each table cell in which element content is to be horizontally aligned.

ALIGN CELL ELEMENTS HORIZONTALLY

Use the ALIGN attribute to center the column head in your table:

1. Return to your text editor to view the source code of your **table_practice_1.html** file.
2. Locate the "Column Span" row, and key the ALIGN attribute and value inside the table data tag (<td>):

```
<td colspan="4" align="center">Column Span</td>
```

3. Save the file and refresh your browser. The "Column Span" text in the first row of the table is now centered. As is the case with the VALIGN attribute, there must be enough horizontal space within a cell for this attribute to work.

Table Text Appearance

The text appearing in tables can be modified just like any other text in an HTML file. However, elements and attributes that affect text appearance (text tags) do not work at the table level. Instead, they must be used to mark the text contained in each table cell that is to be modified. They should not be placed inside the table data tags, but should surround the text bracketed by the table data tags.

action

CHANGE TABLE TEXT APPEARANCE

Use text tags to change table text appearance:

1. Return to your text editor to view the source code of your **table_practice_1.html** file.
2. Locate the table rows containing the "Column Span" and "Row Span" text. Key the bold and font text tags:

```
<td colspan="4" align="center"><b>Column Span</b></td>
</tr>
<tr>
<td rowspan="3" valign="bottom"><font size="2">Row
Span</font></td>
```

3. Save the file and refresh your browser. The "Column Span" text is now in bold, and the "Row Span" text appears in a smaller font.

There is an alternative to using bold tags to bold the text of row or column headings. **Table heading tags** (<th></th>) can be used in place of table data tags to change the text in a row or column heading to bold.

Add table heading tags to create vertical and horizontal table headings:

1. Return to your text editor to view the source code of your **table_practice_1.html** file.
2. Delete the tags that you keyed earlier to mark up the text as indicated here:

```
<td colspan="4" align="center"><b>Column Span</b></td>
</tr>
<tr>
<td rowspan="3" valign="bottom"><font size="2">Row
Span</font></td>
```

3. Key text heading tags to replace the table data tags (<td>):

```
<thtdcolspan="4" align="center">Column Span</td></th>
</tr>
<tr>
<thtdrowspan="3" valign="bottom">Row Span</td></th>
```

4. Save the file and refresh your browser. The column and row headings should now appear in bold.

Background Color

The background color (BGCOLOR) attribute and value can be used to set the background color of a table or the individual cells within a table. Placing a background color attribute and value inside a table start tag sets the background color for the entire table. Placing a background attribute and value inside a table heading tag (<th>) or table data tag (<td>) sets the background color for that cell. Setting the background color for a cell overrides the background color of the table if both have been specified. If no background color is specified for a table, the table background will be the same color as the Web page background. This could cause problems if the Web page background color clashes with the element content of the table.

Use background color attributes and values to change the background colors of your table:

1. Return to your text editor to view the source code of your **table_practice_1.html** file.
2. Key background color attributes and values to change the background color for the table and for the table heading:

```
<table border="1" align="center" cellpadding="15"
cellspacing="10" bgcolor="00ffff">
<tr>
<th colspan="4" align="center" bgcolor="3399ff">Column Span</th>
</tr>
```

3. Save the file and refresh your browser. Your table now has a light blue background, with a darker blue heading column (see Figure 3.16).

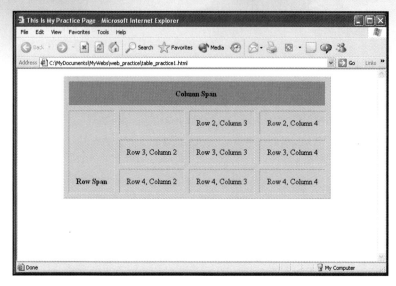

FIGURE 3.16

Background color attributes and values can be used to change table and table cell background colors.

Stacked Tables

You can stack tables on top of each other. When using tables to control layout it is better to use several short tables rather than one long table. Longer tables take a browser longer to load, so you should avoid them whenever possible.

STACK TABLES

Stack two tables to control the page layout:

1. Return to your text editor to view the source code of your **table_practice_1.html** file.
2. Select all of the code for your table, from the table start tag (<table>) to the table end tag (</table>). Copy the selected code.
3. Key several line break tags after the table end tag of the table you just copied:

```
</table>
<br />
<br />
```

4. Paste the table code that you copied just below the last line break tag you entered.
5. Save the file and refresh your browser. There are now two copies of your table on the page, separated by several lines of white space (see Figure 3.17).

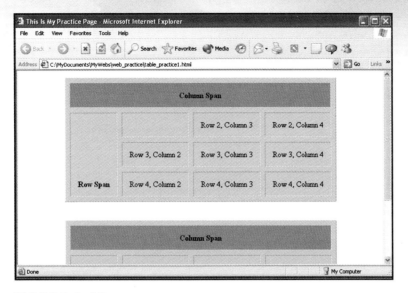

FIGURE 3.17
Stacking tables is an effective method for controlling Web page layout.

Nested Tables

Tables also can be nested, or placed inside another table. There is no limit to the number of tables that can be nested inside one another, but for clarity's sake, it is not a good idea to nest too many tables. Nesting tables is another way to use tables for layout control.

NEST TABLES

Nest a table within the table you have already created:
1. Right-click to view the source code of your **table_practice_1.html** file.
2. Replace the content of the fourth cell in the second row of the first table in the file by keying the following:

```
<td>Row 2, Column 4
<table border="1">
<tr>
<td>Nested Table</td>
</tr>
<tr>
<td>Nested Table</td>
</tr>
</table>
</td>
</tr>
<tr>
<td>Row 3, Column 2</td>
```

3. Save the file and refresh your browser. You now have a small table within the first table on your page (see Figure 3.18).

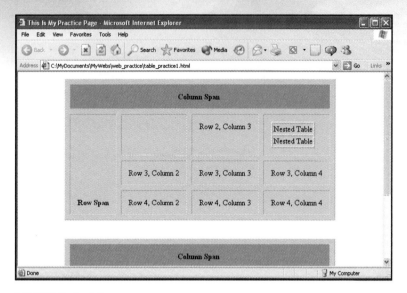

FIGURE 3.18
A small table is nested within a larger table.

Make Tables Invisible

When using a table for layout control, you will usually want table borders to be invisible. This can be accomplished by setting the values for the BORDER and CELLSPACING attributes to "0". You must do this to create an invisible border, even if you did not originally key BORDER and CELLSPACING attributes. This is because some browsers will use a default value of 1 for these values unless you specify otherwise. This is particularly true for the CELLSPACING attribute. If you do not enter a zero value for cell spacing, spaces might appear between table cells.

CREATE AN INVISIBLE TABLE

Follow these steps to make the borders of your table invisible:
1. Right-click to view the source code of your **table_practice_1.html** file.
2. Change the BORDER and CELLSPACING attributes inside the first table's start tag (<table>) to 0:

```
<table border="0" align="center" cellpadding="15"
cellspacing="0" bgcolor="00ffff">
```

3. Save the file and refresh your browser. The first table should now appear without any table borders.

Table Captions

The optional CAPTION element (<caption></caption>) can be used to provide a caption for your table. The ALIGN attribute can be used with the caption tags, and the possible values are "top", "bottom", "left", and "right". A caption start tag (<caption>) must be followed by a caption end tag (</caption>). Current browsers will display the caption centered above a table if you do not enter an ALIGN attribute and value. Text tags can be used to mark up the caption text. The caption tag should be located just after the table start tag, and before the first row start tag.

USE CAPTION TAGS

Add a caption to your table using the caption tags:
1. Return to your text editor to view the source code of your **table_practice_1.html** file.
2. Key a caption tag just below the TABLE element as shown here. Note that bold tags are being used to create bold text:

```
<table border="0" align="center" cellpadding="15"
cellspacing="0" bgcolor="00ffff">
<caption><b>This Is a Practice Table</b></caption>
```

3. Save the file and refresh your browser. The table caption should now appear in bold text centered above the first table.
4. Experiment with entering different values and text formatting tags.

design
project

1. Use a search engine to gather information on resources about good Web page design. Look for sites that you think would be helpful to you and to others, and pick a list of favorites. Make sure to gather notes that include any reference material that will be needed later, such as URLs, publishers, and author. You will be comparing and annotating these resources on your Web site, so be sure to gather this information as well. Feel free to conduct any additional research you feel might be beneficial. Bookmark the sites so you can easily locate them again. Write a report summarizing your findings.

2. Examine other Web pages to see how they use tables to control page layout. Right-click to view the source code of page layouts you find attractive to see whether you can understand how they used tables to control their layout.

3. Conduct a search for Web sites that offer guidance on creating and using tables in HTML. Bookmark any of these sites that you find helpful so that you can use them as a resource when working with tables.

4. Create a new Web page (or pages) and use Copy and Paste to insert the content of the report you created for the Research Assignment. Use the knowledge you have just gained to create tables for your Web pages. Some of the tables you create may be conventional tables, and you might want to begin entering data you have gathered into them now. Other tables you create will be used to control the layout of your Web pages.

4

Usability and Accessibility

cyber visit

RAYMOND PIROUZ

Web Designer, Author, Instructor, Product Developer

Design Viewpoint

"Good interface design facilitates flawless communication between the messenger and the audience. It helps the visitor to focus on the content of a Web site rather than their position within it. It can positively reinforce the brand by emoting structure, stability, and trust."

"The World Wide Web will totally revolutionize the way human beings communicate and advance as a species (if it hasn't begun to do so already)."

Resume

Working online since the 1980s; former art director at Rubin Postaer Interactive; received World Studio Foundation award for design and advertising excellence; authored several Web related books and articles; has taught Web design at UCLA and R35.edu.

Clients

American Honda, Cathay Pacific & iBank, Panasonic/Monty Python, Toyota, and the Globus Project, among others.

Designer's Home Page

www.raymondpirouz.com/

Insights

"By working closely with your creative directors and copywriters, your goal as the designer is to help your visitors quickly find any and all of the information available on your Web site. This can be accomplished through a number of methods: a solid navigation, utilitarian search engines and pull-down menus, and creatively crafted and typographically rich copywriting that entices and leads the user."

PORTFOLIO

Visit Raymond Pirouz's home page at www.raymondpirouz.com/.

Raymond Pirouz is founder of **R35, Inc.**

Raymond began his career as an Art Director for **Rubin Postaer Interactive**, where he established himself as an expert in the field of advertising on the Internet, creating award-winning campaigns for major clients including American Honda, Cathay Pacific Airlines & American Century Mutual Funds.

At R35's Communication Design Studio, Raymond's clients have included American Honda, Cathay Pacific & iBank (Rubin Postaer Interactive), Panasonic/Monty Python (THINK NEW IDEAS, INC.), Toyota (Saatchi & Saatchi LA), Rational Software Corporation, Virgin Records, California Institute of Technology (Caltech), NASA/JPL/States Of Art and The Globus Project (USC) among others.

An honors graduate of the prestigious **Art Center College of Design**, Raymond is dedicated to sharing his knowledge with others. In 1997, Raymond taught an advanced web design class at UCLA extension and has since then taught studio & sponsored project courses at the Art Center College of Design in Pasadena, California.

In 1997, Raymond's vision inspired the launch of **shop.R35.com**, an eCommerce site that embraces Raymond's vision of *Design for Modern Living*™.

Raymond Pirouz created this Web site (www.r35.com/) for his own business—R35: Design for Modern Living. The mission of this company is clear from the site: "to help you surround yourself with the most beautiful, thoughtfully designed, and practical furniture, lighting, accessories, and technologies, so you can work, learn, and play better."

Welcome to R35 : *Design For Modern Living*™

Get LIVE answers to your questions WITH ONE CLICK.

At R35, our mission is to help you surround yourself with the most beautiful, thoughtfully designed and practical furniture, lighting, accessories and technologies so you can work, learn and play **better**.

Whether you are shopping for your new or existing home, office or corporate headquarters, we have the know-how and the products—backed by **exceptional customer service**—so you can make the most out of any environment.

As an authorized **Herman Miller for the Home** retailer, we represent products by world famous designers such as **Charles & Ray Eames**, **Isamu Noguchi**, **Alvar Aalto** and **George Nelson**. In addition to Herman Miller, we represent other fine manufacturers such as **Offi**, **Vitra** and **Health Postures**.

We invite you to **shop at R35** and experience *Design For Modern Living*™.

By Raymond Pirouz
(5/19/98)

Typography--the art of communicating through specifying, positioning, and layering type--may have met its match in the World Wide Web. Modern-day typographers are often stymied by the fact that their creations are rendered inconsistently across the various Web browsers and platforms. No matter how careful your design, you simply can't be sure that users will see what you intended.

▶ High-tech type tips
▶ White-space tips
▶ Page-scale type tips
▶ Balanced-page type tips
▶ Colored-type tips
▶ Download the software
▶ List all tips

View Raymond Pirouz's tips about typography—the art of enhancing communication by "specifying, positioning, and layering" of type—at builder.cnet.com/webbuilding/pages/Graphics/Type/. Controlling type on the Web is much trickier than in print.

Objectives

➤ Explain the meanings of "usability" and "accessibility" and the significance of each concept for Web design.

➤ Describe usability standards and guidelines compiled and verified by the National Cancer Institute.

➤ Outline the accessibility standards and guidelines from the World Wide Web Consortium Web Accessibility Initiative.

➤ Explain some of the major techniques for ensuring Web sites are accessible to all users.

➤ Discuss the effect that usability and accessibility have on the use of enhancements such as scrolling text, font color, graphics, movies, and audio files.

The parameters, principles, and generations discussed in Chapter 3 provide a means for judging where a site is successful and where it can be improved; however, devising a plan and producing such improvements requires a more specific and applied level of guidance. This guidance comes from the standards and guidelines that have been established through the leadership of two groups in particular—the National Cancer Institute (NCI) and the World Wide Web Consortium (W3C).

The usability and accessibility guidelines and standards presented in this chapter are the beginning of a site design framework. This framework will become a useful tool for upgrading current sites or designing new ones. It is essential for new (and current) designers to consult at least these major sources as a substantive guide for methods and practices. Also, it is important to begin practicing the habit of regularly updating these guidelines to reflect changes and developments in the field.

INTEGRATING USABILITY STANDARDS AND GUIDELINES

usability
The degree to which a Web site is efficient and easy to use. Ease of use, efficiency of the design, visual consistency, and a clear focus on meeting the needs of users are hallmarks of usability. A usable Web site should also be memorable, result in few errors, and provide a level of satisfaction for the user.

Usability—the quality that makes a Web site efficient and easy to use—is a primary concern that drives Web design standards and guidelines. Usability is defined as the measure of the quality of users' online experiences, including factors such as the:

• Ease with which they are able to learn how to use the site.
• Efficiency with which they can use it.
• Ease with which they can remember a site's address and how to use the site when they return.
• Number and severity of errors users make.
• General sense users have of whether they like using the system.

Usability is as important to the site's owners as it is to its users. Web sites need to be efficient and easy to use or they will lose visitors, which could result in the loss of revenue. Visitors who experience the smallest degrees of confusion or frustration while on a site will leave. In the physical world, it is accepted that driving to another store, finding a different doctor or lawyer, calling and scheduling another plumber might be worse than sticking with a present supplier. As a result, customers might continue in a business relationship even if that relationship does not fully meet their expectations. However, in the virtual world, shopping, research, and scheduling can be done much more quickly, so changing suppliers is much more common. A usable Web site is a valuable site, to both the owner of the site and the people who access it.

According to design experts Jakob Nielsen and Donald Norman: "Over time, people gravitate to the sites that treat them well and are easy to use. Sheer design Darwinism: survival of the easiest. Usability is not a luxury on the Internet. It is essential to survival."

In spite of the importance of usability for the success of a Web site, usability problems are pervasive on the Web. Nielsen reports the common usability barriers listed in Table 4.1. As you look at the table, notice that all usability problems cited by Nielsen relate in some way to the parameters presented in Chapter 3. For instance, the first problem cited by Nielsen can be restated as a failure to engage audiences (the engagement parameter). Each problem Nielsen states can be matched with one of the parameters covered in the previous chapter.

TABLE 4.1 Common Usability Barriers

Barrier	Description
Lack of Goal Support	Difficult for users to accomplish what they want because the site focuses too much on self-promotion and "branding messages."
Confusing Information Architecture	Site structure is not intuitive.
Navigation Problems	Users lose track of where they are, where they have been, and where they want to go next.
Search Problems	Users cannot identify relevant pages from lists of search results.
Content Problems	Text is difficult to scan, making it hard for users to jump ahead to the specific information they want.
Speed Problems	Download is too slow.
Consistency Problems	Different areas look different or behave differently, leading users to complain that the site "does not feel like a unified whole."

Source: Nielsen, J. "Users First," www.zdnet.com/.

Implementing Usability Guidelines

This section reviews the guidelines compiled by the National Cancer Institute (NCI), a federal agency with the responsibility of making information about cancer and cancer treatments available to the public. NCI's Web usability guidelines make up one of the more useful sets compiled so far. NCI collected, distilled, and categorized information from the many already existing guidelines to create its list. Guidelines on the NCI list receive scores based on "levels of evidence," ranging in strength (high to low), from research studies to observational evaluations and usability tests to expert opinions.

NCI's guidelines were initially provided to assist NCI Web managers, designers, and authors in improving their overall communications and Web design efforts when developing informational sites in health-related areas. However, because "the general principles of design and usability are applicable to anyone who works with information Web sites," as the NCI's Web site puts it, organizers decided to make the guidelines available to other federal agencies and to the general public.

Root Link www.usability.gov/
Direct Link www.usability.gov/guidelines/intro.html
Why Go? To view the NCI's compilation of the top Web design and usability guidelines, as judged by NCI's rating system. The introductory page explains NCI's rationale and process.

All guidelines listed on NCI's usability site are classified into 14 categories (see Table 4.2). To simplify this discussion, NCI's categories are regrouped into related topics as follows:

- An organized design process
- Design considerations
- Hardware and software
- Page layout
- Architecture of the site

TABLE 4.2 NCI's Research-Based Web Design and Usability Guidelines

Guideline Category	Specific Guideline
1. Design Process	Set and state goals. Set performance and/or preference goals. Share independent design ideas. Create and evaluate prototypes.
2. Design Considerations	Establish level of importance. Reduce users' workload. Be consistent. Provide feedback to users. Include logos. Limit maximum page size. Limit use of frames.
3. Content/Content Organization	Establish level of importance. Provide useful content.

continues

Guideline Category	Specific Guideline
3. Content/Content Organization—Continued	Put important information at top of hierarchy. Use short sentence/paragraph lengths. Provide printing options.
4. Titles/Headings	Provide page titles. Use well-designed headings.
5. Page Length	Determine page length. Determine scrolling versus paging needs.
6. Page Layout	Align page elements. Establish level of importance. Be consistent. Reduce unused space. Put important information at top of page. Format for efficient viewing.
7. Font/Text Size	Use readable font sizes. Use familiar fonts.
8. Reading and Scanning	Use reading performance or user preference. Enhance scanning. Determine scrolling versus paging needs.
9. Links	Position important links higher. Show links clearly. Indicate internal versus external links. Use descriptive link labels. Use text links. Avoid mouseovers. Repeat text links. Present tabs effectively. Show used links.
10. Graphics	Use graphics wisely. Avoid using graphics as links. Avoid graphics on search pages.
11. Search	Consider importance of search engine. Indicate search scope. Enhance scanning.
12. Navigation	Keep navigation aids consistent. Use text-based navigation aids. Group navigation elements. Place navigation on right.
13. Software/Hardware	Determine connection speed. Reduce download time. Consider monitor size. Consider users' screen resolution. Design for full or partial screen viewing.
14. Accessibility	Use color wisely. Design for device independence. Provide alternative formats. Provide redundant text links. Provide user-controlled content.

Source: National Cancer Institute (www.usability.gov/guidelines/index.html)

AN ORGANIZED DESIGN PROCESS   Efficiently building a Web site requires knowing the best ways of organizing a Web development project. NCI makes specific suggestions on how best to organize a Web development project.

In the early stages of the design process, designers should be open to different design ideas. Developers should not rely exclusively on the initial design ideas of one person or group. Instead of being satisfied with the first idea or a single individual's opinion, it is best to "saturate the design space" with ideas before making decisions. Designers should be open to alternatives before taking a single direction.

It is important to set specific goals based on performance and preferences. These goals help designers build better Web sites and guide the design of usability tests that address measurable specifics. Three examples of possible performance and preference goals include:

- 90% of users should be able to find the information they need in less than one minute.
- 90% of users should say they like the site and will return.
- Site users are able to move efficiently through the site to the content that is of specific interest to them.

The primary goals of the Web site should be articulated clearly at the beginning of the design process. A Web site can undergo numerous changes, but the fundamental mission should not change. The primary goals help the Web developers keep track of their mission. Clearly articulated goals reduce the extent of fundamental revisions that could occur during the design process.

As the design process continues, the design team should work to create and evaluate illustrative models of the site. An iterative design process includes cycles, and each cycle produces a **prototype** of the site. Each prototype is evaluated by the design team and the client to see how well it works and what problems it might create for the user. Prototypes can be created on paper or on-screen and often do not include coding. After a prototype is approved, programmers code the prototype. Finally, the prototype is tested, corrected, and modified until the site is complete. This topic is covered in more detail in Chapter 6, *Phase II: Design and Produce*.

DESIGN CONSIDERATIONS   As the design process continues, the work should be guided by general design considerations that directly affect the look and feel of a site as well as its content. NCI provides guidelines that focus on the design process in order to make the final Web site easy to use.

For example, the design should reduce the user's workload. Computers are machines that perform routine tasks effortlessly. It makes sense, then, to use this power to the advantage of Web users. Anticipate what users will need and provide the tools to spare them from having to perform routine tasks the computer could perform for them. For example, calculations, estimations, and recall of account numbers and passwords are tasks that the computer can perform so users can concentrate on those tasks that actually require their thought and input.

Providing tools commonly used in accomplishing a task will reduce users' workloads. This site at www.virtualtourist.com/ includes features that make it easy to plan international trips: a time converter, a currency converter, a metric converter, a language translator, and travel warnings from the U.S. State Department.

Web sites should have a unified design. Similar information and functions should appear consistently throughout the site, thus creating unity and making it easier to find specific things on the Web site. Unity also improves navigation. To help achieve unity in a site, titles should appear on every page and banners and navigational elements should be placed in the same spots and should look the same. Recurring text, buttons, and graphics should be in consistent positions. Consistent layout makes it easier for users to evaluate categories and decide where information they seek will be located. Logos create unity by identifying individual pages as belonging to a site, and they are an effective way to ensure that users know where they are.

Users bring expectations about the location of Web page elements because of their experiences on other sites. These expectations drive design experts to strive for more global levels of consistency beyond a single site or even a single designer's sites.

Web designs should limit the use of **frames**.

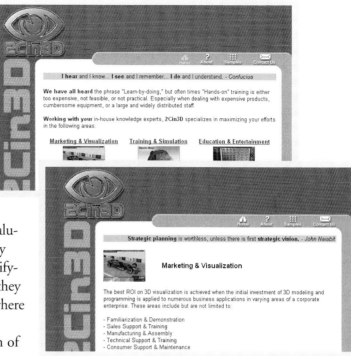

The design at www.2cin3d.com/ works by maintaining a frame-like look where the text changes from page to page, but the borders and logo remain the same. However, this look is accomplished using tables to control layout and thus is not subject to the difficulties caused by frames.

Frames provide a way of displaying multiple Web pages on a browser at the same time. Each frame can be coded to scroll or to remain static, and selecting links within one frame can affect what is displayed in another currently displayed frame. Frames offer layout control in much the same way as a table, although no table cell can be scrolled independently from another cell. Thus, one frame can act as a permanently available navigation window while other frames change from content that is completely viewable to other content requiring the user to scroll down to view it in its entirety. Splitting pages into frames can be confusing to users, and might yield unexpected results in terms of URLs, bookmarking, and printing. Thus, frames should be used only when other design solutions are not adequate.

frames

Multiple, independently controllable sections on a Web page. One master HTML file identifies all of the separate HTML files making up the frameset. Originally created by Netscape and now part of the HTML 4.0 specification. Defined with HTML frameset tags (<frameset>) and frame tags (<frame>).

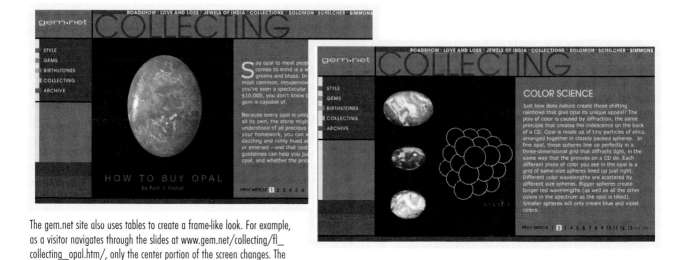

The gem.net site also uses tables to create a frame-like look. For example, as a visitor navigates through the slides at www.gem.net/collecting/fl_collecting_opal.htm/, only the center portion of the screen changes. The navigation bars on the top and left of the page remain the same.

This site uses frames well. The heavy use of graphics would cause the site to load slowly (www.rockwelltour.org/frameset.html). The initial page loads the picture of Norman Rockwell and the graphic banner for the site; once loaded, these are kept throughout. Thus, only the new images for selected pages need to be loaded as the visitor continues to navigate the site.

Another design consideration is best use of Web page titles (the text that comes between the title start tag (<title>) and the title end tag (</title>) in the HEAD element (<head>) of the HTML code. Each page on a Web site should have a descriptive and unique title. Titles do not appear as part of the active screen. Instead, titles show at the top of the browser window and become the default text that shows for lists of favorites or bookmarks. Also, titles are used by search engines to determine which pages to include on a list of results for a particular search.

Another example of one reason to use frames: www.jungletheater.com/frameset.html keeps the key navigational tools and information in a frame at the top of the screen while visitors scroll down the rest of the page to see what is available.

HARDWARE AND SOFTWARE Computer configurations (the combination of hardware and software being used) directly affect the experiences users have as they visit sites. A Web page displayed at a certain size looks and feels different from the same page displayed at another size. Pages that load slowly try users' patience, especially when the elements causing the delay prove irrelevant to the purposes of the site. Because different users have different hardware and software configurations, designers must build sites that perform under the most common situations or adjust to differing situations. To guide Web designers, NCI compiled several guidelines concerning hardware and software.

Web designers make every effort to reduce download time of the Web pages. Web pages should load quickly enough to keep users interested in staying at the site. What is a good download time? Web users rate downloads of up to 5 seconds as "good," downloads of 6 to 10 seconds as "average," and downloads over 10 seconds as "poor." Although it is difficult to specify how long casual users of Web sites might wait for a page to download before moving on, NCI cites statistics indicating that the average time is about 10 seconds.

Obviously, access speeds affect how quickly a page downloads. Designers should design for connection speeds of 56 Kilobits per second (KBps). Most users (60%) use a 56 Kbps modem or slower. Actual connection speeds are about 38% slower than this. This means that a 56 Kbps connection averages an actual data transfer speed of about 35 Kbps. At this connection speed, a 30 KB page would take about 8 seconds to download, a 40 KB page would require almost 13 seconds, and a 50 KB page close to 16 seconds. Thus, only the 30 KB page would download within the 10-second maximum of how long users generally will wait without losing patience. Although faster access speeds are already available and becoming more widespread, many users do not have such access and could be excluded from sites that presume a fast user connection.

DO YOU KNOW?

Question Before packet switching, when "message switching" was used, how long did it take for a message to travel from the source computer to its destination?

Answer Message-switching methods could take hours. Traveling on a message-switching circuit, complete messages traveled on the network and then had to wait at each point for earlier messages to be sent on. This meant that a short message (such as "Hi") could wait a long time for longer messages to be sent if the longer messages were sent first. This method was aptly compared to sending smoke signals.

Designers must consider that screen resolution influences how clear the page will look on a screen. Screen resolution also affects the size at which the page is displayed. Screen resolution is measured in pixels ("pixel" is short for "picture element"). As a general rule, as shown in Figure 4.1, the greater the number of pixels, the clearer the page will be. The higher screen resolution allows more pixels to be displayed on the screen, which means that more of the Web site's content appears within the vertical space of the monitor (although with the lower resolution, the content still fills the screen's horizontal space). A higher screen resolution results in smaller type on the screen, which can be hard to read, but it also can save users from having to scroll down the page if all contents fits within the frame. Two studies referred to by NCI indicated that the largest number of users (53%) were using screen resolutions of 800 × 600 pixels, so the guidelines recommend designing for this resolution. There are practical consequences for such a strategy, however, and it is advisable to test designs on various screen resolutions to determine the best possible solution. (See Table 4.3 for recent statistics on screen resolution usage.)

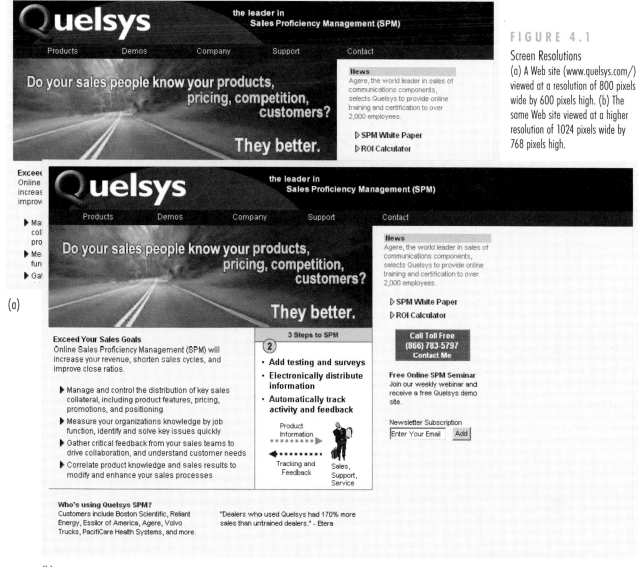

(a)

(b)

FIGURE 4.1

Screen Resolutions
(a) A Web site (www.quelsys.com/)
viewed at a resolution of 800 pixels
wide by 600 pixels high. (b) The
same Web site viewed at a higher
resolution of 1024 pixels wide by
768 pixels high.

TABLE 4.3 Statistics on Screen Resolutions

Screen Resolution	Number of Users*	Percentage
800 × 600	180.3 million	51%
1024 × 768	125.6 million	36%
1280 × 1024	13.5 million	4%
640 × 480	13.0 million	4%
1152 × 864	10.6 million	3%
1600 × 1200	2.5 million	1%
unknown	4.4 million	1%

*Numbers rounded to nearest hundred thousand.

Source: "Resolution stats," April 2002 (www.thecounter.com/stats/2002/April/res.php). Copyright 2000-2002 INT Media Group Incorporated.
All rights reserved.

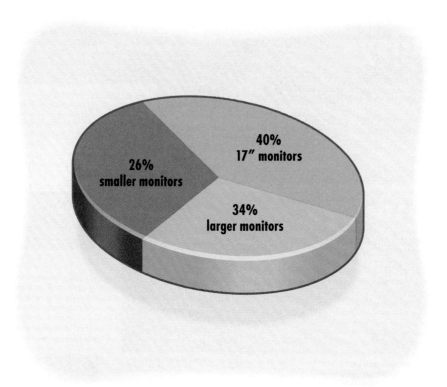

Designers must consider monitor size, which also affects users' abilities to view Web pages. Larger screens are easier to read than smaller screens, and it turns out that about 40% of users use 17-inch monitors, while 34% use larger monitors. Only about 26% use monitors smaller then 17 inches (including laptops; see Figure 4.2). Because they are so common, the NCI usability guidelines recommend designing for a 17-inch monitor.

Even with a 17-inch or larger monitor, some users will view Web sites in partial screen view, and designers must consider these view options. Partial-screen design allows a user to have multiple Web page windows open, displaying side by side with another partial-screen Web page in a browser. This eliminates the need for the user to toggle back and forth between pages in order to view them simultaneously. Some designers use flexible pages (based on percentages rather than fixed widths) that adjust according to the window size.

PAGE LAYOUT NCI cites six guidelines, four of which have high levels of support, regarding page layout. Layout, an issue that some might consider a concern primarily for graphic designers, actually requires the attention of information architects, writers, and editors.

Elements on the page should be aligned according to some clear arrangement. A page without some kind of alignment scheme appears chaotic to the eye. Thus, comparable items of information on a page should appear to follow some consistent alignment scheme.

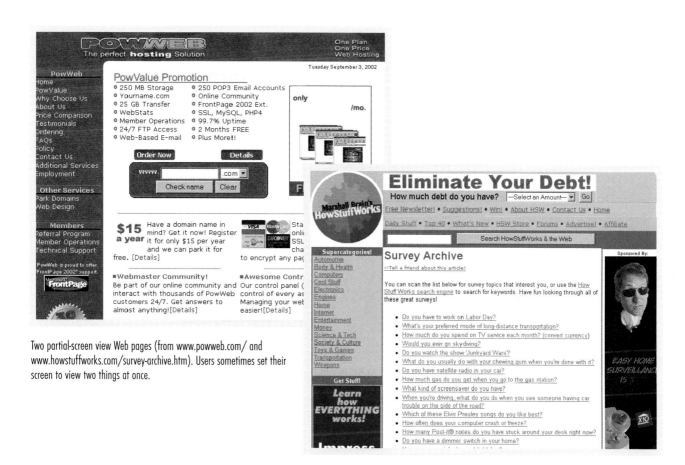

Two partial-screen view Web pages (from www.powweb.com/ and www.howstuffworks.com/survey-archive.htm). Users sometimes set their screen to view two things at once.

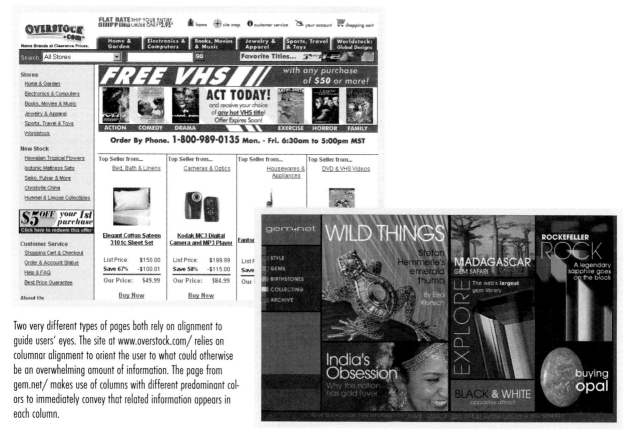

Two very different types of pages both rely on alignment to guide users' eyes. The site at www.overstock.com/ relies on columnar alignment to orient the user to what could otherwise be an overwhelming amount of information. The page from gem.net/ makes use of columns with different predominant colors to immediately convey that related information appears in each column.

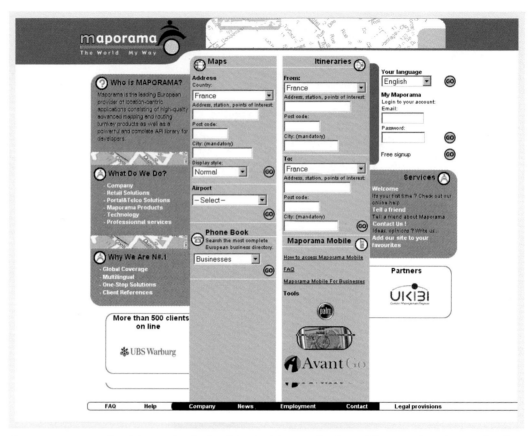

The site at maporama.com/share/ places two large headings ("Maps" and "Itineraries") at the top of the page, pushing information about the company to the sides, where it is accessible but less prominent. This is an example of placing what users will want at the top of the page, above the promotional information about the company that runs the site.

On pages that will be scanned quickly, designers should reduce unused space. An example is a home page where the primary purpose is to provide links or categories. The greater the density, the faster the scanning, as long as density does not impede scanning. A balance needs to be struck between density and legibility, but as a general rule, Web pages should contain less white space than arrangements of the same information on paper.

Placing important information at the top of the Web page makes scanning easier. Therefore, the most important information should appear at the top of any page, menu, or list. Most readers will scan a Web page by looking at the top center of the page, then looking left, then right, and then systematically moving down the total page in the same fashion. Therefore, all critical content and navigation options should be at the top of the page. All major choices should be visible without scrolling, because when users do not see anything of interest to them on the visible portion of the page, they might not bother to scroll down to see the rest.

Developers should use the layout that provides for the most efficient viewing and use of information on each page. This layout is determined based on the most common use of each page. The structure of each page should facilitate scanning to help users know which large chunks of the page they might be able to ignore in terms of their particular goals. Studies report that between 75% and 79% of users scan a new page, while only 16% read all of the text word for word. Most users (78%) tend to focus first on text, not graphics.

Page length should be based on the intended use of the page. If reading speed is important, and response time is reasonably fast, the Web site should use short pages that are linked to other pages, rather than long pages that require the user to scroll to information. Home pages, navigation pages, and pages that need to be quickly browsed or read online should be short.

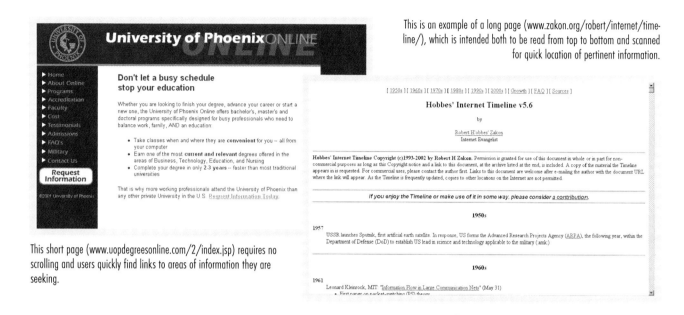

This is an example of a long page (www.zakon.org/robert/internet/time-line/), which is intended both to be read from top to bottom and scanned for quick location of pertinent information.

This short page (www.uopdegreesonline.com/2/index.jsp) requires no scrolling and users quickly find links to areas of information they are seeking.

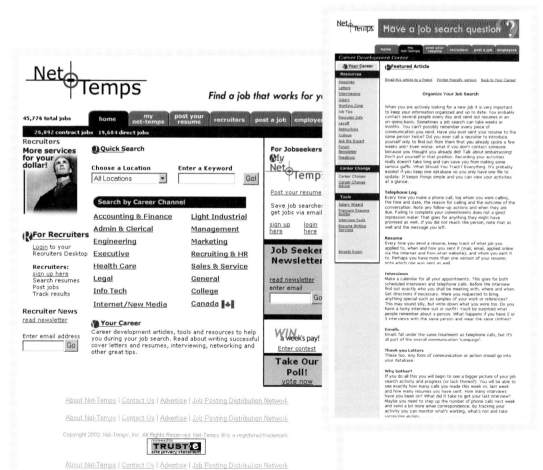

The same site might use short pages in combination with long pages. The site at nettemps.com/ uses a short page for an introductory home page. The page at www.net-temps.com/careerdev/index.htm?type=article&id=1 1 is the first page of a long article and so is appropriate for a long page design.

Long pages are used to simplify page maintenance; match the structure of a paper counterpart (such as an article); and make pages more convenient to download, print, and read or scan together as a full set of "destination" content. Pages should always provide feedback to inform users where they are in a site.

Good Web designs use many carefully selected headings, with names that conceptually relate to the information or functions they describe. Headings provide cues that orient users and inform them about the page's organization and structure. Headings also classify information on the page, helping users to scan text to look for particular areas of interest. Considering that headings are sometimes removed from the context of the page to be used in a table of contents, for example, it is important that headings communicate clearly even when they stand alone.

Visit www.linksys.com/ and navigate throughout the site to see an example of a site that provides feedback about where you are within the site. The page shown in this screen capture (www.linksys.com/Products/product.asp?grid=23&prid=20) shows that you are in the Products section of the site, reviewing information about the EtherFast Cable/DSL Router.

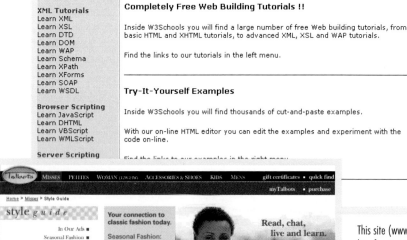

This site (www.w3schools.com/), which lists free training opportunities for computer-related topics, categorizes the many choices with clear headings.

Another example of how good headings communicate a site's structure. This page is at www.talbots.com/styleguide/default.asp?BID=&h=Ma.

Readability improves with sentences and paragraphs that are relatively short. Sentences should contain 20 or fewer words and paragraphs should contain fewer than 5 sentences. Bulleted lists are helpful in breaking text out so that it can be viewed more readily.

Users tend to prefer shorter line lengths (55 characters per line) but read faster when line lengths are longer (100 characters per line). When performance is the most critical goal, use longer line lengths to increase reading speed. If user preference is more critical, use shorter line lengths. The screen capture of the Norman Rockwell site provided earlier in this chapter is an example of a site that uses short line lengths. Although the short page might be easier to read, the long page, with its text set wide, is set up for quick scanning. Users can read a great deal of material without having to scroll continuously.

Web pages enhance scanning by using clear links, headings, short phrases and sentences, and short paragraphs. Users tend to scan a page, stopping to read more closely only when they find something that is of interest to them. Research shows that users have difficulty finding a specific piece of information when the page contains dense text. Rather, users tend to look for alternatives to reading by resorting to a modified scanning strategy of reading the first sentence and then scanning for links on the page.

Web designers should use familiar and readable fonts. Although it is possible to specify any typeface a designer might have available, it is best to stick with the main types of fonts supported by all browsers: Arial, Helvetica, and Times New Roman. Times New Roman is an example of a serif font (because the letters have extensions at the ends of their strokes), whereas Arial and Helvetica are examples of sans serif fonts (because their strokes do not have the serif extensions; "sans" means "without"). If a designer wants to use a font other than these standards, this situation is often handled by turning the text into a .gif file to be embedded in the page as an image. This practice is practical, however, only for small blocks of text, otherwise the resulting page would be slow to load. Thus, this practice is usually reserved for banners, headings, navigational links, and other short items.

For font size, use at least a 10-point font to achieve the best possible reading performance. Fonts smaller than 10-point slow the reading performance of users and, particularly for people over age 65, it might be better to use at least 12- or 14-point fonts. As a rule of thumb, font size 3 (an HTML attribute to determine text formats) characters on the screen equal 12-point characters of the same font in print.

Root Link www.eyewire.com/
Direct Link www.eyewire.com/products/type/
Why Go? To learn basics and find more detailed information about typefaces and the practice of typography.

Mixing serif and sans serif fonts within the text may decrease reading speed. Also, the fancy-looking "cursive" scripts are generally difficult to read. They should be avoided for long passages that contain important information.

Graphics should enhance content or lead to a better understanding of the information being presented. Large graphics often take a while to download, and should add

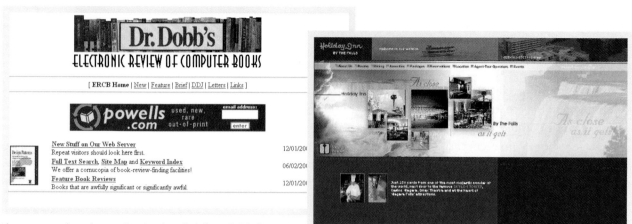

The site at www.ercb.com/ uses small graphics almost like bullets to the left of descriptive text.

Holiday Inn's site offers many choices on its home page (holidayinn.com/). It provides hotel guests with one-click access to information about hotel rooms and dining accommodations, making reservations, locations, and money-saving packages.

value to the site's content to be worth the wait from a viewer's perspective. When using graphics, designers should use small graphic files to reduce download time.

Designers should avoid using graphics on search pages because graphics do not have a positive value in terms of users' success with searching. Also, designers should avoid using graphics as links because clickable images generally confuse users. If graphics are used as links, provide alternative text that is sufficiently descriptive to clearly identify the image as a link to something of importance. Also provide a redundant text link to the same page or piece of information.

ARCHITECTURE OF THE SITE Effective Web sites have a hierarchy that is appropriate to the information on the site. Information should appear quickly, without the user having to click through extraneous levels of pages. The more steps users must make to find what they are looking for, the greater the likelihood of their making a wrong choice or abandoning the process.

Links should change visually in some way to indicate to users which links they have already visited. After a target page has been visited, all locations on the site where the link to that destination page occurs should change color. If the color (or some other cue) does not change on all visited links, users repeatedly return to the same set of pages, not knowing they are going back to the same pages again and again. For links that use standard text, most browsers automatically change the color of visited links and the cache of a computer will keep track of visited links between visits. When graphic links are used, similar visual cues can be designed.

In addition to showing used links, the guidelines direct designers to consider the following ideas when designing links.

- Position important links higher on the page; at a minimum, they should be above the scroll line.
- Show links clearly, using the text-underline cue when possible.
- Do not require users to move the mouse to find hidden links (where the pointer changes to the hand icon). Users are confused when no immediate visual indicator shows where the links are on the page.

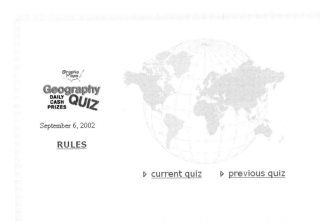
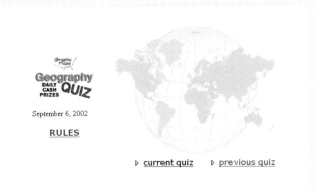

If a visitor takes the current quiz at www.graphicmaps.com/geoquiz.htm and then
returns to the home page, the link to the current quiz changes to show that the current quiz link has been visited already.

- Indicate internal versus external links so that users know when they will be moving off the Web site to a page on a different site.
- Use descriptive link labels so that users are not forced to ponder the differences between various link destinations, or to follow a link in order to know what is there.
- Use text links, not image links, because these are preferred by users and can be set to change color after the link destination has been visited.
- Repeat text links using several versions of descriptive labels to ensure that the most important content can be accessed by more users, using whatever label is most meaningful to them. When information is critical to the success of the Web site, providing more than one link name to the same content enables users who do not respond to one label to respond to another.
- When using folder tabs as links, present tabs effectively so that they look like "real-world" tabs on folders found in a file drawer. This increases the likelihood that users will understand that these are meant to represent tabs, and will know to click on them appropriately.

Web sites should provide printing options so that destination documents and resources can be printed in their entirety. Documents can be broken into sections on separate pages, so a printable version can make it easy for users to print the entire document with one click. Printable versions also can ensure that text to the right side of the screen actually prints on the paper. Sometimes this text can be chopped off when printed. Also, Web sites should contain useful and usable content that supports the Web site goal of each page.

Navigation aids should be consistent and grouped in close proximity. Whenever possible, place navigation aids on the right side of the screen. Users tend to be more efficient at using navigation aids on the right side of the screen rather than the left side. This increased efficiency is because links on the right are

Travelocity.com at www.travelocity.com/ colors the tab relating to the page the user is visiting. All other tabs are left uncolored to create a clear distinction.

Visit amazon.com for an example of a site that enables users to search all or part of the site. The drop-down box on the left of the screen allows you to search All Products or a specific category of products such as Books, Popular Music, Classical Music, or DVDs.

Navigational links on the right side of the page make them quicker to access with a mouse, as the scroll bar is also located on the right side of the page. The site at get-crafty.com/ has right-hand navigational links that appear almost integrated with the text.

closer to the scroll bar, thus allowing for quicker movement between scroll bar and index items. The benefits of this are particularly strong for laptops.

Search facilities are helpful on some sites, but do not add value on others. Sites that benefit from search utilities are those that are large and complex (100 pages or more), particularly when the amount of content is continually growing. When search capabilities are provided on a Web page, the page should communicate the range of the search that will be performed. Will the search be limited to the content of the site pages, or will a database beyond the pages be included? It is helpful to give users the option of controlling the scope of their search, for example, to be able to search within a section or subsection, or to search the site globally.

Testing Usability

Web designers must test sites to confirm that they will work for both novice and experienced users. To determine the degree to which the objectives of usability are met, usability studies are conducted with small groups of actual users. Usability tests are generally performed using five to twelve users, more for sites where multiple types of users will be visiting. Data are collected one-on-one, recorded through an interview process that combines actually watching users perform functions, and asking them, as they do so, what they are doing, what they are thinking, what they are experiencing, and other questions to clarify usability issues as they surface. Usability testing will be discussed in greater depth in Chapter 6.

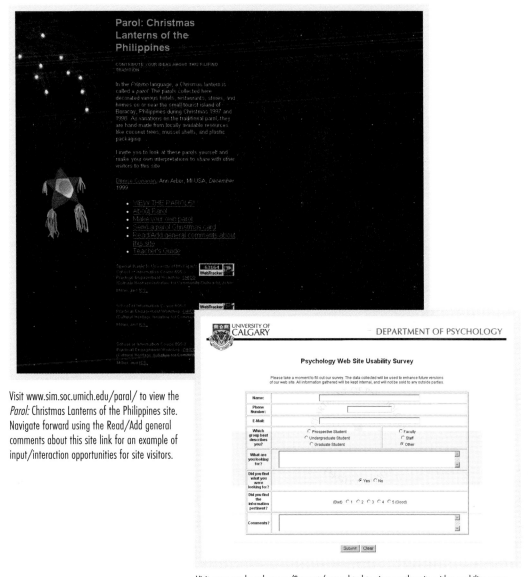

Visit www.sim.soc.umich.edu/parol/ to view the *Parol:* Christmas Lanterns of the Philippines site. Navigate forward using the Read/Add general comments about this site link for an example of input/interaction opportunities for site visitors.

Visit www.psych.ucalgary.ca/Support/survey.html to view another site with a usability survey.

Metrics—or measurements—that are gathered to measure usability include factors such as:

- How much time it takes for users to complete the test tasks
- How many errors users make in the process
- The ease with which users learn to use the site
- How well they remember how to use the functionality of the site on subsequent visits
- How satisfying they find their experience with the site to be.

Based on what is found during usability testing, and via general comments from users, changes are made to improve the overall experience and usability of the site.

Over the years, millions of visitors have been observed and queried by expert Web designer/developers to ensure that their online experiences are positive and useful, and thus that they will be likely to return. These measures of user experiences have led to important guidelines and standards about what has proven effective in terms of ensuring the usability of a Web site.

One usability study has concluded that the best sites are usable less than 60% of the time. According to another study, over 60% of Web shoppers give up looking for the item they want to buy online. Yet another study indicates that approximately 40% of users do not return to a site where their first visit is a negative experience. These are some of the statistics quoted by researchers such as User Interface Engineering, Zona Research, and Forrester Research, Inc.

Using the results from two searches that you perform, one for information and one to complete a purchase, do "mini-studies" to check these statistics and either confirm or refute the findings. Review all three tests (see Table 4.4) and the data you will need to collect to fill in the blanks. To prepare to develop rough personal statistics to compare to the reported statistic, conduct the following two searches:

TABLE 4.4 Usability Study Report

Reported Statistic	Test to Arrive at Personal Statistic	Problem Frequency	Personal Statistic	Confirm or Refute?
60% of the time, users are unable to find information they seek on a Web site (research by User Interface Engineering).	From the results of search 1, select 10 results at random and visit the sites. Give yourself 1–2 minutes at each site to locate information you need. List the sites where you succeeded and the sites where you failed.	Unable to find info: _____ Able to find info: _____ (Total sites = 10)	Unable to find info _____% of the time.	Confirm Refute (circle one)
Over 60% of Web shoppers have given up looking for the item they wanted to buy online (study by Zona Research).	From the results of search 2, randomly select 10 places to shop. Give yourself 1–2 minutes at each site to locate the item to be purchased. List the sites where you succeeded and the sites where you failed.	Unable to find item: _____ Able to find item: _____ (Total sites = 10)	Unable to find item _____% of the time.	Confirm Refute (circle one)
40% of users do not return to a site when their first visit is a negative experience (study by Forrester Research).	From the sites you visited for the first two mini-studies, review the lists of the sites where you were unable to find what you're looking for. Write the word "no" next to sites where you would not plan to return.	Would not plan to return: _____ (Total sites = 20)	I do not plan to return to _____% of the sites where I was unable to find what I needed.	Confirm Refute (circle one)

Source: National Cancer Institute, "Usability Basics" (www.usability.gov/basics/index.html).

- **Search 1: Information Search** The goal is to research the differences between ISDN (Integrated Services Digital Network) and DSL (Digital Subscriber Line) technologies. Search for sites that explain the differences between these two types of connections to the Internet and that help you decide which type of connection is best for you.
- **Search 2: Product Search** The goal is to locate a discounted copy of Macromedia Flash MX software for potential purchase. Search for sites that sell Macromedia Flash MX at less than the suggested retail price. You need to know what Macromedia charges for its current version of Flash MX and then compare other vendors' prices to that.

INTEGRATING ACCESSIBILITY STANDARDS

Along with issues of usability, Web designers also need to consider the **accessibility** of a Web site. Although the terms usability and accessibility are sometimes used to mean the same thing, they also possess more precise meanings. Usability refers generally to those qualities that make a Web site easy or hard to use, whereas accessibility refers more exactly to the criteria a Web site needs to follow to be used by Web users with special considerations: physical or mental disability, on the one hand, and specialized Web access devices on the other hand. Accessibility, then, is a special category within usability.

Accessibility has been a goal of the Web design community for some time. The World Wide Web Consortium (W3C) began its Web Accessibility Initiative in 1997. As Tim Berners-Lee, director of the W3C, says on the W3C Web site, "The power of the Web is in its universality. Access by everyone regardless of disability is an essential aspect."

As the Web has matured, early enthusiasms with the Internet and Web technology have been replaced with increasing attentiveness to the vast and varied needs of the user population in all of its diversity. These needs include the ergonomic requirements of individuals who might not be able to use their hands, eyes, or brains as most people do. These needs also include the technological modifications required to make Web sites available to different types of access devices. These two groups can overlap, especially as more workers—disabled or not—participate in the workforce by "telecommuting," that is, participating in the economy through telework.

Access to the Web is increasingly becoming a means for access to employment. A growing proportion of the workforce is affected by the restructuring of the workplace towards "telework." Telework, both for telecommuters (who occasionally work on their employer's site) and "virtual professionals" (who never meet face-to-face with their employer), is a trend that had impacted over 20 million workers by 2001 and is predicted to involve 55% of the work force by 2004. Telework is increasingly being recognized not as a luxury, but as "a necessary component of the evolving structure of modern work. . . . It is the most important workplace trend of the twenty-first century," according to *The Telecommuter*.

accessibility
In its specific sense, accessibility refers to removing barriers to the site, including those that prevent people with disabilities—visual, physical, cognitive, or neurological—from using the World Wide Web. An official activity of the W3C, whose goal is to provide "unprecedented access to information [on the Web] for people with disabilities."

The Department of Labor, in its executive summary of the October 2000 national symposium on "Telework and the New Workplaces of the Twenty-First Century" in New Orleans, compared the "historic transformation of the workplace" from this shift towards telework to the transformative changes brought about by the Industrial Revolution. One significant prediction made at this conference was that "the Information Age may return workers to their homes, and connect them via modern technology to the 'virtual office.' Such a shift holds huge implications for how we work and how we live."

This rapidly moving workplace trend impacts heavily the 16.9 million people with disabilities who are of working age (18.7% of all people 15 to 64 years old). Of these, fewer than a third (only 28% or 4.7 million) are employed. Of the 12.2 million not working, almost four out of five (9.6 million) want to be working, according to information available at www.disabledperson.com. For these 9.6 million individuals, access to the Web can mean access to work. At a minimum, Web access can provide a means for these individuals to match up with employers who are proactive about recruiting people with disabilities.

Web access technologies are changing. People are now accessing the Web by using mobile phones and personal digital assistants (PDAs)—sometimes for work, sometimes for personal reasons—and these devices are appearing everywhere. Will all of these formats be included in the vision of worldwide, universal access? Certainly, that is the goal. Standards for accessibility are important because they establish uniform goals for all software and Web developers to achieve, and the expectation that the Web will achieve its original vision.

Root Link www.dol.gov/
Direct Link www.dol.gov/asp/telework/p3_4.htm
Why Go? To learn about employment trends, including current statistics on employment in the United States and tips and leads for job hunters. Learn more about the subject of telework at the Direct Link.

Root Link www.recruit-ability.com/
Why Go? To see how one Web site is seeking to encourage communication between "disabled" job seekers and employers. "We are striving to improve the economic status of people with disabilities."

How People with Disabilities Use the Web

A variety of disabilities can impact Web access. What impact does motion on the screen have on a person with epilepsy? What are the needs of people who have used computers for so long and so continuously that they suffer from repetitive stress syndrome and must shift to other means of access? What does and does not make intellectual sense to a person with limited ability to grasp complex concepts? Addressing these questions, although difficult, will ensure that all perspectives can be voiced and heard, a central promise of the Web.

To understand some of the additional needs brought to the Web by people with disabilities, it is helpful to review specific examples of these users, the challenges they face, and the requirements necessary for successful use of the Web. Examples of this use are listed in Table 4.5. One example of a feature that makes Web pages more usable is the **access key,** which allows a user to substitute keyboard commands for use of the mouse to select functions. An access key is defined within the HTML code. In addition to HTML techniques to improve accessibility, **assistive technology**, such as screen readers, also improve the ability of many to use the Web.

——————— access key
A keystroke combination that provides keyboard access to a part of a Web page. Eliminates the need to use a mouse.

——————— assistive technology
In the language of the World Wide Web, refers to technology that provides access to the computer system itself for people with physical or mental impairments. Also refers primarily to software, as most technologies are software rather than hardware.

T A B L E   4 . 5 Web Requirements for Various Disabilities

Disability	Description	Web Users' Need
Color Blindness	Some color combinations are indistinguishable to people with color blindness. For example, for those with red/green color blindness, colors often contrast poorly, appearing to be similar shades of brown.	The ability to substitute personal style sheets for those used on a site. This allows certain color combinations to be substituted with others that are easier for a user to view.
Repetitive Stress Injury	An injury that results from frequently performed operations (typing, using a mouse).	Keyboard and voice commands that replace use of the mouse to select functions; access key feature; speech recognition software and alternate keyboards.
Auditory Impairments	Deafness, difficulty hearing in certain situations, difficulty hearing certain types of sounds, and tinnitus (painful ringing in the ears caused by sudden sounds).	The ability to view text that describes audio content. The ability to deactivate sound.
Visual Impairments	Blindness, blurred vision from visual conditions such as glaucoma or cataracts, difficulty watching moving or blinking items.	Text that describes each image, video, or other complex visual element; screen-reading software that reads text that might be difficult for some to read.
Memory Impairments	Reduced ability to recall information.	Navigational structures that offer clear guidance without assuming that earlier messages and directions will be remembered; a consistent and clear organizational structure for the Web site.
Cognitive Disability	Difficulty with complex concepts; more time needed to learn what others learn quickly.	Graphics rather than text to relay navigational cues; clear, simple language rather than complex language.
Attention Deficit Disorder	Difficulty focusing; easily distracted.	Controls that allow users to turn off distracting visual or audio elements; moving elements and multimedia that are active are set to stop after a brief time.
Seizure Disorders	Brain reactions (seizures) to animations, blinking text, or certain frequencies of audio.	Controls to allow users to turn off visual and auditory elements that have the potential for triggering seizures.

input*refresh*

WIRELESS IS HERE

Issues pertaining to visual, mobility, auditory, and other disabilities have relevance for Web access on handheld devices, in hands-free environments, and in workplaces with high noise levels. In other words, access is an issue not just for those with disabilities, but also for those who access the Web from alternative devices—for instance, those who do their work away from an office building (telework).

Compliance with accessibility standards supports access for all users whatever device they might be using to access the Web—desktop or laptop PC, voice browser, mobile phone, or automobile-based personal computer. According to industry leaders, including Carlene Ellis, VP of Education for Intel, Web access via wireless technologies is expected to approach the current level of over 500 million people using PC-based access. Ellis cites the prediction that the number of people using wireless access will have grown from the 2001 level of 6 million to over 80 times that figure (484 million) by 2005.

Dr. Kevin Kahn, Intel Fellow and Director, Communications Architecture, Intel Corporation, relates the rapid growth of wireless technologies to the emerging importance of mobility. "As PCs have become more ubiquitous, users have found it increasingly important to have access to them and the Internet when they are at places other than their desks. Taken together, these new wireless capabilities will fuel a revolution in how and where we access the Internet." Table 4.6 lists some of the devices now being used to access the Internet.

TABLE 4.6 High-tech Devices for Accessing the Web

Device	RAM/Storage	Description
RIM BlackBerry 5810 Wireless Phone/Handheld PDA	8 MB RAM	Includes "always-on" e-mail access, SMS (Short Message Service) messaging, a wireless Web browser, an electronic organizer, fully functional cell phone, Java 2 Micro Edition OS, custom Java applications, and the ability to talk on the phone while using the device's other features.
Sony DCR-IP7BT Camcorder	8 MB memory stick	Incredibly compact and lightweight, with direct network capability, precision color viewfinder, 10x optical/120x digital zoom, picture stabilization technology, MPEG movies and digital still photos recorded on memory stick media, and USB computer interface.
Personal Removable USB Storage Device	128 MB	Small enough to fit on a key chain, with 1 MB data transfer rate. Has its own central processing unit (CPU). Plug-and-play operation with no driver required. Works with both Mac and PC.
Cybiko Handheld Multifunctional Communications Computer	2.5 MB	Offers hundreds of downloadable games and applications, a personal organizer, text editor, graphing scientific calculator, multilanguage translator, walkie-talkie, voice recorder, MP3 player accessory with USB connector, wireless connectivity with other Cybiko users (for e-mail, intranet, data transfer, and multiplayer games), and 200m communication range.

Root Link www.trace.wisc.edu/

Direct Link www.trace.wisc.edu/world/web/index.html

Why Go? An academically based organization that aims to "prevent the barriers and capitalize on the opportunities presented by current and emerging information and telecommunication technologies, in order to create a world that is as accessible and usable as possible for as many people as possible." Part of the University of Wisconsin's College of Engineering.

The Importance of Compliance

Because federal law has for some time required that federal buildings, projects, and services be available to everyone—including those with disabilities—Congress decided to amend the Federal Rehabilitation Act, originally passed in 1973, to state that all Web services procured by the federal government should also be made accessible.

The "Federal Accessibility Standards for Web-based Internet Information and Applications," Section 508 (1194.22) of the U.S. Rehabilitation Act, is based on the Web Accessibility Initiative of the W3C. The amendment requires accessibility on all Web projects funded by the U.S. government. In other words, to do Web design work that is funded by the U.S. government requires that all finished work meet the accessibility standards supported by the legislation.

The guidelines contained in this legislation mirror those written by the W3C and have the same primary goals. The guidelines are intended to ensure that Web pages work on different types of devices, connect with technologies to assist those with disabilities, and are easy to understand and navigate:

- Graphics or multimedia must have text labels or descriptors that describe what would have been seen. This can be accomplished using the HTML ALT element (<alt>) to provide a verbal descriptor of graphic images.
- Information conveyed by color also must be available when color is missing.
- Table rows and columns must have headers that identify the data clearly.
- Frames must have titles so they can be identified and navigated when they are not being seen.
- Screen flicker must not be at a rate between 2 and 55 Hz.
- The use of advanced technologies (JavaScripts, Java applets) to provide functionality, present a page, or control form input, must also be accompanied by a means for these functions to be performed using assistive technologies.
- The use of time limits for user response must be accompanied by an alert system and a means to request more time.

These standards for compliance were published in December 2000 and took effect in 2001. They apply as requirements for all federal and federally-funded Web sites. Although compliance is not regulated for private sector Web sites, it is self-regulated through the profession's leadership and the W3C.

There are three areas of potential financial loss as an expense of noncompliance: loss of business from potential clients and customers, loss of contracts or subcontracts that involve federal funding, and loss from liability.

Root Link usability.gov/
Direct Link www.usability.gov/accessibility/508.html
Why Go? To view an updated list of federal accessibility requirements.

Root Link www.access-board.gov/
Direct Link www.access-board.gov/sec508/508standards.htm
Why Go? To view a full-text version of accessibility standards on the Federal Register site. Also accessible from the Section 508 home page at section508.gov/.

The expense of lost business can be fairly sizable. In the United States, an estimated 8% of the population "has visual, learning, cognitive, auditory or physical dexterity disabilities severe enough to affect their ability to access the Web," according to an article from ZDNet. In Europe, the figure is 11% and is expected to reach 18% by 2020, according to a proposal for a European Thematic Research Initiative Concerning eAccessibility for All. These people control $175 billion in discretionary income, says Michael Paciello, author of *Web Accessibility for People with Disabilities*.

Costs associated with loss of contracts or subcontracts relate to the current requirements (effective since 2001) that the section 508 standards and guidelines be met on any and all projects that are in some part funded by the federal government. This applies to all suppliers, as well as to the primary contractors. Companies who do not provide accessible interfaces to people with impairments or disabilities "will be unable to sell to this market," according to front-end.com.

In terms of liability, lawsuits already have been filed and won on the subject of online accessibility. For example, in August 2000, Australia's Disability Discrimination Act supported a successful lawsuit against the Sydney Organizing Committee for the Olympic Games, as a result of which monetary damages were awarded. In the United States, America Online agreed out-of-court to do a major accessibility overhaul as a result of a lawsuit launched by the National Federation for the Blind under the Americans with Disabilities Act, according to information from www.508now.com.

Implementing Accessibility Standards

This section reviews the guidelines recommended by the W3C through its Web Accessibility Initiative (WAI). Although the W3C's standards are not regulatory, they carry weight with the Web design profession, not only because the W3C's founder invented the Web, but because the W3C conducts activities in so many aspects of Web design, all with a view toward making the Web truly useful.

The W3C's stated mission is "to lead the Web to its full potential, which it does by developing technologies (specifications, guidelines, software, and tools) that will create a forum for information, commerce, inspiration, independent thought, and collective understanding." Its work extends into just about every aspect of Web development. W3C activities are summarized in the goals and operating principles listed in Table 4.7.

TABLE 4.7 W3C Goals and Operating Principles

Goal	Operating Principle
Universal Access	To ensure that the Web is available to all people, whatever hardware, software, or network infrastructure they use and whatever their native language, culture, geographical location, or physical or mental ability.
Semantic Web	To use forms of expression that computers can interpret and exchange independently—that is, without human intervention.
Trust	To promote a Web environment that allows collaboration among users while it "offers confidentiality, instills confidence, and makes it possible for people to take responsibility for (or be accountable for) what they publish."
Interoperability	To allow users to access the Web with whatever software they like, thus avoiding fragmentation and proprietary, vendor-dependent technologies in favor of interchangeable components based on open computer languages and protocols.
Evolvability	To plan toward a Web that "can easily evolve into an even better Web, without disrupting what already works," by applying principles of simplicity, modularity, compatibility, and extensibility.
Decentralization	To avoid bottlenecks in Internet and Web traffic by using distributed systems. This allows the increased traffic to find the quickest routes to their destinations. The added flexibility will reduce vulnerability.
Multimedia	To support creativity by providing a framework for interactivity and richer media using languages such as Scalable Vector Graphics language (SVG) and the Synchronized Multimedia Integration Language (SMIL).

Source: www.w3c.org/WAI/References/QuickTips/. © 2000, 2001, W3C (MIT, INRIA, Keio). Used with permission.

Root Link www.w3.org/WAI/
Direct Link www.w3.org/TR/WCAG10/
Why Go? To learn all about the accessibility guidelines directly from the source. (Click on Guidelines in the list of links on the right side of the Root Link page.) The Direct Link leads to a list of the guidelines and provides helpful resources such as checklists, techniques for achieving accessible designs, training resources, and evaluation and repair tools.

The W3C has compiled specific recommendations on what developers can and should do to achieve the W3C's standards. These guidelines and checkpoints make up what the W3C considers "best practice" for Web designers. These accessibility guidelines explain how to make Web sites accessible to all people, both those with disabilities and others whose access is, for some reason, momentarily or generally compromised or otherwise substandard. This categorization includes users who:

- Have difficulty seeing, hearing, moving, or processing some types of information, easily or at all.
- Have difficulty reading or comprehending text.
- Do not have, or are unable to use, the keyboard or mouse.

- Use a text-only screen, a small screen, or a slow Internet connection.
- Do not speak or understand fluently the language used for the site.
- Access the Web when their eyes, ears, or hands are busy or interfered with (for example, driving, working in a noisy environment).
- Use an early version of a browser, a different browser, a voice browser, or a different operating system.

Web designers are called upon to consider these and other potential barriers and to plan for them as part of the design process. Accessibility solutions do not necessarily mean that graphics must be eliminated. However, accessibility needs to become a constant consideration. A well-designed site provides, at the very least, alternate and equivalent information for those who are unable to access the site using the primary medium.

In general, the W3C's accessibility guidelines aim to ensure graceful transformation when the site is accessed using alternative means, in order that content still is understandable and navigable. "Graceful transformation" means that pages remain accessible despite any constraints imposed by users' physical, sensory, or cognitive disabilities, work constraints, or technological barriers. Another hope is that "user agents" (software and devices used to access Web content such as graphical browsers, text browsers, voice browsers, and mobile phones) will advance to be able to handle automatically issues relating to transformation, thus reducing the burden on Web developers to take into account the bewildering variety of differing conventions among software manufacturers.

On the W3C site where these accessibility guidelines are presented in detail, each guideline is accompanied by a rationale explaining the reason for the guideline and a list of the users who will benefit. Each checkpoint includes its priority level, notes about how the checkpoint would be applied, and a clarifying example. Table 4.8 provides a list of the guidelines, and corresponding checkpoints and priority levels.

TABLE 4.8 W3C Guidelines

Guideline	Checkpoint	Priority
1. Provide equivalent alternatives to auditory and visual content.	Provide a text equivalent for every non-text element (for example, via alt tags, longdesc tags, or in element content). This includes images, graphical representations of text (including symbols), image map regions, animations (for example, animated GIFs), applets and programmatic objects, ASCII art, frames, scripts, images used as list bullets, spacers, graphical buttons, sounds (played with or without user interaction), stand-alone audio files, audio tracks of video, and video.	1
	Provide redundant text links for each active region of a server-side image map.	1
	Until user agents can automatically read aloud the text equivalent of a visual track, provide an auditory description of the important information of the visual track of a multimedia presentation.	1
	For any time-based multimedia presentation, synchronize equivalent alternatives with the presentation.	1
	Until user agents render text equivalents for client-side image map links, provide redundant text links for each active region of a client-side image map.	3

continues

TABLE 4.8 W3C Guidelines—Continued

Guideline	Checkpoint	Priority
2. Do not rely on color alone.	Ensure that all information conveyed with color is also available without color, for example from context or markup.	1
	Ensure that foreground and background color combinations provide sufficient contrast when viewed by someone having color deficits or when viewed on a black-and-white screen.	2 images 3 text
3. Use markup and style sheets properly.	When appropriate markup language exists, use markup rather than images to convey information.	2
	Create documents that validate to published formal grammars.	2
	Use style sheets to control layout and presentation.	2
	Use relative rather than absolute units in markup language attribute values and style sheet property values.	2
	Use header elements to convey document structure and use them according to specification.	2
	Mark up lists and list items properly.	2
	Mark up quotations. Do not use quotation markup for formatting effects such as indentation.	2
4. Clarify natural language usage.	Clearly identify changes in the natural language of a document's text and any text equivalents (for example, captions).	1
	Specify the expansion of each abbreviation or acronym in a document where it first occurs.	3
	Identify the primary natural language of a document.	3
5. Create tables that transform gracefully.	For data tables, identify row and column headers.	1
	For data tables that have two or more logical levels of row or column headers, use markup to associate data cells and header cells.	1
	Do not use tables for layout unless the table makes sense when linearized. Otherwise, if the table does not make sense, provide an alternative equivalent.	2
	If a table is used for layout, do not use any structural markup for the purpose of visual formatting.	2
	Provide summaries for tables.	3
	Provide abbreviations for header labels.	3
6. Ensure that pages featuring new technologies transform gracefully.	Organize documents to be read without style sheets. For example, when an HTML document is rendered without associated style sheets, it must be possible to read the document.	1
	Ensure that equivalents for dynamic content are updated when the dynamic content changes.	1
	Ensure that pages are usable when scripts, applets, or other programmatic objects are turned off or not supported. If this is not possible, provide equivalent information on an alternative accessible page.	1
	For scripts and applets, ensure that event handlers are input device-independent.	2
	Ensure that dynamic content is accessible or provide an alternative presentation or page.	2

continues

Guideline	Checkpoint	Priority
7. Ensure user control of time-sensitive content changes.	Until user agents allow users to control flickering, avoid causing the screen to flicker.	1
	Until user agents allow users to control blinking, avoid causing content to blink (that is, change presentation at a regular rate, such as turning on and off).	2
	Until user agents allow users to freeze moving content, avoid movement in pages.	2
	Until user agents provide the ability to stop the refresh, do not create periodically auto-refreshing pages.	2
	Until user agents provide the ability to stop auto-redirect, do not use markup to redirect pages automatically. Instead, configure the server to perform redirects.	2
8. Ensure direct accessibility of embedded user interfaces.	Make programmatic elements such as scripts and applets directly accessible or compatible with assistive technologies.	1*
9. Design for device-independence.	Provide client-side image maps instead of server-side image maps except where the regions cannot be defined with an available geometric shape.	1
	Ensure that any element that has its own interface can be operated in a device-independent manner.	2
	For scripts, specify logical event handlers rather than device-dependent event handlers.	2
	Create a logical tab order through links, form controls, and objects.	3
	Provide keyboard shortcuts to important links (including those in client-side image maps), form controls, and groups of form controls.	3
10. Use interim solutions.	Until user agents allow users to turn off spawned windows, do not cause pop-ups or other windows to appear and do not change the current window without informing the user.	2
	Until user agents support explicit associations between labels and form controls, for all form controls with implicitly associated labels, ensure that the label is properly positioned.	2
	Until user agents (including assistive technologies) render side-by-side text correctly, provide a linear text alternative (on the current page or some other) for all tables that lay out text in parallel, word-wrapped columns.	3
	Until user agents handle empty controls correctly, include default, place-holding characters in edit boxes and text areas.	3
	Until user agents (including assistive technologies) render adjacent links distinctly, include non-link, printable characters (surrounded by spaces) between adjacent links.	3
11. Use W3C technologies and guidelines.	Use W3C technologies when they are available and appropriate for a task and use the latest versions when supported.	2
	Avoid deprecated features of W3C technologies.	2
	Provide information so that users can receive documents according to their preferences (for example, language, content type, and so on).	3
	If, after best efforts, you cannot create an accessible page, provide a link to an alternative page that uses W3C technologies, is accessible, has equivalent information (or functionality), and is updated as often as the inaccessible (original) page.	1

*Priority 1 if functionality is important and not presented elsewhere. Otherwise, priority 2.

continues

TABLE 4.8 W3C Guidelines—Continued

Guideline	Checkpoint	Priority
12. Provide context and orientation information.	Title each frame to facilitate frame identification and navigation.	1
	Describe the purpose of frames and how frames relate to each other if it is not obvious by frame titles alone.	2
	Divide large blocks of information into more manageable groups where natural and appropriate.	2
	Associate labels explicitly with their controls.	2
13. Provide clear navigation mechanisms.	Clearly identify the target of each link.	2
	Provide metadata to add semantic information to pages and sites.	2
	Provide information about the general layout of a site (for example, a site map or table of contents).	2
	Use navigation mechanisms in a consistent manner.	2
	Provide navigation bars to highlight and give access to the navigation mechanism.	3
	Group related links, identify the group (for user agents), and, until user agents do so, provide a way to bypass the group.	3
	If search functions are provided, enable different types of searches for different skill levels and preferences.	3
	Place distinguishing information at the beginning of headings, paragraphs, lists, and so on.	3
	Provide information about document collections (that is, documents comprising multiple pages).	3
	Provide a means to skip over multi-line ASCII art.	3
14. Ensure that documents are clear and simple.	Use the clearest and simplest language appropriate for a site's content.	1
	Supplement text with graphic or auditory presentations where they will facilitate comprehension of the page.	3
	Create a style of presentation that is consistent across pages.	3

Because these guidelines and checkpoints are an ongoing project and subject to change, obtain updated versions of these guidelines regularly. To help understand and learn these accessibility guidelines and checkpoints, the W3C's guidelines have been categorized here into three main topics as shown in Table 4.9, then discussed in greater detail. These topics (which are not those of the W3C) are a convenient way to organize the guidelines so they become easier to learn. Also, because some of the guidelines overlap, the categories shown here contain references to the guidelines from the W3C.

TABLE 4.9 A Framework for Mastery of the W3C Guidelines

Adaptability	Provide alternatives to auditory and visual content (guideline 1). Mark code for natural language (guideline 4). Ensure graceful transformation (guidelines 5 and 6). Do not rely on color alone (guideline 2). Provide user control (guideline 7). Provide for access on full range of devices (guidelines 8 and 9).
Structure	Use style sheets (guideline 3). Provide information to ensure users make full use of the site (guidelines 12 and 13). Ensure clarity and simplicity (guideline 14).
Compliance	Use interim solutions (guideline 10). Use W3C technologies and follow the guidelines (guideline 11).

Root Link www.aware.hwg.org/
Why Go? To learn techniques for writing accessible HTML code. A section of the HTML Writers Guild site that contains links to accessibility guidelines, tips and techniques, classes, and authoring software.

ADAPTABILITY Eight guidelines have to do with adaptability—ensuring that Web sites are set up to be ready to adapt to the needs, special or otherwise, of all users. A Web site that meets the requirements of adaptability does the following:

- Provides alternatives to auditory and visual content.
- Marks code for natural language usage.
- Ensures graceful transformation between primary and alternative modes of communication.
- Provides for user control of features, including the ability to turn them off.
- Provides for user access using any of the full range of devices.

Not everyone who uses the Web has software that allows them to view images or movies, listen to sounds, or run programs written in languages other than HTML. This is more than a matter of providing alternatives to "bells and whistles" on a site. For instance, graphics-based navigational aids will not appear on a Web site if a user has a text-only browser or has disabled the browser's graphics capabilities. In addition, individuals with auditory or visual impairments need alternatives to audiovisual content to enable them to navigate and make complete use of a site.

The guidelines specify that alternatives should be provided to the Web site's primary mode of communication. The design of the site should "provide equivalent alternatives to auditory and visual content." Also, the design should "not rely on color alone." By providing alternatives, Web pages are made accessible despite any potential constraints including physical, sensory, and cognitive disabilities; work constraints; and technological barriers. Necessary alternatives include:

- Text equivalents for non-text elements
- Redundant text links when images are used for linkages
- Auditory alternatives for multimedia presentations
- Alternate means of conveying information when color has been used to communicate

Visual elements must have text equivalents and audio elements must have visual equivalents. When color is used for communication and/or contrast, the meaning still must be clear and contrast must be sufficient when color is not available.

To help screen-reading software convert text into audible speech, the text should be marked with tags that identify the language. This makes the conversion to audio much easier for the screen reader "to facilitate pronunciation or interpretation." In other words, tags must be correctly coded so screen readers will know when to switch to a different "speech engine." This allows languages to sound more natural than if the computer were reading one language with the pronunciation rules of another language. The same principle applies for software that converts text into Braille and for users who might be viewing a Web site without graphics. When headings are properly used, the tables should "transform gracefully." In other words, tables should be fully understandable when they are accessed through auditory means such as a screen reader. For tables containing data, the column and row headings need to be clear, so that as the data is read aloud, moving down the column or across the row, the communication is complete. Users also must be able to access data in table cells using voice commands (when using a mouse is not possible).

This guideline is relevant also when an abbreviation is used. The first time an acronym or abbreviation is used, the expanded version it represents must be provided. Screen-reading software will know how to interpret abbreviations if they are identified in the code. For example, if "USDA" is marked as an abbreviation, the screen reader will know to pronounce each letter individually and not pronounce the four letters as one word.

For individuals who access a Web page's table with a screen reader or who view only a portion of the page at a time (users with blindness or low vision using speech output or a Braille display or other users of devices with small displays), the W3C makes specific suggestions on how designers can accommodate these types of users. "Transformation" suggests that the same content can be displayed in several ways without loss of information, a critical objective when designers are trying to make the Web accessible to all.

When a table is used for layout purposes, the content must make sense when read linearly. If a table used for layout will not make sense when read in a linear fashion, an equivalent alternative needs to be provided.

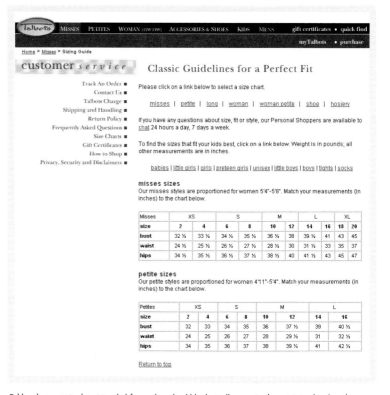

Tables that contain data intended for readers should be logically organized, containing headers that clearly identify the types of data in each row and column. This page from www.talbots.com/howto/combo_sizing.asp does this task well.

This site (intellicast.com/) nests tables within other table cells to force screen readers to proceed down columns of related information. This practice must be balanced against other considerations: download time increases with the number of tables used on a page, especially if they are nested tables.

When tables are used to control page layout, screen readers can have difficulty coverting the text to speech. To ensure access, the content in the table should make sense when it is read linearly, as it will be by text-to-speech readers. In fact, the W3C guideline says that designers should avoid the use of tables for layout purposes.

Web sites should be designed to "ensure that pages featuring new technologies transform gracefully." The new technologies referenced here include dynamic content elements controlled by JavaScripts, Java applets, and Flash movies. The intent of these guidelines is to ensure that users are able to grasp the meanings to be communicated even when they are unable to view these dynamic elements. Verbal descriptions of these elements must be sufficiently clear to communicate the message even when these elements are not being viewed as intended. Also, pages should still work when they are accessed using older browsers or when users have turned off certain features such as dynamic content, scripts, and applets. When new technologies such as style sheets, dynamic content, JavaScripts, Java applets, or other objects are used, Web pages should be organized so that they can be read without the style sheets. Also, the text equivalents of dynamic content must be updated when the dynamic content changes. These guidelines are important to make it possible for Web sites to be accessed no matter what device users employ to view them.

Another issue of adaptability of the site to user needs is to provide for user control of elements. For example, the user should be able to stop the motion of animated, blinking, scrolling, or automatically updating objects on Web pages. This guideline is geared toward individuals with certain types of mental and physical impairments and toward users who access the Web with devices that impose limitations on such Web page enhancements. User control of screen activity is essential, particularly to people with photosensitive epilepsy, because seizures can be triggered by flickering or flashing that ranges from 4 to 59 flashes per second, with peak sensitivity at 20 flashes per second.

These user control guidelines are important for people with cognitive or physical disabilities who are unable to read moving text quickly enough or at all. Movement can cause distraction that makes the rest of the page unreadable for people with cognitive disabilities. Screen readers are unable to read moving text. These guidelines involve designer responsibility at least until user agents and assistive technologies provide their own means for providing adequate user control of screen dynamics.

This site (www.techjourney.com/) has changed from its earlier three-column design to this one-column design to facilitate use of the site by screen readers, which otherwise would proceed through each column before proceeding to the next.

Until users can control on-screen motion such as flickering, blinking, movement in pages, and automatic refreshing or redirection of pages, the W3C guidelines state that these forms of on-screen motion should not be used. Also, elements such as JavaScript and Java applets should be directly compatible with, and accessible by, assistive technologies.

Designers should "design for device independence." Device independence is the W3C's term for making Web pages accessible to all devices, no matter what type of input or output device the user employs. For instance, a mouse, a keyboard, the user's voice, and a head wand are all types of input devices, but Web pages interface with them in very different ways. This guideline ensures that users who are using any of these pointing devices (or none at all) still are able to access and interact with all parts of the site, including forms that require them to input information.

Designers should use client-side **image maps** where possible and ensure that elements on the page can be accessed using any type of pointing device. Also, there should be a logical tab order among on-screen links, form controls, and objects. That is, by using the Tab key (or voice commands) to move among on-screen elements, users should be taken to the next logical active area and not bounce from one part of the screen to other, unrelated parts of the screen. Keyboard shortcuts should be available for moving among these elements.

image maps
Graphic navigation aids. Images are divided into sections, each of which links to another page when clicked or accessed.

At www.linksys.com/, the main navigation buttons at the top of the page are image map hot spots on a single GIF image named "home_top3.gif."

Some of the more restrictive checkpoints, such as those that limit on-screen motion, will continue in effect only until user agents support necessary user control of these elements. The W3C recognizes that site designer/developers are being limited and that these accessibility needs would be "more appropriately met by user agents." A special area of the W3C site provides updated information specifically about user agent support for accessibility features and encourages Web designer/developers to consult this page regularly for updates on the current status. When user agents adequately support this accessibility need, providing user control of on-screen motion, these checkpoints should become less strict.

STRUCTURE There has always been a distinction between an HTML document's content and its structure. Now that Web coding is moving toward XHTML, this distinction is growing in importance, especially when the goal of universal access is adopted.

As the W3C defines it, "content" refers to what a document says to a user, whereas "structure" refers to a document's logical organization (larger portions of a document, such as an introduction, a chapter, or a section, and smaller portions of a document, such as a paragraph, a block quotation, and so on). A third term the W3C uses is "presentation," which refers to how the document "is rendered (for example, as print, as a two-dimensional graphical presentation, as a text-only presentation, as synthesized speech, as Braille, and so on)." As used in this book, "structure" refers to more than what the W3C means by the term; it refers to the logical layout of pages, as well as to the logical and understandable navigation, functionality, and content—the "bones" of the site.

Four of the Web content accessibility guidelines specify how Web sites should be structured. A Web site that meets the requirements for logical structure does so through:

- Using style sheets correctly to control layout and presentation.
- Providing context, orientation, and navigation information and mechanisms to ensure that all users are able to make full use of the site.
- Ensuring clarity and simplicity so that sites are fully understandable to all users.

Designers should "use markup tags correctly to control elements such as text and image layout, lists, and quotations." As an example of the misuse of markup, the W3C site mentions using a heading tag (h1, h2, h3) to change the size of the font within one structural item (for example, a paragraph). This could create confusion when a screen reader accesses the screen. In other words, presentation markup should be used for presentation effects, and structural markup should be reserved for communicating information about structure to the browser (or assistive technology). These methods need to replace commonly used practices that produce desired effects on the screen at the expense of some users' abilities to understand the organization of the page and navigate it effectively. In addition, designers should

Root Link www.assistivetech.com/
Why Go? To visit the organization (started in the 1980s at Boston Children's Hospital) that developed MultiVoice, MultiPhone, and WriteAway, some early solutions for disabled individuals. Look at its two versions—graphics version and text version—to see how accessibility can be provided effectively.

use style sheets to control layout and presentation, and generally use markup properly or according to the best practices.

Web sites should provide a navigational context so that users can orient themselves and see immediately how to navigate the site. Elements should be grouped logically and Web sites should provide contextual information about the relationships among these elements. Such information is (and should be designed to be) useful to users in their attempts to understand how the page fits together and works. Navigation mechanisms need to be clear and consistent. These considerations are essential to people with cognitive disabilities or visual disabilities, but also benefit all users. Navigation buttons that use simple names are an example.

Designers should identify frames by providing titles for the pages in each frame and by providing a text equivalent to describe how the frames fit together if this is not apparent from the title alone. In addition, large blocks of information should be broken up into manageable chunks, and controls should be labeled. Also, designers should clearly identify the target for each link, again using descriptive text. Navigation should be consistent. Links that pertain only to one group of users should be so identified, so others will know to bypass them. Search functions should allow for searches by users of all different skill levels, and descriptive labels should be provided as the beginning part of headings, paragraphs, lists, and collections. Addressing these requirements will make the Web site more understandable.

The Encyclopedia Britannica site (www.britannica.com/) groups information much like the company's printed encyclopedias do—a familiar device used to great effect on this Web page.

Holding to standards of clarity and simplicity will make documents easier to navigate and understand. Language should be clear, page layouts consistent, and graphics easy to recognize.

COMPLIANCE Although the W3C cannot compel designers to abide by its recommendations in the same way the federal government can, its influence is such—and its membership is so broad—that designers who ignore its guidelines make acceptance of their work harder.

Designers should take responsibility by complying with the latest versions of the guidelines. For now, designers need to attend to operations that hopefully will someday be handled by user agents. For example, until user agents allow users to control extra windows and pop-ups, these should not be used without first informing the user. Web pages must be designed to allow users to exercise control or to view the pages without such control.

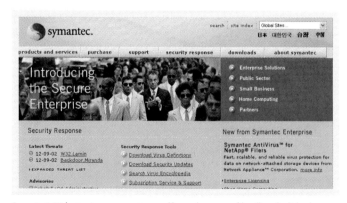

Symantec's Web site at www.symantec.com/ has a clever way of handling the links that enable users to view the site in languages like Chinese that use a different alphabet. Links in the upper-right portion of the page are written in the characters of the languages named, but the alternative text identifies the language in English.

When a page cannot be made accessible, provide an alternative page that is. Designers also need to address problems with the way screen readers and other assistive technologies read forms, tables, and adjacent links—at least for now. For example, to prepare forms to be read by current screen readers, each label for an input field in a form needs to be placed on the same line and immediately preceding the input area it refers to. To prepare tables requires designers to compensate for the fact that user agents are unable to handle blocks of text that are presented side by side. For current assistive software to recognize where one link ends and the next begins, markings need to be included that distinguish between adjacent links.

To ensure correct compliance with the accessibility guidelines, and to know what **deprecated HTML** tags to avoid, requires that Web designers continuously monitor the W3C site at www.w3.org/, where updated versions of the guidelines undergo a review process. To assist Web designers with the task of applying these guidelines, the W3C site offers many tools, including a section on techniques for accomplishing compliance with each checkpoint and the processes to use to test for compliance.

It is important for Web designer/developers to learn and apply all priority 1 and priority 2 checkpoints and to be aware of priority 3 checkpoints. Web sites that conform to all of the checkpoints receive a Triple-A rating. If all priority 1 and 2 checkpoints are met, it will receive a Double-A rating. Web sites that meet all priority 1 checkpoints receive an A rating.

Another useful tool provided to designers free of charge from the W3C site is a set of laminated Quick Tip Cards, available by completing the form at: www.w3.org/WAI/References/QuickTips/qtform.htm. The information on these cards is shown in Table 4.10.

TABLE 4.10 Quick Tips to Make Accessible Web Sites

Tip Category	What to Do
Images and Animations	Use the ALT attribute to describe the function of each visual.
Image Maps	Use client-side maps and text for hotspots.
Multimedia	Provide captioning and transcripts of audio, and descriptions of video.
Hypertext Links	Use text that makes sense when read out of context. For example, avoid "click here."
Page Orientation	Use headings, lists, and consistent structure. Use CSS for layout and style where possible.
Graphs and Charts	Summarize or use the LONGDESC attribute.
Scripts, Applets, and Plug-ins	Provide alternative content in case active features are inaccessible or unsupported.
Frames	Use no frames and meaningful titles.
Tables	Make line-by-line reading sensible. Summarize.
Check Your Work	Validate. Use tools, checklist, and guidelines at www.w3.org/TR/WCAG/.

Source: www.w3.org/WAI/References/QuickTips/. Copyright © 2000, 2001, W3C (MIT, INRIA, Keio). Used with permission.

Testing Accessibility

As increased attention has been given to issues of accessibility, organizations such as the W3C through its Web Accessibility Initiative, the National Cancer Institute, as well as the regulatory bodies of the federal government, have provided necessary leadership and guidance to Web designers who are in the process of making the shift to code that is "compliant" in terms of accessibility. Tools for testing accessibility electronically, and even repairing noncompliant code, have emerged and are becoming useful. Samples of these tools include software packages that do the following:

- Create accessible, dynamically generated graphs and charts; for example, Corda Technologies (www.corda.com/)
- Simulate colorblindness when viewing a Photoshop image on a Web screen; for example, Colorfield Insight (www.colorfield.com/insight/)
- Check Web pages for accessibility when using screen readers; for example, Bobby (www.cast.org/bobby/)

As an initial testing process, use the five steps defined in Table 4.11 to test your Web pages.

Validation tools, including the three mentioned here, are described and, in some cases, made available to check Web sites for compliance. Some of these tools also repair accessibility problems. Some examples of such tools are listed in Table 4.12.

TABLE 4.11 Accessibility Testing

1. Select a representative sampling of different kinds of pages from the Web site to be reviewed; must include entry page(s) ("welcome page," and so on).

2. Use a graphical user interface (GUI) browser (such as Internet Explorer, Netscape Navigator, or Opera) and examine the selection of pages while adjusting the browser settings as follows: *(Note: For reviewers who have disabilities, certain of the following steps might need to be done with another person who does not have the same disability.)*

   - Turn off images, and make sure that the information is presented in an appropriate sequence relative to the visual presentation on the GUI site.

   - Turn off the sound, and make sure audio content is still available through text equivalents.

   - Change the font size (larger and smaller) in the browser, and observe whether the page is still readable.

   - Set screen resolution to 640 × 480 and observe whether or not this forces the page into horizontal scrolling.

   - Change the display color to black-and-white (or print out the page on a black-and-white printer) and observe whether color contrast is adequate.

   - Put away the mouse and tab through the links and form controls on a page, making sure that you can access all links and form controls, and that the links clearly indicate what they lead to.

3. Use a voice browser (such as Home Page Reader) or a text browser (such as Lynx) and examine the Web site while answering these questions: *(Note: Experienced users of screen readers can substitute a screen reader for a voice or text browser, but, if blind, might need a sighted partner to compare information available visually; if sighted, listen to it with eyes closed, then open eyes and confirm whether the information is equivalent.)*

   - Is equivalent information available through the voice or text browser to that available through the GUI browser?

   - Is the information presented in a similar logical order as when viewed through the GUI browser?

continues

TABLE 4.11 Accessibility Testing—Continued

4. Use two accessibility evaluation tools and note any problems indicated by the tools, for example:

    - **WAVE** An online accessibility assessment tool that flags any items on a Web page that should be examined for potential accessibility problems, and provides a description of what the problem might be.

    - **Bobby** An online or downloadable accessibility checker which provides a semi-automated assessment of accessibility problems on a Web page or group of Web pages; it can identify many problems on sites, and lists problems which it is not able to evaluate automatically and which require manual review.

    - **A-Prompt** A tool that identifies potential accessibility problems and provides guided editing to correct the problems.

5. Summarize the results.

    - Summarize the types of problems encountered, as well as best practices that should be continued or expanded on the site.

    - Indicate the method by which problems were identified, and clearly state that this was not a full conformance evaluation.

    - Recommend follow-up steps, including full conformance evaluation, which includes validation of markup and other tests, and ways to address any problems identified.

Source: www.w3.org/WAI/eval. Copyright © 2000–2001, W3C (MIT, INRIA, Keio). Used with permission.

TABLE 4.12 Validation Tools

Tool	Description
AccessEnable	An online Web site evaluation and correction product line that is able to make site-wide automatic fixes as well as interactive fixes to satisfy federal and other Web accessibility standards.
AccVerify and AccRepair	AccVerify performs verification and reports all errors or noncompliance with the standards, differentiating between 508 and W3C standards. AccRepair corrects these accessibility failures.
PageScreamer	Verifies and corrects noncompliant Web content. Provides text equivalents for every nontext element. Provides the ability to identify rows and columns in HTML tables. Ensures identification of frames for navigation. Identifies and alerts the user to server-side image maps.
W3C HTML Validation Service	An easy-to-use HTML validation service that checks documents for compliance. Services are available through the W3C Web site.

web **4.2** activity

ACCESSIBILITY AND FLASH

One hesitation some designers have about making their sites accessible is that doing so might mean they must remove all the flare and creativity that makes the site stand out. Explore the possibilities in this regard by reading about accessibility on the Macromedia site. Macromedia is known for Flash, the software as well as the concept. To do this activity:

1. Read the discussion about accessibility on the Macromedia site. Begin your reading at www.macromedia.com/macromedia/accessibility/.

2. Review the chapter material about accessibility, including the tables of accessibility checkpoints in the chapter, to answer the question: "What needs to be done to have both Flash and accessibility in a single site?"

3. Write a one-page brief entitled "How a Site Can Be Accessible Yet Still Have Flash!"

apply & practice

Online Quiz

As a review of the key concepts in this chapter, define the terms in the following list:

accessibility
access key
assistive technology
deprecated HTML
frames
image maps
prototype
usability

After you are confident that you understand this chapter's content, go to this book's Internet Resource Center (IRC) at www.emcp.com/ and take the self-test online quiz for this chapter. Review any questions you answered incorrectly, and then study the related chapter material again. Retake the online quiz as many times as you need to achieve full mastery (90–100%).

Topics Roundtable

1. As a designer, what position will you take on usability and accessibility issues? Why?
2. Talk about a Web site you consider to have accessibility and/or usability difficulties. What impact does this have on you? What impact do you think it has on the site?
3. What kinds of changes would be necessary to improve the site you discussed in Topic 2?
4. How would you explain to a future client the processes and needs for Web site accessibility and usability?
5. Do accessibility and usability necessarily make it difficult or impossible to create appealing and interesting Web sites? How can designers successfully achieve the best of both worlds?
6. To what degree does the NCI site model as well as specify usability standards and guidelines? To what degree does the W3C site model accessibility? Provide examples.

window to the web

CREATING LISTS AND FEEDBACK FORMS FOR WEB PAGES

➤ Create unordered lists.
➤ Create ordered lists.
➤ Create definition lists.
➤ Nest lists.
➤ Use tables for list alignment.
➤ Create feedback forms.
➤ Write a report on career opportunities in the Web design field, formatting that material in HTML.
➤ Add lists and forms to your Web resource site.

technical walk-through

Using lists is an effective way to enhance Web page utility and attractiveness. Presenting items or short pieces of information in list form makes them easier for readers to digest. The items in a list may not involve any particular order (an **unordered list**), or they may involve a sequence or hierarchical order (an **ordered list**). Unordered lists are also referred to as **bulleted lists**, and ordered lists as **numbered lists**. The functionality of lists can be further increased with HTML by linking the items on a list to related content located elsewhere on the Web page, or to a Web page located on another site.

Feedback forms offer another method for improving Web pages. Feedback forms make a site truly interactive by allowing the exchange of information between those running a site and the visitors to the site. Forms can be used to handle requests from visitors, to gather information, or a combination of these functions.

Unordered Lists

Unordered lists start and end with **unordered list tags** (<ul></ul>). Each item in an unordered list begins with a **list item tag** (<li>). The list item tag is not a paired tag, so no end tag is necessary. However, to be ready for XHTML, it is a good idea to get used to keying a list item end tag (</li>). When the list of items is complete, you must close the list with the unordered list end tag (/ul).

The style of bullet in an unordered list can be specified by keying a TYPE attribute and value. Keying a TYPE attribute and value in an unordered list tag (<ul>) creates the specified bullet style for all the items in the list. Keying a TYPE attribute and value in a list item tag (<li>) affects the bullet style for only that item. The default bullet style is a solid circle called "disc." The other two bullet style choices are a hollow circle ("circle"), and a solid square ("square").

Create an unordered list:

1. Use your text editor to open the **shell.html** file.
2. Save the shell.html file as **list_practice_1.html** using the Save As command.
3. Key a title as indicated here:

```
<!DOCTYPE HTML PUBLIC "-//W3C//DTD HTML 4.01 Transitional//EN"
"http://www.w3.org/TR/html4/loose.dtd">
<html>
<head>
<title>This Is My Practice Page</title>
</head>
<body>
</body>
</html>
```

4. To create an unordered list, key the tags and element content between the body tags of the HTML shell as shown (providing a heading for the list is optional, but if used it should be keyed before the unordered list start tag):

```
<body>
<p>
This Is an Unordered (Bulleted) List:
<ul>
<li>Apples</li>
<li>Oranges</li>
<li>Grapes</li>
<li>Peaches</li>
<li>Bananas</li>
</ul>
</p>
</body>
```

5. Save the file and use your browser to open and view it. You have just created a simple unordered list, with a title at the top of the list (see Figure 4.3).

6. Return to your text editor to view the source code of the **list_practice_1.html** file.

7. Key the TYPE attributes and values as indicated here, keeping the other list items as they are:

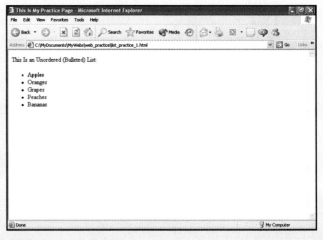

FIGURE 4.3

The unordered list tags (<ul></ul>) and list item tags (<li></li>) are used to create lists of items that are not numbered or ranked by importance or priority.

```
<ul type="square">
<li type="circle">Apples</li>
<li type="disc">Oranges</li>
```

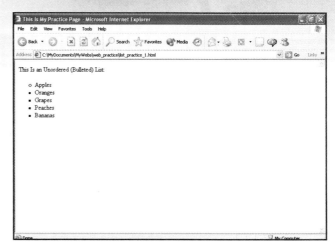

8. Save the file and refresh your browser. Keying a "square" bullet style value in the unordered list tag has made "square" bullets the default bullet style for this list. However, keying "circle" and "disc" bullet style values in the first two list item tags overrides the default bullet style for those items. The first two list items therefore appear as "circle" and "disc" bullets, while the remaining three list items revert to the default bullet style as specified in the unordered list tag (see Figure 4.4).

9. Experiment with using different bullet style values on this list practice page.

FIGURE 4.4

Three different bullet styles can be specified for unordered lists: "disc," "circle," and "square." The solid circle bullet ("disc") is the default bullet style unless another default is specified as part of the UL element.

Ordered Lists

Ordered lists are similar to unordered lists, but use numbers or letters for list items rather than bullets. Ordered lists start and end with **ordered list tags** (<ol></ol>). The list item tags (<li></li>) are used for each item, and function just as they do in unordered lists. Ordered lists are closed by the ordered list end tag (</ol>).
The number or letter style for ordered lists can be specified using a TYPE attribute and value inserted in the ordered list start tag. Keying a TYPE value of "I" or "i" creates uppercase or lowercase Roman numerals. Keying a TYPE value of "A" or "a" creates uppercase or lowercase letters, and keying a TYPE value of "1" creates a numbered list. If no TYPE attribute and value are keyed, the default style is a numbered list.

CREATE AN ORDERED LIST

Create an ordered list:
1. Return to your text editor to view the source code of the **list_practice_1.html** file.
2. Modify your unordered list by changing the list heading, changing the unordered list tags (<ul>) to ordered list tags (<ol>), and deleting the bullet TYPE attributes and values:

```
This Is an Ordered (Numbered or Lettered) List:
<ol>
<li>Apples</li>
<li>Oranges</li>
<li>Grapes</li>
<li>Peaches</li>
<li>Bananas</li>
</ol>
```

3. Save the file and refresh your browser. Your list now appears as a numbered list (see Figure 4.5) since this is the default ordered list unless otherwise specified.

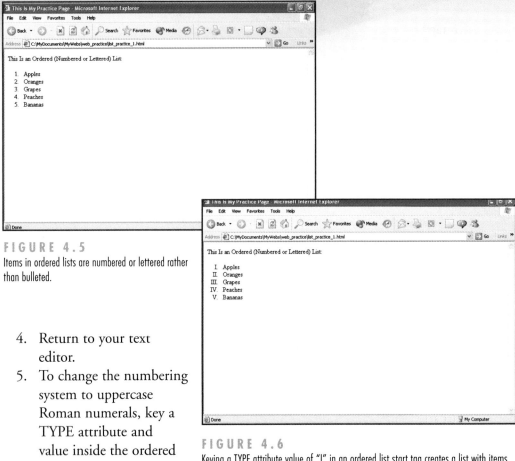

FIGURE 4.5
Items in ordered lists are numbered or lettered rather than bulleted.

FIGURE 4.6
Keying a TYPE attribute value of "I" in an ordered list start tag creates a list with items numbered in uppercase Roman numerals.

4. Return to your text editor.

5. To change the numbering system to uppercase Roman numerals, key a TYPE attribute and value inside the ordered list tag:

```
<ol type="I">
```

6. Save the file and refresh your browser. The list is now ordered in uppercase Roman numerals as illustrated in Figure 4.6.

Definition Lists

A definition list contains items as well as a further definition or description of each item. Definition lists begin with a definition list start tag (<dl>), followed by definition term tags (<dt>), and definitions tags (<dd>). Definition lists are closed by definition list end tags (</dl>). Just like list item tags, definition term tags and definition tags work without end tags, but it is a good idea to use them to be ready for XHTML.

CREATE A DEFINITION LIST

Create a definition list:

1. Return to your text editor to view the source code of the **list_practice_1.html** file.

2. Change the heading for your list:

```
This Is a Definition List:
```

3. Change the ordered list tags to definition list tags (<dl></dl>), change the list item tags to definition term tags (<dt></dt>), and add definition tags (<dd></dd>) and content:

```
<dl>
<dt>Apples</dt>
<dd>Apples grow on trees in temperate climates.</dd>
<dt>Oranges</dt>
<dd>Oranges grow in tropical climates.</dd>
<dt>Grapes</dt>
<dd>Grapes are used in wine making.</dd>
<dt>Peaches</dt>
<dd>Peaches are my favorite fruit.</dd>
<dt>Bananas</dt>
<dd>Bananas are exported around the world.</dd>
</dl>
```

4. Save the file and refresh your browser. You have created a definition list with short definitions under each definition term in the list (see Figure 4.7).

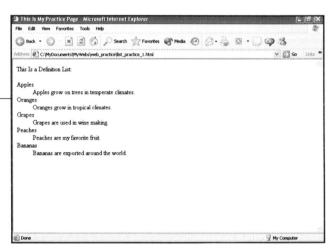

FIGURE 4.7

Definition lists consist of a list of terms, with each term followed by a short definition or description.

Line Breaks

Lists can appear too crowded, especially if they are in smaller fonts. Line break tags can be used to improve the appearance of a list by creating white space between the items or definition terms in a list. Because the list item or definition term tags break lines by default, two line break tags are needed to create additional white space between items in a list.

USE LINE BREAKS WITH LISTS

Insert line breaks to create more white space between items or terms in a list:

1. Return to your text editor to view the source code of the **list_practice_1.html** file.
2. Key two line break tags after each definition tag:

```
<dl>
<dt>Apples</dt>
<dd>Apples grow on trees in temperate climates.</dd>
<br />
<br />
<dt>Oranges</dt>
<dd>Oranges grow in tropical climates.</dd>
<br />
<br />
<dt>Grapes</dt>
<dd>Grapes are used in wine making.</dd>
<br />
<br />
<dt>Peaches</dt>
```

```
<dd>Peaches are my favorite fruit.</dd>
<br />
<br />
<dt>Bananas</dt>
<dd>Bananas are exported around the world.</dd>
<br />
<br />
</dl>
```

3. Save the file and refresh your browser. The terms in your definition list are now separated by additional white space, making the list more attractive and easier to read.

Text Tags

Text tags can be used to modify the text in lists and work just as they do with normal text.

Use text tags to modify the text in your list:

1. Return to your text editor to view the source code of the **list_practice_1.html** file.
2. Modify the text in your definition list by inserting text tags:

```
<body>
<font size="4">
<p>
<h1>This Is a <i>Definition</i> List:</h1>
<dl>
<dt>Apples</dt>
<dd>Apples grow on trees in temperate climates.</dd>
<br />
<br />
<dt>Oranges</dt>
<dd>Oranges grow in tropical climates.</dd>
<br />
<br />
<dt>Grapes</dt>
<dd>Grapes are used in wine making.</dd>
<br />
<br />
<dt>Peaches</dt>
<dd>Peaches are my favorite fruit.</dd>
<br />
<br />
<dt>Bananas</dt>
<dd>Bananas are exported around the world.</dd>
<br />
<br />
</dl>
</p>
</font>
</body>
```

3. Save the file and refresh your browser. The text now appears in a larger font, in a level 1 heading font, and the word "Definition" in italics, as illustrated in Figure 4.8.

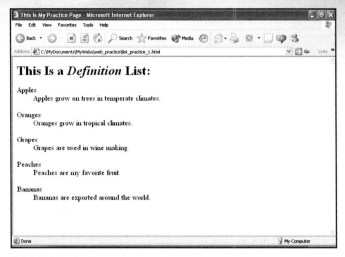

This Is a *Definition* List:

Apples
    Apples grow on trees in temperate climates.

Oranges
    Oranges grow in tropical climates.

Grapes
    Grapes are used in wine making.

Peaches
    Peaches are my favorite fruit.

Bananas
    Bananas are exported around the world.

Done   My Computer

FIGURE 4.8

Text tags can be used to modify text in lists.

Sublists

Sublists are lists that branch off from a list item. They can be created by nesting a list inside an existing list item.

CREATE SUBLISTS

Create a nested list:

1. Return to your text editor to view the source code of the **list_practice_1.html** file.
2. Delete all the code between the body tags.
3. Key the code to create an ordered list between the body tags:

```
<p>
Creating a Nested List
<ol>
<li>Apples</li>
<li>Oranges</li>
<li>Grapes</li>
<li>Peaches</li>
<li>Bananas</li>
</ol>
</p>
```

4. Select and copy all the code from the <ol> start tag to the </ol> end tag.
5. Position your cursor just after the word "Bananas" in the last line item. Hit the Enter key to move to the next line.
6. Paste the list you copied inside the "Bananas" list item.
7. Save the file and refresh your browser.
8. The list you nested now appears as a sublist branching off from the "Bananas" list item in the original list.

9. Change the font size, numbering style, and text in the nested list by keying code and element content:

```
<p>
Creating a Nested List
<ol type="I">
<li>Apples</li>
<li>Oranges</li>
<li>Grapes</li>
<li>Peaches</li>
<li>Bananas
      <font size="2">
      <ol type="a">
      <li>Big Bananas</li>
      <li>Small Bananas</li>
      <li>Green Bananas</li>
      <li>Yellow Bananas</li>
      <li>Storing Bananas</li>
      </ol></font>
      </li>
</ol>
</p>
```

10. Save the file and refresh your browser. The nested list should now appear as a sublist of the "Banana" list item. The main list should be in uppercase Roman numerals and the nested list in lowercase letters (see Figure 4.9).

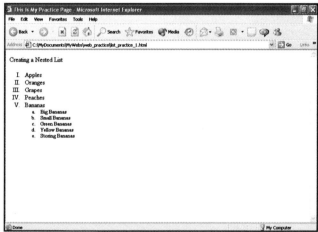

FIGURE 4.9

A list can be nested inside another list, producing a sublist branching off from the list item where the nested list was inserted.

List Alignment

Alignment attributes do not work well with lists, so the best way to horizontally align a list is to place it in a table.

ALIGN THE LIST

Align the list using a table:

1. Return to your text editor to view the source code of the **list_practice_1.html** file.

2. Place your list in the center column of a three-column table by keying the HTML code to create a table:

```
<p>
<table width="100%" border="1">
<tr>
<td> </td>
<td>
Creating a Nested List
<ol type="I">
<li>Apples</li>
<li>Oranges</li>
<li>Grapes</li>
<li>Peaches</li>
<li>Bananas
     <font size="2">
     <ol type="a">
     <li>Big Bananas</li>
     <li>Small Bananas</li>
     <li>Green Bananas</li>
     <li>Yellow Bananas</li>
     <li>Storing Bananas</li>
     </ol></font>
     </li>
</ol>
</td>
<td> </td>
</tr>
</table>
</p>
```

3. Save the file and refresh your browser. You will notice that although the table is located in the middle column of the table, it is not centered on the screen because table cells are left-aligned by default.
4. Return to your text editor.
5. Center the list by specifying a WIDTH attribute and value of 33.3% in all three table cell start tags in order to equalize the column sizes as indicated below:

```
<p>
<table width="100%" border="1">
<tr>
<td width="33.3%"> </td>
<td width="33.3%">
Creating a Nested List
<ol type="I">
<li>Apples</li>
<li>Oranges</li>
<li>Grapes</li>
<li>Peaches</li>
<li>Bananas
     <font size="2">
     <ol type="a">
     <li>Big Bananas</li>
     <li>Small Bananas</li>
     <li>Green Bananas</li>
     <li>Yellow Bananas</li>
     <li>Storing Bananas</li>
     </ol></font>
     </li>
</ol>
</td>
<td width="33.3%"> </td>
</tr>
</table>
</p>
```

6. Save the file and refresh your browser. The list should now appear centered in the middle of the browser screen.
7. Return to your text editor.

8. Delete the BORDER attribute and value from the table start tag (<table>).

9. Save the file and refresh your browser. The table is now invisible, but still anchoring the list in the center of the screen (see Figure 4.10).

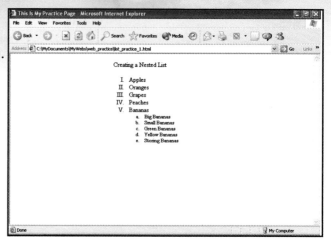

FIGURE 4.10

An invisible table has been used to center the list on the browser screen.

Forms

Forms allow Web site visitors and Web site operators to exchange information, making visiting a Web site a truly interactive experience. Forms are used for many different kinds of activities, including ordering products, making payments by credit card, registering for permission to use a Web site, filling out surveys, and much more (see Figure 4.11).

One of the most common methods of processing the information in forms is accomplished with the assistance of a **protocol** (often referred to as a program) known as **Common Gateway Interface**, or **CGI**. CGI programs are located on Web servers and are not resident in HTML files or Web browsers. When a form has been completed, a user is usually instructed to click on a button to submit the information. When the information arrives at the Web server, the CGI program passes the data to another program for processing, and then assists in transforming the data into a format such as an HTML page or e-mail that can then be directed as a response, according to the instructions contained in the code for the form (see Figure 4.12).

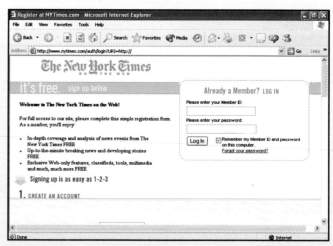

FIGURE 4.11

An online registration form for the *New York Times*. Applicants who complete and submit this form receive a message from the newspaper informing them that they are now permitted to access news articles on the *New York Times* Web site.

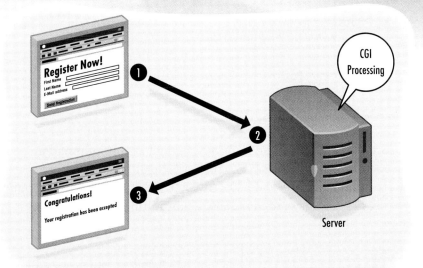

FIGURE 4.12
Forms submitted by users go to a Web server where a CGI program resident on the server will be used to process the information and form a response.

Forms start and end with **form tags** (<form></form>). Inside the form start tag (<form>), the method used for processing the form is specified, either "get" or "post." "Post" is the most commonly used method. The method employed by servers varies, so you will need to know what method your Web host uses. Next comes an "action" that directs the form to the correct location for processing. This action is in the format of a path to the server that will handle the processing. The form start tag (<form>) is followed by input tags that specify the type of form input, such as text, check box, or radio button. A form is closed by a form end tag (</form>).

The NAME attribute is keyed inside the INPUT element so that the origin of the user-entered information can be identified when it is returned after processing. Each data item needs its own unique name to identify it. These names should not contain spaces or reserved symbols. The SIZE attribute specifies the width of the text field, and the MAXLENGTH attribute specifies the maximum number of characters that can be entered. Note that the NAME attribute is supported by all browsers, but that XHTML processors will use the ID attribute rather than the NAME attribute whenever both are available.

In the following action steps, you will learn how to create a simple feedback form. However, to make the form interactive, you must contact your Internet Service Provider (ISP) or system administrator to find out what process they use for forms and what kind of instructions to the server need to be included in your form Web pages. As an alternative, data entered into the form can be sent to an e-mail address by using the action mailto: followed by an e-mail address (`action="mailto:me@myaddress.com"`).

action
action

CREATE A BASIC FEEDBACK FORM

Create a basic feedback form with a single text field for entering a name:
1. Use your text editor to open the **shell.html** file.
2. Save the shell.html file as **forms_practice_1.html** using the Save As command.

3. Key a title:

```
<!DOCTYPE HTML PUBLIC "-//W3C//DTD HTML 4.01 Transitional//EN"
"http://www.w3.org/TR/html4/loose.dtd">
<html>
<head>
<title>This Is My Forms Practice Page</title>
</head>
<body>
</body>
</html>
```

4. To start the form, key the following form method and action information between the body tags. If you know an actual server path, you can delete **"server path"** and key the actual path. (If you will be using the e-mail option, use **action="mailto:me@myaddress.com"**, substituting the e-mail address you wish to use.)

```
<form method="post" action="server path">
```

5. To create a single text field, key the following code below the line containing the FORM element you just entered:

```
Name: <input type="text" name="name" size="50" maxlength="25" />
```

Note: The text "Name:" will appear as a label on the screen. The code **name="name"** identifies the input field and will not appear on the browser's screen.

6. Close the form by keying a form end tag:

```
</form>
```

7. Save the file and open it in your browser. You should now see the word "Name:" followed by a blank text field box (see Figure 4.13). If you had keyed the label for the text field after the input element, the text field box would appear first.

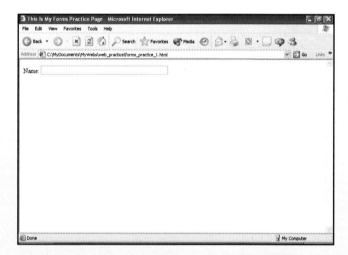

FIGURE 4.13
A text field allows users to input text into a form.

8. Repeat Step 5 to create additional text fields for "Mailing Address" and "E-Mail Address." Key two line break tags between each text field INPUT element so that they appear on separate lines. Adjust the width of the box and number of characters that can be entered into the text fields as appropriate for the expected content. Create names for these data fields that clearly identify the data.

9. Save the file and refresh your browser. Your browser should now display three text fields for name, mail address, and e-mail address.

Check Boxes

Check boxes save time by allowing users to check a box rather than key text. Since it is possible to select more than one check box at a time, they are best used for input that is easily categorized and for which users might need to indicate more than one choice. For example, the following question could be answered by selecting more than one box if the user has owned more than one of these different makes of automobile:

```
Please indicate which of the following automobiles
you have owned:
❑ Toyota
❑ Chevrolet
❑ Oldsmobile
❑ Mazda
❑ Porsche
```

CREATE CHECK BOXES

Create check boxes for your form:

1. Return to your text editor to view the source code of the **forms_practice_1.html** file.
2. Key two line break tags (<br />) below the last text field INPUT element in the form:

```
E-mail Address: <input type="text" name="e-mail address"
size="50" maxlength="25" />
<br />
<br />
```

3. Key the code for creating check boxes under the last line break tag. Note that each check box INPUT element must have a different name.

```
Which of the following computer programs have you used before?
You may check more than one box:
<br />
<br />
Microsoft Word: <input
type="checkbox" name="Word" />
Microsoft Excel: <input
type="checkbox" name="Excel" />
Microsoft PowerPoint: <input
type="checkbox" name="PowerPoint" />
```

4. Save your file and refresh your browser. Your form now has a series of three check boxes that visitors can use to indicate their experience (see Figure 4.14). Because no line break tags were entered between the check box items, they appear on the same line.

FIGURE 4.14

Check boxes make using forms easier by allowing visitors to check a box rather than having to key information.

Radio Buttons

Radio buttons are used for input when users are able to make only one choice from among a group of items. This is useful for information such as age groups (0–21, 22–45, and 46–60), in which where there can only be one correct answer. Unlike check boxes, all radio buttons for a single item on the form should be assigned the same name, such as **name="age"**. This is because only one answer for age group will be submitted out of all the possible choices. Because the radio buttons all have the same name, a unique value must be indicated for each button. Using the age group example, the values assigned for radio buttons would be **value="0-21", value="22-45", value="46-60"**.

Add radio buttons to your form:

1. Return to your text editor to view the source code of the **forms_practice_1.html** file.
2. Key two line break tags below the code for the last check box:

```
Microsoft PowerPoint: <input type="checkbox" name="PowerPoint" />
<br />
<br />
```

3. Key the code for creating radio buttons under the last line break tag:

```
Please indicate your opinion of the design of this Web page:
<br />
<br />
<input type="radio" name="opinion" value="excellent" />
Excellent<br />
<input type="radio" name="opinion" value="good" />Good<br />
<input type="radio" name="opinion" value="fair" />Fair<br />
<input type="radio" name="opinion" value="poor" />Poor
```

4. Save your file and refresh your browser. Your form now has radio buttons that visitors can use to indicate their opinion of your Web page design (see Figure 4.15). The radio buttons appear before each choice because this time you keyed the INPUT elements before their labels. Each radio button also appears on a different line because of the line breaks you keyed.

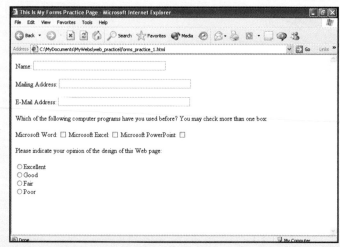

FIGURE 4.15

Radio buttons are circular buttons that users can click on to indicate a preference or choice.

5. If you want a check box or radio button to be a default selection, use the CHECKED attribute with the value "checked" in the check box or radio button INPUT element that you want to make the default choice. Then users will only need to enter something if their response is different. Try this by checking the "Excellent" INPUT element:

```
<input type="radio" name="opinion" value="excellent" checked />
Excellent<br />
```

Note: Browsers currently allow the attribute and value—**checked="checked"**—to be minimized to just the attribute because the two are the same. However, XHTML does not allow minimized attribute values.

6. Save the file and refresh your browser. The "Excellent" radio button is now the default selection.

Drop-Down Menus

Drop-down menus are handy for questions in which the user must choose from a long list of choices, such as a list of states. With a drop-down box, the user only has to scroll down and select the appropriate state. Without a drop-down box, a radio button for every state would have to be listed on the form, which would make the form crowded. The size of the drop-down box and whether or not users can select more than one choice can be specified.

CREATE A DROP-DOWN BOX

Create a drop-down box for your form:
1. Return to your text editor to view the source code of the **forms_practice_1.html** file.
2. Key two line break tags below the code for the last radio button:

```
<input type="radio" name="opinion" value="poor" /> Poor
<br />
<br />
```

3. Create a drop-down box by keying the following code:

```
My Favorite Color:
<br />
<br />
<select name="color">
<option>Black</option>
<option>White</option>
<option>Green</option>
<option>Yellow</option>
<option>Blue</option>
<option>Purple</option>
<option>Orange</option>
<option>Red</option>
</select>
```

4. Save the file and refresh your browser. You have just created a drop-down box that visitors can use to choose their favorite color (see Figure 4.16). Note that the drop-down box will drop down only if there is sufficient screen space below the drop-down box. If there is not enough space, the box will drop "up."

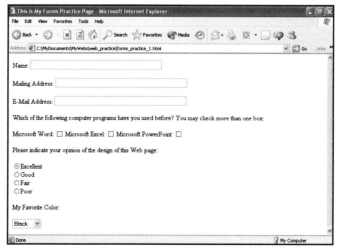

FIGURE 4.16
Drop-down boxes save Web page space by allowing users to select from a long list of items that can be viewed by scrolling down the list.

5. You can indicate the number of choices that are visible at a time in the drop-down box window, whether or not users will be able to make multiple choices, and which item will be highlighted by default. To choose more than one item, users must hold down the Ctrl key while selecting an item. Try these functions by keying the following text and code:

```
My Favorite Colors: (Hold down the Ctrl key to choose more than
one color.)
<br />
<br />
<select name="color" size="3" multiple="multiple">
<option>Black</option>
<option>White</option>
<option selected="selected">Green</option>
<option>Yellow</option>
<option>Blue</option>
<option>Purple</option>
<option>Orange</option>
<option>Red</option>
</select>
```

6. Save the file and refresh your browser. The drop-down box window should now show three colors, green should be highlighted, and you should be able to select more than one color can be by holding down the Ctrl key while making selections.

Text Areas

Text areas provide a space for visitors to key their comments. You can specify the size of the text area by indicating the number of columns and rows it will occupy.

Create a text area for your form:

1. Return to your text editor to view the source code of the **forms_practice_1.html** file.

2. Key two line break tags below the select end tag:

```
</select>
<br />
<br />
```

3. Create a text area by keying the following code:

```
Use the space below to enter any comments you may have:
<br />
<br />
<textarea name="comments" rows="10"
cols="75">
</textarea>
```

4. Save the file and refresh your browser. You now have a large text box where visitors can key comments (see Figure 4.17).

Submit and Reset Buttons

Submit buttons are used to submit the information that has been entered into a form so that it can be processed. Reset buttons reset the form by erasing any information that was entered into the form prior to clicking the Reset button.

FIGURE 4.17

Text areas create a space that Web site visitors can use to key comments.

Add Submit and Reset buttons to your form:

1. Return to your text editor to view the source code of the **forms_practice_1.html** file.

2. Key two line break tags below the text area end tag:

```
</textarea>
<br />
<br />
```

3. Create Submit and Reset buttons for your form by keying the following code:

```
<input type="submit" value="Submit" />
<input type="reset" value="Reset" />
```

4. Save the file and refresh your browser. Submit and Reset buttons appear at the bottom of the form (see Figure 4.18). Changing the value for a button will change the text that appears on the button. Clicking the Submit button forwards your form to a Web server for processing after you have the correct instructions coded in the page.

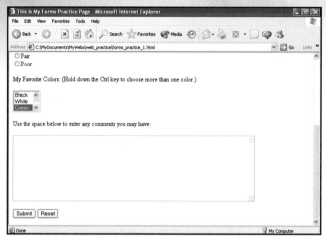

FIGURE 4.18
The Submit button submits the form for processing. The Reset button clears the form of any previously entered selections or text.

design
project

1. Use a search engine to research career opportunities in the Web design field. Search for Web design sites, employment databases, job recruitment sites, government information, or any other resources that would be helpful for someone looking for a career in Web design. Create a list of your favorite sites. Make sure to gather notes that include any reference material that will be needed later, such as URLs, publishers, and author. You will be comparing and annotating these resources on your Web site, so gather this information as well. Feel free to conduct any additional research you feel might be beneficial. Bookmark the sites so you can easily locate them again. Write a report summarizing your findings.
2. Conduct a search for Web sites that offer guidance on creating and using lists and forms in HTML. Bookmark any of these sites that you find helpful so that you can use them as resources when working with lists and forms.
3. Ask your ISP or system administrator for information on what you will need to do for your forms to function interactively. As an alternative, use the option of sending the input data to your e-mail address.
4. Create a new Web page (or pages) for the report you created for the Research Assignment. Use what you have just learned to create forms and lists for your Web pages. This form might be used to seek visitors' opinions of your Web resource site, gather information about the people who visit your site, or gather any other information that you feel suitable. Create lists to organize information. Think of how the items on a list can be linked to other information on your Web site or other Web sites. Enter comment tags to indicate items or areas that you plan to link in the future.

CHAPTER

5

Phase I: Prepare and Plan

cyber *visit*

LYNDA WEINMAN

Writer, Designer, Animator, Teacher

Design Viewpoint

"I help media designers and communicators understand how to use professional tools and design to enhance visual communication through Web, print, and motion graphics."

Resume

Former animator and motion graphics teacher at Art Center College of Design in Pasadena, California; owner of the Ojai Digital Arts Center, a teaching facility devoted solely to the World Wide Web.

Clients

Web designers and instructors from around the world.

Designer's Home Page

www.lynda.com/

Insights

". . . the Web has the potential to be one of the most significant publishing mediums in history. The Web stands to revolutionize the way we communicate and distribute information and artists will play a huge role in establishing the look and feel of this extraordinary medium."

"I taught art to undergraduate and graduate students at the Art Center College of Design for many years and always told my students that it's not enough to know a program or technique—it's much more important to know how to learn a new one. The nature of software programs and techniques is that they will always change, so it's almost more important to learn how to learn than to know everything about something that will eventually become outdated."

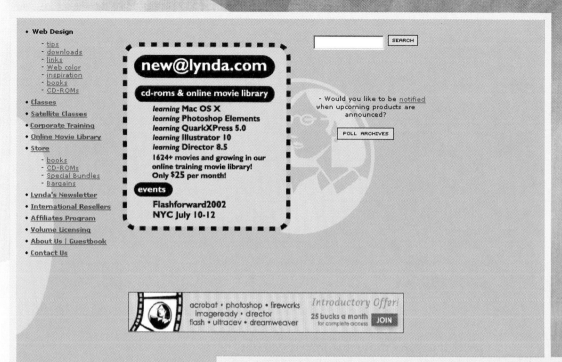

Lynda Weinman's home page at www.lynda.com/.

www.htmlbook.com/

Objectives

➤ Describe the Web site design process model, differentiating among the three main phases.

➤ Demonstrate four areas in which designers need to educate themselves to prepare for a Web design project, using a subject area about which you have considerable knowledge.

➤ Define the main steps in performing a needs analysis.

➤ Demonstrate the techniques for establishing a Web site's needs.

➤ Demonstrate how the needs analysis becomes the basis for goal statements.

➤ Translate needs into goals for the Web site, aligning these goals with types of purposes and their associated parameters.

➤ Write user profiles and create scenarios for each main profile.

➤ Create a site Project Plan that includes a Site Specifications and Standards document and a Project Management Plan.

After learning the concepts and best practices of Web design, the next step is the design process that leads to a well-designed site. The next three chapters take a detailed look at the organizational phases involved in building a site that satisfies the site design client's needs and also appeals to users.

This chapter, and those that follow, describe, not prescribe, a typical process. Although this description covers the major aspects involved in the Web design process, no two design firms or in-house design staffs will organize a project in exactly the same way. Nonetheless, an overview of which procedures should be handled is valuable, regardless of how different firms or in-house staffs handle the details. Designing a Web site is a complex, creative process requiring the organization of a myriad of tasks. No matter who composes the design team—specialists combining their abilities in the various aspects of Web design, or a single contractor taking all of it—learning how the process can be organized into a series of steps helps remove the sense of being overwhelmed by the complexity of the work.

There are typically three major phases of a Web design project, and each phase has a corresponding set of tasks. The first phase starts by defining the site's goals (based on needs) and writing a site project plan. The second phase continues with the design, production, and approval of a working prototype of the site. The third phase includes the launching of the site and its continuous improvement. Figure 5.1 illustrates this process. Each phase results in a finished product that serves as a basis for the next phase. It is a complex and sometimes lengthy process, but by proceeding methodically through each phase, a design team can keep its eyes on the goal without losing its way or enthusiasm.

In the first phase, which is the subject of this chapter, a design team's goal is to reach consensus with the client about the site's purposes and anticipated users, the client's expectations for the site (including expectations regarding potential users), the technical specifications for the site (including the standards to which it will conform), and, of course, how much work will be involved and how much the design work will cost. During this phase, developers clearly document the scope of the work they are to accomplish, how that work will be carried out, and the process for collaboration between the client and the designer(s).

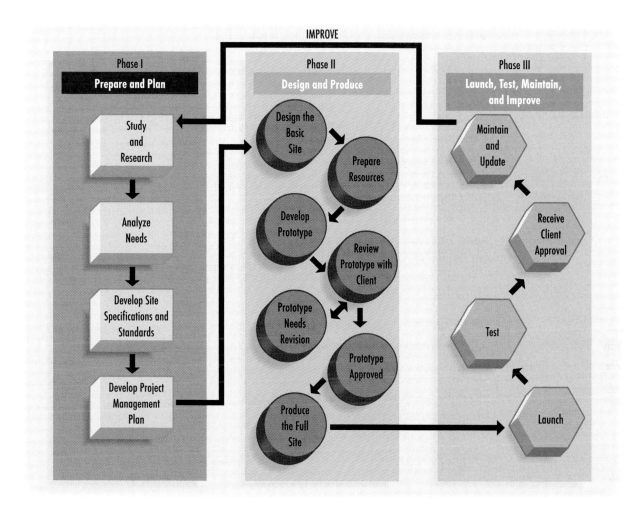

FIGURE 5.1 The Web Design Process Model

This first phase is where all the research and planning takes place and only preliminary work in coding, graphic design, and content gathering occurs. Yet it is critical, because this phase (ideally) results in a complete understanding of the needs, goals, and plans for the site, an understanding that helps designers balance the client's expectations against time and budgetary constraints. The major document to be produced by the end of this phase is the site Project Plan, which is composed of two parts: the Site Specifications and Standards document, and the Project Management Plan.

The second section of this chapter discusses how to conduct the needs analysis. How to develop the Project Plan (made up of the Site Specifications and Standards document, and the Project Management Plan) is presented in the third section. The first part of this chapter, however, discusses the important step of preparing the design team for conversing with the client. Immersing itself in the client's world is one of the most important first steps a design team can take.

PREPARING THROUGH STUDY AND RESEARCH

Understanding the content and language of the subject matter of a Web site is invaluable when designing and developing a site. Knowledge of the subject matter is essential to being able to discuss the business intelligently with a Web design client in order to build the client's assurance that the design team will handle the content of the site accurately. When interviewing for and bidding on a new Web design project, consider knowledge of the business a marketing tool; a client is more likely to agree to work with a design team that clearly understands the content area.

Four areas of study and research are essential during the preparation and planning stage of a Web site project:
- Content area (including commonly used language)
- Client company (or organization, institution, business)
- Target market (current visitors to an existing site and potential visitors to a new one)
- Competition and their Web sites

Content Area

Before even the earliest planning meetings with a site design client, a Web design team should have researched the content area enough to be able to discuss the subject intelligently. Understanding the content is critical to speaking about it clearly and creating a functional and responsive design. Although the team will not be expected to know the subject thoroughly, the team must demonstrate that it has cared enough to begin to learn it. The team's ability to work somewhat independently of the client depends on understanding the fundamental aspects of the content area. The team cannot present what it does not understand.

To learn about a content area fundamentally means to learn the subject's main topic as well as its primary methodologies. To design a site for an oceanographic institution, for instance, might require developers to learn how their particular client's research relates to that of other institutions. Designing for a scientific organization might require designers to brush up on the principles of the scientific method. This is important because the client might have special ways it wants to discuss its activities, and an understanding of how scientists conduct research should affect how the team announces the client's results. Other material that is worth learning has to do with the history of the subject, its major figures, and events. The goal here is to focus on the big picture.

Research can be an important way to avoid being influenced by personal biases—those of the designer or the client. Personal biases can steer the design in the wrong direction. The client company will certainly have major influence on the goals and directions of the Web site. But the designer, who can function as an objective observer, can help clarify the Web site's goals and even call attention to things the client might not know. For example, businesses are sometimes less able than outsiders to evaluate their own customers, particularly how, why, and when those customers will become visitors of the Web site.

Everyone on the design team might not need to be educated about the subject matter to the same degree. With a large team, on which site-building tasks are to be parceled out to members with particular expertise, only certain members might devote time to this portion of the project.

DO YOU KNOW?

Question How did programmers retrieve data from Turing's revolutionary Automatic Calculating Engine (ACE) that came out in 1958?

Answer Programming a computer in the 1950s was complicated by the fact that data was not always accessible whenever a program needed it. This had to do with the way data was accessed in memory. ACE used a technique to access the rotating mercury delay line memory that made it possible to get out a certain segment of data just when it was needed. Programmers needed to account for these timed releases of data in order to retrieve data when it was needed, calculating exactly when elements of data would be available and extracting them at just that point in time. If the timing was wrong, the program ran slowly while waiting for the necessary information to come around again. But by the time ACE appeared in 1958, it was virtually obsolete. Magnetic forms of memory (tapes) had made data more accessible by making it available nearly all the time.

To begin to understand a completely unfamiliar subject, the first source of information to consider is the client. Ask the client to provide materials—either its own marketing materials or standard materials the client consults. Read this material thoroughly. Take note of any questions you have, and determine whether you can answer these questions on your own. If not, ask the client for clarification.

Designers also can conduct Web searches to study the content area. In addition to providing valuable information, a Web search in the client's content area will reveal what other organizations in your client's content area have done on their Web sites. The client's competitors or organizations affiliated with the client might have features on their sites that the design team might want to emulate, avoid, or improve. Designers also can look for organizations that sponsor informational sessions on the subject. Aside from the Web, printed sources such as books, journals, newspapers, and magazines are still good sources of information. Libraries, both physical and virtual, are invaluable sources.

Another practical way of learning a content area is focusing on the subject's vocabulary, especially the key words. By mastering two or three dozen words that are particular to the content area and learning to use them correctly, a designer will be prepared to communicate about the significant concepts in that topic area. To compile a list of the critical vocabulary for the content area, use materials from the client or other sources. Learn what these terms mean and practice how to use them correctly. Be on guard especially for words that might seem familiar but take on specialized meaning within this area. For example, the word "communications" means something different in computer networking than in counseling; "parameter" means something completely different to a computer-applications programmer using Java than it does to a Web designer.

Root Link www.yourdictionary.com/
Direct Link www.yourdictionary.com/diction4.html#business
Why Go? To discover comprehensive language tools. Language-related products and services are available in more than 260 languages and in specialty fields ranging from economics to entomology and from literature to sociology.

Consider, for example, a project to design a Web site about British car restoration. Some of the key words for the designer to learn and be ready to use are listed in Table 5.1.

Familiarity with language aids designers while they build the site, but it also instructs writers as they attempt to devise a suitable, appealing writing style; guides artists as they choose appropriate artwork, logos, and photographs; aids content organizers as they create effective architecture; informs programmers of special requirements for which they need to provide code; alerts designers to fitting images or ideas that can serve as navigational metaphors; and allows the design team to envision the features that will appeal to the client and the client's target market.

TABLE 5.1 Specialty Language for British Car Restoration

Term	Meaning
boot	luggage compartment or trunk
bulkhead	firewall
concours	a level of judging competition for restored cars
drop head coupe	convertible
dynamo	generator
estate car	station wagon
key sockets	trim detail judged in competition
luggage rack	trim detail judged in competition
mandatory deduction	items that, when incorrectly restored, lead to the loss of points in competition
originality	element that is judged in competition
overall condition	element that is judged in competition
paint quality	element that is judged in competition
saloon	sedan
silencer	muffler
stone shields	trim detail judged in competition
vintage	a car that is 25 years old or older

The Site's Sponsor

A number of important things should be known about the client company for a Web design project, including a full understanding of its business; its reputation; its goals, products, or services; its long- and short-term plans; and its leadership and vision. Ask to see the company's mission statement. Ask questions about the basics:

- Is it a multinational company, a domestic business with several offices throughout the country or world, a regional business with a few locations, or a one-room operation?
- What is its main business? What are its secondary businesses?
- Is it a well-known organization? A start-up? A long-time participant?
- Is the client trying to change its image or obtain standing in a new area of its business?
- Who are the leaders of the organization?
- What is their vision for the future of the company?
- Why are they interested in having a presence on the Web?

Answers to these questions definitely affect plans for a Web site. Businesses will most likely have databases they want linked to their site, if not for customers' use then certainly for use by employees. Multinational companies will have languages to translate among and might need language-specific versions of each of its pages. If the company's customers are from around the world, ways should be made for individuals of any nationality to make use of the site, whether this means providing versions in four of the most widely used languages or in languages known to be of concern to the client. Companies whose main business is selling products directly to customers will be interested in displaying photos and information to encourage sales. Companies that have numerous departments (legal, manufacturing, sales, and purchasing, for instance) might want to have separate areas to facilitate information exchange within and possibly between departments.

Clarify what the site sponsor thinks a new Web site can do for its business. The following questions can help identify the site design client's goals for the site:

- What is the rationale for creating a new site (or redesigning an existing one)?
- How will the new site affect the existing company?
- Will the site increase sales, or will it be used primarily as a way of communicating with customers?
- Will employees benefit from a new Web site? If so, how?
- What existing business documents and resources—databases, for instance—will be incorporated into the Web site?
- Does the company have an **intranet**?
- Will a new site require the client to hire new technical staff, or are its technical personnel sufficient to handle the work?
- Who will host the site, the company or a third party vendor?

Using a systematic process to ask key questions such as these is important, even for an on-staff designer for the site sponsor.

Learning about the clients' design preferences, likes, and dislikes is also valuable. The following questions can elicit this information from the client:

- What sites has the client seen and liked?
- Which sites does the client dislike? Is the site-design client looking for "plain," straightforward functionality, or for something with more technical or artistic splash?
- If a site is being redesigned, what are the most important features to be changed and improved, and which are items that might have to wait?

intranet
A private version of the Internet, usually built to be accessed only by a company's employees. Most often an internal Web site for a company containing information and features that are not for public consumption.

- Is the client company set in its ideas about what the Web site should do, or is it open to possibilities a design team might suggest?

Many design choices are a matter of preference. The designer must accommodate the site sponsor's wishes as constructively as possible, working to balance the sponsor's wishes with the standards and expectations of the Web design field and with the designer's aspirations to provide striking, attention-getting Web sites. A site-design client can have unrealistic expectations, and the designer is sometimes the only barrier between these and unfortunate results. But the designer might also be best able to turn a client's limited vision into something more engaging and vital. Making a concentrated effort to incorporate a client's ideas will benefit the site, and also will increase satisfaction with the final product. However, the client must be able to depend on the designer's expertise to recommend features that will make the site more interesting, useful, appealing, or effective.

Building a strong relationship at the outset will have a positive impact on the ability of the designer to work constructively with the client throughout the project. In a large project, there is much give and take, and many discussions that can touch on important, even sensitive issues. With all the back and forth communication, a relationship built on mutual respect and interdependence is essential for the process to work.

Target Market

Understanding the client's target market, current customers, whether these customers are the intended Web site users, and what additional customers the site might be targeted to attract is particularly important. The designer might pose questions to help the site sponsor work out new or better ways of meeting its customers' demands. The following questions can help get information about the customers:
- What do they find valuable about the company's services, products, or organization?
- Are these customers loyal?
- What special or unique needs do they have?
- What do the client's customers think about the company?
- Are they looking for an improvement in something the company does or offers?

The answers to these questions might result in the designer suggesting a special feature for the Web site: perhaps an improved support page, with links clearly showing access to advice from company representatives, or a gallery showing off the site sponsor's products, with links to a database containing valuable product information that can be sorted by categories the user selects. When tailoring a Web site to a sponsor's business, it is important to understand why customers would come to a Web site and what they would most likely do there.

Competition

A designer should understand as much as possible about what the client's competitors do and how they offer their products and services. The goal is to identify ways that the sponsor's new Web site can improve upon what the competition's sites have to offer.

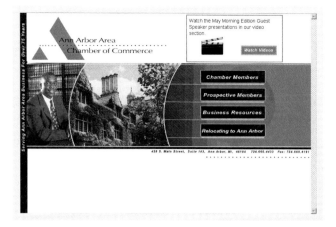 

Comparing several sites of competing or complementary organizations alerts designers to the issues facing the team. For instance, how much information should be available directly from the home page? Here, two different chambers of commerce (www.annarborchamber.org and www.chicagolandchamber.org) approach this differently.

Researching the competition's Web sites can provide important information about parallel and complementary enterprises and agencies. If your client is a chamber of commerce, for example, important additional areas of research would be to investigate what chambers of commerce in other parts of the country have done with their Web sites and what services or goods other area and community agencies and resources offer online. Questions that might help the designer focus on a sponsor's competition include:

- Who are the principal competitors?
- Where are the main competitors physically and virtually located?
- What do the competitors do or offer that the client does not?
- What weaknesses or strengths does the company see in its competitors' products, services, or marketing methods?
- Do the competitors offer rich, robust sites on the Web?

Researching complementary areas can identify which sites the sponsor's site could link up with. A business will not want to link to a competitor's site, nor would its competitors want to do the same. But being listed on the sites of organizations whose users might be likely to explore your client's site is one of the best forms of free advertising. Cross-linking like this becomes one of the important considerations in a Web site design because it increases "traffic" to the site. Given the interconnected nature of the Web, initial research about competing, parallel, and complementary enterprises is critical to getting the most benefit from the site, both for the client and for its users.

Root Link www.si.edu

Direct Links www.mnh.si.edu/vikings/
www.photo2.si.edu/volcano/volcanopix.html
www.pandas.si.edu/pandacam/index.htm

Why Go? A good example of cross-linking. Explore 16 museums and galleries with more than 140 million artifacts and specimens, including the National Zoo and the Smithsonian Institution. Experience a North Atlantic Viking Saga, see pictures of the volcanoes of Indonesia, watch real-time cam photos of the pandas in the National Zoo.

Explore a Web site that covers many topics and evaluate how understanding or not understanding a site's subject matter can influence a Web experience. For this activity, complete these tasks:

The Home and Garden TV site www.hgtv.com/.

1. Go to the Home and Garden TV site at www.hgtv.com/ and explore the site's content and determine how the content is organized.

2. Select one of the site's content areas. You should select a content area with which you are familar. Within that content area, select a specific page to visit.

3. When you have arrived in this specific section of the site, read the page and make notes about the language. List any terms and concepts you do not understand.

4. Follow several links to related articles from this page, and write down additional terms you do not understand.

5. Go back to the home page and select a different content area to explore. This time, pick a content area with which you are unfamiliar. From the page you have selected, follow links, read articles, and copy down any terms you do not understand. Find out the meanings of these new terms. You can do this in whatever way you wish: consult a dictionary or an encyclopedia, or do a Web search.

6. Become comfortable enough with the definitions of these terms to be able to go back to the site (www.hgtv.com/), revisit the unfamiliar content area, and read the same articles you did before. Was it easier to understand them this time?

7. Compare the number of unfamiliar terms from both the familiar and unfamiliar content areas you visited. Which is larger? What does this suggest about where you would need to spend more time educating yourself on a subject area?

8. Write a report that tells which content areas you visited, lists the words with which you were unfamiliar, and the definitions you were able to find. Describe whether concentrating on learning the vocabulary of a content area helped you feel more familiar with the content area itself. Does focusing on vocabulary seem like a method you would use in your own work as a Web designer?

CONDUCTING A NEEDS ANALYSIS

To build new Web sites (including upgrades of existing sites), designers begin with a **needs analysis**. By definition, "need" is based on comparing what exists with what is desired (as shown in Chapter 2). In reality, defining these needs is a matter of clarifying the needs of the site's sponsor and the site's users. These needs should be considered separately, but in the end, they are brought together in an informal written document called the needs statement. Without a needs statement, the goals for a Web site remain vague.

> **needs analysis**
> The fundamental definition of the needs the Web site will meet. Based on what the site design client needs the Web site to accomplish and what visitors to the site will expect the site to provide.

Defining the Client's Needs

For a new or redesigned Web site, the process of establishing the needs of the client generally involves exploring the plans the client is considering for the site. Different plans emerge from every department that will make use of the site, however, and coordinating all these plans can be a major challenge. The following steps can help the designer sort through the client's needs:

- Interview the right people, including the decision-makers.
- Use techniques for collecting information from the client.
- Define goals based on specific needs.

Because so much is riding on the achievement of a clear definition of the needs for the Web site, this step in the process relies on well-developed procedures for eliciting information, sifting through it to decide what is important, and then writing a needs statement that leads to clear objectives for the design team to work toward in designing the Web site.

SOURCES OF INFORMATION To begin defining the client's needs, the initial question is, "Who represents the collective viewpoint of the client?" Within an organization, company, institution, or business, there are multiple viewpoints of what the Web site can and should do, and these viewpoints are based on the specific roles and responsibilities of the various "stakeholders."

With any organization, opinions will vary among different stakeholders about what a Web site should accomplish. If the client is an organization, the officers, agents, and membership will each have their own set of Web site needs. This will happen within a business, too. For example, the needs of marketing may be, and probably are, distinct from the needs of the service department, or the product designers, or the company's leadership.

The correct source of information about needs differs with each Web design project, but some sources are generally important. The highest level of management within the enterprise generally decides on the overall strategy for the Web site. Upper management knows what information should be shared or not shared, how current customers are to be handled differently from new ones, and what image the company should project. High-level management also determines the financial, personnel, and technical resources that are available for this project.

Although upper management needs to be involved in the needs analysis that will form the basis of the Web site's goals, others within the company—those in middle management and other key information sources—are more likely to be helpful in providing specific information about the site's prospective users and their needs. Middle management and other company professionals can help designers with user profiling, identifying and supplying content, and other essential functions that clarify and bring together the substance of the site.

TECHNIQUES FOR COLLECTING INFORMATION TO ASSESS NEEDS After the people within the organization who can provide information have been identified, the design team will need to know how to mine their experience and imaginations for ideas on what the Web site's needs are. The needs analysis can be developed by using any of a number of information-gathering strategies. Interviewing and brainstorming are two of the more popular strategies for identifying client's needs.

Interviewing can be a useful strategy for arriving at a clear understanding of the needs and associated goals of the site. Interviews can be conducted individually or in small groups, using face-to-face meetings, telephone interviews, or online interviews. Whatever process is followed for interviews, it is essential to:

- "Sell" the value of the interview, to help the interviewees see that their input is needed.
- Prepare questions in advance and use the same question check sheet for all interviews to ensure consistency in the range of questions asked and information gathered.
- Schedule interviews in advance, even if they will be conducted by phone, and state how long the interview will take.
- Be sensitive to the fact that time is very valuable—gather the responses needed, and sign off promptly.

Interview questions are tailored to the specifics of the enterprise and content area of the site design client. For purposes of the needs analysis, these questions elicit responses about what exists—how it is special as well as how it is limited—and what is desired, thinking beyond the limits of what now exists. The following are typical interview questions:

- What types of products, services, means of interaction with sales, and service support does your company offer customers now?
- What are the main strengths of what your company makes available to customers now? How do you know that these are important to the customers?
- Which of these strengths do you want to see carried over to the Web site?
- What beyond current interactions and offerings to customers do you want to see?
- What beyond current interactions and offerings do your customers want?
- How do you see the Web site working together with your existing ways of interacting with customers? Would there be changes to your existing ways of interacting with customers as a result of the Web site?
- What do you *not* want to see happen in terms of interactions with customers after the Web site is in place?
- What do you consider most important after customers have both the Web site and your current means of interacting with them available?

Brainstorming is a process in which participants bring out as many ideas as possible, in this case about what exists and what is desired. All ideas are accepted in brainstorming, without censoring them for practicality, cost, or clarity. Ideas can be written down on separate pieces of paper and placed on a large board without worrying about how they are related to each other. The goal is to encourage ideas without imposing limits, at least at the outset. Eventually, all ideas generated during the brainstorming process are evaluated and grouped, and decisions are made about which ideas are workable and good. But during the brainstorming session itself, no idea is censored.

Ask participants not to censor their thoughts too strictly; let them express even ideas that might at first seem too ambitious. As long as participants are on track, sharing ideas about what the Web site might be or do, no ideas should be eliminated from the brainstorming session. As a moderator, make sure that participants do not criticize each other's suggestions during the brainstorming process. Equally important is keeping the focus on the task at hand—exploring what exists and what is desired to determine the needs of the Web site. Have the group focus on issues they will be able to agree on—for instance, what the group does not want to see when the site is developed (this could produce useful insights about design). Agreement about what to avoid can lead more smoothly to agreement on what needs the site will fill, and what it is to accomplish.

Use the following as examples of questions that encourage brainstorming what is desired, thinking beyond the limits of what exists:

- What products, services, and modes of interaction exist now?
- What are the special qualities and limits of what exists now?
- What opportunities does having a Web site present beyond the limits of what exists now?
- What can a Web site do for us beyond other methods of marketing and promotion?
- How should a Web site relate to our existing methods of business and interaction?
- What do we *not* want our site visitors to experience on our site?
- How might users of our site value interaction with each other as well as with us?
- How might users want to interact with us? What people within our organization might want to interact?

Figure 5.2 shows an example of some ideas that might be generated in a brainstorming session. These ideas can be evaluated and organized after the session is completed.

brainstorming
Idea-generating process in which fresh new ideas are sought from participants. Creative thinking is the primary goal, so ideas are not judged, rejected, or put to a test to determine whether they are practical or attainable.

FIGURE 5.2 Results of a Brainstorming Session

DEFINE GOALS After gathering information from interviewing or brainstorming, design teams can begin compiling a list of the goals to which the client enterprise and its representatives can agree. The point at which the team involves the client in this process depends on the client's time constraints and expectations. It might be wise for the designers to do some of the preliminary work of sorting through the needs and crafting associated statements of goals. Designers might have a sense of which goals will have the greatest support, and be able to compile a preliminary list based on the insights gained from conversations. The team should share its list of Web site goals with the client for additions, adjustments, and approval. Present this list, accept their changes, and make sure those changes are incorporated into the list of goals.

The **normative technique** is a more formal process for focusing on a final list of goals, working from the ideas generated during brainstorming. Ideas that have been written down are grouped into related topics. Then, the group of participants selects some number of topics they think are most important. Ideas receiving the most votes rise to the top of the list and remain for the next round of discussion and voting until a distilled list of goals to be met by the Web site is chosen. Figure 5.3 shows an example of how the information from the brainstorming session (refer to Figure 5.2) was organized and evaluated. The resulting list of goals defines the client's needs and focuses the efforts of the Web design team. Goals further down the list might be set aside for development in future versions of the site.

FIGURE 5.3 Normative Technique Example

Defining the Needs of the Users

Information about the targeted users of the site is equally essential to evaluating the needs of a successful Web site and to its design. Part of the process of gathering information involves seeking details about the characteristics, habits, and preferences of individuals most likely to use the site. Who are they? How old are they? What language do they speak? Where are they located? What do they want? How much experience with computers can they be expected to have? For purposes of the needs analyses, information again is gathered about what exists and what is desired.

SOURCES OF INFORMATION   Agents of the client company (or other enterprise) who deal with customers on a regular basis are the best sources of information about users' needs. Service personnel will understand best what the service needs will be. Sales personnel will understand best the issues that customers/visitors will raise as part of the buying or exploration process. Faculty and advisers will understand best the needs of potential students. Conference planners will understand best the needs of potential attendees, speakers, and vendors. Always seek out those who understand the issues facing the company's customers, who have frequent personal contact with them, or who deal frequently with the issues they raise.

If opportunities exist, directly interview those individuals who fit the profile or profiles for the targeted users of the site. Before these interviews, compile a list of assumptions and guesses about what people of this profile will want when they arrive at the site, and what their characteristics will be. Create a check sheet of questions that will guide the interview process to test these assumptions and to gain additional information. A survey is another option for collecting valuable material about potential users. Figure 5.4 provides an example of a user survey.

USER DIVERSITY: INTERESTS, KNOWLEDGE, AND SKILL   When evaluating users' needs, it is important to anticipate the diversity of interests, knowledge, and skills users will bring to the site, both in terms of the Web site's content and its technology. To understand this diversity, answer the following questions:

- What distinct groupings of users will the site attract and what will each group be looking for at the site?
- What prior content knowledge will the visitors bring to the site? How many visitors will be unfamiliar with the subject?
- How many visitors will be experienced in using the Web? How many will be inexperienced?

For instance, a small crafts business that wants its Web site to advertise products and announce classes it offers to individuals in its surrounding area might define its likely users in general terms as "individuals who enjoy doing craft projects as hobbyists and who look for opportunities to find great deals on supplies, discover new projects to do, learn new techniques and time-saving tips, and talk crafts with other enthusiasts." This general description might be broken down based on levels of interest, knowledge, and skill, supplemented with statements such as "Most users do not have vast experience with the Web, although some users do" and "Most users will have medium skill levels in their craft of choice, but some will be exploring crafts that are entirely new to them."

This general description regarding users' interests, knowledge, and skill can be turned into an illustration showing major categories of user interest. This illustration allows you to see relationships among needs that later can be translated into possibilities for major Web site sections. Figure 5.5 is an example of a user diversity diagram. Interests branch into five main categories: supplies, projects, skills, interaction, and showcase. Within each of these categories are more specific interests, some of which go beyond what can be addressed traditionally by a crafts store in a neighborhood.

Two news sites based on different user interests. *Time* magazine (www.time.com/) attracts users whose interests vary widely, from international and national news on the one hand to sports and entertainment news on the other. Because *The Week* (www.theweek-magazine.com/) focuses primarily on international news, visitors to this site might not vary as much. Notice that the Web site for *The Week* has many fewer links than does the site for *Time*.

USER SURVEY

1. Where do you live? [AK ▼]

2. What age group are you in? ▢ 5–17 ▢ 18–30 ▢ 31–40 ▢ 41–50 ▢ 51–60 ▢ 60+

3. What language do you speak? [English ▼]

4. How comfortable are you using technology?
   ▢ Very comfortable ▢ Fairly comfortable ▢ Somewhat comfortable ▢ Very uncomfortable

5. What form of connection do you have to the Internet?
   ▢ Modem ▢ ISDN line ▢ DSL ▢ Cable ▢ Satellite

6. What crafts do you engage in, and what is your skill level in each? (Select all that apply.)
   Knitting
   ▢ Beginner ▢ Intermediate ▢ Advanced
   Crocheting
   ▢ Beginner ▢ Intermediate ▢ Advanced
   Needlepoint
   ▢ Beginner ▢ Intermediate ▢ Advanced
   Embroidery or Counted Cross Stitch
   ▢ Beginner ▢ Intermediate ▢ Advanced

7. What are your main reasons for engaging in crafts? (Select all that apply.)
   ▢ To create items to decorate my home   ▢ To make items to sell at craft shops and fairs
   ▢ To make items to give as gifts   ▢ To master a skill   ▢ To relax

8. Which of the following activities would you like to do on a craft Web site? For each, mark if you can do that activity at your local shop. If you would rather do the activity at your local shop, indicate that as well.
   Purchase supplies
   ▢ Would like to do on a craft Web site   ▢ Can do locally   ▢ Prefer to do locally
   Learn new crafts
   ▢ Would like to do on a craft Web site   ▢ Can do locally   ▢ Prefer to do locally
   Interact with other craft enthusiasts
   ▢ Would like to do on a craft Web site   ▢ Can do locally   ▢ Prefer to do locally
   Seek expert advice on crafts
   ▢ Would like to do on a craft Web site   ▢ Can do locally   ▢ Prefer to do locally
   Find answers to questions
   ▢ Would like to do on a craft Web site   ▢ Can do locally   ▢ Prefer to do locally
   Get new ideas for projects
   ▢ Would like to do on a craft Web site   ▢ Can do locally   ▢ Prefer to do locally
   Purchase gifts
   ▢ Would like to do on a craft Web site   ▢ Can do locally   ▢ Prefer to do locally
   Find projects to teach my child to do
   ▢ Would like to do on a craft Web site   ▢ Can do locally   ▢ Prefer to do locally
   Showcase my work
   ▢ Would like to do on a craft Web site   ▢ Can do locally   ▢ Prefer to do locally

FIGURE 5.4 Sample User Survey for a Crafts Site

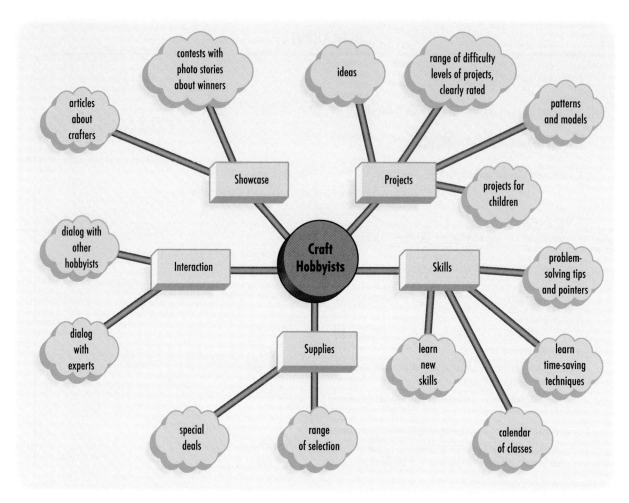

FIGURE 5.5 User Diversity Diagram
This illustrates the different categories of interest visitors of a craft Web site might have.

It might be that every visitor to the site is interested in everything the site's sponsor plans to offer on the site. On the other hand, some sites might attract visitors who are more finely differentiated, and the site needs to pay close attention to the unique challenges of attracting and keeping each kind of visitor. For example, a news organization might have some visitors who are interested only in world and national news while others are interested primarily in sports or entertainment news.

USER PROFILE After all of this user information is gathered, it is used to develop a set of user profiles. To make these profiles seem real, give a name to each type of user. To create sample profiles, combine the information obtained from the user survey and other sources. Group user responses and characteristics to come up with a profile to describe each type of user. As an example, the following are three profiles that represent the various types of people who will come to the crafts site.

Celeste is a 53-year-old who loves quilting and embroidery. She is fairly comfortable with the Web, uses an ISDN line, and would visit the site to make purchases and to interact with others who enjoy the same crafts.

Matt is a 25-year-old who is too busy to shop and uses the Internet as a ready solution to this. He is very comfortable with the Web, uses cable, and would visit the site to make a purchase primarily when he needs to locate a gift.

Terry is a 32-year-old who has just moved into her first home. She is very comfortable with the Web, uses DSL, and would visit the site to learn new crafts and to get project ideas to decorate her home.

Fictional profiles help the Web site designers understand the site's visitors. These user profiles will be used later to create scenarios of "typical" visits from each type of user, start to finish. Walking through these actual visit scenarios helps align the site design, and even helps the goals of the site better fit what users will want to do when they arrive at the site.

Profiles help clarify the purpose of a site, but they also help anticipate problems having to do with usability. As the number of non-technical users moving online continues to grow, this can be a serious issue. One writer described the confusion of a client who had entered information into an online form and then did not know what to do next. Although the Submit button was at the bottom of the form, the client had no idea that the box marked with the word "Submit" was a "button" or that she needed to click on this button to send information. The word "Submit" was meaningless to her in this context, since she did not understand that to "Submit" meant to send the data she had entered. Thus, to write a profile for every level of computer experience and for every level of familiarity with the content (as outlined previously) is to foresee possible problems with the types of users that could visit the site.

Creating a Needs Statement

As a summary of the findings about the users' and client's needs analysis, a needs statement is written to include information about what the client expects from the Web site, what users will want from it, and how these two sets of interests come together. The following is an example of a needs statement.

Context: The sponsor of this crafts site wants to surpass other sites in terms of meeting users' needs, the better to form long-term relationships.

Desired: The sponsor of this crafts site wants to surpass other sites in terms of meeting users' needs; stimulating their interest in learning and excelling in crafts; and providing a virtual venue for mentoring, teaching, interacting, and showcasing exemplary craft projects and creations, the better to form long-term relationships between the sponsor and the site visitors, and among site visitors.

Exists: On sites of this type, users typically find project ideas and sometimes patterns, supplies available for purchase, tips and "how-tos" about various crafts, and calendars for local craft presentations and classes.

Needed: The differences between what is "desired" and what "exists" include:
- Exchange venue for craft customers
- Means and process for showcasing exemplary craft projects

- Process for stimulating interest in learning and excelling in crafts, both those that visitors already engage in and ones that are new to them that they will need to learn
- Exchange process among site visitors for mentoring and teaching each other
- Regional matching and exchange process, including support for arranging small local sessions, possibly with invited experts ("learning on demand")

The language should be specific about what client and users expect, but plans about how they come together should remain general at this point. After all, planning a site's look, feel, and organization has yet to be done and is at the heart of Web design. But if a needs statement cannot produce a general idea of how the Web site will satisfy users' desires or how the Web site will promote the interests of the client, the needs statement has failed.

When looking at the needs statement, designers can then ask which parameters the site should support and which Web site generation the design team should aim for. If the parameter of engagement will be a requirement, the site will need to conform to the qualities of a generation 4 Web site design because this site will exist, in part, to encourage connections and interaction among site visitors. To state this outright is in part to devise a statement of the site's purpose, which should be a prevalent concern early in the design process. And, of course, along with generation 4's parameter of engagement comes the requirement for the site to support all other parameters: communication, visual appeal, and utility. The reasons for this should also be clear. Returning to the example of the crafts site, every site needs to communicate; a site that encourages interaction among visitors, provides instruction to hobbyists, and allows enthusiasts to purchase online requires utility; and all these goals require visual appeal, without which a site will fail to entice.

Thus, from the needs statement comes a clear idea of the Web site generation of the project, the parameters it will support, and the site's purpose. The needs statement should be considered a foundation to the goals and plan for the site, one to which the design team returns as the project goes through the various stages of development. By looking at what desires lie beyond what now exists, developers can more clearly see the goal for the Web site, and its value to the business. This helps identify the qualities that will be crucial to the site's success. Following the needs analysis process before arriving at a goal or goals for the site is a means of avoiding the tendency to think within the confines of what already exists for a site's owner, of providing merely an electronic version of what the site's owner already has.

By combining users' needs with the client's needs, main navigational possibilities begin to appear to support the design and prototype efforts in the second phase of the site design project. For instance, the crafts store's needs are for the Web site to promote and support craft hobbyists, encourage people to purchase craft supplies, and create opportunities for learning new craft hobbies and planning projects, all in an effort to stimulate business and the number of returning customers. As shown in Figure 5.6, these needs naturally overlap with users' interests, thus suggesting the main categories of user interests are likely to support the client's needs as well. Linking client needs to related user interests through general categories is one way to come up with the main navigational sections of a Web site.

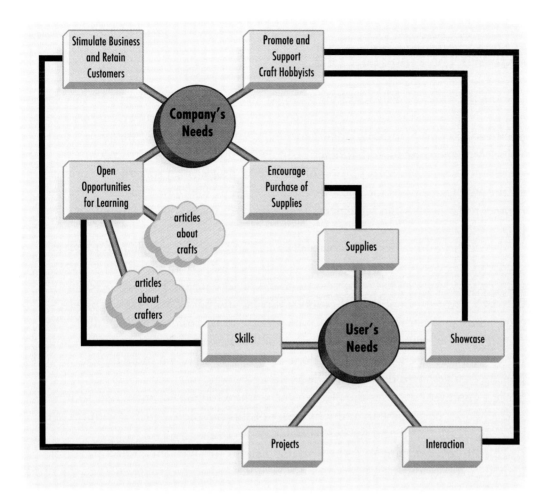

FIGURE 5.6 User and Client Needs Combined

 **activity**   **USER PROFILES AND SITE PATHS**

Explore a Web site to determine three profiles of users who might be expected to visit that site and report your experience from the viewpoint of each user.

Go to the MSN House and Home Advisor site (houseandhome.msn.com/default.aspx) and explore the site. Create three profiles of possible users of this site, describe them, give them names, and identify their needs. Assuming the role of the first user profile, enter the site. Search for what you need. Make notes and copy screen captures to describe what you find that is of value to you. Visit the site again, assuming each of the remaining two roles.

Write a two- or three-page report with supporting screen captures, and provide the following:

1. A summary of each of the three roles and what you experienced using the site from the viewpoint of each user profile.

2. Your general observations about how the site anticipated varying user profiles to provide experiences that were different, customized, and valuable to people who fit that profile. Explain how the site supported or did not support the user profiles you developed.

CREATING THE PROJECT PLAN

Site Specification and Standards document
The formal, detailed statement of the product the Web design team will produce for the client. Essentially a contract defining the nature, scope, and duration of the work to be performed.

Project Management Plan
A detailed description of how the work will be carried out, those responsible for doing the work, locations of existing material, indications of material needing to be created, types of resources to be included (text, audiovisual, or data files), and deadlines.

Defining the project involves writing a project plan. Although project plans vary somewhat by designer and project, the plan generally includes two essential sections: a **Site Specifications and Standards document** that defines the results of the project and a **Project Management Plan** that describes how the project will be carried out. The Site Specifications and Standards portion of the overall project plan specifies the product, and the Management section specifies the process. The site project plan is a written document that defines the agreements that have been reached between the Web developers and the client.

The design firm writes this project plan and presents it to the client for review. Because of this document's importance, it is usually not written in one review cycle but might require several cycles of presentation and revision to reach a clear agreement. With each new version of the definition and plan, another layer of expectations, assumptions, and clarifications rises to the surface, to be explored and handled. The time for such back and forth between client and designer is better spent at this point than later when more work has been done and it becomes much more difficult to make extensive changes. This document reflects the agreements that have been reached and, after it is approved, serves as the plan for the work to follow. For many Web projects, the facilitation, development, and refinement of this site project plan document is its own project task, to be paid for by the client.

This approved document is the working plan for the Web site project. If adjustments are made to this plan later, they can be noted using direct references to the plan. When these adjustments cause delays and additional expenses, this also can be noted with references to the originally approved plan.

Site Specifications and Standards Document

As stated previously, the product portion of the formal agreement between the client and the design team is called the Site Specifications and Standards document. The purpose of this document is to formalize the needs statement that was developed as a result of the needs analysis process, and to agree upon at least the following six elements as part of the project plan:

- **Goal Statements** The needs statement information is translated into measurable goals.
- **User Profiles and Scenarios** Early ideas about the types of users who will use the site.
- **Content Requirements and Sources** List of the content required for the site in detail.
- **Technical Requirements** Description of the technical requirements for the site.
- **URL Selection** Information on available URLs should be part of the initial planning.
- **Clarified Expectations** Expectations regarding client "identity" and creative direction.

This document is important to ensure that commonality of expectations has been established between the client company and the design team creating the Web site. Even when the Web site design team is composed of staff members who are internal to the site sponsor, it is essential to develop this document, obtain agreement on its main points and issues, and then follow it after agreement has been reached and the project begun.

GOAL STATEMENTS   Based on the needs-analysis information gathered earlier, it is time to write an official statement of goals for the site. A Web site cannot be all things to all people, although the needs analysis might have made the client think that its Web site should try to meet all of the identified possible needs. Arriving at a clear goal statement for the site requires making choices. The Web designer can help the client understand that a Web site without a clear purpose is headed for problems. Designers, clients, and users will not benefit from such sites.

To avoid an undefined goal, translate the findings from the needs analysis into a specific, measurable statement of purpose. This statement will be a more specific version of the general needs analysis, comparing each needs statement with the purposes for Web sites covered in Chapter 2 and summarized in the following list:

- Assist the search for knowledge
- Support decision making and problem solving
- Help users accomplish tasks
- Provide opportunities for interconnection
- Provide opportunities for recreation

A Web site's goal statements should be written in terms that are clearly understood and can be measured. A goal statement can be too general. For example, a too-general goal statement might say that the site will "improve customer service." This statement does not indicate how the improvement will be measured, so the site sponsor will not know if the Web site is achieving this goal. A measurable version of this vague goal statement could be modified to read "the site will provide 24/7 access to answers about common problems and how to resolve them, and will decrease telephone service calls by 20%." This statement is more specific: it explains what types of questions users can have answered on the site and provides a goal that is measurable (reducing service calls by 20%). (See Chapter 4 to review the usability.gov/ Web site's guidelines concerning performance and preference goals.)

Consider another example: For a popular theme park Web site, a goal statement might be "to provide information to people with disabilities to help them know they would have a positive experience visiting the park." A more measurable version of this goal statement might be "to increase the number of people with disabilities visiting the park by 200 per month by providing Web site information and interaction that demonstrate that they would have a positive experience visiting the park."

It might be hard to arrive at clear goal statements without first writing a set of goals as a means to guide discussion. Even if the client has provided extensive input concerning the Web site's needs, a design team might need to evaluate and develop these ideas to fit the team's criteria. These goals might turn out to be replaced by other, more concrete, realistic goals. Goals might change to respond to a new vision of the Web site's purpose. At this stage, it is important to write down specific goals that can at least begin the discussions that will eventually lead to a Web site with a clear purpose. These goals are presented and adjusted as needed. Because of greater experience with Web sites and how they are constructed, the designer can bring to the goal statements additional substance and potential. In particular, the designer can help the client see how connections and links can be made to expand the value of the site, assisting with the "teaching" task of helping the client see the potential and power of the Web as a hyper-medium. The designer can help push the Web site goals beyond the "legacy" concepts of what exists for the "brick-and-mortar" business, toward what more will be possible given the 24/7 interconnectedness of the Web.

USER PROFILES AND SCENARIOS A second important part of the Site Specification and Standards document consists of user profiles and scenarios, which are preliminary ideas about the specific types of users who will use the site and why. These user profiles and scenarios are preliminary to, and become the basis for, detailed navigational plans for the site's informational structure (a process covered in detail in Chapter 6, *Phase II: Design and Produce*). Nonetheless, while compiling the user profiles—written earlier to determine users' needs—and defining the user scenarios, the design team will most likely begin to identify some of the navigational possibilities.

Returning to the crafts site example, outline sample scenarios for actual sessions using the site. Using profile 3, Terry, the following are examples of possible scenarios.

Scenario #1 Terry enters the site to explore ideas for projects she could do herself to decorate her home. Beginning with a visit to the Craft Project Ideas section of the site, she uses the scroll-down list to explore several types of projects (embroidery, rug making, crewel, knitting, crochet) and selects two projects that she wants to create: one an embroidery project and the other a hooked rug. She then wonders how difficult it will be to learn these crafts and goes to the Crafts Corner section of the site where she goes through the online tutorials and prints out instructions to get her started. While there, she joins two discussion groups already in progress, one with people who enjoy embroidery and the other with people involved in rug making. Reassured that she will be successful, she visits the Everything-You-Need Shop section of the site to purchase the basic project kits including the Tools and Supplies Needed list for each project. She purchases everything on the list and expects that this list will be complete for each project. She completes her order, and arranges to have everything delivered to her this week, using the express shipment option.

Scenario #2 Terry has completed the hooked rug, and it is a beauty. She decides to return to the site to get instructions about how and when to enter her rug in the Crafts Showcase. She learns that she will need a digital picture of the rug and makes plans to create and upload one to the showcase area. While she is on the site, she decides to purchase her next hooked rug project kit. She also reads the recently posted notes from her two discussion groups and responds with her own comments. Two of the members of the hooked rug discussion group are from her area, so the three of them exchange e-mails and plan a meeting. Her embroidery discussion group is talking about some new Christmas stocking kits. Terry moves to the shopping section of the site to take a look and check on prices. She ends up purchasing a rug kit and three of the stocking kits, again using the Tools and Supplies Needed list provided with each project to make sure she will have everything she needs to complete the projects.

Scenario #3 Terry's 9-year-old daughter is interested in Terry's embroidery projects, so Terry decides to look for project kits that would be appropriate for her daughter, who is just beginning to learn crafts. She believes that it is important for her daughter to be successful in each project she takes on so she does not become frustrated and lose interest. She visits the Spotlight on Crafts E-zine section of the site and uses the search utility to look for articles about what would be a good sequence of projects for her daughter's age group. She also explores the section of the site called Kid's Krafts Korner, and finds a new set of discussions, teaching tools, and project ideas. She decides to show her daughter this section of the site and lets her make her own choices about what to do first, but provides some guidance concerning a good sequence of craft project challenges. They will shop together this evening.

The purpose of developing scenarios is to anticipate the ways the site will be used, and to imagine what a typical user will need to be successful and what will encourage the customer to come back. In the sample scenarios for the Terry profile of users, for example, it is clear that it is important to provide Tools and Supplies Needed lists to go with each project so that when orders arrive users will have everything they need to get started. Substantive content (articles, tutorials, discussions) is needed as well as products available for purchase. There might need to be a special area for children, with its own content and themes.

As well as providing ideas about the main areas of the site, looking at scenarios also provides the beginning of a navigational structure for the site. In this crafts site example, some of the areas (and associated navigation) for the Terry profile of visitor would include: Crafts Project Ideas, Crafts Corner, Kid's Krafts Korner, Everything-You-Need Shop, Spotlight on Crafts E-zine, and Crafts Showcase.

Now, look at an example with a bit more complexity than that of the crafts store. Consider a project in which the design team's responsibility is to develop the Web site for a new annual business and technology expo. Profiles of visitors to the site would be developed for each of the following groups: sponsors, speakers, exhibitors, and attendees. Each type of visitor has a different fundamental interest in the expo, and thus each needs to find specific types of information from the Web site. Scenarios of use based on these profiles make some areas of the site interesting only to particular groups, and not to others. For example, a sponsor might want to know who the speakers are, but would not necessarily want to sign up to be a speaker. Other areas of the Web site might be of interest to more than one group, but for different reasons. For example, exhibitors and visitors might want to view a list of exhibitors. An exhibitor might want to learn about which competitors are going to be exhibiting at the conference, while a visitor might want to know what different types of exhibits there will be.

The design team might start by focusing on one of the four defined groups of users, the attendees. The general profile might state that anticipated attendees are "individuals who are involved in local businesses, as owners or employees, with interests in networking with other business people and gaining access to additional information about technology and how they might take advantage of it." This profile could be refined. For instance, some attendees might be business owners who are planning to attend the expo only to check out the exhibits. The following list shows an example of the profiles developed for the anticipated attendee group of visitors to the Business and Technology Expo site.

- Business owner or employee
  - Wants to network with other businesses
  - Wants information about technology
  - Needs to decide whether to attend expo
  - Might also want to consider speaking or exhibiting

The design team then uses these profiles to identify what use scenarios the typical attendee might want to follow when visiting the Web site. For example, the following list of questions might be asked by a potential attendee:

- What is the conference about and what is its purpose?
- What benefits would I receive if I participate in the expo?
- What will the speakers be presenting?
- Who will be exhibiting?
- How can I register as an attendee?
- When and where is the expo? How do I get there?

In addition to these questions, some of the attendees might want to consider becoming speakers or exhibitors, two of the other profiles of anticipated Web site visitors. Figure 5.7 illustrates some of the anticipated questions visitors might ask and the corresponding places of information on the Web site they might visit to inform their decisions about the advertised event.

The Web designers must also consider that several of the defined visitors might ask the same questions, but the answers would be different depending on their user profiles. For example, the answer to the question "What benefits would I receive if I attend?" would be different if an attendee, a speaker, an exhibitor, or a sponsor asked the

FIGURE 5.7 Possible Visitor Scenario

question. This question might require unique responses, but each visitor type would get the same answer to the question about the time and location of the expo.

Working through actual scenarios of Web site use as part of developing the Site Specifications and Standards is an essential part of the documented agreement. Later, these scenarios will be used by the design team to determine the practical relations among the bits of information available on the site and to construct the site with a focus on usability. Although different types of users can end up visiting the same pages, they might do so in a completely different order, with a different intent, and for a different goal. Chapter 6 will show how to organize material by focusing on the information particular users will want to find and when they will want to find it, as well as by focusing on the logical sequence of the material itself.

CONTENT REQUIREMENTS AND SOURCES A third part of the Site Specification and Standards document involves listing the content required for the site in as much detail as possible. This includes all content types: text, images, and any other media that will be used. The client also might use forms routinely to collect information about their customers; these will need to be incorporated into the site. Company logos and their various renderings will certainly be needed. For the Business and Technology Expo site, for example, content includes registration forms, sponsor logos, maps to the location, and a map of the exhibition area.

Much of the text and graphic material for the site might be available in electronic format. These materials can be in a variety of file formats, but as long as the files are digital, they can be converted. It is always more expedient to convert from one digital format to another, using copy and paste or other conversion options, than to input material from scratch. For example, images might be in file formats that can be converted to GIF or JPG files. Documents in word processing files can be converted to HTML files, inserted into Web pages using copy and paste, and then revised as needed. Directories of sales or service staff in a company database can be extracted and converted for use. Some material might not be in digital format, but many types of documents are easily converted with the use of scanners, **OCR** software, and image-editing software.

One useful strategy for listing and organizing content elements is to develop a complete matrix (or table) of all content elements, including where and how to obtain those that already exist, and which elements need to be developed from scratch. For each element of content cited in the matrix, fill in these essential details:

- Description of the element
- Type of content
- Whether the content already exists in some form
- For each element that already exists:
  - Current format
  - Who has a copy

Figure 5.8 shows how such a matrix might look. To make this more useful, the matrix becomes part of the Project Management Plan, with information added to indicate completion dates and who is responsible for each item.

OCR
Optical Character Recognition. A process by which a computer recognizes printed or written characters when they are not available as binary codes (as in a word-processed document). An image of the text is scanned into the computer, and each character is analyzed and translated into a character code.

Description	Type of Content	Does Content Exist?	Format of Existing Content (File Name)	Who Will Create or Adapt?
photograph for home page	image	yes	JPG file (image1.jpg)	design team
background art for home page	image	yes	JPG file (image2.jpg)	design team
copy for home page	text	yes	DOC file (maintext.doc)	client
text for primary link pages	text	no	X	client
Readme file	text	no	X	design team
navigation bar	art	yes	GIF (nav.gif)	design team
product images	imago	yes	product0001.tif product0836.tif	client
product descriptions	text	yes	product0001.txt product0836.txt	client
company mission	text	yes	DOC file (mission.doc)	client

FIGURE 5.8 Web Content Matrix

At this point, a number of standard questions must be resolved. If material already exists, is it copyrighted, and is it necessary to obtain permission to use it? The design team is responsible for ensuring that all copyright issues are resolved. For content that needs to be adapted or created, what are the specifications for file size, image quality, sound, or video elements? For any new elements that will be developed, planners need to think about the required approval processes. After approval, how will these approved files be transmitted to the designers and what range of changes will be allowable before additional approvals are necessary?

It might not be possible during this stage of the project to list every item that will be used on a Web site. Many details become clear only after a portion of the work has been done and unforeseen needs give rise to the need for more material. At this stage, a design team should aim for agreement about the major materials needed and their sources, to produce early models. Major materials needed early in the project include content elements for the home page and primary routes through the site. Material that will play a major role in accomplishing the purpose of the site or that will constitute a substantial portion of the site might also be included in the list of content needed early in the design process.

TECHNICAL REQUIREMENTS A fourth part of the Site Specifications and Standards document is a complete description of the technical requirements for the site and how they will be handled. If the site is to be internally hosted by the client company, some of the essential questions that must be answered in the Site Specifications and Standards document are:

1. Will the existing information technology (IT) staff handle the additional work involved in this or will additional personnel be needed?
2. Will sufficient internal staff resources be provided for both the technology and the user support needs?
3. What will be the impact in terms of security of essential internal resources such as proprietary information, payroll and financial information, student records, and whatever other information is private and critical to the enterprise? What are the needs for **encryption** and **secure data sending**?
4. Will there be programming requirements that are necessary to communicate between the Web site and internal resources and databases?
5. Will the designer be able to gain access to the internal system to upload files and otherwise accomplish the tasks needed for the design and development of the site?

If the site is to be externally hosted, there are an equal number of essential tasks and questions. First, the range of options for host services must be reviewed and compared. (These options are presented in Chapter 7, *Phase III: Launch, Maintain, and Improve the Site.*) Investigate the cost of external hosting. Not all services charge the same. The cost, of course, is affected by the services a hosting service provides, and these issues should be investigated carefully. A Web-hosting service must meet the requirements of the site. Support should include the following assurances:

- Host capabilities (for example, server capacity) are adequately expanded as additional clients and needs are added.
- Host capabilities include "redundant" systems as backup in case one system goes down and the other needs to step in to pick up the load.
- The host provides 24-hour server support to ensure that there are no lapses in service.
- The host provides 24-hour client support services, as needed, while the site is being developed and implemented.
- The designer (or design team) can count on the host site installing on their servers whatever extensions are needed for the site to operate (see Table 5.2).
- Arrangements can be made to use the host site as a "staging" site during the design and development phases of the Web site project, and before the site goes "live."

Issues relating to the technical requirements of the site should be resolved in advance and these plans and any associated constraints should be incorporated as part of the site project plan. These are not matters to leave until later, when assumptions that have been made about resources turn out otherwise, and the site is unable to function properly because of something that could have been resolved earlier or handled differently from the outset.

During the process of formally planning for the technology requirements of the project, adjustments can be made to the scope of the work, moving some expectations to future phases of the Web site project. In-depth discussions of the technology requirements also might lead to a change in general strategy. For example, an initial plan to host the site internally might change to a plan for using an external host after a full understanding of the support requirements for the Web site project have been considered.

---

encryption
Conversion of data into secret code so it will be unreadable if viewed by someone not intended to receive it. Only intended recipients should be able to decrypt data to make it readable again. Widely used to protect sensitive data against eavesdropping or theft during transmission via the Internet.

---

secure data sending
Ensures the security of online financial transactions. Identifies the merchant and all banks involved in a transaction by using a "digital wallet" application. Prevents identity fraud by any party involved and keeps credit card numbers secure.

TABLE 5.2 File Types, Software, Tools, and Extensions

File Type	Software Tools	File Extension	Notes
HTML	Beginner's level: FrontPage Professional level: Macromedia Dreamweaver, or Adobe Golive	.html (or .htm)	• Files can be created in HTML format, or created in another format and then converted. Examples of files that can be converted include Word documents, PowerPoint presentations, Excel spreadsheets, and Access databases.
Graphics	Bit-mapped images created using paint programs such as MS Paint, edited using image-editing programs such as Adobe Photoshop; vector-based images created using drawing programs such as Adobe Illustrator, and CorelDRAW	Graphics Interchange Format (.gif, .gif97a, .gif89a)	• Needs no plug-ins and works in all browsers. • Limited to 8-bit color palette (256 colors) and best for solid-color images. • Supports transparency (making the image's background color transparent so it can better integrate into the page). • Allows interlacing (building the image from blurry to sharp while it is still being downloaded).
		Joint Photographic Experts Group (.jpg, .jpeg)	• Supports millions of colors; best for continuous-tone images such as photographs. • Allows selection among various degrees of compression. • Does not support transparency, so all images are rectangular. • Progressive JPG images allow quick previews, as with interlaced GIFs.
		Portable Network Graphics (.png)	• Highly flexible, supporting 256 as well as millions of colors. • Uses "lossless" compression (no data is lost during compression). • Supports variable levels of transparency. • Combines methods for GIF interlacing and progressive JPG to provide views as file downloads. • Provides gamma correction when an image produced on a Macintosh is displayed on a PC (too dark), or when an image produced on a PC is displayed on a Macintosh (too light).
Animation	Animated gif images (2D or 3D) are bit-mapped animation created using a range of software tools such as Fireworks, ImageReady, Live Motion, GIFmation, and GIF Construction Set.	Animated GIF format (.gif98a)	• Multiple images stored within a single file. • Image sequence played back or "streamed" to simulate motion. • Image begins showing immediately, while file is being downloaded. • Requires no special plug-ins or players. • Continues motion for a specified number of loops or indefinitely.

continues

File Type	Software Tools	File Extension	Notes
Shockwave	Presentations generally created in a multimedia authoring tool such as Macromedia Director or Authorware.	Shockwave multimedia format (.dcr)	• Supports streaming, interactive, multi-user content, including animation, video, sound, and graphics. • Requires Shockwave player to be installed on user's system. (Shockwave player is included with Windows and Macintosh operating systems, and with Netscape and Internet Explorer browsers.) • Presentations use a "cast" of multiple objects, controlled in scenes using a timeline (called a "score") to control the order and duration of the actions, and the transition effects between actions. • The cast can be created in a range of graphic formats, including .gif, .jpeg, and .png.
Flash movies	Either vector-based (and thus compact) or bit-mapped files with a range of built-in action and the potential for incorporating MP3 (near-CD quality) audio; very popular for vivid and exciting animation.	Flash format (.swf)	• Compressed, view-only format specifically designed for efficient delivery of graphics and animation over the Web. • Already developed codes for a range of actions available for selection. • "Morphing" function is available to create the intermediate images (tweening). • Viewers need Flash player installed, but this is widely distributed and free. • Objects can be imported from a wide range of graphics production tools.

URL SELECTION For a new site, selecting a URL should be part of the initial planning; this information should be included as part of the Site Specifications and Standards document. Conduct research to determine whether the proposed address is available (the client's idea for a name might already have been taken by somebody else). As with any naming process, there are likely to be a number of proposed candidates. Designers will be performing a valuable service to the client by helping choose the best option from among the top choices.

Naming the Web site bears careful consideration. The URL will be an important handle to the Web site and needs to be easy to remember and appropriate. Some memorable options might need to be dismissed because other sites with similar names would not make for positive associations. Some might be too close to the names of competitors, leading to the danger that a visitor coming to this client's site might end up at the site of the competition by mistake. Whatever URL is selected needs to be one that visitors can both remember and key easily.

input *refresh*

NECESSARY SYSTEM MAINTENANCE FOR WEB USERS

Probably one of the most important, yet overlooked, ways to ensure productivity and to reduce downtime when something goes wrong is to maintain the computer system's health. With a little diligence, harmful viruses and computer problems can be a thing of the past. Learn how to improve the computer's overall performance, recover lost data, schedule and perform preventive maintenance tasks, troubleshoot, and detect potential problems before they become apparent.

Several computer maintenance utilities are available to make short work of these tasks. Cleaning up a system sounds highly technical, but it usually involves clicking "Clean Now" (or something similarly intuitive).

Windows system tools can handle the basics of cleaning up unnecessary files, defragmenting the hard drive, scanning the drive for errors, and determining system information. The Maintenance wizard is available to schedule and perform these tasks automatically. Programs such as Norton System Works and McAfee's suite of utilities offer more advanced features than Windows system tools and can handle all this and much more.

SYSTEM MAINTENANCE CHECK For example, Norton System Check finds disk problems and Windows problems, improves performance, and gives the computer a preventive maintenance checkup. If one of the peripheral devices causes trouble, Norton also offers a diagnostic test to track down and fix problems. Norton's Speed Disk "defragments" the computer's hard disk (removes the gaps that result when files are added, changed, or deleted) and optimizes the remaining files by rearranging them for fastest access.

SYSTEM TRACKING AND RECOVERY Norton's Registry Tracker gives the computer user a bit more insurance, allowing recovery from unwanted changes to the system. To be prepared for such a recovery operation, Registry Tracker keeps track of changes made to Registry keys, text files, and data files and folders on the computer system. "Image" is another handy utility that takes a snapshot of the computer disk's critical file information, saving the disk's boot record, file allocation tables, and root information to a special file that can be recovered in the future.

Norton's Rescue Disk copies critical setup data and startup files to a set of removable disks. If the computer has trouble starting, the rescue disk set can usually get the computer running again. After the computer is running, the programs stored on the rescue disk set can help the user diagnose and fix computer problems, and restore the computer to full functioning.

Another essential item to remember after a computer crash is to allow Scan Disk, or one of the Scan Disk equivalents, to run to perform the function of closing files that were left open at the time of the crash.

SYSTEM INFORMATION If a system problem is serious and requires assistance from online or telephone technicians, it is important to provide these technicians the detailed information they need to assist with troubleshooting. Questions technicians ask can sound technical and intimidating. What kind of processor does the machine use? What type BIOS? What is the bus type? How many ports does it have—how many of these are serial and how many parallel? How much memory does it have, and what percent of the memory is being used? To answer these questions, the user needs to know exactly what is on the system. All of this information is available on the System Information screen, with selection tabs for System, Display, Printer, Memory, Drive, Input, Multimedia, Network, and Internet.

SYSTEM EFFICIENCY AND CLEANUP An essential element in keeping your computer running efficiently is to keep your computer "clean". Internet cache, Internet history, the Recycle Bin, temporary files, and lost cluster files all take up space on your hard drive.

Windows System Tools utilities, Norton System Works utilities, and McAfee utilities all have the capability to find and delete these wasteful files. They even have settings that enable a scheduling agent to automatically clean the computer at predefined times.

Another way to improve performance is by removing any unnecessary startup items that are wasting resources and slowing the boot up process. To see which programs are being automatically started up and brought into RAM when a computer boots up, look at the "system tray" (on the same line as the Start button). All of these programs begin using resources as soon as the computer boots up, whether or not they are opened or used. To determine what some of these programs are, hover the mouse cursor over each icon, and look at the text that describes what program it indicates as being active. If some of the programs that are active are unnecessary, they can be removed from the system tray by following the sequence illustrated in Figure 5.9.

As a general rule, do not turn off a startup item if you do not know what it does. Items that need to be activated during the startup process include Scan Registry, System Tray, any scheduling agents, and virus-protection software. Some examples of programs that do not need to be activated on system start-up include RealPlayer, MSN Messenger, Yahoo Messenger, Quick Time, Microsoft Office Startup, as well as many others. When a start-up item is removed, it should no longer appear in the system icon tray, but it still can be activated intentionally.

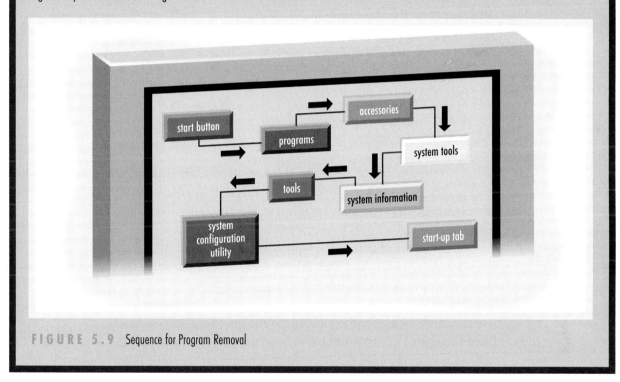

FIGURE 5.9 Sequence for Program Removal

After a URL has been selected and the research has been conducted to ensure that the URL has not already been taken, the address must be registered. This process takes time. It is a big decision, so a client probably will not make this decision in haste; it involves a registration process, which itself eats up time, and also requires coordinating efforts with the client's purchasing department. Thus, this procedure is best set in motion early in the project and as part of the written project plan.

Root Link www.internic.net/
Direct Link www.internic.net/whois.html
Why Go? To request a name and to register a domain name on the Internet.

Another issue to consider concerns who will be listed as the owners of the site. When a Web site is registered with Network Solutions (the original and most widely used Internet registrar), the names of all owners are listed in **whois**, along with contact information. This information is available to the public (by federal law), so care should be exercised in deciding who will be listed as owners of the site.

CLARIFIED EXPECTATIONS Finally, as part of the Site Specification and Standards document, it is important to state in writing any additional expectations the client has. For example, there might be expectations about the creative direction of the Web site project. If the client has particular preferences as to styles, colors, or other design issues, it is best to clarify these before substantial amounts of time have been spent designing and developing the site. This prevents wasting time and the potential for negative feelings and responses from the client. As with other requirements for the site, these expectations need to be part of the written agreement. If necessary, these elements might be circulated among those who will impact decisions about the client's site.

Project Management Plan

In addition to the Site Specifications and Standards document, a second part of the site project plan that needs to be in writing before moving forward is the Project Management Plan. The Project Management Plan includes the following details:

- **Scope of Work** A definition of the level of effort required, based on goals. Includes a definition of the phases of the work when the site is to be developed in stages.
- **Work Process, Tasks, and Subtasks** A statement of the work for the project, broken down into tasks and subtasks.
- **Roles and Collaboration Process** Specifics of who will complete each task, and the needed collaborations and contributions of the client and its agents.
- **Time Lines and Checkpoints** A map of the project across time, with specified times at which schedule and progress will be reviewed, and adjustments made when needed.

Again, even when the design team is composed of internal staff of the sponsor company, it is important to create and receive agreement on this formal Project Management Plan.

SCOPE OF WORK The scope of the initial site design project needs to be defined and agreed to in advance, taking into account the objectives of the site and the limitations of time and budget. Features that go beyond the scope of the current project can be added during subsequent projects. The Project Management Plan should state in writing the scope for the portion of the site's development that is to be accomplished as part of the current agreement, making reference to potential additional versions of the site that might follow in the future. An effective scope statement clearly defines when the project ends.

Developing a clear scope statement is important to the success of a project because it establishes in advance the terms measured by time and money. The scope statement performs these key functions:

- Forms the basis for the agreement between the client and the design team.
- Provides a basis for future decisions about the project, including what can and cannot be added into the project while in progress.
- Determines when the project has been completed.

A project scope statement might define a project to create a basic site as follows:

> Create a homepage and five derivative pages, using off-the-shelf technology. The client will supply edited text and digitized images that can be converted to Web format. The project will be accomplished within a one-month time span, with the level of effort defined as 60 person-hours.

This is a different scope of project than one that includes interfacing with client databases, providing for shopping facilities and secured payment by credit card, and creating entry screen animations designed in Flash. It is essential to develop a common understanding of the project scope from the outset so that all assumptions are clearly delineated and agreement is reached as to when this project ends and the next begins.

For example, the scope of the Business and Technology Expo site might be defined as follows:

> **Products/Deliverables** A basic Web site, using information provided by the Expo leadership team, will be developed using Dreamweaver and Flash. The site will include an animated entry page; a homepage; information pages for attendees, presenters, and sponsors; registration pages; and logos, write-ups, and links to all Expo sponsors' Web sites.

> **Level of Effort** The work is to be accomplished by a four-person design team within a four-week time frame, with a level of effort of 160 person-hours per week for a total of 640 person-hours.

> **Benchmarks** The prototype will be presented by Week 3 of the project, and changes made based on feedback, cycling through the presentation and revision process up to three times during that week. Throughout the prototype and full development phases of the project time line, edited copy will be provided by the client and placed into pre-established locations on the site's pages. The final product will be delivered by the end of Week 4, by the pre-agreed date needed for Expo registration to begin three months prior to the event. Updates and insertions of material as it is received will be performed by the design team until the project delivery and sign-off date, at which point subsequent revisions and updates to the site will be turned over to a Web site manager designated by the client.

WORK PROCESS, TASKS, AND SUBTASKS To define the project in terms of tasks, begin with the objectives and the basic design process model (as shown earlier in Figure 5.1). Consider how each major phase of the project is to be accomplished, and break it down into tasks and subtasks. This process of defining the project in terms of tasks must be carried out in sufficient detail to ensure that all contributors to the project know what to do and how to do it. It is also important to think through and plan how the various tasks will impact each other. This will have major implications in terms of the project time line. For example, some tasks can be completed simultaneously, while others will depend on the completion of an earlier task (or tasks) before they can be started.

For example, returning to the Business Expo site, the project task of "Prepare Resources" would be broken into subtasks such as:

1. Produce list of resources needed for site.
2. Determine priority levels of resources based on when they will be needed.
3. Assign resource-collection responsibilities for those resources that exist.
4. Assign resource-creation responsibilities for those resources that do not exist.
5. Create a repository and file transfer process for resources to be gathered together.
6. Upload and log resources as they become available.
7. Adapt resources to the design formats and file types planned for the site.
8. Prepare and distribute regular reports of missing elements and their priority levels.

ROLES AND COLLABORATION PROCESS   With a clear and complete list of tasks and subtasks, assignments can be made, including:

- Who will do which tasks?
- How are tasks handed off to the next person responsible for working on a task?
- What communications process and plan will be used so that those assigned to dependent tasks know the status of earlier tasks and are able to plan their time and work?

When gathering resources, the design team needs to know who has what and who knows what within the client organization. Technical logistics of file exchange should be considered, as well as important decisions about cost versus quality when a resource is to be created from scratch, and when it will involve rewriting and/or repurposing existing materials. These questions must be asked:

- How will the client assist?
- Who within the client organization will be the key source of information?
- Who will be assigned when materials need to be located, created, or converted to digital formats?
- What will be the priority level given to this participation from the client organization's staff?
- What approvals will be needed, and from whom, when decisions must be made that will impact the project costs and/or time line?

TIME LINES AND CHECKPOINTS   These tasks and subtasks are then plotted across time. Checkpoints and times when review and input are needed are inserted and highlighted so that all are aware of the key time constraints, deadlines, and goals.

In a well-planned project, the various tasks and subtasks are plotted to produce a project time line. Tools such as Microsoft Project can be used to produce a **Gantt chart** (shown in Figure 5.10) to map out the entire project, how and when it will be conducted, and who will conduct it. Each subtask in the Gantt chart is further defined in terms of the following:

- **Assigned Duration** The length of time required to complete the task.
- **Assigned Resources** Both personnel and other resources needed to accomplish the work.

Gantt chart
A project management tool that plots tasks and subtasks against time, showing the duration and interdependencies of tasks.

- **Dependencies** Relationships among tasks, where a delay in one task will result in the delay of another.

This process makes explicit all requirements and expectations, including the key point of when the initial Site Design project will end and another project for Site Maintenance begin, should the client want to continue to receive services.

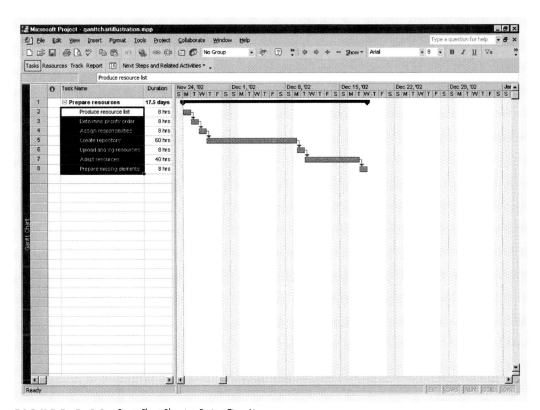

FIGURE 5.10 Gantt Chart Showing Project Time Line

For this activity, you will visit the Disney Online site and will practice looking at a site in terms of user profiles and scenarios of use based on those profiles. For this activity, complete the following tasks:

1. Visit the Disney Online site at Disney.go.com/park/homepage/today/flash/index.html and explore the various paths and options to become familiar with the site.

2. Create two user profiles for potential visitors to the site. Be as specific as possible about these users and their situations, characteristics, and needs.

3. Using your first profile, note a scenario of use for the site in which this person uses the site to accomplish something in particular. Be creative about this, but imagine that your profile person actually wants to accomplish the defined purpose.

4. Visit the Disney Online site to accomplish this purpose and navigate the site in order to do so.

5. Create a second scenario of use for this first user profile, and again navigate the site to accomplish the purpose stated in the scenario.

6. Now, use your second profile to design two scenarios of use and follow through with them on the Disney site.

7. Write a one-page profile and description of scenarios for each of your two profiles, adding your comments about the degree to which the site was successful in meeting the needs of each profile and scenario of use combination.

apply & practice

Online Quiz

As a review of the key concepts in this chapter, define the terms in the following:

brainstorming	OCR
encryption	Project Management Plan
intranet	secure data sending
needs analysis	Site Specifications and Standards document
normative technique	whois

After you are confident that you understand this chapter's content, go to this book's Internet Resource Center (IRC) at www.emcp.com/ and take the self-test online quiz for this chapter. Review any questions you answered incorrectly, and then study the related chapter material again. Retake the online quiz as many times as you need to achieve full mastery (90–100%).

Topics Roundtable

1. What is one area in which you are relatively expert? What are some of the specialized terms used by people who are expert in that area? Explain what some of these terms mean.

2. What is one retail business that you frequent and purchase from regularly? Describe what "exists" already when you visit this store or service in person. What would you like to have available as you deal with this business that goes beyond what exists from face-to-face encounters? Compare what exists to what you want, and from this make a list of the unmet needs that offer potential for this enterprise's Web site to go beyond what is already in place in its physical setting.

3. What is your user profile when you visit a site such as Amazon.com, Travelocity.com, or Disney.com? What would be a typical scenario of use for you when visiting each of these sites?

4. If you were taking the lead in planning a site for your family reunion in the Smoky Mountains, what content would you list that would be needed on the site? Where would you obtain these content elements?

5. Give some examples of URLs that are easy to remember and appropriate to the site and enterprise with which they are connected. Give some examples of URLs that are not easy to remember or use. What are some of the critical points about URL names that you would relay to a client during the URL selection process?

6. If you were forming a site design team to carry out a site design project you had been awarded, what would be some of the key understandings you would want with team members from the outset of the project? What characteristics of team members would you look for and consider most important as you selected members of the team?

window to the web

WORKING WITH IMAGES

➤ Download images from Web pages.
➤ Insert images on Web pages.
➤ Add borders to images.
➤ Use images as a Web page background.
➤ Add alternative text to images.
➤ Create a report on copyright-free graphics resources, formatting that material in HTML.
➤ Gather and insert images into your Web pages.

technical walk-through

Text-only Web pages are monotonous, making it difficult to attract and maintain viewer interest. The use of images enhances Web pages and increases the chances that viewers will want to stay and view their content. Images can play several roles on a Web page. Some are used because they are attractive, while others are used for informative purposes. Many images fulfill both these roles at the same time. Images can often supplement text, or even eliminate the need for text altogether. Images can even perform a functional role when they are used as links to other information or resources.

Images

Many different digital image formats exist, some of which are unsuitable for use on Web pages. The ideal image format for Web page use is supported by all browsers and uses a compression technique that produces small image files. The three image formats that meet these requirements are GIF (Graphics Interchange Format), JPEG (Joint Photographic Experts Group), and PNG (Portable Network Graphics).

GIF images are the images most commonly used on the Web. The GIF format has several variations. One allows interlacing and transparency. **Interlacing** allows images to be displayed gradually, somewhat like a picture slowly coming into focus. **Transparency** allows the background color of a Web page to show through an image. A more recent GIF variation produces **animated** (moving) graphics. The GIF format only supports 256 colors, so it might not be suitable for all images. As a general rule, GIF is the best format for displaying drawings or illustrations.

JPEG images support more than 16 million colors and are therefore the best format to use for photographs. When used to display large images, a JPEG file will be smaller than a comparable GIF file because of the compression technology used.

PNG images are relatively new and are only supported by version 4.0 and later browsers. They offer interlacing and transparency, and produce smaller file sizes than the GIF or JPEG formats.

Web page images are not saved as part of a Web page document as they are in text files. Instead, they are located in separate files, with an HTML image source tag to direct the browser to the image's location so that it can be retrieved and displayed as part of the page. Because a Web page is thus made up of multiple files, the time required for the browser to retrieve all the necessary elements to show the page is a function of the total of all the various files involved. To ensure that a Web page does not take too long to load, it is important that image file sizes are kept relatively small. Many experts recommend that a single Web page be no larger than 100 KB (kilobytes) in size, with the smaller the better. Thus file sizes of the HTML pages plus all images added together should be less than 100 KB whenever possible. The excessive use of images on a page should also be avoided to keep the cumulative file size down. The exception to this rule is if the same image is repeated on a page, as this does not increase loading time because each image file only needs to be brought in once.

For these step-by-step exercises, you will need several images in GIF, JPEG, or PNG formats. Download these images from one of the many sites offering free graphics (see Figure 5.11) unless you already have files available for use. The following lists the URLs for several popular sites offering free photos, clip art, and other image types that can be used copyright-free for non-commercial purposes:

- Free Graphics at www.freegraphics.com/
- ClipArt.com at www.clip-art.com/
- Freefoto.com at www.freefoto.com/

You also can copy images off of any Web page, but you should be aware that these images are protected by copyright law *unless* specifically stated otherwise. If there is any doubt, contact the Web site owner for permission before using any image on your own site. Even when a site offers copyright-free graphics, it is essential to read and comply with the "terms of use" required by the owner of the images.

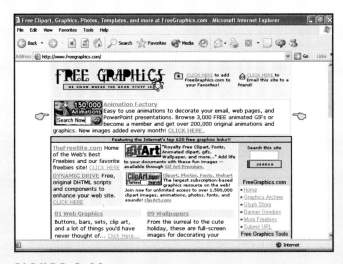

FIGURE 5.11

A number of Web sites offer copyright-free use of images for noncommercial purposes including Free Graphics at www.freegraphics.com/.

Copy images for use on your own Web pages:

1. Log on to the one of the free graphics sites described earlier.
2. Browse through the different image topics to find an image you like.
3. Click on the image thumbnail (a postage stamp sized reduction of the actual image) to enlarge it.
4. After the enlarged image is displayed, right-click to display an options list. Click on Properties to learn more about the image's size, format, and dimensions (see Figure 5.12).

FIGURE 5.12

This properties box indicates that the picture displayed is a JPEG image with a file size of 25,735 bytes (25.7 KB). The image's dimensions are 600 x 400 pixels.

5. After you have viewed the image properties, click OK. Right-click to display the options list again.
6. To download the image to your computer, select Save Picture As (*Internet Explorer*) or Save Image As… (*Netscape*) to open a File dialog box.
7. Use the File dialog box to indicate the folder or directory in which you want to save the image. Images for Web pages should be kept under the same root folder or directory as the files for your Web pages. If you are using a lot of images, you might want to create a subdirectory especially for images. Be sure that the images you choose are in GIF, JPEG, or PNG format. After you have indicated where you want to save the image, click Save.
8. Open the program you use for file management and make sure the image has been successfully downloaded to the location you indicated.

Image Tags

The image tag (<img />) has no end tag, so the closing slash is inserted within the open tag. All of the information relating to an image is contained within the image tag. All image tags contain an SRC (Source) attribute indicating the image file name and the path leading to the location of the image. When your images are stored in the same directory (or folder) location as your Web page files, an IMG (Image) attribute path will contain only the name of the image file between quotation marks: `<img src="name_of_image.extension" />`. Each directory (or folder) within a path is separated by a forward slash (/). For example, if you created a subfolder or directory named "images" in which to store your images, the path to those image files would follow this format: `<img src="images/name_of_image.extension" />`. You will learn more about creating paths in the next chapter's Window to the Web section. It is very important that the file name and path specified in the code matches exactly the actual file name and folder location of the file. A single difference between the code and the actual file name and path will result in the image failing to load. If everything is correct, the browser will be able to locate the image and display it in the designated spot on the page.

INSERT AN IMAGE

Place an image on a Web page:

1. Use your text editor to open the **shell.html** file.
2. Save the shell.html file as **images_practice_1.html** using the Save As command.
3. Key a title as indicated here:

```
<title>This Is My Images Practice Page</title>
```

4. Key an image tag between the body tags as indicated in the following code. Be sure to replace "*image_name*" with the exact file name of your image, and be sure to enter the correct file extension (.jpg, .gif, or .png). (Pay attention to upper and lowercase letters in the filename.) For now, your image should be located in the same root folder or directory as the images_practice_1.html file. If you are using a separate folder for images, adjustments will be necessary to direct the browser to the folder location where the image files are to be found.

```
<body>
<img src="image_name.extension">
</body>
```

5. Save the file and refresh your browser. If you used the right type of image and the file name and path you indicated was correct, your image should now be displayed in the upper-left corner of your browser's screen (see Figure 5.13).

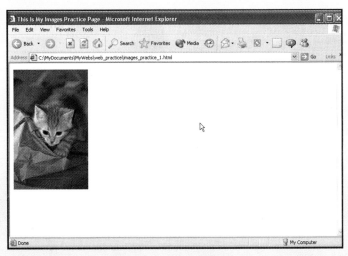

FIGURE 5.13
Image tags instruct browsers to locate and display images.

Image Height and Width

The height and width of an image in pixels should always be specified in an image tag (height="*size in pixels*" width="*size in pixels*"). A browser will display an image even without this information. However, it might take longer because the browser will need to download the image first to estimate the size of the image file, potentially slowing the time it takes to load the text on a page. When an image's dimensions are specified in pixels, the text portion of the Web page loads first, followed by the downloaded image.

Attempting to change the height and width of an image using specifications in an image tag is not a good strategy, for two reasons: it will not reduce the size of the file, and it might lead to image distortion. If you need to resize an image or reduce its file size, you need to use an image-editing program such as Adobe Photoshop or IrfanView. To determine the dimensions of an image, you can use your file-management program to locate the image file and then right-click to select Properties. The Properties box displays the height and width of the image in pixels. If you have already keyed an image tag in your Web page file, you can see the dimensions by viewing the image through the browser, and then right-clicking and selecting Properties from the options box that appears.

SET IMAGE HEIGHT AND WIDTH

Specify height and width dimensions in an image tag:

1. Return to your text editor to view the **images_practice_1.html** file.
2. Key height and width dimensions in pixels inside the image tag as indicated in the following code. Be sure to replace "*size in pixels*" with the actual size for the image you have chosen.

```
<img src="image_name.extension" height="size in pixels"
width="size in pixels" />
```

3. Save the file and refresh your browser. The image should appear exactly the same size as it did before, but now will load more quickly.
4. Return to your text editor to view the images_practice_1.html file.
5. Increase the values for the height and width of the image.
6. Save the file and refresh your browser. Your image will probably appear distorted (see Figure 5.14). Even if the image size is bigger or smaller, the size of the file remains unchanged because the height and width specifications only change the appearance of the image on the browser and not the file itself. The actual image is resident in another file and remains the same.
7. Change the dimensions back to their original values and save the file.

FIGURE 5.14

Changing image dimensions in an image tag will only change the image as it appears on the browser's screen, and often results in distortion. The image file itself remains unchanged.

Alternative Text

An alternative text description (ALT attribute) should be included in all image tags. Some viewers might be using text-based browsers, or they might have turned off the image-viewing capability of their browsers to increase the speed with which pages load. Many visually impaired people use browsers that can read Web pages aloud. An alternative text description allows all these viewers to know the subject of an image without having to view it. With the most recent browser versions, the ALT attribute text will be displayed when the cursor is rolled over the image or image location.

ADD ALTERNATIVE TEXT TO AN IMAGE TAG

Add an alternative text description to your image:

1. Return to your text editor to view the **images_practice_1.html** file.
2. Key an ALT attribute (alt=) and text description inside the image tag as indicated here. Change the text so that it is appropriate for the image you have selected.

```
<img src="image_name.extension" height="size in pixels"
width="size in pixels" alt="Description of image." />
```

3. Save your file and refresh your browser.
4. If you have a recent browser version, you should see the alternative text description when you roll the cursor over the picture. Those with image-viewing capability turned off will see an outline of the image with the alternative text description contained inside the outline (see Figure 5.15).

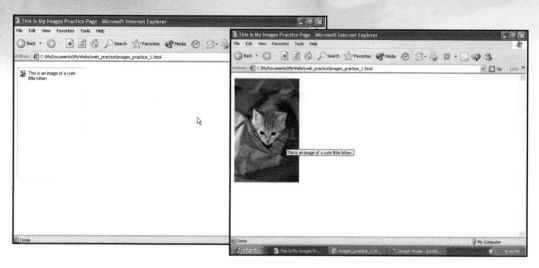

FIGURE 5.15

FIGURE 5.15

If a browser's image-viewing capability has been turned off, an outline of the image containing the alternative text is visible (left). The latest browser versions show an alternative text description when the mouse cursor is rolled over an image (right).

Vertical Image Alignment

The bottom of an image is aligned with any text in the Web file, by default. The vertical relationship of an image to adjacent text can be controlled using an ALIGN attribute (align=) and one of three vertical values: "top," "middle," or "bottom."

CONTROL VERTICAL ALIGNMENT

Vertically align your image with text:

1. Return to your text editor to view the **images_practice_1.html** file.
2. To see how your image behaves with text, key some text below the image tag as indicated here:

```
<img src="image_name.extension" height="size in pixels"
width="size in pixels" alt="Description of image." />
This is an experiment to see how vertical alignment can be
specified.
```

3. Save the file and refresh your browser. You will notice that the bottom of your image is in line with the text.
4. Return to your text editor.
5. Key an ALIGN attribute with a "top" value as indicated here (substituting the actual file name, image size, and alt text for your image):

```
<img src="image_name.extension" height="size in pixels"
width="size in pixels" alt="Description of image." align="top"
/>
```

6. Save the file and refresh your browser.
7. The top of your image should now be in line with the text.

8. Experiment by keying an ALIGN attribute with a "middle" value to place the image in the middle of the text (see Figure 5.16)
9. When you are finished, delete the ALIGN attribute and value and save the file.

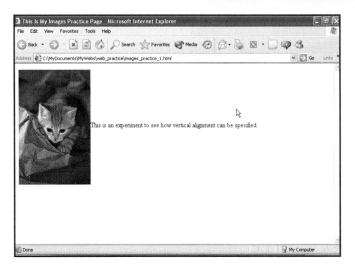

FIGURE 5.16
Images can be vertically aligned in relation to adjacent text by using the ALIGN attribute with one of three vertical alignment values: "top," "middle," or "bottom."

Horizontal Image Alignment

The ALIGN attribute can be used with "left" and "right" attributes to align an image to the left or right side of a Web page. This causes any text on the page to wrap around the right side of a left-aligned image, and to the left side of a right-aligned image. Only one ALIGN attribute can be used inside an image tag, so if an ALIGN attribute has been used to align the image vertically, you also cannot key an ALIGN attribute to align it horizontally. Tables can be used for horizontal image alignment, so this does not create a problem.

CONTROL HORIZONTAL IMAGE ALIGNMENT

Use the ALIGN attribute to control horizontal image alignment:
1. Return to your text editor to view the **images_practice_1.html** file.
2. Delete the text below the image tag and replace it with text as indicated here using copy and paste to produce the repetitions. You can substitute your own text if you like.

```
<img src="image_name.extension" height="size in pixels"
width="size in pixels" alt="Description of image." />
This is an experiment to see how vertical alignment can be
specified.
This is a horizontal image alignment test. This is a horizontal
image alignment test. This is a horizontal image alignment test.
This is a horizontal image alignment test. This is a horizontal
```

image alignment test. This is a horizontal image alignment test. This is horizontal image alignment test. This is a horizontal image alignment test. This is a horizontal image alignment test. This is a horizontal image alignment test. This is a horizontal image alignment test. This is a horizontal image alignment test. This is a horizontal image alignment test. This is a horizontal image alignment test.

3. Key an ALIGN attribute with a value of "right" inside the image tag:

```
<img src="image_name.extension" height="size in pixels"
width="size in pixels" alt="Description of image." align="right"
/>
```

4. Save the file and refresh your browser. The image on your browser screen should now appear on the right side, with the text wrapped to the left (see Figure 5.17).

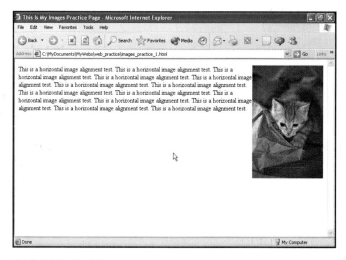

FIGURE 5.17

The ALIGN attribute can be used to wrap text around an image located on the left or right side of a page.

The Line Break Tag with a CLEAR Attribute

A CLEAR attribute (clear=) can be added to a line break tag (<br />) to instruct a browser to stop text from wrapping around an image and to resume below the image. It must be used in conjunction with a left or right horizontal ALIGN attribute. In the case of a right-aligned image, using a line break with a CLEAR attribute value of "right" causes any text located after the insertion point to resume again after it has "cleared" the object, in this case the image, that was the subject of the right alignment. If a line break clear value of "left" was entered, it would have no effect on the text because there is no left-alignment for the text to clear. An "all" value causes text to resume after it has cleared either a left- or a right-aligned image.

Place a line break tag with a CLEAR attribute with a value of "right" in your Web file to stop text from wrapping around the image:

1. Return to your text editor to view the **images_practice_1.html** file.

2. Key the line break tag (<br />) and CLEAR attribute inside the text to force the text to resume below the right-aligned image:

```
<img src="image_name.extension" height="size in pixels"
width="size in pixels" alt="Description of image." align="right"
/>
This is a horizontal image alignment test. This is a horizontal
image alignment test. This is a horizontal image alignment test.
This is a horizontal image alignment test. This is a horizontal
image alignment test. This is a horizontal image alignment test.
This is horizontal image alignment test. <br clear="right" />
This is a horizontal image alignment test. This is a horizontal
image alignment test. This is a horizontal image alignment test.
This is a horizontal image alignment test. This is a horizontal
image alignment test. This is a horizontal image alignment test.
This is a horizontal image alignment test.
```

3. Save the file and refresh your browser. All the text after the insertion point of the line break tag should be located below the image (see Figure 5.18).

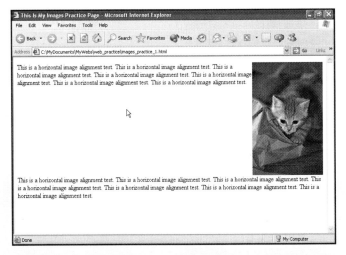

FIGURE 5.18

A line break tag with a CLEAR attribute and value (<br clear="right" />) has been inserted in the text of the HTML file, causing the text located after the insertion point to stop and resume again below the image.

Horizontal and Vertical Image Space

If you look at your image, you will see that the text closely abuts the image. Using an HSPACE (horizontal space) attribute (hspace=) inside the image tag creates white space on the image's horizontal borders. The value for the horizontal space is indicated in pixels. Vertical space can be created using a VSPACE (vertical space) attribute (vspace=).

Create horizontal and vertical white space around an image:

1. Return to your text editor to view the **images_practice_1.html** file.

2. Key horizontal and vertical white space attributes and values inside the image tag:

```
<img src="image_name.extension" height="size in pixels"
width="size in pixels" alt="Description of image." align="right"
hspace="20" vspace="20" />
```

3. Save the file and refresh your browser. The image is now surrounded by white space on all sides (see Figure 5.19).

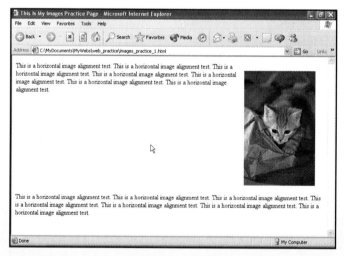

FIGURE 5.19

HSPACE and VSPACE attributes have been placed inside the image tag to create white space between the image and the text surrounding it.

Borders

Entering a BORDER attribute and value inside an image tag creates a border around an image. The border value is indicated in pixels. If you do not want a border around an image, enter a border value of "0" to avoid the possibility that some browsers might create a border around the image by default.

Add a border to your image:

1. Return to your text editor to view the **images_practice_1.html** file.

2. Key a BORDER attribute and value inside the image tag:

```
<img src="image_name.extension" height="size in pixels"
width="size in pixels" alt="Description of image." align="right"
hspace="20" vspace="20" border="5" />
```

3. Save the file and refresh your browser. The image is now surrounded by a thick black border (see Figure 5.20).

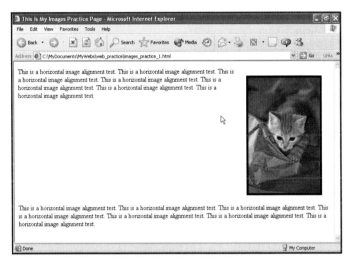

FIGURE 5.20

Keying a BORDER attribute and value inside an image tag instructs the browser to draw a border around the image.

Image Control with Tables

Image layout is easily controlled using tables. Combining your knowledge of table construction with what you have learned about creating and controlling images will allow you to create just about any Web page layout. It is a good idea to specify a BORDER attribute and value of "1" when working on tables for page layout. This makes it easier to troubleshoot the table if something goes wrong. After the table is finalized, you can change to a border value of "0" to make the border invisible.

Center your image by placing it inside a table:

1. Return to your text editor to view the **images_practice_1.html** file.

2. Delete all the code between the body tags.

3. Key the code necessary to create a three-column table, and place an image tag with a path to the image you want to appear in this location on the page, as indicated in the following code. Note that because this table will be invisible, it is not necessary to key non-breaking character entities ( ) to prevent the first and third cells from collapsing.

```
<body>
<table width="100%" border="1" cellspacing="0">
<tr>
<td></td>
<td align="center">
<img src="image_name.extension" height="size in pixels"
width="size in pixels" alt="Description of image." />
</td>
<td></td>
</tr>
</table>
</body>
```

4. Save the file and refresh your browser. The image appears within the second cell of the layout grid created by the table.

5. Change the border value from 1 to 0.

```
<body>
<table width="100%" border="0" cellspacing="0">
<tr>
```

6. Save the file and refresh your browser. The image you placed inside the table should appear in the center of your screen (see Figure 5.21), with the layout table now invisible.

FIGURE 5.21

Tables can be used to place images exactly where you want them on a Web page. This image has been centered using an invisible table.

7. It will take some time before you are entirely comfortable using tables and images together, so it is a good idea to practice this skill. Use the knowledge you have learned so far to reproduce the image and text layout in Figure 5.22.

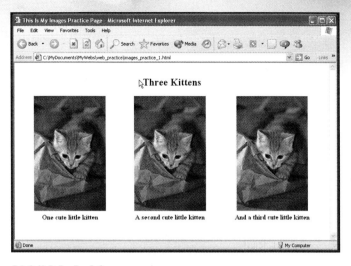

FIGURE 5.22

Use the skills you have learned so far to reproduce the image and text layout pictured in this browser screen.

Background Images

An image can be used as a Web page background by keying a BACKGROUND attribute inside a body start tag (<body>). The background attribute includes the path to the image file that will be used.

CREATE A BACKGROUND IMAGE

Create a background image:

1. Use your text editor to open the **shell.html** file.
2. Save the shell.html file as **background image_practice_1.html** using the Save As command.
3. Key a title:

```
<title>This Is My Background Image Practice Page</title>
```

4. Key the file name and extension for the image you want to use as a background inside the body start tag (<body>):

```
<body background="image_name.extension">
```

5. Save the file and use your browser to open and view it. The image you selected should appear as the background to the Web page (see Figure 5.23). If the dimensions of the image you used were too small, the image will "tile," or be repeated across the screen. This might be an effect that you want, but if not, you can use an image editor to adjust the image's dimensions. Your image also might be too dark for any text to be visible. This can be remedied by using an image editor to adjust the image's brightness, by changing the color of the text to increase the contrast, or by creating a table with a solid background to contain the text.

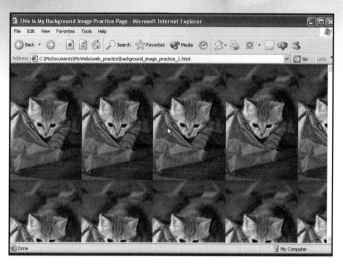

FIGURE 5.23

An image can be used as a Web page background. A BACKGROUND attribute with a path and file name for the background image was placed inside the body start tag to produce this effect.

Animated GIFs

Animated GIFs produce images that move on your Web page. The HTML code used to place an animated image on a Web page is exactly the same as that used to place a non-animated image. The only difference is that the image file is an animated GIF. Software is available to produce animated GIF images. Also, it is possible to locate and download animated GIF files from one of the free graphics sites listed earlier in this section. Download an animated GIF file for use in the following action.

ANIMATE AN IMAGE

Use an animated GIF file to produce an image that "moves" on your Web page:

1. Use your text editor to open the **shell.html** file.
2. Save the shell.html as file **animated_image_practice_1.html** using the Save As command.
3. Key a title:

```
<title>This Is My Animated Image Practice Page</title>
```

4. Key an image tag with the file name and extension for one or more of the animated GIF images that you downloaded:

```
<body>
<div align="center">
<img src="image_name.gif" />
</body>
```

5. Save the file, and open and view it with your browser. The animated GIF file you selected should "move" on your screen just like a miniature cartoon (see Figure 5.24).

FIGURE 5.24
Animated GIF files can be used instead of regular GIF images to create small cartoon-like images that move on your Web pages.

design project

1. Use a search engine to gather information on resources for copyright-free graphics similar to the graphics sites you used for this Window to the Web. Look for sites that you think would be helpful to you and to others, and pick a list of favorites. Make sure to gather notes that include any reference material that will be needed later, such as URLs, publishers, and authors. You will be comparing and annotating these resources in your Web site, so be sure to gather this information as well. Also, make notes about the terms of use requirements for using the graphics available from each of the sites you plan to include. Feel free to conduct any additional research you feel may be beneficial. Bookmark the sites so you can easily locate them again. Write a report summarizing your findings.

2. Examine other Web pages to determine how they use images to attract and inform viewers. Right-click to view the source code of the pages to see how they control image placement. If you see techniques you like, try to understand how they work so you can use those techniques on your site.

3. Create a new Web page (or pages) and use copy and paste to insert the text from the report you created about copyright-free graphics. Use the knowledge you have just gained to place images on your Web pages. Do not go overboard and place too many images or your pages will become slow to load and will turn off viewers with slow Internet connections. The images you use should be attractive, but they must serve a purpose and be related to the theme of your Web site. Be creative—use images in a variety of ways, not just as static illustrations. They can be used to divide sections, serve as table headings, and illustrate concepts—your imagination is the only limit. Some of your images can be used to link to other sections, or even other Web pages. Use comment tags to indicate any images that you want to use as links after you have learned that skill in the next Window to the Web. Provide alt text for all images you incorporate into your site.

CHAPTER

6

Phase II:
Design and Produce

cyber
visit

ROBERT DIETZ

Designer, Principal of Platform Creative Group

Design Viewpoint

"There are two main goals. First, usability. Regardless of how beautiful a site is, if it's not usable, it doesn't solve the communication problem. Second, making sure it's appropriate to the target demographic. For the people you are reaching, it's important that you design to them and not to yourself."

Resume

BFA, University of Washington; in 1995 began Dietz Design, which became Platform Creative Group, Inc. in 2001.

Clients

Nordstrom's, Rainier Investment Management, Adobe Human Resources department, Corum Group, and MSN.

Designer's Home Page

PlatformCreative at www.platformcreative.com/.

Insights

"Think. Results. (Pretty simple, huh?)"

"We find success working with clients who understand that differentiating themselves from their competition is about more than just design, it's about the messages they convey."

"Designers can end up projecting who they are and what they would like instead of what the target demographic would like. Site design is not about the designer's preferences. Apply the sensibilities you have developed to create for your target group, not for yourself."

PORTFOLIO

PlatformCreative at www.platformcreative.com/.

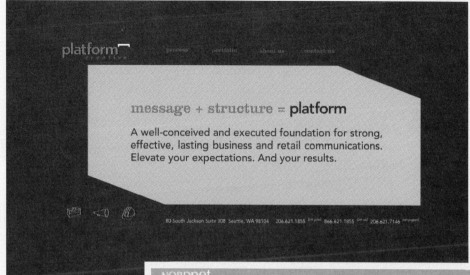

Nordstrom's Intranet

Objectives

➤ Outline the design process for Phase II of a Web site project, explaining the process and tasks for each part.

➤ Describe each set of tasks for Phase II and state how they are best handled.

➤ Identify the tools to be used for Phase II and explain how they are used to produce Web sites.

➤ Create a basic site design, structure, site map, and navigation plan.

➤ Describe how to prepare resources from those already available and how to create what is missing.

➤ Develop a site prototype for presentation to the client.

➤ Conduct reviews with the client, facilitating feedback exchange to reach agreement on changes and follow-up.

Having taken the first steps of a Web design project—becoming familiar with the subject matter, gathering preliminary content, defining the client's and the users' needs and the general purpose of the site, organizing the process, and coming to agreements with the client—the design team can begin work on the design and the prototype. This is an exciting part of designing because it calls for creativity, but it is also a stage in which methodical steps help keep the process organized so the team's creative efforts do not flag under a load of new, unfamiliar content elements.

DESIGN THE BASIC SITE

Phase II of a Web site project involves a cycle of the following steps (see Figure 6.1):

• Design the basic site.
• Prepare resources.
• Develop the prototype.
• Present prototype and obtain approval.
• Produce the full site.

Despite the seeming simplicity of this list of steps, meeting these basic objectives requires performing a large number of tasks.

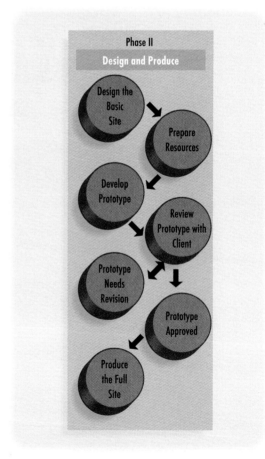

FIGURE 6.1 The Design and Produce Cycle

Create the Basic Design

Before tackling the details of the code or creating the graphics of a Web site, the first step in producing a Web site's design is to decide on the most basic features of the site—that is, what users will be able to do and how. Based on initial profiles of the types of users who will visit the site, begin to plot out how they would find what they came to the site for. Will they browse through options or search for them? What types of communications will be available on the site: bulletin boards, chat rooms, e-mail? Is audiovisual material appropriate, and, if so, what will be its purpose? At this initial stage of design, keep the design team thinking about the "big picture."

Design is more than just specifying the look and feel of the site. It involves coordinating the site's purpose with its technical and interpersonal features. Although it is tempting to just begin coding, intensive work on pages, graphics, layout, navigation, or any detailed aspect at this point is premature and detrimental to the overall project. Expert designers (and programmers) use the rule-of-thumb "the sooner you begin to code, the longer it will take."

DO YOU KNOW?

Question How many people did Tim Berners-Lee predict would be needed to create his initial vision of the Web? How many months did he think this project would take to accomplish?
Answer Berners-Lee thought it would take two people 6 to 12 months to complete the Web's first version.

With these general concepts of who the users will be and what they will do on the site in mind, it becomes possible to draw rough sketches of what the site's home page will look like. Figure 6.2 is an example of such a sketch. Many details will not yet be established, but even general ideas can suggest possible ways of organizing the material on the page. Some of the initial text (such as the purpose of the site) can be roughed in. Basic decisions such as where art is placed also can be made; realize, however, that some decisions made now might be revisited later and so should be made with the acknowledgment that changes are likely.

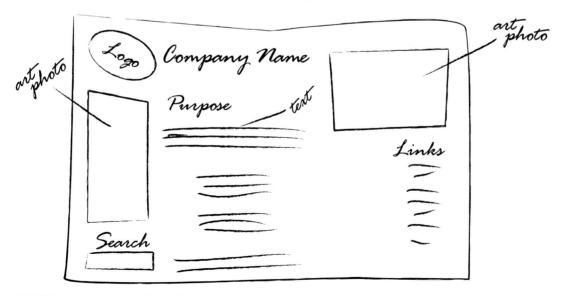

FIGURE 6.2 A Rough Sketch of a Home Page

INTEGRATE CONCRETE INFORMATION The design team can still focus on the big picture even if preliminary design ideas are based on concrete information that the client supplies. Some good design ideas come from working with concrete information. A client's mission statement could immediately suggest how much emphasis should be placed on e-commerce, for instance. As a result of the preparation the design team undertook (covered in Chapter 5), the team will be in a position to make some general decisions about which features will receive prominent treatment and which will play a supportive role.

Because the Web site will be entirely digital anyway (and thus it will be easy to move copy around using cut and paste), it can be productive and beneficial to rough in some actual elements of the site to experiment with basic design concepts. Again, this is not inconsistent with focusing on the big picture. Take some of the content the client has provided and create a set of demonstration pages consisting of ideas for the home page and several pages linked to it. Use some of the text the client has provided, such as the purpose statement for the Web site.

This early phase and these demonstration pages will not include finished copy material or complete designs of fully functioning Web pages. Rather, the emphasis is on considering preliminary ideas on how text and images will look together on the page. Initial plans for interactivity can be sketched in as well. Forms that users might fill out and ways for users to contact the site's sponsor, individuals listed on the site, or other users can be generally described. These pages should show rough ideas: where links might go, where text might go, and so forth. Figure 6.3 is an example of a rough demonstration page. The anchor tags need not be included, or if they are, the HREF attribute can be left empty, because the target pages have yet to be planned, named, and placed in the file structure. Because this stage is still exploratory, focus on the most elemental of HTML codes, not on JavaScript or database connections. Focusing on the big picture means exploring ideas and considering alternatives without committing yet to one plan in particular.

BE FLEXIBLE The work the design team does at this stage must be approved eventually by the client, which is another reason not to become overly invested in a favorite design idea at this point. Use a highly flexible process to rough in and experiment with the initial design. Consider multiple options and use tools that accommodate all of them. Paper and pencil sketches, note cards or sticky notes on a wall, or idea-modeling software provide better support for the process than anything that might move the project too quickly toward more "locked in" designs. As the guidelines from the usability.gov Web site say, saturate the design space with as many ideas as possible so you are sure to pick the best ones to show the client.

Root Link www.inspiration.com/

Direct Link www.inspiration.com/vlearning/index.cfm

Why Go? To learn about visual-learning techniques: alternative ways for organizing thinking as thoughts occur. Try out a trial version of Inspiration, an idea-modeling program that allows you to create diagrams freely as ideas come, generate outlines from the diagrams, and produce idea and concept maps for use in organizing the information for a Web site.

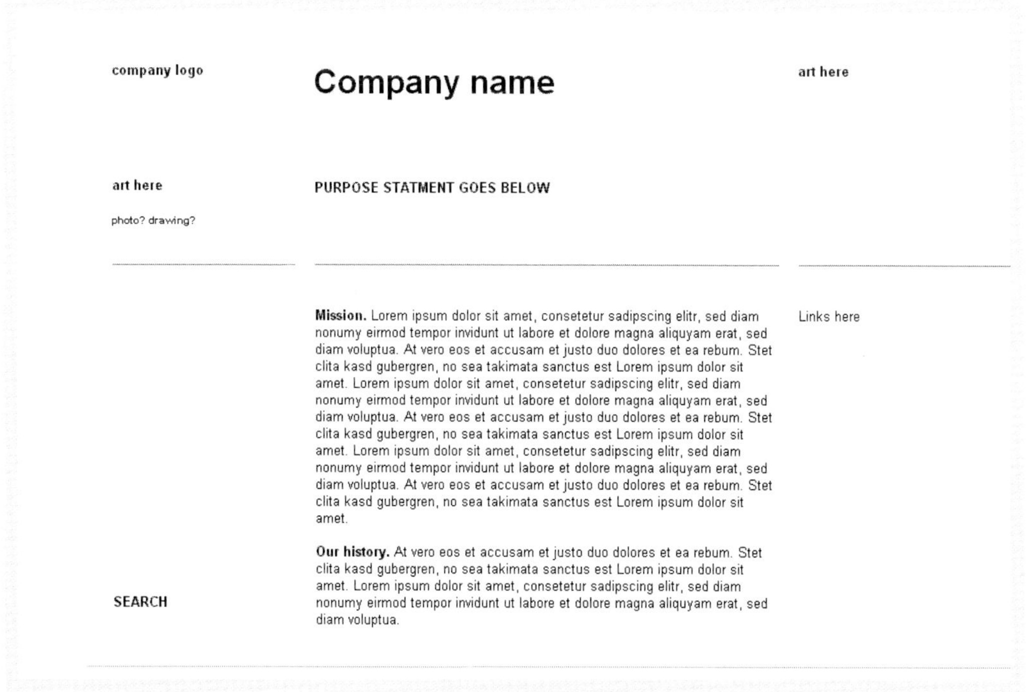

company logo   **Company name**   art here

art here   PURPOSE STATMENT GOES BELOW

photo? drawing?

_____   _____   _____

Mission. Lorem ipsum dolor sit amet, consetetur sadipscing elitr, sed diam   Links here
nonumy eirmod tempor invidunt ut labore et dolore magna aliquyam erat, sed
diam voluptua. At vero eos et accusam et justo duo dolores et ea rebum. Stet
clita kasd gubergren, no sea takimata sanctus est Lorem ipsum dolor sit
amet. Lorem ipsum dolor sit amet, consetetur sadipscing elitr, sed diam
nonumy eirmod tempor invidunt ut labore et dolore magna aliquyam erat, sed
diam voluptua. At vero eos et accusam et justo duo dolores et ea rebum. Stet
clita kasd gubergren, no sea takimata sanctus est Lorem ipsum dolor sit
amet. Lorem ipsum dolor sit amet, consetetur sadipscing elitr, sed diam
nonumy eirmod tempor invidunt ut labore et dolore magna aliquyam erat, sed
diam voluptua. At vero eos et accusam et justo duo dolores et ea rebum. Stet
clita kasd gubergren, no sea takimata sanctus est Lorem ipsum dolor sit
amet.

Our history. At vero eos et accusam et justo duo dolores et ea rebum. Stet
clita kasd gubergren, no sea takimata sanctus est Lorem ipsum dolor sit
amet. Lorem ipsum dolor sit amet, consetetur sadipscing elitr, sed diam
SEARCH   nonumy eirmod tempor invidunt ut labore et dolore magna aliquyam erat, sed
diam voluptua.

FIGURE 6.3 Demonstration Page

PRESENT THE DESIGN TO THE CLIENT After devising several possibilities, select only the best models to present to the client, because it is unnecessary (and unwise) to show the client every design idea. Choose those that best achieve the client's goals for addressing users and enabling them to accomplish worthwhile tasks. Consider whether the team's plans support the appropriate parameters of Web design and whether they uphold the standards of the Web site generation for which the team is aiming.

As these ideas are presented to the client, listen to the client's reactions. Determine the most reasonable way to respond to the client's concerns. Consider what should be done, make adjustments, and return the modified designs to the client for reactions. Do this over and over until the client and the design team agree on the general direction of the design. The flexibility of the tools and processes the team chooses will prove important assets during this exchange with the client. And, clearly, working with the client will establish good communication and clarify expectations. Several visits with the client might be necessary before the design team arrives at a clear idea of the basic design. But after the team and the client have come to some agreement about the direction of the design, work can proceed to the next stage.

Root Links www.extremeprogramming.org/
www.agilealliance.org/
Direct Links www.extremeprogramming.org/what.html
www.agilealliance.org/articles/index/ (also look at www.agilemanifesto.org/)
Why Go? To read about two software-development processes that emphasize contact with the clients during the development process. Written primarily for application software development teams, but applicable to Web design teams.

Select Editing Tools and Development Platforms

Although much of the planning at this stage can still be done using paper and pencil and hand sketches, the team should be thinking about which Web-development software to use. Even though it is possible to design entire sites by producing original HTML code, most designers use the considerable benefits of Web design editing software, and then make adjustments to the code (known as "tweaking" the code), as needed. This process takes advantage of the time savings of editing software, while preserving control of the final site. Many designers have a favorite package and do not switch just for the sake of variety. But some tools are more efficient in certain circumstances. Thus, determining which package to use is an important consideration.

Choices of tools range from WYSIWYG ("what you see is what you get," pronounced "wizzy wig") products that are fairly easy to learn but allow less control to the designer to tools for which the learning curve is somewhat steeper but are more powerful and flexible and better support designer control. Many editing packages include tools that simplify adding code-intensive features such as a **rollover**. Other tools might offer help in creating **active server pages (ASP)** and other programs that increase the functionality of a Web site. If a database is to play a role in a Web site, some HTML packages facilitate connections to **ODBC-compliant databases** and other data technologies. (See the Input/Refresh, "Some Common HTML Editing Packages" later in this chapter.)

Whether the basic HTML code is generated by hand or by using an editing package that generates the code, to make Web pages interactive and dynamic this basic HTML code needs to be supplemented with scripts, applets, and applications that perform tasks HTML was not designed to do. For example, data is processed behind the scenes of the Web page and is achieved with the help of such additions. By itself, HTML is insufficient for complex functionality.

These additions allow interaction with users, providing information a user requests, for instance; they support business functions, allowing individuals and businesses to order products and services from a Web site; and they can provide animation and other enhancements to make a Web page more interesting and appealing.

Having established the necessity of these add-ons, the next concern is the location from which the add-ons perform their tasks. Although most add-on scripts and programs originate from the Web server, sometimes the program scripts or applets are sent to the user's computer so that the data processing occurs there and results can be more immediate. Placing the program scripts or applets on the user's computer cuts down on the amount of work done on the server, which can become bottlenecked from being kept busy processing hundreds (perhaps thousands) of requests at the same time. But with commercial transactions, such as making an airline reservation, buying a book,

rollover
Sometimes called a "mouseover." Changes the look of a page element (usually a graphic image) when the user rolls the mouse over it.

active server pages (ASP)
A server-side scripting environment that supports dynamic Web pages by performing a variety of functions, including accessing information from databases stored on the server. Does not require Microsoft products to be developed; scripts can be written using VBScript, JavaScript, and PerlScript.

ODBC-compliant databases
Databases that conform to the Open Database Connectivity (ODBC) standard, developed by Microsoft. The ODBC standard is an interface that allows a single application (such as a Web page) to access various types of databases without requiring special programming. Write one program; link to many different databases.

Root Link www.design-bookshelf.com/
Direct Link www.design-bookshelf.com/Database/index.html
Why Go? To find books that teach necessary Web-building skills, including programming with databases. Contents include descriptions of each book to make choosing a specific title easier.

joining a professional organization, or registering for a conference, access to a database usually requires data-processing programs to run on the **back end**.

Numerous tools—scripting, markup, and programming languages—can be used to develop these enhancements to a Web page. Each tool has its strengths and weaknesses, not to mention its group of loyal followers. A given task, such as creating a screen animation, generally can be accomplished with any one of several tools. For now, however, it is important only to recognize that a Web page frequently consists of more than HTML tags and going beyond text-only sites or sites with limited graphic appeal usually involves using one or more of these tools (see Table 6.1).

No matter which add-ons are included in a Web site, in one way or another, they must be integrated with the base HTML code. Although add-ons can be developed as a separate part of a project, they must ultimately be tested with the HTML code to make sure they do not cause unforeseen problems.

TABLE 6.1 Web Page Enhancement Tools

Web Coding Tool	Notes
Markup Languages	
HTML (Hypertext Markup Language)	The main language of the Web. Interpreted line by line by the browser; specifies how to display the Web page.
DHTML (Dynamic Hypertext Markup Language)	A collective term that designates a combination of certain HTML tags and programming or scripting languages. Allows for "dynamic" pages—pages that change content according to information or instructions the user provides.
XHTML (Extensible Hypertext Markup Language)	The emerging standard for Web pages. Revises HTML practices so they conform to the more rigorous set of requirements of XML.
XML (Extensible Markup Language)	Like HTML, a markup language, but it allows coders to choose the markup labels associated with the data in a file (for instance, phone numbers on a Web page could be marked with a label such as <phonenum> instead of being surrounded with <p> or <blockquote> tags). Allows the addition of "extensions" to the existing language commands.
Scripting Languages	
JavaScript	Inserted into HTML code. Syntax similar to C language. Uses "functions."
ActionScript	JavaScript-based scripting language used with Flash (a Web-development tool).
Jscript	Syntax similar to VBasic. Uses subroutines. Runs on Explorer, but not Netscape.
ASP (Active Server Pages)	Microsoft's scripting environment; works along with HTML to create dynamic Web pages.

continues

TABLE 6.1 Web Page Enhancement Tools—Continued

Web Coding Tool	Notes
Programming Languages	
Java	Programming language developed by Sun Microsystems and Netscape. On the Web, usually used to write "applets," or small applications, that run inside a browser window and allow users to perform advanced functions while visiting a site.
C/C++	Popular and powerful language, used to program CGI (Common Gateway Interface) actions and exchanges.
Perl (Practical Extraction and Reporting Language)	UNIX-based language used to program CGI actions and exchanges.
Client-Server Exchange Tool	
CGI (Common Gateway Interface)	Interface for exchange between server and client. Server-side script retrieves "cookie" data from client, and then performs action.

Analyze and Organize the Information for the Site

With the preliminary content and rough design for the site, and with the additional guidance provided by user profiles and scenarios developed in Phase I (Chapter 5), the design team should be ready to deal more explicitly with the architecture of the site. The architecture is developed by dealing with the informational content, which must be broken down, and then restructured into a logical organization that supports the needs, interests, and lines of inquiry of each anticipated user profile and associated scenario. At the end of this process, this organization leads to a structure that supports the design of the navigation interface of the site to assure that users are able to access what they need.

DECONSTRUCT INFORMATION Breaking down and reorganizing the site's informational content is intended to take best advantage of the hypertextual medium of the Web. This is an important step, and not the simplest to achieve.

For many designers, there is considerable impetus to organize a site's information in the same way the legacy materials of the enterprise—brochures, catalogs, announcements, schedules, product descriptions, forms and applications, or newsletters—are organized. Consider the example provided in Chapter 5: a Web site for a local business and technology expo. The print materials for the expo might include items such as:

- A brochure describing the expo in general terms—for as many interested parties as possible
- Three different registration forms, one each for participants, exhibitors, and sponsors
- Sponsors' lists, with additional information about each sponsor to be included on the Web site as one of the benefits of sponsorship
- Exhibitors' lists, with the booth number and location each has been assigned

input/refresh

SOME COMMON HTML EDITING PACKAGES

Many software packages help designers build Web sites, handling details for designers without requiring them to code "by hand." Details of some of the most common packages are discussed here, but for a complete list of Web site integrated development environments (IDEs), visit one of the technology Web sites mentioned in this chapter and elsewhere in the book (ZDNet and WebMonkey, for instance).

MICROSOFT FRONTPAGE FrontPage is a WYSIWYG product for creating quick Web sites, incorporating graphics and images, and setting up basic frames and forms. The FrontPage package includes these functionalities:

- Customizable business-ready themes
- Graphics (clip art, backgrounds, buttons, and banners)
- Rudimentary dynamic HTML animation effects
- Tables and frames
- Cascading Style Sheets (CSS)
- Forms for input
- Site-management reports
- Automatic link fix-up

FrontPage integrates well with Microsoft Office products, including Word, Excel, Access, Outlook, and PowerPoint. Forms can be designed to send results to an existing e-mail address or to a database. The designer can work directly with the HTML code in FrontPage to make changes when needed, but FrontPage takes many liberties with the code itself and can be a frustration to designers who have particular needs and changes they have decided to make. Also, for some functions to run correctly, the host server must have FrontPage "extensions" installed.

MACROMEDIA DREAMWEAVER Dreamweaver is a "start to finish" solution for professional Web site design, with workflow support for teams of designers working together on a site. Dreamweaver uses "round-trip" HTML, which allows the designer complete control over the final code. Dreamweaver works hand-in-hand with Fireworks, enabling graphic and graphic text enhancements, such as multilevel pop-up menus. Other functionality includes the ability to:

- Create dynamic navigation with JavaScript rollovers and pop-up menus
- Create nested tables, coding entirely by hand, or drawing directly on Dreamweaver tools
- Create extensions, media, and data
- Maximize team efficiency with support for version control
- Launch, edit, and optimize graphics

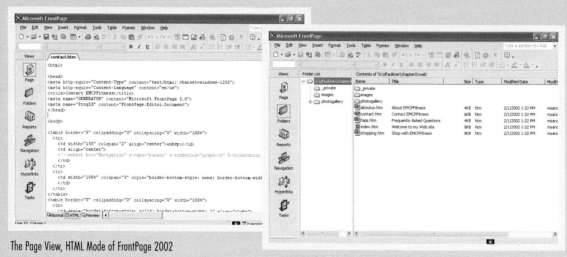

The Page View, HTML Mode of FrontPage 2002

The Folders View of FrontPage 2002

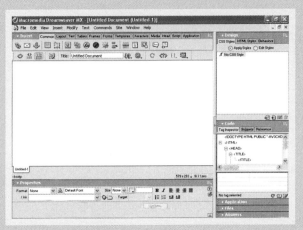

The Dreamweaver Environment

- Update Fireworks images, HTML, and JavaScript directly from within Dreamweaver
- Instantly add graphical bullets, buttons, or an entire Web photo album to the site

ADOBE GOLIVE GoLive supports the production and management of professional, dynamic Web sites, and enables the management of workflow for a site design team. GoLive integrates with other Adobe tools, such as Photoshop, Illustrator, and LiveMotion, to support the production of original and adapted eye-catching images. LiveMotion and Illustrator files can be edited from within GoLive by using the "smart links" tool to launch these applications, using the full functionality of the graphics package to alter the image, and simultaneously updating the site as changes to the image are made. Existing code can be imported without corrupting or inappropriately modifying the current file. Graphical elements can be linked from the Web page to ODBC-compliant databases. Support for ASP makes it easy to incorporate e-commerce capabilities, using GoLive "dynamic links" to operate the site as a business.

- Presenters' lists, with titles and descriptions of the sessions they will be offering
- Business resources—companies and individuals who are available to publicize their services
- Information to recognize the contributions of the officers and chairpersons on the leadership team who have provided time, resources, and effort to make the expo possible

To reuse this material in its current form—to upload the material as is to a host—results in a content-based, not a user-based, site structure; no one would consider that the best use of the Web's hypertextual medium. Another possibility is to upload every printed brochure to the same Web site and make each brochure a major section on the site, using links to facilitate moving to the desired sections of the material from the home page, as in Figure 6.4. This home page is an example of taking previously printed material and simply uploading it to a Web site. At this point, the Web site does not show that much thinking has gone into how the site's users will want to access the information on the site. Yet, making the content of each brochure available with the appropriate link takes a step toward Web-based information architecture.

If each link takes a user to content that is not linked directly to other content, the organization still does not favor the user. In fact, such a decision makes a return to the home page necessary each time the user wants to view different information as shown in Figure 6.5.

One way to solve the problem of forcing the user to return repeatedly to the home page is to provide the same set of links in a navigation bar on each page. From the page containing general information, the user could immediately access registration forms by following the Registration Forms link. However, will every user be interested in every registration form? Or, what if the link in the navigation bar takes the user to a long page through which the user must search for appropriate information? Simply providing links among all pages might not be the best way to consider which users will want which information.

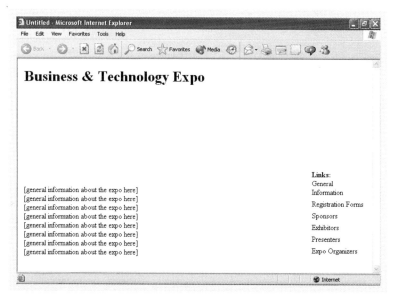

FIGURE 6.4 The Business and Technology Expo Home Page
Categories used as links on the right side of the page have been taken from the printed brochures on whose information the Web site is based.

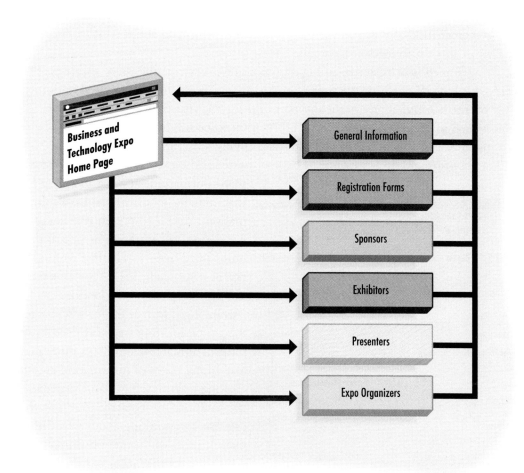

FIGURE 6.5 Content-Based Structure
In a content-based structure, the visitor has to return to the home page to view information about another topic.

On the other hand, considering which interests users have and their potential lines of inquiry leads to many possibilities for organizing the site, thus allowing for multiple ways in which the same information could be accessed. The following list identifies some options for accessing information on the business and technology expo site.

- Business owners signing up to participate in the expo as exhibitors might want to follow links to presenters' information. Also, they might want to become presenters.
- Presenters might follow links to information about who is exhibiting. They also might take an interest in becoming an exhibitor or perhaps even a sponsor and want to know the requirements and benefits for these.
- Visitors planning to attend might note a particular presenter on the list, and then want to learn more about the business this presenter represents. They also might want to see whether that business is among the exhibitors.

One possibility for organizing the expo's information in a more user-friendly way is suggested by Figure 6.6. The figure shows what might happen after a user has successfully registered as an exhibitor (assume this individual has met all of the requirements for exhibiting and has gone through the registration procedure). What would the user be interested in doing just after successfully registering as an exhibitor? Getting information on becoming a presenter or sponsor? Getting more information on exhibiting or on another aspect of the expo? A designer cannot know for certain, but should have some inkling of what else a visitor would need to do at this stage. Reducing the number of links through which a user must travel increases the usability of a Web site. Being able to increase usability in this way requires detailed thinking about which options will be of most interest to users at particular times.

Providing choices as shown in Figure 6.6 requires anticipating users' interests. That means thinking through what a user of a particular type might be interested in doing while on the site and at any particular point during that user's visit. But providing choices such as these also requires the information to be subdivided into chunks that are directly relevant to these specific interests. Giving a user the choice of getting information about becoming a presenter is best supported if the user can be taken directly to that information, not just to a long page that contains all of the standard information relevant to presenters. Thus, the navigation bar on the right side of the home page (refer to Figure 6.6) might not be a sufficient means for directing the user to specific information.

Arranging information for a Web site—that is, performing steps involved in information architecture—is more than just taking pages of information and creating links among them. To make information immediately accessible to users means thinking about what information users will want and thinking of ways to make that information readily

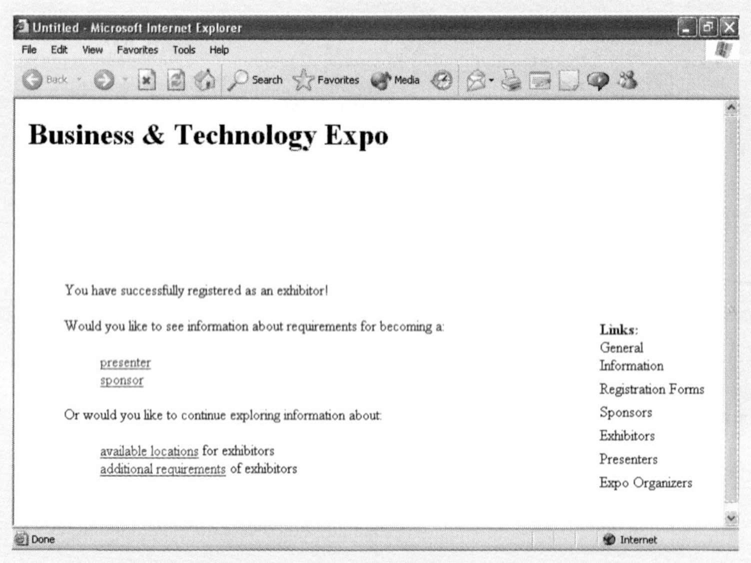

FIGURE 6.6 An Exhibitor's View of the Business and Technology Expo Site
After registering to become an exhibitor, the user is provided options based on anticipating what the visitor might want to do next.

available. This requires breaking the information down to the elemental level, and then structuring the information anew, according to its anticipated uses by targeted users.

The definition of "element level" depends on the nature of the material and on the use for which the material is being broken down. A promotional brochure might appear to be a piece just as it is. But just like a brick wall is made of individual bricks, so a promotional brochure is made up of elemental bits of information. Information that tells how to contact the Web site's owner or sponsor, for instance, could be considered an elemental piece of information. But this contact information consists of elemental bits, too: individual's name, company's name, street address, city, state or province, postal code, phone numbers (voice, fax, and cell), and e-mail address are all elemental pieces of information. On the other hand, subdividing this information might be unnecessary if all of the elements will always be used together, as one piece. Defining the logical organization of information requires some common sense—some thought, for instance, of how the information will be used, not just identifying atomic pieces of information.

If the information for the Web site of a business and technology expo is to be taken from existing brochures, some information is probably repeated in every brochure: dates and location of the expo, phone numbers and addresses (including e-mail and Web addresses), and the names of individuals to contact. Within each brochure, however, some information is unique, yet still capable of subdivision. For instance, in the brochure with information for presenters, there might be a list of presenters already scheduled, a list of topics on which they will speak, topics of interest for which the expo has not found presenters, and locations and times for presentations at the expo site. In the brochure with information for exhibitors, there is likely to be information of a similar nature, and the same could be the case for a brochure with information for sponsors. Table 6.2 lists these fictional possibilities.

The way to break down information into elemental pieces certainly depends on the nature of the material. If the designer is working from previously printed brochures, some of the categorizing might already be done, but perhaps not all the work. In other cases, designers might have to start from the beginning to break down large blocks of information into constituent parts. In either case, it helps to write bits of information down on small pieces of paper (Post-It Notes, index cards). You might tear existing literature into sections (making sure you have enough copies not to lose information printed on the back of the pages), and then proceed section by section, writing down small pieces of information on smaller, note-sized sheets.

TABLE 6.2 Possible Informational Hierarchies in the Business and Technology Expo Brochures

Presenters	Exhibitors	Sponsors
list	list	list
requirements	requirements	requirements
registration form	registration form	registration form
topics	categories	contributions
speech times and locations	exhibit times and locations	

RESTRUCTURE INFORMATION INTO HIERARCHIES
After the information has been broken down into elemental parts, the parts are regrouped to fit the Web's hypertextual foundation. Through regrouping, elements of information are made available from multiple points within the site, as is appropriate to the various patterns of use.

To determine an informational element's place in the hypertextual regrouping, place each piece of information in a hierarchy showing **superordinate** and **subordinate** relations among the different pieces of information. A superordinate element forms a category (for example, "Presenters") in which other terms fall (for example, "list of presenters" and "requirements for becoming a presenter"). These terms are subordinate to "presenter" because they fall within that category.

To continue down the hierarchy, individual presentation topics are subordinate terms under the category "Presentation Topics," which shows that a category can be both subordinate and superordinate at the same time. In Table 6.3, "Presentation Topics" is shown as a superordinate category under which a list of elements falls. However, it is also a subordinate category under "Presenters" as shown earlier in Table 6.2. Determining the placement of informational elements within hierarchies and taxonomies, and thus within Web pages, is to be based on meaning, not on prior organization.

It is important to test for incorrect categorizing. Errors in subordination occur when items are placed in the wrong category (for example, if "A" were categorized under "Numbers" rather than "Letters"). Errors in superordination occur when comparable categories are placed in an incorrect hierarchical relationship (for example, if "Vegetables" were categorized under "Fruits") rather than on equivalent levels. These simple examples are representative of a difficulty that might be more challenging to spot when working with complex material, so it is important to build skills in dissecting information into its elements and then identifying the relationships among those elements.

See Table 6.4 for ways in which information can be incorrectly categorized. Structure 1 illustrates an error in superordination: not all superordinate terms have been placed at the correct level. (Vegetables should be on the same level as fruits, not on a subordinate level.) Structure 2 illustrates an error in subordination: a subordinate element (grapes) has been placed under the wrong superordinate element (vegetables). Structure 3 illustrates errors in both superordination and subordination.

What does the designer do with these chunks of information after they are at the elemental level and classified correctly? Not all informational elements should be link targets somewhere on the Web site. Although the goal is to make each piece of information

superordinate, subordinate

In information architecture, relative terms that describe the relationships among individual pieces of information. A term is superordinate if it forms a category under which other pieces of the available information can fit. Likewise, the same term is subordinate if it can be included in a broader category within the available pieces of information.

TABLE 6.3 Subordinate Entries Under "Presentation Topics"

Presentation Topics
Server-side scripting with JSP
New JavaScript tips and tricks
Building e-commerce sites with RAD
Finding a content-management system for your business
Web programming with C++

T A B L E 6 . 4 Errors in Subordination and Superordination

Structure 1	Structure 2	Structure 3
1. Fruits	1. Fruits	1. Fruits
a. Vegetables	a. Apples	a. Vegetables
b. Apples	2. Vegetables	b. Beans
c. Grapes	a. Beans	c. Apples
	b. Grapes	d. Grapes

available from multiple points in the site, all of the necessary steps have not yet been taken to determine which pieces of information should be targets for links and which should be information contained within a target.

To determine whether every piece of information results in a link, continue taking the informational elements from Table 6.2 and determine whether they can be grouped in ways that suggest useful links to the information. The table shows three columns of information; however, information across columns also can form groups because the information that some cells contain serves similar functions. For example, an item called "list" appears in each column. Offering users a choice of lists might be helpful. Think also about the requirements for exhibiting, for presenting, and for sponsoring. A user might want to know the requirements for all of these. Thus, similar information across several already-established superordinate categories might turn out to belong in other superordinate categories, which themselves might become candidates for targets for links on the site. These new categories might prove to be more valuable as link targets than the elemental information they contain. To decide whether a category or the information within it is the target for a link, the designer must balance ease of use (by reducing the number of links to travel through) against visual clutter that could result from providing links to numerous informational pieces.

Another way to determine how to establish useful links is to look at all of the elemental pieces of information and the categories in which they have been grouped, and ask whether another superordinate category might provide access to the information users might want. For the business and technology expo site, for instance, one possibility is to make the superordinate categories of exhibitors, sponsors, and presenters subordinate to a new superordinate category called "Expo Participants" (see Table 6.5). This could be helpful for someone unfamiliar with the site to become acquainted with the major ways people can participate in the expo. It answers a possible question such a visitor might have: "How can I find out how to participate in the expo?" Providing a link entitled "Ways to Participate" or "How Can I Participate?" could lead to an introductory paragraph that explains in a few sentences the major types of participants. From that paragraph, a visitor could then navigate (by following one link) to the section that describes the particular category of interest. Thus, creating additional superordinate categories by analyzing the information and considering how users might want to access it can result in useful navigational tools.

TABLE 6.5 New Superordinate Category

Expo Participants
Presenters
Exhibitors
Sponsors

Root Link www.worldwidelearn.com/
Direct Link www.worldwidelearn.com/webdesign-courses.htm
Why Go? To browse a listing of online courses from diploma- and degree-granting institutions. Check out the link to a free, six-lesson course in information architecture: go to www.worldwidelearn.com/webdesign-courses.htm and find the link "Introduction to Information Architecture."

Root Link www.uscit.com/
Direct Link www.useit.com/papers/webwriting/rewriting.html
Why Go? To read articles by Jakob Nielsen, a leading authority on Web usability. The paper on rewriting for the Web contains a lot of tips for organizing information for presentation on a Web site.

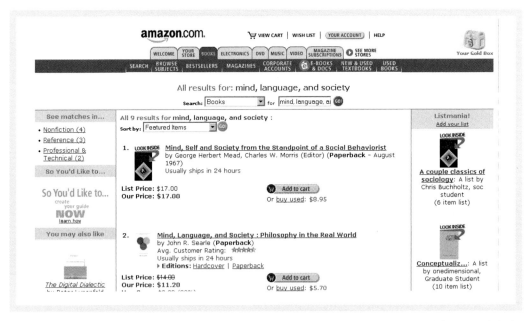

Amazon's Web site at www.amazon.com/ is well organized so that information can be easily accessed. A visitor can search for the title of a book or for books by a specific author. But amazon.com goes far beyond this minimal type of functionality.

Select a Physical Structure

The next step is to select a physical structure—a flowchart or cluster diagram, in a sense—that best arranges the regrouped information in ways that fit naturally with how users will travel through the site. This critical decision is vital to determining the usability of the site.

Why not provide the links that allow users to get anywhere from everywhere? Why worry so much about the physical structure of the site? Choosing the physical structure provides some guidelines by which a design team decides where links go (and which links go there). Skipping over this step in constructing the site's informational and navigational structure can lead to sites that appear to have placed links indiscriminately, without a consistent plan. At worst, without the guidance of a physical structure, pages could be missing links to important parts of the site. Going through the process of selecting a physical structure helps design teams produce pages that contain all of the necessary navigational elements.

Some typical site diagrams from which to choose include linear structure, pyramid or hierarchical structure, and star or cluster structure. Variations and combinations of these fit special site designs and include mesh structure, tutorial structure, and catalog structure.

LINEAR AND DUAL LINEAR (GRID) STRUCTURE Because the Web is meant to be multidirectional to support a variety of uses, linear structure, which imposes bidirectional (back and forth) navigation, is used for some parts of a Web site's design but not generally throughout the entire site. A purely linear path could be termed "lock step" and is not appealing when visitors might want to move off in various directions of their own choice. Figure 6.7 provides a linear structure model.

A linear structure would not be appropriate for the business and technology expo site. Linear structure steers users down a path, and escape from this path requires traveling to the end or backing up to the beginning. This structure provides no quick escape for someone who ends up in the wrong section of the site and wants an immediate method for correcting the mistake. In addition, several categories of information have numerous subordinate categories, and a user might want to jump from one subordinate category to another without having to navigate the entire subcategory.

In some circumstances, however, linear structure is useful and important. Some Web sites might begin with entry portals—for instance, a dynamic **splash page** and a linear sequence of related pages—that contain information relevant to use of the site. After this sequence has been traversed, the site's main content appears on a collection of pages arranged in a less bidirectional fashion. On the other hand, exit portals can move linearly through a fixed sequence so that a certain transaction is brought to a close. This linear movement is typical of the purchasing sequence of e-commerce sites.

splash page
An eye-catching page (often multimedia to create a splash) that serves as a Web site's home page or often redirects users to the site's true home page.

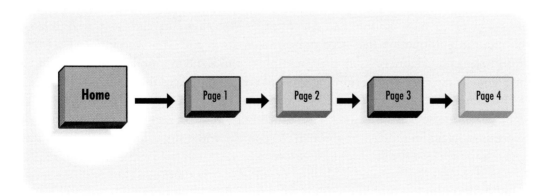

FIGURE 6.7 Linear Structure

This splash page for a Web and print medium design firm (at www.berringa.com/) offers two options by which users can view the site, but does not directly communicate information about the site's sponsor. Its pleasant, uncluttered design captures interest, thus suggesting that the site will be worth exploring.

In this sequence, users can review the items selected for purchase, provide payment and shipping information, approve all final information, place the order, and receive a confirmation page. Finally, tutorials often make use of linear structures because it is necessary to proceed through a tutorial in the sequence imposed by the material being taught.

Variations on linear structure can provide alternatives or allow for side trips. When both horizontal and vertical relationships exist among the informational elements of a site, a 2-D grid structure can best represent the logical connections among them (see Figure 6.8). Such an arrangement allows access to the same information by varying routes (for example, products organized by features as well as by primary classifications). This is still a linear structure because any traveling through it can occur only in consecutive fashion. The difference is that having two dimensions in which to travel does present some options not available in a strict linear structure.

PYRAMID OR HIERARCHICAL STRUCTURE The pyramid or hierarchical structure is one of the most common architectures for Web sites and lends itself well to large collections of information that need to be broken down and organized into levels, from broad to specific. Figure 6.9 shows an example of this structure model. Pages high in the hierarchy contain general information and connect to pages that contain the next (subordinate) level of detail. (Of course, links go in both directions, so pages link to higher levels in the hierarchy, too.) This structure prevents information overload and assists users in finding their way through the content without getting overwhelmed with unnecessary levels of detail early in the process.

Users navigate such a site by "drilling down" through a series of choices to the level where they can find what they want. As users complete one task of drilling down, they can then move up to an earlier, broader level of the hierarchy and follow a different

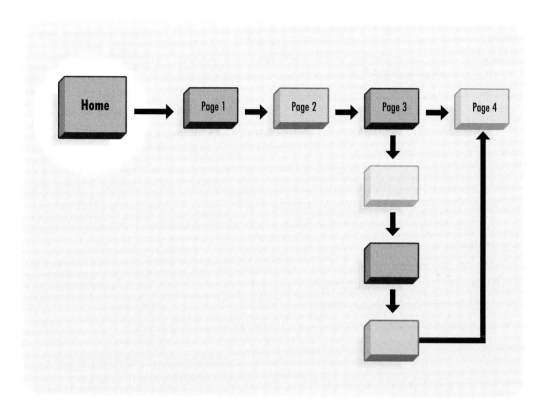

FIGURE 6.8 Linear Structure with Side Trips

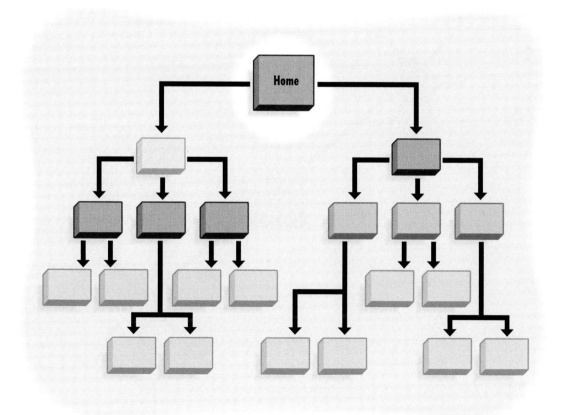

FIGURE 6.9 Pyramid or Hierarchical Structure

path back down into "deeper" levels of specifics. The link labels at the broad level must be clear so that visitors know which path to select to reach the information they are looking for. On sites with this architecture, an alternative to requiring users to drill down is to provide a search utility to locate information within the Web site. This alleviates the frustration that results when users need to move through many levels to reach what they came to find.

Is this an appropriate structure for the business and technology expo site? It certainly offers advantages over the linear structure because at several points a visitor can choose among several options, which seems to be an architectural requirement of the expo site's information. Yet, the pyramid structure provides only a variation of the linear structure. Although a user has options to choose among at various points, each choice can commit the user to a linear path from which escape is difficult if appropriate links are not provided.

STAR OR CLUSTER STRUCTURE Star or cluster structure is useful when users of a site need to move out from a central concept to multiple areas available to be explored as their own entities (see Figure 6.10). In this structure, the main area of the site is an entry to multiple areas that are arranged as their own clusters of information. This structure is appropriate for sites in which the information does not form a hierarchy, but rather forms multiple unified sets of information, each representing its own

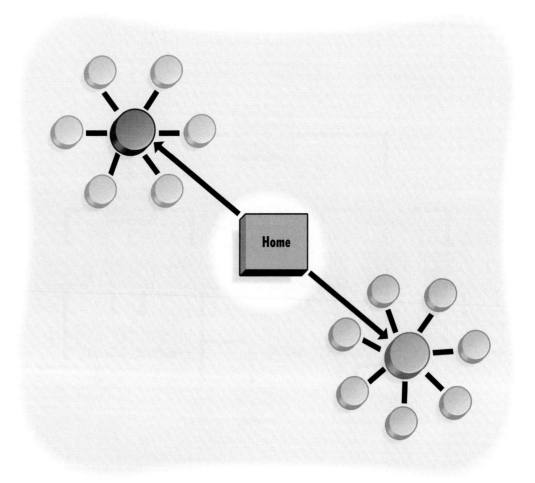

FIGURE 6.10 Star or Cluster Structure

collection. Within a travel site, for example, completely separate areas might be used for destinations, accommodations, air travel, car rentals, and cruises.

Whereas navigation in the hierarchical structure moves up and down the hierarchy, navigation of the star or cluster structure moves out into an area of exploration, within which there is a unified range of navigation possibilities. When exploration of one cluster has been completed, the user moves back to the center to select another area to delve into.

ADDITIONAL STRUCTURES Additional structures are variations or combinations of the linear, the pyramid, and the star structures, such as the mesh, tutorial, and catalog structures. Small sites use structures that can be described as a mesh of information, where every page is accessible to every other page (see Figure 6.11).

Tutorial structure is like a multimedia training program, in which a topic is broken down into learning segments (pyramid, with linear structure), but each learning segment is essentially linear (see Figure 6.12). A more interactive variation for each learning segment employs linear organization with side trips: the basic sequence is interrupted, when needed, to handle misconceptions or errors in learner responses to questions.

Catalog structure (see Figure 6.13) supports sites in which the pattern of use is to look through a set of products for consideration, narrow down the choices to make selections, and then move through a sequence of interactions to complete the purchase, arrange for shipping, and receive confirmation. This can be accomplished using a hierarchical structure (to allow branching into the types of products that are of interest) combined with a cluster structure (allowing exploration and selection of products of a certain type), and moving to a fixed linear structure for purchase and checkout. Depending on the way information is broken down into elements, a single element might be categorized under two or more superordinate categories. Instead of showing

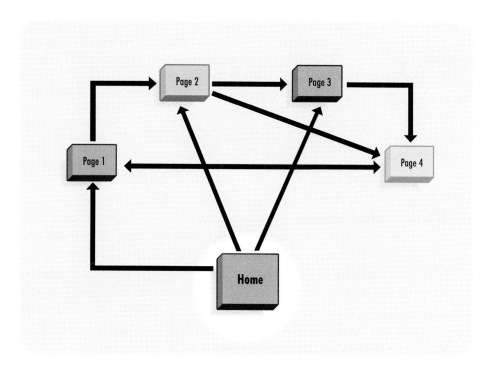

FIGURE 6.11 Mesh Structure

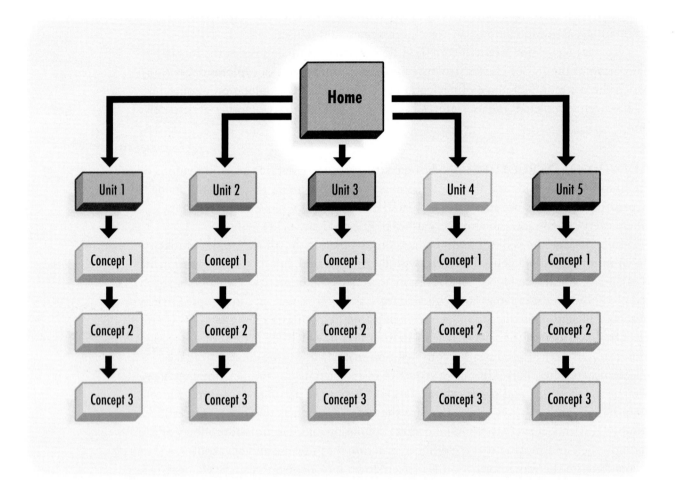

FIGURE 6.12 Tutorial Structure

these as repeated elements in the physical structure, it is clearer to include each element only once, with arrow lines showing multiple routes to the element. This is a better way to represent the element in terms of how the Web site will be structured, because each element will likely be its own separate Web page.

Create the Site Map

site map
A visual representation of the organization of information on a Web site rendered in linear charts or 3-D pictures. Shows where categories of information are placed and usually uses the major links as labels for the informational categories.

When the design team has chosen the physical structure that fits naturally with the reorganized information, a roughed-in visual version of how the site will be structured needs to be created. This step produces a **site map** and involves taking the physical structure and transferring chunks of information onto it. It is important to begin thinking now about the categories in which the elemental pieces of information have been organized. Connections among pages should be represented as connections among categories of information, especially in the non-linear structures. A cluster can show how informational elements are connected to the main hub. A hierarchy can show an original set of choices, and then the sequence of pages available through each.

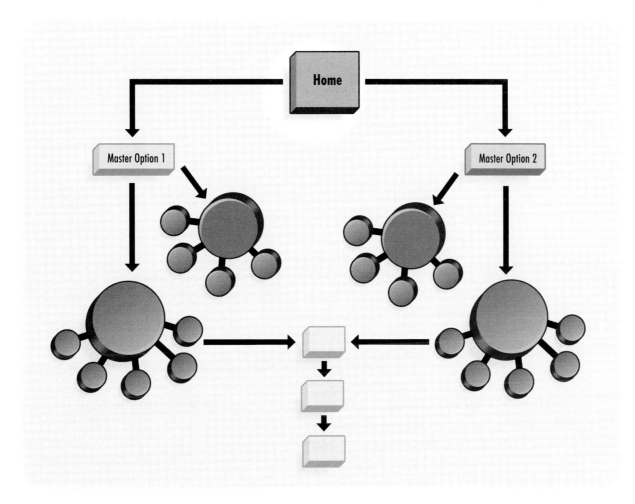

FIGURE 6.13 Catalog Structure

These drawings can quickly become overly complex and difficult to read. To simplify the drawings as much as possible, omit the lines for links that are standard and can be assumed, such as the standard link back to the site's home page. This rough version of the site's structure allows the design team and the client to see at a glance how the site will be arranged and the various paths through the site. Keep a range of site map models in mind, rather than narrowing down to a few selected examples, because these maps will vary tremendously based on the site project.

Using any process that employs symbols to illustrate process, linkages, and relationships among elements, create one or more rough maps of the site in a format that can be easily visualized and discussed. These site maps will be used for design team walk-throughs of the site, and later for presentation to the client.

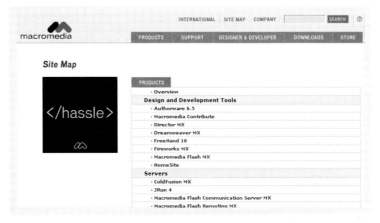

Site maps illustrate a site's organization using a way of representing the hierarchy. For example, the site map on the Macromedia site (www.macromedia.com/sitemap/) shows major categories broken down into subcategories in a graphical outline form.

Navigating a site, as discussed at length in Chapter 4, needs to be entirely "transparent" to the user. The goal is to offer navigation that focuses on the needs and interests of the users, considering what the users will want to do at each point during their time on the site.

To design the navigation plan, envision the actual scenarios of use, considering the actual "people" who were profiled:

- How will they arrive?
- What will they see first?
- What will they need to see to determine where to go next?
- Where might they want to go next? Then where will they want to go?
- What will bring them to discover and use what they came for?
- What will they want to do to bring closure to the experience?

To implement a plan that supports these scenarios requires making decisions such as the following:

- Which links will be placed in consistent locations on all pages and which links will be provided only at certain appropriate spots within the site?
- What will determine the difference between links that appear on all pages and links that appear on specific pages?
- Which options can be nested within other options so they become available when they are needed and sought out?
- How will the basic map of the site be communicated so visitors have a sense of orientation and control rather than feeling they are "lost" and wandering aimlessly?

Ideally, the user will be able to navigate the site intuitively, without needing to first learn how. The navigation plan should be simplified as much as possible, with limited screen clutter from options that are not likely to be necessary at that point. Navigation design strategies such as drop-down menus can be used to provide a full range of selections without creating unnecessary clutter and confusion on a given page. The navigation plan should give the impression that the site is operating in response to the users, providing up-to-date information, personalized to their needs and questions.

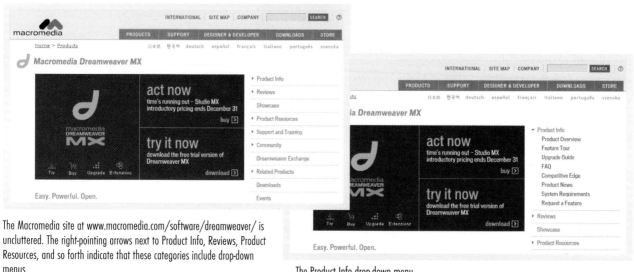

The Macromedia site at www.macromedia.com/software/dreamweaver/ is uncluttered. The right-pointing arrows next to Product Info, Reviews, Product Resources, and so forth indicate that these categories include drop-down menus.

The Product Info drop-down menu.

Robust designs allow search features to save users time and get them to the specifics they are looking for without the frustration of delays or wandering around. They process user input immediately, responding to users' requests and setting in motion the next steps (for example, making a reservation, processing an airline ticket and seat assignment, acknowledging an order, and setting up delivery). These designs provide links to needed information or tools "just in time" to help users make use of what is already available on the page being viewed. They create a path to be followed by site visitors as they pursue their particular interests and needs.

Identify Possible Cross Links

As well as designing the navigation plan that enables the user to travel within the site, it is important to think beyond the site to how users will locate and arrive at the site, and where else they might want to go when they leave. In particular, how will visitors arrive at the site if they are not already familiar with it? The answer to this question requires thinking through and planning how the search engines will locate and classify the site, and what descriptive information about the site will be made available when it appears as one of the results of the search. This part of the process requires determining the search terms likely to be used by those who would benefit from locating this site. These likely search terms and site descriptions can be included as part of the site's meta tags. The selection of these terms is crucial, and should be appropriate to the content of the site. Another important consideration is that visitors who arrive via a search often begin on a page deep within the site. For such visitors, there must be clear paths to take them to a higher level of the site so they will have a fuller experience of the site's benefits.

The plan for cross links is an important part of design thinking. Two basic questions help a design team think through these plans.
- From what other sites might visitors be linked to yours?
- Where else might visitors want to go during their visit to the site, or when they are ready to leave your site?

Not only should a design team consider which links out to other sites should be included on the site being designed, the team should also ask what kinds of sites should link in to the site being developed. Cross links are an important source of traffic to a Web site. If your site is the target of a link from another site, you have a greater chance of increasing the number of visitors to your site than if you relied solely on Web search matches to the terms within the meta tags in your site's header section. So an important part of promoting the site is determining which sites would want to link to your site and communicating with these other sites to make this happen. A competitor of your site is unlikely to steer traffic away from its own site, so design teams probably would not contact competitors' Webmasters. For example, one hardware store will not want to direct visitors to its competitor. However, a site that gives advice on home maintenance might link to either hardware store or to both. Pricing or purchasing tools and supplies is a natural outgrowth of obtaining home maintenance advice, so the link is appropriate.

Determining which sites might be interested in linking to the client's site can be done after the team decides which sites to link to. Think of providing supplemental value to the site's visitors by linking out, and then ask what types of sites would consider linking in to the client's site as a means of providing supplemental value to their users.

A Swedish artist, Bengt Elde, is known for doing artwork the size of several warehouse doors. The originals of this artwork are remarkable, and each one has a story. The artist's son has a shop on a corner of a major shopping street in Stockholm from which he sells copies of the originals in various forms, including postcards, Christmas cards, wall hangings, posters, coasters, ties, scarves, decorative magnets, and serving trays.

The purpose of this activity is for you to create a site structure for a new Bengt Elde Web site, where it will be possible to view the artwork and to make purchases of the various gift items available from the corner shop in Stockholm. The Swedish version of the Web site (www.elde.se/) offers images of the original artwork plus some text (in Swedish) about the artist. The new site will offer everything available through the shop, as well as views (images) of the original artwork and its stories, and text (in English or Swedish) to provide information so site visitors can learn about the artist.

The following is a list of the elements that will be viewed on the new site.

- Original painting of *Tree of Life*
- Christmas cards with *Tree of Life*
- Christmas cards with *Snow Tree*
- Christmas card of *Ship at Sea*
- Original painting of *Blue Forest*
- Double-width postcards with *Blue Forest* (also *Ship at Sea, Snow Tree,* and *Tree of Life*)
- Scarf of *Stockholm Waterfront*
- Commentary about Bengt Elde's work
- Original painting of *Elves and Santa Parade*

- Serving tray with *Tree of Life*
- Story of how the *Tree of Life* painting came about
- Cloth hanging with *Snow Tree*
- Serving tray of *Ship at Sea*
- Scarf with *Blue Forest*
- Coasters with one each images of *Blue Forest, Snow Tree, Tree of Life,* and *Stockholm Waterfront*
- Original painting of *Walking Street*
- "About the artist" write-up
- View of original artwork *The Spade*

- Wall hanging with *Tree of Life*
- Original painting of *Snow Tree*
- Original painting of *Ship at Sea*
- Poster of *Ship at Sea* (also *Tree of Life* and *Snow Tree*)
- Serving tray with *Blue Forest*
- Original painting of *Stockholm Waterfront*
- Scarf of *Walking Street*
- Story about how the *Elves and Santa Parade* painting was created
- Story of the painting of *The Spade*

Use the methods discussed thus far to create a structure from these elements that allows users to take various paths through the site according to different interests.

Visitors might be interested in:
- Learning more about the artist and his work
- Purchasing gift items based on the originals
- Learning about and viewing the original artwork of Bengt Elde
- Learning about Swedish art and how Bengt Elde's work fits in with that tradition
- Learning about Swedish art work available for purchase in Stockholm

Visit the Bengt Elde Web site at www.elde.se/ and look around. For this activity, you do not have to take into account the existing site or incorporate anything from it, although you do need to acquaint yourself with Elde's style of art.

When you are ready, look at the previous list and write down each informational element on a separate card or Post-It Note. Group the elements according to appropriate superordinate categories. Consider categories that you think might improve users' access to the individual pieces of information. (This might require thinking of categories that are not the most obvious as you look at your cards.) Place the elements in various arrangements. Try several possible structures until you have arrived at the optimal structure for the Web site. The structure should be able to expand to incorporate additional items as they become available.

Prepare a brief report (one or two pages) that presents the site structure you propose for the Web site. Include sketches to illustrate your proposal.

PREPARE RESOURCES

As the design team heads into its work of organizing content for use on the Web site, many issues arise concerning how all the material should be handled. These issues affect schedule, workflow, and choice of technologies. First, because much of this process of collecting and organizing content involves interaction with the client, there can be some delays in obtaining all of the material. When a design team discovers what material is missing, it is time to establish whether the client is to provide it (even whether the client has the material) or whether the design team is to create it. Whatever decision is made, more time might be necessary before the material is ready for inclusion in the design. The decision also should be made in light of the Site Specifications and Standards document; this document clearly states who will be responsible for providing a specific item.

Second, because the quantity of collected materials can become extensive, it becomes critical to keep these resources organized and to have a system for identifying gaps in order to adapt or create what is missing.

Third, for projects involving a design team, resources must be accessible by all members of the team, with a clear system for version control to ensure that all team members are using the most current version of each of the dozens or hundreds of files.

Fourth, accessibility and usability considerations take time to address: reducing file sizes for rapid transmission, adapting colors for clear visibility, streamlining elements of functionality to ensure they will work efficiently and not be frustrating or inconvenient to users. These and other issues can require testing and adjustment of resource elements that will be incorporated into the site. In other words, preparing resources takes time.

The main types of Web resources include text, graphics, multimedia of other types, and dynamic and interactive elements. Each of these resource types, and the tasks to prepare them so they can be used on the Web, is supported by powerful tools that can save time, increase quality, reduce transmission times and other inefficiencies, and otherwise make a tremendous difference between a Web site that is barely adequate and one that is efficient, effective, attractive, approachable, and user-centered.

TEXT In breaking information down into elemental parts (as covered previously), a design team might have been dealing with text that must be repurposed for the Web and brought up to date. Names, addresses, phone numbers, and e-mail addresses can all change; but other changes might be made to text as well. In the best case, such changes will not affect the informational analysis performed in the previous step. In the worst case, that step would need to be performed again.

Another editorial issue that arises in handling the text is making sure that copy exists for all major sections of a Web site. Again, the best situation is for a design team to have all this material when performing informational analysis, but clients are not always prepared to deliver final copy at that stage of planning. Nonetheless, it is critical that, as the team moves into the production phase, it gathers or creates all text necessary to place on the site and tracks what needs to be provided if missing. Material that should be gathered for the site includes several types of copy:

- Content copy communicates the information and concepts of the site.
- Guide copy communicates what is at the other end of each link.
- Interactive copy communicates what users are to do or what responses they need to provide.
- Alt-text copy tells what the images or graphics are when they are not visible.

In the interest of keeping all content organized, technical staff might set up an electronic filing system for the project, including any safeguards that keep all staff working on the most current versions of the files. Technical staff might have to convert files to a format that can be used by all members of the team. Although conversion from one electronic format to another is something most word processors now handle with considerable ease, they insert extraneous code that will need to be removed for optimal functioning of the page.

The key to adapting text to the needs of the Web site is converting all text to digital format. Much of the text-based content for the Web site might be provided by the client in electronic format. Other content might be provided in print format. After the text is digitized, it can be copied, pasted into place, and edited.

When sources of text are not yet converted to digital format, two important technologies bridge this gap:

- **Voice-to-text** Entering text by speaking and having the audio input converted to digital format using voice recognition technology.
- **Print-to-text** Entering text using a scanner to create a literal image of the page, and then using OCR (Optical Character Recognition) software to translate text to editable digital format.

With voice-to-text, text is read into a microphone, interpreted by the voice recognition software (such as Dragon Naturally Speaking or ViaVoice, or available in some operating systems such as Windows XP), and then corrected. This is a rapid process for inputting a considerable amount of text material from which Web site copy can be generated. Current versions of voice recognition software support entry via tape recordings. This is an excellent option when material for the site has been gathered in print form that is best used to provide excerpts, or when material is available from interviews or brainstorming and planning sessions with the client. Be aware, however, that this technology is not perfect and requires some time to prepare and correct. The software must be "trained" to recognize distinctive ways individual users pronounce words. Even then, trained voice-recognition software often makes guesses at what is being said, and the results are sometimes curious, even amusing. Do not use voice-to-text technology, therefore, without carefully proofreading the output.

> **Root Link** www.dragonsys.com/
> **Direct Link** www.dragonsys.com/naturallyspeaking/
> **Why Go?** Naturally Speaking is a well-known voice-to-text program. The company that produces this software also has other programs that handle other conversions (paper document to digital document, for example).

With print-to-text technology, printed text is scanned and, with the help of OCR software such as OmniPage, converted to digitized text. The OCR tools have become highly accurate and readily useful. OmniPage claims accuracy rates of better than 99% and is able to preserve tables and spreadsheets to look like the originals with data properly entered. OmniPage retains original page layouts, including columns, graphics, tables, and text style (font size, bold, and italic). Another benefit of OmniPage OCR is support for multiple languages, including French, German, Italian, Portuguese, Spanish, and Swedish. This means, among other things, that it is prepared to interpret accent marks that are not normally used in English; languages that use other writing systems would require different software altogether.

> **Root Link** www.ocr.com/
> **Direct Link** www.ocr.com/products.htm
> **Why Go?** To find information about software that converts paper documents to digital format. Software from this company can handle a variety of different languages.

Once digitized, all material needs to be regarded as rough copy and adapted to the purposes, design, and intent of the Web site. This is where the editorial staff takes charge. Editors are responsible for writing or rewriting copy so that it communicates clearly in the context of the site's architectural plans. Clear communication certainly calls for writing text that fulfills the purposes for which it is intended (remember the communication parameter of Chapter 3). But when converting the client's material for use on the Web site, an especially important consideration is aiming for a Web-appropriate tone. At an absolute minimum, the Web site must go beyond the marketing materials and eliminate the "glitz," hard sell, and slickness that is acceptable in traditional advertising circles, but is generally considered objectionable to Web users.

Editors, for their part, play a major role in shaping the textual content to fit the architectural plans for the site.

GRAPHICS   Preparing graphics for use as part of a Web site again requires collecting images from the client, converting printed images to digital format using a scanner or a digital camera, and organizing them for use by members of the design team. Some

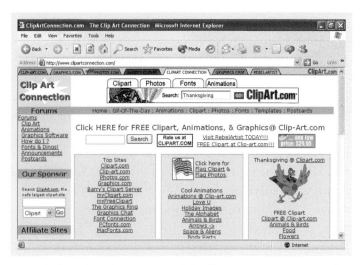

An example of a site (www.clipartconnection.com) that offers connections to many sources of art, images, and even fonts for use on Web pages.

images that are already in digital form might still need to be converted because Web browsers support only images that are in GIF, JPG, or PNG formats, although other formats might be supported in the future. Another task in preparing image files for use on a Web site is to optimize them so that the file size is as small as possible, while adequate quality is retained.

There are many potential sources of graphical components for a Web site, including logo art, photographs, line art, clip art, models, charts and graphs, backgrounds, buttons, banners, and horizontal rules.

Logo art might be available from the client in digital format or in print copy that can be scanned. New photographs can be taken using digital cameras, or regular film can be developed in digital format or in regular format and then scanned from prints. (Thus, old photographs can easily be converted to digital format.) Vast resources of photos are available online, some for a fee, and some free. Every form of art work—line art, clip art, animated clip art, backgrounds, buttons, banners, and horizontal rules— also are available online, or from resource collections on CDs that provide tens of thousands of options. Models can be created using shape objects in graphics packages, or even using the rudimentary drawing tools available with Microsoft Office or other suites of standard software. Charts and graphs can be created readily in any spreadsheet package by creating quick data tables, and then using the charts and graphs utilities to convert the data to bar charts, pie charts, or other visual communications formats.

Root Link www.dgl.microsoft.com/
Direct Link Select any of the categories at www.dgl.microsoft.com/
Why Go? To preview and download photos and artwork that can be used in Microsoft Office documents, which can be published on the Web.

Because large image file sizes cause delays in downloading a Web page, close attention to file sizes is essential. File sizes can be reduced using compression and sampling technologies. Another important strategy is to use vector art where possible. Whereas many standard digital images used in print are stored as "raster" or bit-mapped data, causing large file sizes because each pixel in the image is saved as its own data point, vector art is stored as a set of start points and trajectories. For example, a line stored as a bit map would include hundreds of data points. Stored as a vector, the same line would involve three elements of data—starting point, the direction, and the length.

It is difficult to recommend a specific limitation for file sizes, because download times are affected by numerous variables. In general, consider reducing file sizes if a page seems to take an excessive amount of time to download, something that can be tested only after the files have been designed and coded. For more information on dealing with file sizes, look at recommendations on the usability.gov site under Design Considerations or on the w3.org site, where information can be found by doing a site search for "file size."

Powerful graphics tools to support raster art and vector art include Adobe Photoshop (raster, with some vector features) and Illustrator (vector). Photoshop is used to create and optimize new (or to adapt existing) high-quality images using a complete Web graphics toolset. Photoshop makes it easy to create buttons, navigation bars, and other Web elements using the new vector shape tools and font styles. An important use of Photoshop is to optimize graphics and images using its sophisticated compression tools, and then preview side-by-side versions of the files to determine the best balance between image quality and file size.

Root Link www.adobe.com/products/photoshop/main.html
Direct Link www.adobe.com/products/tryadobe/main.jhtml#product=39
Why Go? To learn about this popular image-editing program. The Direct Link takes you to a page from which you can download a free trial version of the program (although the trial version does not allow you to save, export, or print your work).

Illustrator supports the creation of original artwork in vector-based SVG (Scalable Vector Graphics) and ShockWave Flash (SWF) file formats. Illustrator allows the development of layers, and the application of transparency to any object or layer. Vector graphics can be easily edited, applying variations in colors, patterns, and text formatting. Text can be placed on any path or wrapped around any shape. Drop shadows and transparency effects (such as mist, soft shadows, and fades) can be applied to text and graphic objects, saved in various combinations as graphics styles, and applied to other objects or layers. Illustrator files can be exported to Photoshop (and vice versa), LiveMotion animation software, and various Web design packages (such as Dreamweaver and GoLive) as small, vector-based SWF and SVG files, or as GIF, JPEG, and PNG files.

Root Link www.adobe.com/products/illustrator/main.html
Direct Link www.adobe.com/products/tryadobe/main.jhtml#product=27
Why Go? To learn about Adobe's well-known Illustrator drawing program and to download a trial version (trial version does not allow saving, printing, or exporting files you create).

ANIMATION/SCREEN DYNAMICS Multiple tools are available to prepare the animated and dynamic visual resources for a Web site, some of which are more appropriate to the Web than others. At the simplest level, rollovers and animated GIF files are readily available from any number of sources, or can be created using software packages designed for this purpose. These files provide a rudimentary level of screen dynamic. Because these image files incorporate motion as a permanent feature of the image, this motion is continuous, and can become annoying and distracting quickly. Also, as discussed in Chapter 4, moving images that do not allow for user, or even designer, control can produce difficulties in terms of accessibility.

More sophisticated site dynamics now are becoming prevalent, but they also are more complex in terms of preparation because they involve the creation of objects, and programmed controls of these objects. One powerful tool for producing these higher levels of on-screen dynamics is Macromedia Flash MX, and its associated scripting language, ActionScript.

Flash/ActionScript can be used to create distinctive user interfaces, site navigation, and other Web applications without programming. Functionalities increase the productivity of the workflow and the quality and effectiveness of the dynamic elements incorporated into the site. These functionalities include:

- Drawing tools for inserting shapes, applying colors, and selecting objects in a drawing
- Inspector interface tools for inspecting the technical details of Web page elements
- Optimization time line and smart motion guides to help create and control animation
- Tools such as outline colors mode for working with layers in Flash graphics

Flash is recognized as a means to deliver unique, high-impact Web experiences that attract and excite visitors by mixing and synchronizing MP3 streaming audio with vector and bit-mapped graphics, interactive buttons, and animations. New functionality

A rollover changes an object when the curser is rolled over it. In this example (www.disney.go.com/), when the cursor is rolled over the graphic for Kids Island Home, the list of options for this part of the site appears.

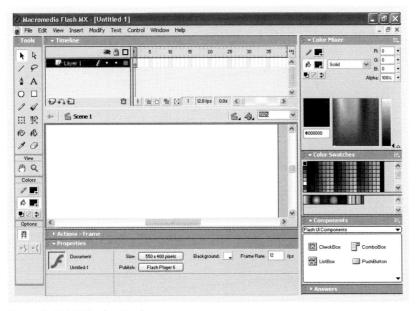

Macromedia Flash MX Developer Panels

for input forms supports data gathering and e-commerce applications, and enables input data to be passed to a Web server. The Flash interface places commonly used tools in "panels," which are available to the designer/developer while work is being done on a page or part of a page. The same page can be viewed by different individuals on a design team, with each individual choosing different panels for his work. A developer—responsible for coding—might use panels to show source code while working on a page. A designer—responsible for the look and feel of the page—might choose panels that help control colors or that create art to be used in a Flash movie.

Adobe LiveMotion enables designers to create interactive graphics, animations, and live motion, and then drop these compositions into a Web site. Features of this tool allow designers to:

- Draw and edit Bezier curves with a pen tool
- Apply visual effects such as distortion, 3-D effects, and special filters to objects
- Add these live effects without changing other attributes
- Open and edit Adobe Illustrator and Photoshop files directly within LiveMotion, making changes that update in the LiveMotion composition
- Create dynamic behaviors such as rollovers, sound triggers, and actions that launch interactivity
- Independently animate the attributes of an object (such as position, special effects, and text)
- Export finished LiveMotion compositions to the GoLive Web design environment

Root Link www.adobe.com/products/livemotion/main.html
Direct Link www.adobe.com/products/tryadobe/main.jhtml#product=33
Why Go? To read information about this Web-authoring program that offers support for Flash/ActionScript. The Direct Link takes you to a page from which you can download a trial version (expires after 30 days).

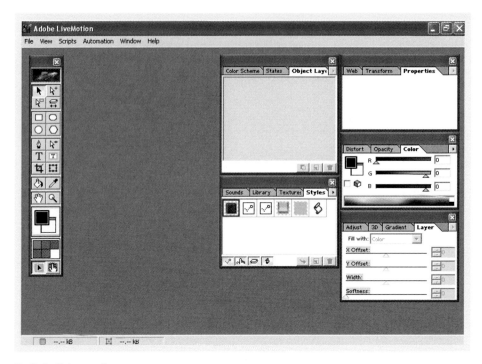

Live Motion Environment Screen

MULTIMEDIA Preparing multimedia files for a Web site involves many of the same issues as other elements, including keeping file sizes low so they will open quickly in the browser window. Other important issues include determining whether elements are appropriate for the purpose of the site, copyright issues (see Chapter 7, *Phase III: Launch, Test, Maintain, and Improve the Site*), browser compatibility, and making provisions to include plug-ins (such as RealPlayer, QuickTime, and others) when they are needed to present the element.

Some of the multimedia elements that can be included in a site design are:
- Sounds/music
- Voice audio
- Video clips

Root Link www.home.about.com/compute/
Direct Link www.graphicssoft.about.com/cs/multimedia/
Why Go? For sources of multimedia software. You can get to the Direct Link by selecting the Multimedia link under Graphics Software on the Root Link page.

Various tools exist to work with these multimedia files: Peak (for the Mac), Sonic Forge, and Cool Edit are popular and powerful programs. With these multimedia programs, speech and song lyrics can be changed and corrected, sound effects added, and files converted to different formats. Precise editing of sound tracks makes it easier to remove minute imperfections. Many programs support digital signal processing and can be used to open QuickTime and MPEG movies for editing.

INTERACTIVITY To prepare a Web site for interactivity sometimes requires going beyond HTML code, although the basic Web input process, a form, begins with HTML. Various types of form fields are set up in the HTML code, including radio buttons, check boxes, drop-down selection lists, and input boxes. Data-handling options include sending input to e-mail. However, this option is not immediately interactive, because there is a delay between submitting the data and receiving feedback or results. Other means are required to make the site seem interactive in real time.

The two types of real-time response strategies are **server-side strategies** and **client-side strategies**. Server-side strategies involve various means by which the data is processed on the server that houses the Web site and back-end databases that drive the site. With server-side strategies, the data is exchanged and processed using programs developed with CGI, ASP, or various other programming options. All of these server-based response strategies involve some degree of delay because the data must be transmitted to the server to be processed, and then a response must be generated and transmitted back to the user.

Client-side processing strategies include Java applets, JavaScript, or other programs and scripts that can be processed locally on the user's computer. Because the processing activity is performed locally without the need to transmit data back and forth, the results are more immediate and give a better sense of interactivity and exchange. Java applets are miniature programs written in Java, compiled, and then embedded in the Web site as executable files. Scripts, however, use interpreted languages—JavaScript, J-script, or ActionScript—that can be written directly into the HTML code. Scripts are executed line by line by the browser as it moves down through the lines of code.

Although scripts are incorporated directly into the HTML code, it is still wise to create these segments of code and test them in advance, collecting them together systematically so that they can be incorporated, where needed, when the site is put together. JavaScript is a viable tool for this purpose, as is ActionScript, at a more limited level. Microsoft JScript operates only on Internet Explorer, and thus is not a good option because best practices, as well as compliance with W3C guidelines and standards, dictate that sites be accessible from any platform and multiple browsers.

Bankrate.com (www.bankrate.com/brm/mortgage-calculator.asp?nav=mtg&page=calc_home) provides a form that calculates the payments on a mortgage immediately, based on amounts to be financed and interest rates.

server-side strategies
Actions performed by programs or scripts on the server computer (for example, a Web-hosting server or an intranet host), often called a daemon. Server-side programs offer more complicated types of transactions: access to large databases that are being actively updated or to calculations that would be too complex for desktop computers to handle.

client-side strategies
Refers to actions occurring on a local (an individual's) computer. Actions are performed by codes or scripts that are downloaded from a server and then executed on the local computer. Good for programs that manipulate or change data without requiring access to a database while the programs are running. Saves processing time on the server.

Use Organizational Aids

As resources are being prepared for use in producing the site, they can stack up into dozens, even hundreds, of files of various types. Some of these files will be used at multiple places within the site. On an ongoing basis, it will be necessary to identify any gaps in resources, and assign someone to follow up with the task of locating, adapting, or creating the missing resources. Access to all of the gathered files must be quick and efficient, and it must be assured that all members of the design team are using the most recent version of each resource.

This means it must be easy to determine the contents of each file without opening them repeatedly to find out. The content and status of each resource must be kept up-to-date, using a logical system for file names, folder locations, and other pertinent log information (such as the date the file was created, its original author, the date it was last revised, and the last person to revise the file). For those files that are in the process of being adapted, other information should be maintained so that all members of the design team know at any point in time that they are using the most current version. When various individuals on a design team have been assigned to work on particular elements and files, there must be a clear way of tracking progress and completion of these tasks, as well as supporting and managing file sharing, and other logistics. In addition to tracking the status of files and resources among the members of the design team, clear records must be maintained of resources that are moving back and forth between the client and the designers.

Tasks and tools that aid in this organization process, thereby saving significant amounts of time and confusion as the project progresses, include file logs, resource matrices, databases, and online resource banks. Software tools to support these include Microsoft Word (or other word-processing programs), Excel (or other spreadsheet programs), and Access (or other database programs). Photo log utility programs such as CompuPic and Portfolio are useful for tracking visual resources in thumbnail versions that can be viewed, classified, and cataloged quickly.

For small projects (fewer than 25 files), it might be sufficient to create and keep a text-based log of resources, setting up a table (or matrix) in either Word or Excel (or an equivalent program). Columns in this table should be set up to keep track of the current information on each resource, such as file name, file type, file size, as well as the source, condition, adaptation work needed, and person responsible for that adaptation work, for each file. Figure 6.14 is an example of a simple Word log used to track files.

For medium-to-large projects, using a database tool is much more efficient for sorting, tracking, and providing up-to-date progress reports about resources. An Access database can be set up quickly, with fields to contain each of the data elements mentioned previously, and any others that would help keep track of the tasks of gathering, adapting, or creating resources needed for the site.

File Name Type	File Size	File	Source	Status	Work Needed	Person Responsible
index	.html	30 KB	Eric	in progress	check links	Jeff
logo	.gif	256 KB	client	in progress	reduce file size	Jeff
navbar	.gif	200 KB	Simone	in progress	create image map	Lisa
map	.gif	150 KB	Simone	in progress	create	Simone
purpose	.doc	50 KB	Alexia	in progress	edit	Lars

FIGURE 6.14 Sample Log

One of the most efficient and effective ways to manage resources for a Web site is to create an organized online resource bank, with elements accessible and cross-referenced using hyperlinks. As members of the design team complete work gathering, adapting, or creating resources, these elements can be made available for use by the full team by uploading them to a shared resource area for the Web site and providing simple pages with tabular descriptions, with links to the locations for each. The benefit of this system is that resources stored online can be accessed from anywhere, any time. To protect resources, this area should be password-protected, with access limited to the design team and any contributors from the client company who will be providing or working with resources as they are being prepared.

web 6.2 activity

MULTIMEDIA RESOURCES

Knowing all that is necessary to stay on the edge of Web design requires constant and ongoing learning. However, the Web also provides a ready means for that learning. To quote one online project mentor for Web designer/developer students, in a message he wrote about something he had just taught his students: "And, by the way, I had no idea how to do any of that marquee stuff until about two minutes before I did it. I looked it up online. With good searching skills, the entire Internet can become an extension of your knowledge base."

The purpose of this activity is to demonstrate the degree to which you are able to learn new skills using a "just in time" approach to learning. Consider this scenario, and respond to it. Then, report your experience.

You have been invited to an interview tomorrow at a place where you would love to work as a member of a Web site design team. You know from the job description that the individual hired in this new position will be assigned to develop animations (along with other tasks) using Fireworks, the vector-based Macromedia tool that can be used for every part of the image-production process, from creating Web graphics, to animating them, to optimizing the file sizes for the Web. To prepare for the interview, you need to begin to get up to speed on Fireworks as soon as possible.

Your task is to learn to use Fireworks—tonight—at least enough so you can communicate intelligently about the program. To learn about this program, follow this process:

1. Go to Web Monkey at www.hotwired.lycos.com/webmonkey/.
2. Navigate to the One-day Fireworks Tutorial presented by Michael Kay, author of the *Web Wizard's Guide to Flash.*
3. Learn the basics of Fireworks, including:
   - Functionality and features
   - The benefits of being vector based and designed specifically for the Web
   - What you will be able to produce with it
   - Interface
   - How to draw in Fireworks and how to work with files from other graphics programs
   - How to import and edit bitmap images
   - How to edit text and alter shapes, color, and effects of vector-based objects

- How to create movement
- How to optimize animations to keep file sizes small enough for the Web
- How much time you estimate the various Fireworks design tasks will require (as a rule of thumb, double or even triple your estimate)

In your own words, write a two-page description of what tasks you would use Fireworks for and how you would perform these tasks. Include details that will persuade someone reading the report that you have enough familiarity with Fireworks to use it efficiently if you were hired for a job that required this.

PROTOTYPE, REVIEW, AND PRODUCE THE FULL SITE

Before moving on to develop the full site, it is crucial to develop a prototype that can be reviewed by the client. It might take several cycles of prototype building and reviewing to arrive at a design for the full site. After the prototype has been reviewed and approved, the client should sign documents stating that the site meets with full approval. Then, and only then, is the way clear to carry through with the production of the full site.

Develop the Prototype

The prototype is a mockup of elements of the site, not a fully rendered version. Although parts of a prototype are actual working versions of pages, many parts might still be in the form of hand-drawn sketches. The assumption is that much or even all of a design can change—thus, rough models help identify changes and improvements until written agreement can be reached about how the final site will be rendered. Although a prototype is not a full rendering of the site, at this point in the design process, the project begins to take form.

Both technical and visual prototypes are needed. Technical prototypes are developed for interactive elements such as interfaces between the site and a database back-end or other technical plans. Technical prototypes, of course, must be working versions—they must be coded in HTML and, if called for, include scripts and connections to databases (copies of the client's true databases). The purpose of a technical prototype is to provide "proof-of-concept": a small version of each interactive function is tested with a few sample cases and shown to the client for approval. These are then expanded into full versions when they are functioning properly and have been approved by the client.

DEVELOP COMPOSITES The visual prototype consists of a set of mockup pages (also called **composites** or "comps") which provide ways to view and decide among various possible approaches to the look and layout of the pages. Composites show roughed-in versions of the layout of elements, typographical choices (headings, fonts, colors, sizing, emphasis), and the arrangement of graphics.

Although hand-drawn sketches of the home page might have been done in an earlier part of the design process, the sketches or roughed-in pages done at this stage can begin to show more detail and to show internal pages as well as the home page (see Figure 6.15). Presumably, some design elements have undergone development and can

composites —
Rough sketches of Web pages. Intended to show the possible placement of elements on a page, after some decisions have been made as to what will go on the page. Can be hand-drawn or based on rough pages, produced through preliminary coding.

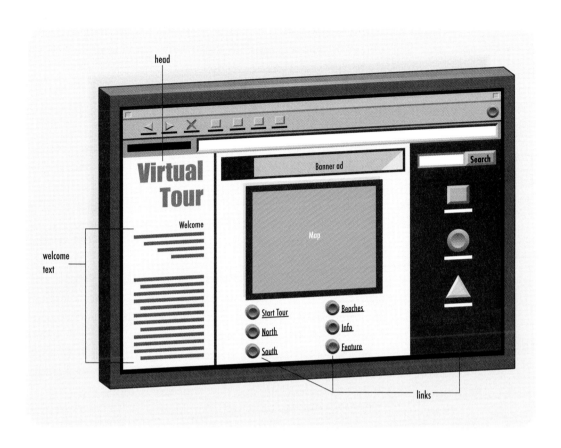

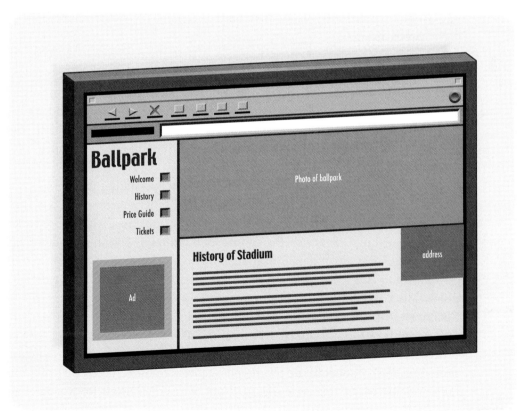

FIGURE 6.15 Home Page Composites

begin to be placed into these sketches. Incremental progress such as this is typical for a Web design project, regardless of its size. It is good practice to prepare several choices of each page. This allows the client greater opportunity to provide input and the designer a chance to learn what the client prefers by assessing actual reactions.

storyboards
Mockup pages arranged in a sequence that shows the paths through a Web site a user might typically take. Mockup pages show as much detail as possible, even though items to be placed on each page might be in development.

DEVELOP STORYBOARDS Comps are then arranged in a set of **storyboards** that shows the ways in which users will move through the site. Thus, home page composites and interior page composites need to be prepared for the storyboard. Using visitor profiles and sample scenarios developed earlier in the Web design process, the storyboard shows what the experience of moving through the site will be like, from beginning to middle to end, for various types of users. (This can result in a large amount of detail. As a result, some pages might be omitted from the storyboard; the most important stopping points in users' journeys through a site are the most critical features to show on the storyboard.)

Connecting lines between mockups show where a screen choice leads. These mockups (and connecting lines) can be created using any expedient method that makes it possible to view and review the storyboard. One storyboard method is to create mockups on note cards or multiple screen captures, printed and cut apart, with one note card per screen. These cards can be posted on a bulletin board and then moved around, with string used to indicate the links among screens (see Figure 6.16). An electronic version of such a storyboard can be created using software that shows mockups and the connections among them.

Storyboards help designers visualize and troubleshoot the screen and interchange sequence as a visitor moves through the site. Because it is a work in progress, a storyboard needs to be flexible to work with and easy to view and review. Designers review the composites and storyboards first; later, the client reviews the material the designers have chosen to show.

Both the designer and client, however, review the designs by "walking through" the storyboards. During the walk-throughs, the designer and client address issues such as:

- What is missing? Is there an organizing page, interim page, or interaction step missing?
- What is superfluous? Are there any screens that serve no purpose and contribute no value? These may either be eliminated or redesigned to "earn their place" on the site.
- Is the design optimal from the larger level of the full experience of the site, for each scenario, for each profile of anticipated visitor?

Many potential problems can be spotted early by walking through the site storyboard, thus saving time and resources that would otherwise be spent without need. Also, walking through the storyboard is a useful means for dividing up work when the site is large enough to require the coordinated efforts of several page designers.

Although the actual details of design are now beginning to be captured in representative form, it still is essential not to get too attached to the prototype designs at this point. The entire purpose of prototyping is to provide a few versions of the basic site design, and then challenge the design until it arrives at a place that is best suited to the requirements of the site and the vision of the client. Tasks done earlier feed into the process. Developing the resources provides essential input into the production of the prototype, and producing the prototype uncovers resource needs that might not have been anticipated. As this cycle is carried out, additional needs for resources are discovered, leading to additional plans for filling gaps or seeking input and material from the client's representatives.

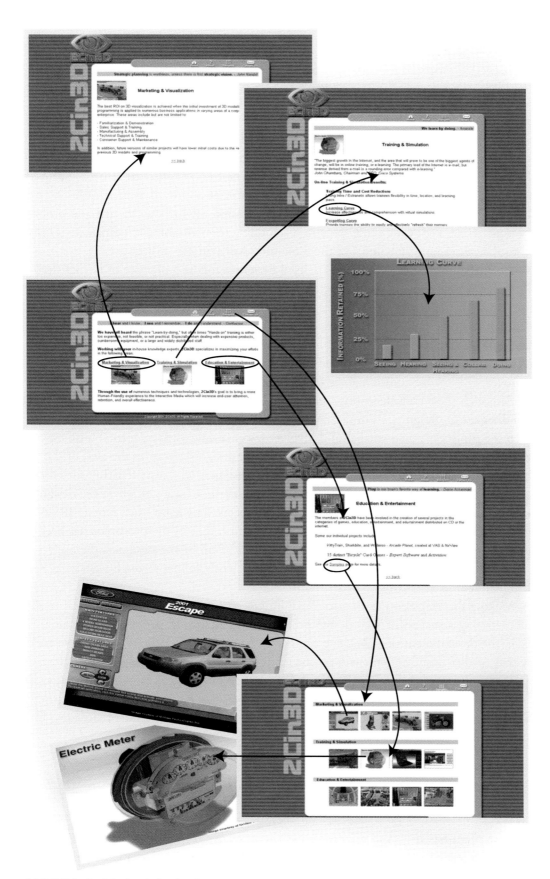

FIGURE 6.16 Sample Storyboard
This storyboard, created from the 2Cin3D site, shows sample screens and how they branch.

Direct Reviews and Obtain Sign-Offs

The prototype and review cycle might be repeated several times, but the process is the same, regardless of the number of repetitions. The design team presents the prototype to the client's representatives—those who have the authority to make final decisions and binding agreements about the site's design—and shows the composites and storyboards, and walks the clients through any sets of sample screens that have been developed. If choices are available, these are discussed. A composite can be approved as is or approved with conditions and changes. The storyboard also can be approved as is or with changes. If changes are extensive, another review session might be necessary, and probably is advisable. Following these steps to reach full agreement about the final site is critical to the success and timeliness of the remaining work on the project.

As final approvals are given, experienced designers follow a practice of having the client sign actual printouts of the approved page composites and storyboard. This is protection for the designers as they carry out the full rendering of the site, following the plan that has been agreed to. The design team must be clear as to when major changes can be made with considerable flexibility and when the official plan is considered to be in place. The client must be informed that changes made after these plans are officially approved will involve additional costs and adjustments to the time line for the project.

Although these considerations seem to apply only in large projects being conducted by a designer or design team under contract for a client, the same principles hold even when the project is much smaller and involves fewer people and less formal business arrangements. These principles also apply when the design team is on the staff of the site's sponsor. They even hold true for individual designers who are preparing sites for their own use. In all site design projects, it is essential to be aware of where the design team is in the design-prototype-review-produce process. The team must remain flexible and open to ideas that will make the site better—until, that is, the prototype has been approved. At that moment, even if the approvals are given by the designers themselves, it is time to stop making casual changes and to efficiently follow through with what has been planned.

Making this transition from great flexibility to efficient productivity is critical to the completion of a successful Web design project. If this change in perspective does not occur, the development of a Web site can become an unending process. This is not to say that further improvements will not be made later, after the site has been launched. But there must come a time in the life cycle of a Web design project when the project moves forward to completion. When this time arrives, it is best to move forward firmly to complete and launch the site as it is currently designed, making note of any ideas for future improvements to be considered at a later time.

Produce the Full Site

After the client has approved the prototype, the next task is to produce a full version of the site. Because prototypes can consist of a combination of coded and hand-drawn renditions of pages, it is necessary to produce complete, coded versions, with all links active and working, all scripts tested, and all graphics and other audiovisual elements created and in place.

The goal at this point is to produce a version that is ready to be uploaded quickly in the next phase (Phase III) of the Web design process. This means that all pages are finalized and the directory structure for the finished site has been followed exactly. Every prototype page is turned into a fully functioning page; if any component was not rendered as a prototype, it must be created; and all navigational paths must be built. Every detail must be right. Otherwise, come launch time, the site will have problems.

At this stage, efficiency is also important. Every strategy that assists in building pages at a productive pace should be used, keeping the focus on preparing the site for launch. As designers become more experienced, they develop ways to make the work process more efficient. A common element of these efficiencies is "enter once, use many." As each piece of work is completed, use it wherever possible to create similar components of the site. Some important examples of this principle include:

- **Save As** When one page has been completed in its proper form and a new page is to be created, open the file of the completed page and, using Save As, give the file the name of the new page. This new file acts as a model for the new page, with many of the features already coded. To make the appropriate changes to the file, overwrite the text and images with new material. This saves the time of setting up the structure for the additional pages and also increases the consistency between pages.

- **Templates** Another possibility is to set up a page template that contains "greeked in" text (nonsense letters, not composed copy). Use copies of this for each of the pages that will follow that format, replacing the "greeked" elements with actual content.

- **Styles and Style Sheets** Use the most generalized level of style control possible. In the logic of "cascading" styles, the browser uses the most specific level of style specified at any given point in the page. Thus, the most efficient process is to set up what will be used at the highest level possible so it can be applied without further attention. Then, the only remaining style (font, size, color, and so forth) determinations needed are those that are different from the normal specifications.

- **Tables** To control placement of text and images onscreen, tables save considerable time and struggle with layout control. Use invisible tables (by setting the borders to 0), establish a page grid, and adjust the heights and widths of the rows and columns to control placement. Remember, however, that tables need to be used so they do not thwart the goals of building an accessible site.

- **Copy and Paste** Use Copy/Paste liberally to save time and prevent error. Even when specifics will change, blocks of code, text, or page elements pasted into place as a placeholder can dramatically increase efficiency.

Such efficiencies, used properly, actually reduce errors. A component used numerous times can be copied without error into every page that uses it, a sure method for cutting down both coding and troubleshooting time. However, these efficiencies do not remove the burden of testing every new page to make sure it works.

An important factor concerns the use of servers. If the design team has been able to upload work-in-progress to the client's server, many of the bugs, especially those regarding directory structure, might already be worked out. If, however, the design team has uploaded its work to a server other than the client's (to avoid using the client's host to store work-in-progress), folder and file paths in the HTML code might need special attention.

Before getting involved in the mechanics of a site's design and layout, experienced Web designers begin with composites. These can be very rough. One designer described it this way: "It can be much easier to obtain goals like this by working on a scratchpad of paper during your design phase. I like to use colored pencils and markers to draw a series of tiny little Web page rectangles to start. This way, in a few minutes, I can try many different layouts, themes, color schemes, and navigation methods."

The purpose of this activity is to create a set of composite sketches by tracing existing Web sites that have been successfully designed. To complete this activity, perform the following tasks:

1. Go to five to eight sites of your choice and print the home pages.

2. Using plain paper and a set of colored marker pens, pencils, or crayons, trace the major blocks where graphics and text, headings and bullets, buttons and links are located. Include details such as the actual text of major heads, Web site's name, and descriptions of graphic components. Come up with a way to show the different screen elements, such as by putting boxes around the headings to show the size and shape, greeking in the text, underlining the links, boxing the graphics, and sketching in the shapes of bullets and buttons. Where needed for clarity, write a note about any special element. The goal is to capture the basics of the page, skipping past extra repetitions of elements after you have captured the ideas.

3. Look through your stack of rough sketches of home page layouts, laying them out side-by-side, and note any similarities or major differences.

4. Write a one- to two-page report describing any patterns you notice. Answer questions such as the following:

   - What major differences exist among the home pages? Do all include text stating the purpose of the Web site? Do some contain no introductory text? How many pages consist entirely of categorized links?

   - How does each page present the navigational possibilities? Are the navigational methods clearly distinguished?

   - Does the arrangement of material (main text, graphics, links) enhance the usefulness of the home page or could the arrangement be improved?

apply & practice

Online Quiz

As a review of the key concepts in this chapter, define the terms in the following list:

- Active Server Pages (ASP)
- back end
- client-side strategies
- composites
- ODBC-compliant databases
- rollover
- server-side strategies
- site map
- splash page
- storyboards
- subordinate
- superordinate

After you are confident that you understand this chapter's content, go to this book's Internet Resource Center (IRC) at www.emcp.com/ and take the self-test online quiz for this chapter. Review any questions you answered incorrectly, and then study the related chapter material again. Retake the online quiz as many times as you need to achieve full mastery (90–100%).

Topics Roundtable

1. How can information architecture—and performing the steps involved in breaking information down and then regrouping it—help a Web site sponsor improve its Web site?

2. Pick an area in which you have a fair amount of knowledge (for example, sports, crafts, gardening, travel, investments, technology). Describe how you might break out and organize the informational elements in this area. How would your organization be different from the ways other Web sites in this area have organized them?

3. How does a hierarchical structure differ from a cluster or star structure, and for what kinds of informational needs is each type of structure best suited?

4. Describe some of the more effective navigation designs on sites you have used.

5. How can animation enhance the presentation of information on a Web site? When would animated images or a Flash movie hinder the presentation of information?

6. What might be some typical problems design teams encounter when they produce a fully working version of a Web site?

> ➤ Understand how links work.
> ➤ Understand the difference between relative and absolute paths.
> ➤ Create internal and external links.
> ➤ Create links for images, e-mail, and file downloads.
> ➤ Format links.
> ➤ Troubleshoot broken links.
> ➤ Add links to your Window to the Web resource site.

technical walk-through

The outstanding feature of the World Wide Web lies in its capability to link information. Links allow users to move easily from one area to another within a file, or to move to files located anywhere in the world. Anyone using the Web can access information seamlessly by moving from link to link with the click of a mouse. The ability to link information is one of the most important HTML skills you will learn.

Links

Link is short for hyperlink. **Hyperlink** is the technical term for the areas within a Web resource that function as links (connections) to other locations within the resource, or as links to resources located elsewhere on the Web. Linking is accomplished by means of HyperText Transfer Protocol (HTTP). A **protocol** is a set of rules governing the transmission of data. HTTP defines how messages are formatted and transmitted on the Web. Hypertext Markup Language (HTML) is used to create documents that will be transmitted using HTTP. Links use a **Uniform Resource Locator** (URL) to point to other resources. The URL functions as an address for any resource located on the Web. There are two types of URLs, absolute and relative.

An absolute URL contains the full URL path needed by a browser to locate and retrieve a Web resource. It identifies the protocol to be used, the server location for the resource, the resource's root directory (or folder), and so on through every directory of the path to the individual file to be displayed. For example, the URL for the front page of the online edition of *USA Today* (http://www.usatoday.com/news/front.htm) can be broken down in the following manner:

- **http://** indicates the protocol to be used. Protocols are always followed by a colon and two forward slashes. Other examples of Internet protocols are FTP (File Transfer Protocol) and telnet.
- **www.usatoday.com/** is the domain name for the USA Today Web site, which identifies the Web server where the *USA Today* Web site's root directory is located.
- **news/** indicates a directory within the site named "news."
- **front.htm** indicates an HTML file named "front" that is located within the "news" directory.

A browser uses the instructions contained in the *USA Today* URL to locate the front.htm file so that it can create and display the *USA Today* front page on a computer screen (see Figure 6.17).

A relative URL (sometimes referred to as a local URL) is a kind of URL shortcut. A relative URL can be used to retrieve any resource located on the same domain server within the same directory structure without the need to include the server location and the directory path that preceded the current location. Using the *USA Today* URL as an example, documents within the "news" directory (the current location) could be linked by using a relative URL consisting only of the name of the document ("*document_name*.html"). If a document is located in a subdirectory of the "news" directory, this would be indicated by a forward slash followed by the name of the subdirectory. Imagine that there was a subdirectory of the "news" directory named "local," and inside the "local" subdirectory there was an HTML document named "city.html." The relative URL used to locate and display this document would look like this: "local/city.html", with the slash indicating that "local" is a subdirectory. Higher

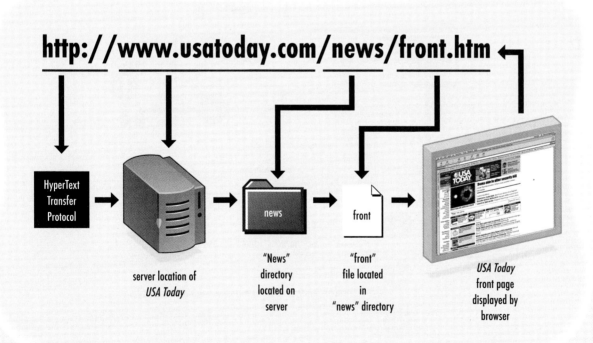

FIGURE 6.17

The URL for the *USA Today* front page indicates the protocol to be used, the Web server hosting the site, and the directory path and file name for the HTML document that a browser will interpret to display the *USA Today* front page.

directories are indicated by two periods and a forward slash (../). Using the *USA Today* example again, a relative URL of "../sports.html" would instruct a browser to move up one directory level from the current location to locate a file named "sports." Figure 6.18 illustrates the different types of relative paths.

When creating your own Web site, it is best to use relative links for your pages. Then, if you ever decide to change domains, you will not need to edit these links. If you use absolute links and then change domains, you will need to edit all your links, which could result in a considerable amount of effort.

Links are not difficult to create, but it is extremely important that they be correct in every aspect. Even the smallest error results in a link that does not work. No mail deliverer is standing by to correct minor mistakes in a URL address. Domain names are not case-sensitive, but the rest of the URL is, so keying a lowercase letter instead of an uppercase letter could result in link failure.

Relative Links

Relative links are all that are needed to link the different resources composing a Web site, as long as their paths point to resources contained within the same domain. These

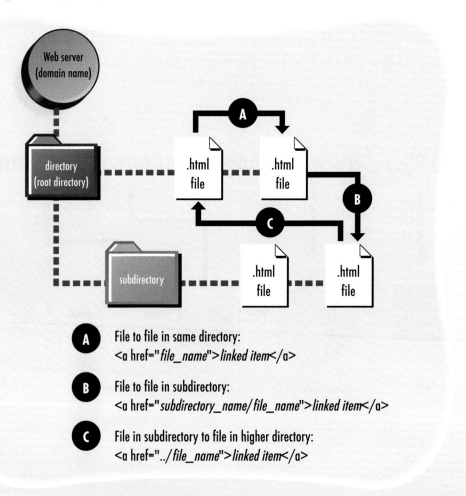

A   File to file in same directory:
         <a href="*file_name*">*linked item*</a>

B   File to file in subdirectory:
         <a href="*subdirectory_name/file_name*">*linked item*</a>

C   File in subdirectory to file in higher directory:
         <a href="*../file_name*">*linked item*</a>

FIGURE 6.18
Files located in the same domain can be linked using relative paths.

relative links continue to work even after the root directory and its contents are uploaded to a Web server to bring the site online.

Relative links are created using **anchor tags** (<a href="*path/filename.htm*"></a>). The "a" in the tag stands for **anchor**, and the "href" for **hypertext reference**. The anchor tags are used to enclose the item (text, an image, and so on) that will become a "link." Text enclosed between the anchor open and close tags appears on browsers in a blue, underlined font. Note that the anchor tag is a paired tag, and that the anchor start tag must therefore be followed by an anchor end tag.

To summarize from the earlier discussion, the path for a relative link consists only of the name of the file to be linked to if the document to be linked to is in the same directory as the document that contains the link. If the file is located in a subdirectory of the directory where the linking document is located, this subdirectory needs to be listed in the path, with each subdirectory followed by a forward slash (/). If the file to be linked to is located in a directory that is located above the directory of the linking document, each directory "up" should be indicated by two periods and a forward slash (../) followed by the file name. All paths and file names used in anchor tags should be enclosed in quotation marks.

Create a relative link in a practice page:

1. Use your text editor to open the **shell.html** file.
2. Save the shell.html file as **links_practice_1.html** using the Save As command.
3. Key a title as indicated here:

```
<title>This Is My Links Practice Page</title>
```

4. Key the code and text between the body tags:

```
<body>
<p>
HTML documents can use relative paths to link to other documents
located within the same domain, or use absolute paths to link
to documents located on other domains.
<br />
<br />
<br />
Links can be made to an e-mail address so that visitors can
send an e-mail message to a specified e-mail address.
<br />
<br />
Links can also be made to image files, and images can also be
made to function as links.
<br />
<br />
If you have material you would like your visitors to be able to
download, you can create links to that material as well.
<br />
<br />
Links are what makes the Web what it is today, an easy-to-use,
endless source of information!
</p>
</body>
```

5. You need to create another page to link to, so open the **shell.html** file again and save it as **links_practice_2.html** using the Save As command.

6. Key a title:

```
<title>This Is My Links Practice Page 2</title>
```

7. Key the paragraph tags and text between the body tags:

```
<body>
<p>
This Web page will be used to practice creating links.
</p>
</body>
```

8. Use your text editor to open the **links_practice_1.html** file.
9. Key an anchor tag with a path to the links_practice_2.html file. Note that because this file is located in the same directory as the links_practice_1.html file, you only need to key the file name and extension between the quotation marks.

```
HTML documents can use relative paths to <a
href="links_practice_2.html">link to other documents</a> located
within the same domain, or use absolute paths to link to
documents located on other domains.
```

10. Save the file and open it in your browser. The "link to other documents" text should now appear as a link, in blue underlined text (see Figure 6.19). When the cursor is passed over the link, it changes into the shape of a hand. Clicking on this link should bring up the links_practice_2.html page on the browser screen. Click the Back button to return to links_practice_1.html.

11. Create a new subdirectory under the web_practice directory (the directory where you save all your practice files). Name this folder **local_files**.

12. Use your text editor to open the **links_practice_2.html** file. Save the file as **links_practice_3.html** in the local_files folder.

13. Change the title as indicated here:

```
<title>This Is My
Links Practice Page
23</title>
```

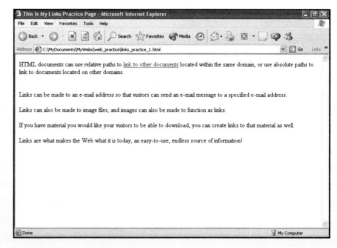

FIGURE 6.19
Hyperlinks, commonly known as links, usually appear in a document as blue underlined text. Clicking on the link instructs the browser to display the linked resource.

14. Use your text editor to open the **links_practice_1.html** file. Locate the anchor tag and change the path to link to the links_practice_3.html file:

```
<a href="local_files/links_practice_23.html">link to other
documents</a>
```

15. Save the file and refresh your browser. When you click on the link, the contents of the links_practice_3.html file should be displayed on your browser.

16. Use your text editor to view the **links_practice_3.html** file. Create a link from this page back to the links_practice_1 file located under the web_practice directory by keying the following anchor tag and path:

```
<body>
<p>
This Web page will be used to practice creating links. Click <a
href="../links_practice_1.html">here</a> to return to the
links_practice_1.html page.
</p>
</body>
```

17. Save the file and refresh your browser. Clicking the "here" link should bring the links_practice_1.html page to your screen. Notice how, in this case, you only needed to type in two periods and a forward slash (../) to indicate that the file was located in a directory one level up, rather than having to name the higher directory.

Internal Links

Relative links can be used to link locations within the same Web page. Internal links to material in a Web page avoid the need for visitors to scroll down the page until they find the information they are looking for. The use of internal page links often takes the form of a Web page with a table of contents at the top. Each element of the table of contents is linked to the location of the relevant material elsewhere on the page. Internal page links also can be used to link material to footnotes, or to create a link from one item to a related item located somewhere else on the page.

To create links within a Web page, the link target must be identified by a **named anchor** start tag and end tag (<a name="*name_of_link*">*target text*</a>). The start and end elements of the tag enclose the link target (the material you want to link to). After the link target has been identified, links to the target material can be created by placing a pound sign (#) before the target name in the anchor tag used to create the link: **<a href="#*name_of_link*">*text*</a>**.

For example, imagine that at the beginning of a Web page you mention that you will be discussing free graphics sites, and that the material dealing with free graphics sites is located much further down the page. The first thing you need to do is use a named anchor tag to identify the target text you want to link to. If the material on free graphics sites began with a header reading "Free Graphics Sites," this text could be designated as a named anchor like this: **<a name="free_graphics">Free Graphics Sites</a>**. You can give the target link any name you like, but it is a good idea to make the name relevant to the target link in some way.

After you have identified the text target to be linked to, you need to create the link to go there. To do this, key an anchor tag enclosing the text about free graphics at the beginning of the page. The reference used for this link must be the same as the name contained between the quotation marks in the named anchor, except that it must be preceded by the pound sign. In this example, the anchor tag to create a link to the free graphics part of the page would look like this: **<a href="#free_graphics">free graphics</a>**. After this coding is complete, when visitors to the page click on "free graphics" at the top of the page, the browser jumps to the section on free graphics further down the page. The link will be in blue underlined text just like any other link.

For an internal link to cause a change on the screen, the link and the link target material must be located some distance apart on the page. If they are close together, the page might not move, or might move only slightly. This is because internal links work by making sure that the target link material is visible on the browser screen. If it is already visible, there is no need for the browser screen to jump to another location.

Create an internal link:
1. Use your text editor to open the **links_practice_1.html** file.
2. Locate the anchor tag and change the path to link to the links_practice_2.html file:

```
<a href="localfiles/links_practice_32.html">link to other
documents</a>
```

3. Key the line break tags, named anchor start and end tags, and text as indicated below. The line breaks push this new sentence off the browser screen so that a visitor would have to scroll down to view it.

```
Links are what makes the Web what it is today, an easy-to-use,
endless source of information!
<br /><br /><br /><br /><br /><br /><br /><br /><br /><br /><br />
<a name="internal_link">This text is a target that will be
jumped to from a link at the top of the page.</a>
</p>
```

4. Go to the top of the file and key the anchor tag to jump down to the target you just created. Note that the name must be preceded with the pound sign, and be identical to the name identified in the named anchor tag.

```
<p>
HTML documents can use relative paths to <a
href="links_practice_2.html">link to other documents</a> located
within the same domain, or use absolute paths to link to
documents located on other domains. They can even be used to <a
href="#internal_link">link to material within the same page.</a>
</p>
```

5. Save the file and refresh your browser. Clicking on the link you just created should cause the browser to jump ahead so that the target sentence at the bottom of the screen is visible. If the target sentence was already visible before clicking the link, go back into the file to key additional line break tags so that the sentence is pushed off the screen view. Save the file, refresh your browser, and try the link again to see the effect.

Internal links also can be used to link to a named anchor tag located in another document. The link to the target document includes the path to the target document, followed by the pound sign (#) and the name of the named anchor. For example: **<a href="*target_document*.html#target">link</a>**. This link would take you to the named anchor of the target located on the target_document.html Web page.

Create an internal link to another document:
1. Because you have already created a named anchor in the **links_practice_1.html** file, use your text editor to open the **links_practice_2.html** file so that you can link from that page to the named anchor in the **links_practice_1.html** page.

2. Key the anchor tag and text:

```
<body>
<p>
This Web page will be used to practice creating links. Clicking
<a href="links_practice_1.html#internal_link">here</a> will link
to the named anchor area in the links_practice_1.html file.
</p>
</body>
```

3. Save the file and refresh your browser. Clicking on the link you just created should bring up the **links_practice_1.html** page, with the section marked by the named anchor visible on the screen.

4. Use your text editor to open the **links_practice_2.html** file. Delete the name of the named anchor in the anchor tag to see what would happen if you did not include the pound sign and the name of the named anchor tag.

5. Save the file and refresh your browser. Clicking on the link should now open the **links_practice_1.html** file at the top of the page instead of the bottom.

External Links

For links to resources outside the Web page domain containing the link, absolute paths must be used. The process of creating links with absolute paths is the same as that for creating links with relative paths, except that absolute paths must contain the entire URL for a linked resource.

There have been cases in which Web site owners have tried to forbid others from linking to their site, or to pages located on their site. The issue of whether or not Web site owners can deny permission to link to their sites has not yet been resolved by the courts. To many observers, the idea of forbidding someone to link to a site or a page makes as little sense as trying to prevent someone from publishing a street address, since a URL is really nothing more than an address. For the moment, you can create links to any site or page you wish. As a courtesy, you should request permission if the linked site is private or noncommercial, as small sites might be overwhelmed if too many people try to link to the site at the same time.

Many URLs are long, increasing the chance that you will make a mistake when keying them by hand. To avoid errors, the best practice is to copy the URL from the Web browser and then paste it inside an anchor tag.

CREATE AN EXTERNAL LINK

Create a link to a resource located outside your Web domain:

1. Open your browser window and log on to the Web page you want to create a link to.

2. Look for the site's URL in your browser's address window located near the top of the browser.

3. Use your mouse to select the URL.

4. Right-click and select Copy from the menu that appears (see Figure 6.20).

5. Use your text editor to open the **links_practice_1. html** file.

6. Key the anchor start and end tags as indicated here. Right-click and select Paste from the menu that appears to place the URL you copied between the anchor tag quotation marks.

FIGURE 6.20

URLs can be copied by using a mouse to select the desired URL in a browser's address bar. Right-clicking the mouse causes a menu to appear on the screen. The URL can be copied by selecting Copy, and then pasted inside an anchor tag path.

```
<p>
HTML documents can
use relative paths
to <a
href="links_practice_2.html">link to other documents</a> located
within the same domain, or use absolute paths to link to
documents <a href="copied URL here">located on other
domains</a>. They can even be used to <a href="#internal_
link">link to material within the same page.</a>
</p>
```

7. Save the file and open **links_practice_1.html** in your browser. If your browser is online, clicking on the link should cause it to display the page you linked to.

Links to Image Files

You can create links to images as well as text. Clicking on a link to an image usually causes the browser to open a new window to display the image. Clicking the Back button returns visitors to the original page.

To link to an image, the relative or absolute path and file name of the image must be placed in the path section of the anchor tag. The image must be in one of the three formats supported by most Web browsers: GIF, JPEG, or PNG.

LINK TO AN IMAGE

Create a link to an image:

1. Use your text editor to open the **links_practice_1.html** file.
2. Key in an anchor tag with a path to an image located in your root directory as indicated here. If you have saved the image in a subdirectory, be sure to precede the name of the image file with the name of the subdirectory, followed by a forward slash.

```
<br />
Links can also be made to <a href="relative path and filename
of image">image files</a>, and images can also be made to
function as links.
<br />
```

3. Save the file and open **links_practice_1.html** in your browser. Clicking on the "image files" link should open a new browser window with the image you selected displayed in the new browser.

4. Return to your text editor and delete the link created in Step 2.

Thumbnail and Button Links

Images can be used as links to other Web resources. This is frequently done when the image is a thumbnail version of a larger image. A large number of thumbnails can be placed on a Web page without creating a cumulative file size that would be slow to load for visitors with less than optimal Internet connection speeds. These thumbnail images can be made into links that enable visitors who want to see a larger copy to do so by clicking on the thumbnail, to have the browser open up the larger image in a new window.

Thumbnail size images also can take the form of control buttons and symbols that can be added to a Web page to link to various resources. "Next Page," "Previous Page," "Home," and "Return" buttons are just a few examples of thumbnail images that can be used to allow visitors easy navigation on your site. Many of the sites featuring free graphics have a number of control buttons that can be downloaded and used free of charge (see Figure 6.21).

A thumbnail link to a larger image is created by using anchor tags to create a link to the larger image, and then placing an image tag for the thumbnail between the anchor start and end tags. The following is an example of how this looks in practice:

FIGURE 6.21

Many free graphics sites have a large selection of Web graphics, including buttons that can be used for many different kinds of links.

```
<a href="image_file.extension"><img
src="thumbnail_image.extension" height="pixel size" width="pixel
size" /></a>
```

Note that the anchor tag path to the image file does not contain height and width attributes. This is because attributes are not allowed within anchor tags. Dimensions for the thumbnail have been included, as they should be any time an image tag is used. If the thumbnail in the previous example was used as a button to link to another page or Web resource, the anchor tag path to the larger image would instead be a path to the link target.

Use thumbnail images to link to larger images, or use them as control buttons. You can use your image editor to create a thumbnail, or you can download a thumbnail image from a free graphics site.

1. Log on to a free graphics site.
2. Locate an image you want to use. Do not click to enlarge the image. Instead, right-click on the image thumbnail.
3. Choose Save Picture As (*Internet Explorer*) or Save Image As (*Netscape*) to save the thumbnail to your root directory, or the subdirectory where you save your images.
4. Now save a larger version of the thumbnail by clicking on the thumbnail, and then downloading the larger image on your screen to your root directory or image subdirectory.
5. Use your text editor to open the **links_practice_1.html** file.
6. Key the anchor and image tags:

```
Links can also be made to image files, and images can also be
made to function as links.
<br />
<br />
<a href="image_file.extension"><img src="thumbnail_
image.extension" height="pixel size" width="pixel size"></a>
<br />
<br />
```

7. Save the file and refresh your browser. The thumbnail image you specified should appear on your page (see Figure 6.22). Click on the image. A new browser window should open to display the larger copy of the thumbnail image.

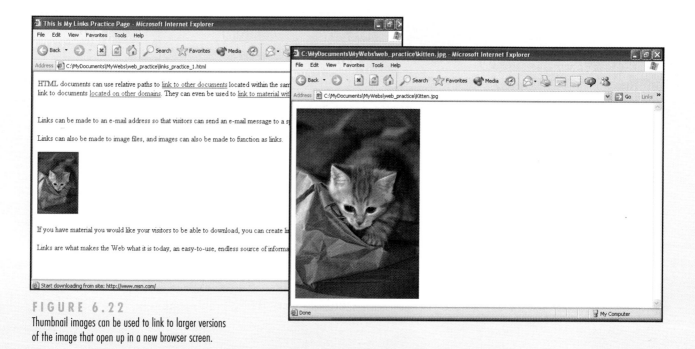

FIGURE 6.22

Thumbnail images can be used to link to larger versions of the image that open up in a new browser screen.

It is a good idea to let visitors know the file size of the image a thumbnail is linked to, especially if it is a very large file. This can be accomplished by inserting an alternative text attribute and text inside the image tag enclosed by the anchor link.

IDENTIFY FILE SIZE WITH ALT TEXT

Use the alternative text attribute to show a visitor the image file size:

1. Use your text editor to open the **links_practice_1.html** file.

2. Key an alternative text attribute and text inside the image tag. Substitute the size of the image in kilobytes (KB) or megabytes (MB) for the "X":

```
<a href="image_file.extension"><img src="thumbnail_
image.extension" height="pixel size" width="pixel size"
alt="Link to X KB or MB image."></a>
```

3. Save the file and refresh your browser. If you are using a recent browser version, the alternative text should appear on the screen when you float the curser over the image (see Figure 6.23).

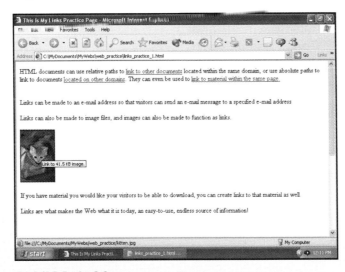

FIGURE 6.23

An alternative text attribute and text can be placed inside the image tag used to create a thumbnail link to a larger image. In this example, the text is used to let visitors know the size of the file they will be opening.

DELETE AN IMAGE BORDER

The thumbnail image has a border. If you want to eliminate the border, follow these steps:

1. Use your text editor to open the **links_practice_1.html** file.

2. Key a border attribute and value of "0" inside the image tag:

```
<br />
<br />
<a href="image_file.extension"><img src="thumbnail_
image.extension" height="pixel size" width="pixel size"
alt="Link to X KB or MB image." border="0"></a>
<br />
<br />
```

3. Save the file and refresh your browser. The image will be borderless.

LINK YOUR WEB PAGES WITH THUMBNAIL BUTTONS

Use a thumbnail as a button to link your Web pages:

1. Visit a free graphics site. Locate a control button suitable for use as a "Back" or "Return" button.
2. Download the button to your root directory or image subdirectory following the same process used for copying images from free graphics sites that you learned earlier.
3. Use your file-management program to rename the button to match its function, such as "Home," "Back," "Return," and so on.
4. Use your text editor to open the **links_practice_2.html** file.
5. Key anchor and image tags as indicated below. Note that the image tag path should be for the thumbnail, and the anchor tag path and file name should be for the Web resource you want to link to. In this case you will be linking to the **links_practice_1.html** page.

```
<p>
This Web page will be used to practice creating links. Clicking
<a href="links_practice_1.html">here</a> will link to the named
anchor area in the links_practice_1.html file.
</p>
<br />
<br />
<a href="links_practice_1.html"><img src="control_button_
image.extension" height="pixel size" width="pixel size"
border="0"></a>
</body>
```

6. Save the file and open **links_practice_2. html** in your browser. The button you specified as a thumbnail should now appear on your browser's screen (see Figure 6.24). Clicking the button instructs the browser to display the content of the links_practice_ 1.html file.

FIGURE 6.24

Small image files in the form of buttons or symbols can be used to link to any kind of Web resource.

Download Links

Links can be created that point to files that can be downloaded. This is useful when material you want to share with visitors is too large to place on a Web page. For example, you could place the contents of a 10-page Word document on your Web page, but it would take up a lot of space and you would have to waste a lot of time formatting the material so that it appeared just as it did in the original document. An easier way of allowing visitors access to this material is to create a link to the file that allows them to download it to their own computers.

A download link is created using an anchor tag. The path and file name of the file to be downloaded is placed inside the anchor tag. A link that would allow users to download a Word file might look like this:

```
Click<a
href="http://www.domain_name.com/download_files/document.doc">
here</a> to download a copy.
```

In the previous example, the word "here" has been enclosed by the anchor tag to make it a link that will allow visitors to download the file specified in the path of the anchor tag.

CREATE A DOWNLOAD LINK

Create a link that allows visitors to download a file from one of your Web pages:

1. Use the file manager to place a copy of a Word file (or other word processing file) in the root directory for your Web site.
2. Use your text editor to open the **links_practice_1.html** file.
3. Key an anchor tag and path to your download file:

```
If you have material you would like your visitors to be able to
<a href="path and filename for download file">download</a> you
can create links to that material as well.
```

4. Save the file and refresh your browser. If your file does not download automatically when you click the word "download," a download dialog box will appear that prompts you to either open the file or save it on your computer.

E-mail Links

An anchor tag can be used to create an e-mail link. Clicking on the link instructs a browser to open a pre-addressed e-mail form on the browser screen. Visitors can key comments and send the e-mail message just as they would normally. The e-mail will go to the address specified in the anchor tag. The path to the e-mail address specified in the anchor tag begins with "mailto:". This is followed by the complete e-mail address. The following is an example of an anchor tag that could be used to create an e-mail link:

```
<a href="mailto:your e-mail address">E-mail Me!</a>
```

An e-mail link only works if the person clicking on the link is using a browser that has been configured to work with an e-mail program, such as Outlook Express or Eudora.

Create an e-mail link on your Web page. If your browser is not configured to work with an e-mail program, consult with your instructor to see which e-mail program you can use and how you can configure your browser to work with that program.

1. Use your text editor to open the **links_practice_1.html** file.

2. Key an e-mail anchor tag that includes your e-mail address:

```
Links can be made to an e-mail address so that visitors can
send an e-mail message to a specified e-mail address. Click <a
href="mailto:your e-mail address">here</a> to send an e-mail
message.
```

3. You also can specify the subject content of the e-mail form by keying the following code and text just after the e-mail address:

```
<a href="mailto:your e-mail address?subject=key in subject
here">here</a> to send an e-mail message.
```

4. Save the file and refresh your browser. If your browser has been configured to work with an e-mail program, it will display an e-mail message form pre-addressed to the e-mail address you specified in the path of the e-mail anchor tag (see Figure 6.25).

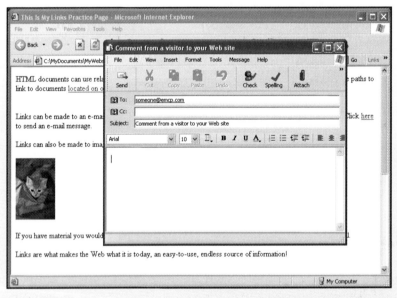

FIGURE 6.25
An e-mail link instructs the browser to display a pre-addressed e-mail form that can be filled out and sent to an e-mail address specified in the e-mail anchor tag. The content of the subject line can be specified in the e-mail anchor tag as well.

Text Markup and Links

Links can be formatted by using text tags, but text tags must not be placed inside the anchor tag.

Change the font size and color of a link by using text mark-up tags:

1. Use your text editor to open the **links_practice_1.html** file.
2. Key the font tags and attributes for your e-mail link:

```
Click <a href="mailto: your e-mail address?subject=Comment from
a visitor to your Web site"><font size="6"
color="green">here</font></a> to send an e-mail message.
```

3. Save the file and refresh your browser. Your e-mail link should now appear in large green text (see Figure 6.26).

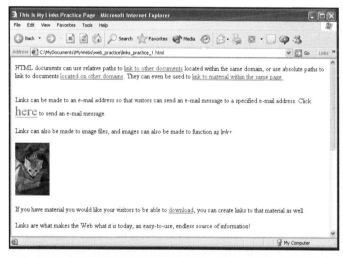

FIGURE 6.26

Text tags can be used to mark up links, but must not be included inside the anchor tags. A font tag with SIZE and COLOR attributes has been used to modify the e-mail link on this page so that it is a different color and size than the surrounding text.

Link Colors

The default color for links is blue underlined text. You can use special attributes inside the body start tag to specify the color of an inactive link (link=), an active link (alink=), and a visited link (vlink=). An **inactive link** is a link that has not yet been clicked on. An **active link** is one that has the cursor hovering over it, and a **visited link** is a link that has already been clicked on to link to another Web resource.

You might have noticed that links change color after they have been used. How long these links remain in a "visited" color is determined by your browser's history configuration. In Internet Explorer, selecting Tools from the menu bar and then selecting Internet Options brings up the Internet Options dialog box, which can be used to clear your browser's history and/or change the cache configuration. Netscape users can select Preferences from the Menu bar to locate their history and cache configuration.

CHANGE LINK COLORS

Change the colors of the links on your page:
1. Use your text editor to open the **links_practice_1.html** file.
2. Key link color attributes and values inside the body start tag:

```
<body link="green" alink="orange" vlink="brown">
```

3. Save the file and refresh your browser. The links on your page should now reflect the color choices you entered in the body tag. If you notice that some of your choices have not been carried out, it might be because your browser is overriding the choices you made. If that is the case you can check your browser's preferences settings to determine whether that situation can be changed. It is not always possible to do that, so if you encounter this problem, it is probably not worth wasting a lot of your time trying to fix it.

Troubleshooting

Creating links can be tricky because there are so many parts that make up an anchor tag element. Even the smallest error—a misplaced quotation mark, an uppercase instead of a lowercase letter, a missed end tag—will cause a link to fail. One of the best things you can do to prevent link failure is to copy and paste file names and paths whenever possible. This prevents the possibility of making an error when keying these components. You can take a number of other steps when troubleshooting a link:

- **Check that all elements of the anchor tag are correct.** Be sure that all of the elements have been included. It is easy to forget to key an anchor end tag.
- **Make sure that a linked resource has not changed locations or been removed.** The URL for an external link might have changed or been removed, so you should verify the link when troubleshooting. A relative link might fail if you have moved or changed the target file on your computer.
- **Verify that you have keyed the correct file extension.** Keying a .gif extension for a JPEG image will cause the link to fail. Be sure that you key the correct file extension.
- **Check to see that there are no missing or incorrect spaces.** Adding a space that is not called for, or omitting a space that is, will cause a link to fail. For example, keying `mail to:` instead of `mailto:` will cause an e-mail link to fail.
- **Look for typographical errors.** It is easy to key .hmtl instead of .html, so check your spelling carefully.

- **Be sure that you did not inadvertently include any text tags inside the anchor tag.** Any tags or attributes that do not belong inside an anchor tag can cause a link to fail.
- **Make sure that the path to the linked resource is correct.** A proper understanding of how paths work is necessary to create correct link paths. Verify that the path you keyed is the correct path.
- **Use the correct case when entering a path.** Keying "Image.gif" instead of "image.gif" for a file named "image.gif" can cause a missing graphic. Be sure to check for the correct case in any code you enter.
- **Do not forget to click "Refresh" after making any changes.** This is a simple requirement that is often forgotten. You must refresh your browser to see the results of any changes you have made to the code.

You will undoubtedly commit many of these errors when you begin creating your own links. Do not be discouraged. Practice will increase your understanding, and you will soon find the number of errors you make rapidly decreasing.

design project

1. Use a search engine to research any additional Web design-related material for your Window to the Web site. Search for information that would be useful to visitors to your site. This might include reviews of books related to HTML and Web design, newspaper and magazine articles, courses in Web design, articles profiling successful Web designers, or other similar items. If you want to include these items on your Web pages be sure to ask for permission if they are copyrighted. In many cases, permission for private or noncommercial use will be granted. Bookmark the sites so you can easily locate them again. Write a report summarizing your findings.
2. Conduct a search for Web sites that offer guidance on creating and troubleshooting links. Bookmark any of these sites that you find helpful so you can use them as a resource when working with links.
3. Incorporate the material in the report you created for Step 1 into your Web pages. Create links to the information in your Web pages, as well as to external resources. Create at least one link to a file that can be downloaded from your site. Create an e-mail link so that visitors to your site can send an e-mail to you if they want to. Create a "Home" button on each page that visitors can click to return to your Home page. Create internal target links to enable movement within and between pages.

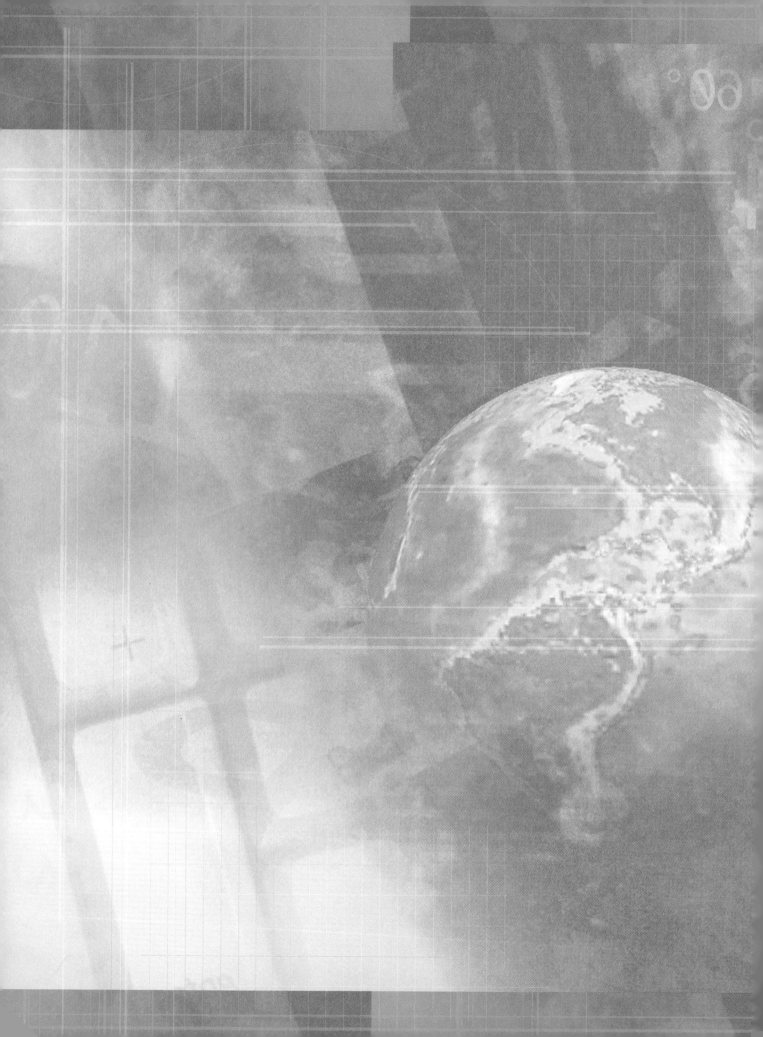

Phase III:
Launch, Test, Maintain, and Improve the Site

cyber
visit

JOHN TOLLETT

Designer, Art Director, Illustrator

Design Viewpoint

"Web design, like most things, can be performed on many levels of expertise, professionalism, and difficulty. It's really easy to create amateurish Web sites that look like they were put together in one hour. There are two aspects of Web design that will determine what league you're in as a designer. One is a visual aspect: making the site look appealing, compelling, or entertaining. The other aspect is technological; knowing how to design and optimize pages and graphics for efficient downloads and display. While you can't be an expert in every area of Web design, you can continually expand your appreciation, knowledge, and awareness of both design and technology."

Resume

Thirty years as an art director, designer, and illustrator for a dozen advertising agencies. Co-founded the Santa Fe Mac Users Group; founding partner of West of the Pecos Web Design (now merged with two other firms and known as PanoramaPoint).

Clients

Georgia O'Keefe Museum, Santa Fe Opera, Performing Arts Register, Santa Fe Convention and Visitors Bureau, Focus Tours, Arizona Public Service Co. (APS), Santa Fe Film Festival, First National Bank of Santa Fe.

Designer's Home Page

PanoramaPoint at www.westpecos.com/.

Insights

"By putting ourselves in the shoes of the people who will visit our site, we can assemble the information the best possible way—using intuition and creativity. It is complex, creative, frustrating, and exciting to build great sites, and a much more time-consuming process than print design because of the huge number of variables that the team must work around."

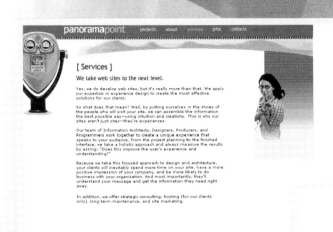

PanoramaPoint at www.westpecos.com/.

Design notes:

Each of the navigation items is a small JPEG slice that has a swap image behavior assigned to it. We used Dreamweaver's Behaviors palette to which image file would be replaced by a mouseover, and which image file would replace the swapped image.

The thin vertical type used in the headline (Plaza Cafe Home Made) was too blurry for our tastes, even though we had used the "crisp" option of anti-aliasing. To make it sharper, we enlarged

www.virtuallastchapter.com/examples/chapter02/plazacafe/index.html

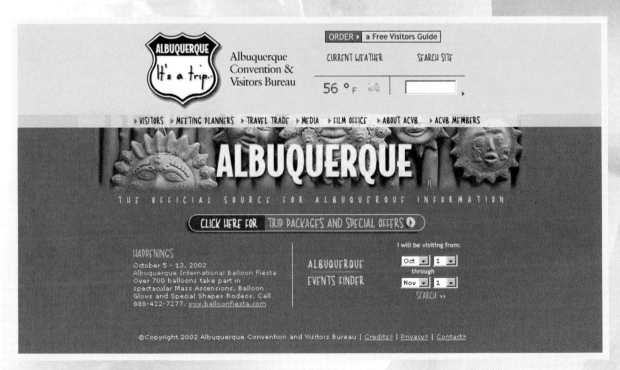

Albuquerque Convention and Visitors Bureau at www.abqcvb.org/.

Objectives

➤ Plan and carry out the launch of a Web site.

➤ Explain the differences between FTP and zip/unzip file transfers.

➤ Perform a general site check including detailed checks.

➤ List and describe the major sources of user data.

➤ Explain how user data can be used to guide revisions of a site.

➤ Differentiate between routine maintenance and updates and plans for a major redesign.

➤ Discuss the ethical, legal, and professional responsibilities of Web designers.

When a fully designed site is launched, the designers' work goes public. This is a moment of excitement, of course, but it should also cause designers to take a deep breath and ask one more time whether everything is set to go. Have all the design issues been addressed? Is the client satisfied with the results? Are all of the designers' responsibilities taken care of? A design team has been entrusted to create a site that will reflect the client's wishes for how it promotes itself in the world. But designers' responsibilities go beyond those to the client and include making sure the site satisfies users and abides by conventions and rules adopted by the World Wide Web community as well as those required by law.

During Phase II of the Web design process, all resources for the Web site were collected and developed; the site was designed and mapped; the prototype was developed, reviewed, tested, and approved; and the final site was produced. During Phase III (see Figure 7.1), the site is launched and tested. Launching and testing a site are responsibilities designers have to their clients; both are covered by the existing contract. Beyond the existing contract, however, could be other work the design team might be asked—and contracted—to do. The site needs to be maintained, which could include monitoring user logs to analyze the amount of traffic on the site or determining whether users are successful at accomplishing tasks. The site might also need updating, which could include making some small changes to improve the usability of the site. Other tasks also could become routine parts of maintaining and updating.

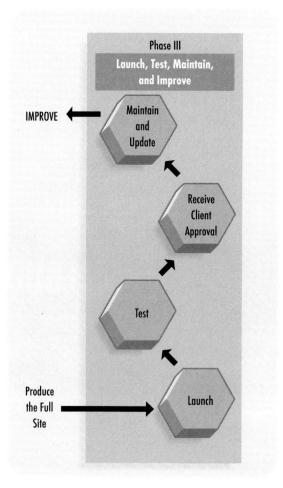

FIGURE 7.1 Phase III: Launch, Test, Maintain, and Improve

At some designated point after the site has been launched (quarterly, biannually, annually), the site could undergo periodic review to determine whether significant improvements can be made and especially to determine whether it can be advanced to a higher level. This would be achieved through a reevaluation in which the site is measured against the four parameters (communication, visual appeal, utility, and engagement) and their underlying principles, as well as guidelines and standards for usability and accessibility. This reevaluation provides the groundwork for planning improvements to the site. But any work contemplated as a result of the reevaluation would certainly require a new plan and contract for work. And, of course, if such work were to be done, the design team would return again to Phase I and proceed through Phases II and III.

LAUNCH AND TEST THE SITE

When launching and testing the site, the following tasks need to be accomplished:
- Upload all files to the host.
- Test the site to ensure that it is working correctly.
- Promote the site.
- Obtain client sign-offs to mark the end of the Web site project.

As with other phases in the design process, multiple iterations of these discrete tasks might be required. This cycle continues until tests are satisfactorily met and necessary changes have been carried out. These are important objectives to meet, because the site design client will not approve the design team's work until the client is satisfied that the design has been implemented thoroughly and adequately. After the client approves the team's work and signs off on the project, a new contract would need to be entered for any further work.

Upload All Files

When sites are published to the Web, all files for the site must be transferred to a host server and placed in the same folder structure as they were on the designer's system. During this upload operation, the main link to the site should be deactivated until everything has been uploaded and tested. Replicating folder structures on the host allows modifications to be accomplished easily: designers can make changes to the "local" version, test it there before uploading changes, and then change the "published" version on the host simply by replacing files in the same locations as on the local version of the site. If, however, any files have new names, or are in different folder locations than they were originally, adjustments must be made at many places in the HTML code so the browser can locate and upload these files. This can involve considerable work, most of it unnecessary if consistent directory structures were followed from the beginning.

Uploading files and folders could be time consuming if it were not for utilities that handle these procedures efficiently. Fortunately, with programs that can automate many of the steps, the task of uploading files is simplified.

FTP PROGRAMS Utilities such as **FTP** and **zip/unzip** programs enable entire file folders and their contents to be uploaded at once. These utilities speed the uploading

FTP (File Transfer Protocol)
A method for transferring computer files from one computer to another. Used when transferring Web files to a server when launching a site or when testing portions of a Web site.

zip/unzip
A program that compresses a set of computer files into a single file. Enables large numbers of files to transmit more quickly over a network. A zipped file must be unzipped on the receiving computer for the single file to return to multiple files that are once again in readable form.

process, and also reduce the risk of errors caused by files being uploaded into different locations (or with different names) than have been specified by the code.

FTP is the standard way for users to copy files between computers on a network regardless of what type of computer or operating system is on either end. By using FTP client software, a user can copy files to and from a computer that runs FTP server software. A Web server almost always runs FTP server software.

To send files to a Web server, the user must know the address of the FTP server, and must have a login ID and password. If the designer is redesigning a site, the client provides these pieces of information, which enable the designer to upload frequently even while the site is being designed. Designers should be careful not to damage existing directories and files, and keep in mind that the client might have limitations on how much uploading and downloading can be done during a one-month period, as well as limitations on storage space. The designer also must ensure that pages do not "go live" before they have been approved. If, however, the design team is responsible for contracting with a host service, the design team will be given the FTP address, user name, and password by the host, and will need to communicate these to the client when the project is concluded and responsibilities are shifted.

Although exact details on uploading differ from one FTP program to another, the idea is the same: select the folders of files to transfer from the computer and instruct the FTP software to make copies of them on the host. Entire Web site directories and subdirectories can be transferred intact, with the structure replicated exactly on the host. The operation is similar to copying folders of files within Windows on a user's system or across a network. The amount of time necessary for uploading files depends on the size of the Web pages and the speed of the connection to the Web server.

As shown in Figure 7.2, a typical FTP program has two windows, one on the left showing folders and files on an individual, local computer, and one on the right showing folders and files on a remote computer. For example, to transfer files between computers using the WS_FTP program, users select folders in the window representing the computer from which they want to transfer files, and then, in the center panel between the windows, click the arrow pointing toward the computer they want to transfer files to. Files can be transferred in ASCII (plain text) format, which is essential for transferring HTML files, or in binary format, which is essential for graphics files. Selecting Auto allows the software to transfer files in a manner appropriate to their type. Buttons to the right of either window allow the user to create folders (also called directories); rename, edit, and view files; or place restrictions on who can use and change files loaded on either computer.

After uploading the Web pages to a server, designers check the resulting Web site using a Web browser pointed at the starting page that was uploaded. They look for broken links and images that fail to display. Understanding and carefully adjusting the relationship between the link code of the HTML

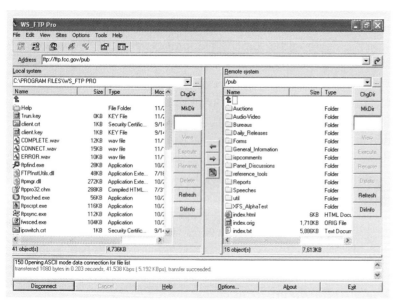

FIGURE 7.2 The Interface of the WS_FTP Program

files and the locations and names of files on the Web server allows the designer to fix any broken links.

FTP is only as good as the structure a design team has created for a site. No FTP program fixes broken links or supplies missing files by itself. Rather, FTP programs are tools to allow the design team to transfer files to the storage space on a remote computer. The skills used to organize local computer's folders and subfolders apply to distant ones as well.

A search on any shareware or freeware Web site for "FTP" will provide a list of FTP utilities to choose from. The sites www.tucows.com/, www.jumbo.com/, and download.com/ all offer a variety of FTP client programs, including SmartFTP, BulletProof FTP, and CuteFTP, to name a few. Commercial software for creating Web pages, such as Microsoft FrontPage and Macromedia Dreamweaver, has built-in FTP tools that help manage the transfer of files. In a pinch, a developer can even drag and drop a file onto an Internet Explorer or Netscape Navigator window to initiate an upload. Table 7.1 lists several FTP software programs that can be downloaded for a free trial period. After a designer chooses one of these FTP packages and gets it installed and ready to run, the specific connection information must be set up for the Web host that will be receiving the Web site files.

TABLE 7.1 FTP Software Options

FTP Program Platform	Where to Find It
FTPPro	1st Choice Software www.ftppro.com/
AbsoluteFTP	Van Dyke Software www.vandyke.com/products/absoluteftp/
Vermillion FTP Daemon	Arcane Software www.arcanesoft.com/
Bit Beamer	Bit Beamer www.bitbeamer.com/en/information.html
File Dog	Edge Publishing www.edgepub.com/fd/
FlashFXP	FlashFXP www.flashfxp.com/
FTP Voyager	Rhino Software www.ftpvoyager.com/
FTP Now	Network-Client.com www.network-client.com/
Robo-FTP	Robo-Soft www.robo-ftp.com/
TurboFTP	TurboSoft www.turboftp.com/
WS_FTP Pro	Ipswitch www.ipswitch.com/Products/WS_FTP/

ZIP/UNZIP PROGRAMS Zip/unzip utilities differ from FTP programs in that they compress an entire structure of files contained in folders to a smaller, single "zipped" file that can be transmitted more quickly. When this compressed file is "unzipped" at the other end, the entire set of files is set up the way they were at the outset, but on the receiving computer. Figure 7.3 illustrates this process.

For example, a personal Web site is saved in a folder named c:\\myweb. Within this folder, there is the index.htm file, 15 additional files, a subfolder named "images" with 8 graphics files, and a subfolder named "sounds" with 3 sound files. The code for the index.htm and other Web page files has references to each of the other files used in the site, including the "path" (folder location) to each file.

For the site to work properly after it has been uploaded to a host, the locations for every file must match those given in the code. To transmit these 27 files one by one, it would be necessary to set up the subfolders for the graphics files and sound files, and then carefully place each file in its appropriate folder. If a file was uploaded to a location that did not match the location specified in the code, the missing image icon would show when the browser was unable to locate the file. Using zip and unzip, these files and their structure are transmitted as a single, compressed file that, when unzipped, restores both the files and the original structure.

Although zip/unzip utilities can significantly speed up the file transfer function, there are important precautions when using them. Although it is highly efficient to work with an entire set of files, the procedure also can lead to a "speedy" loss of files. It is especially critical to move slowly and carefully at each step in the process when

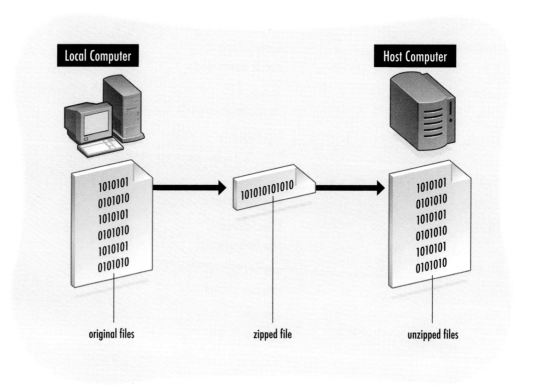

FIGURE 7.3 The Zipping Process
A zip program takes a set of computer files and compresses and combines them into a single, smaller file. The zipped file is transmitted across a network to another computer, where the file is decompressed and restored to multiple files in their original forms.

unzipping the compressed file. If any file included in the zip file is an older version of the file than the one already on the site, the danger is that the older version will overwrite the newer one, causing loss of valuable work. One way this can happen is when one member of a design team makes changes to a file and uploads it without notifying the rest of the team. Later, when the entire site is uploaded, an older version of the file might overwrite a new one in error. If the design team has been careful to exercise systematic version control to keep updated files in order, they will avoid this danger.

Zip/unzip utilities are available through download sites such as www.tucows.com/. Table 7.2 provides a list of common zip utilities. Through these download sites, it is possible to acquire and experiment with these important tools on a free trial basis. If they prove to be valuable, they can be purchased. At some point, Web designers need to acquire both types of utilities (FTP and zip/unzip) as these are essential tools to work with entire sets of files, instead of one file at a time, and to transmit them systematically to the host.

FILE MAINTENANCE   Similar functions are made available through advanced site-design software such as Dreamweaver, which provides utilities such as FTP for handling uploads. These programs have added features such as version control, which helps keep track of pages that have been changed since the last upload. Dreamweaver also offers a system for file "checkout" that is useful when multiple members of the design team are working together. When one team member is working on a file, Dreamweaver shows it as being "checked out," thus preventing others from attempting to work on that file at the same time.

File management tools are powerful utilities and can be tremendously helpful. But they also can do considerable damage in a short time if they are not used with caution. It is essential to know how these utilities work, and to think through each stage of the process, to avoid making errors that can be costly in terms of time and resources.

To help eliminate errors, designers should make notes (in a notebook or word-processing file) to help keep track of what needs to be uploaded, what has been uploaded, and even what changes might need to be made after uploading a directory or file. Whatever process is used to upload a Web site, details must be followed through consistently and carefully, using a systematic means to keep track of all critical information. This is important to avoid broken links or missing graphics.

Being systematic about the uploading process also will be important later when it is time to transfer duties from the site design team to those who will maintain and update the site regularly, possibly a member of the site sponsor's staff. During the initial

TABLE 7.2 Zip/Unzip Utilities

Name	Where to Find It	Platform
PKZIP	www.pkware.com/downloads/	DOS, UNIX, Windows
WinZip	www.winzip.com/	Windows
MacZip	mac.tucows.com/	Macintosh
StuffIt Expander	www.stuffit.com/expander/index.html	Windows, Macintosh, Linux, Solaris

uploads, it is best to plan the specifics for passing off future revision and upload tasks to the site maintenance and update team. Considerations that will assist in this transfer process include parsing on a clear system for keeping track of site files, and simplifying the organization of files so that the person who will be following up with site maintenance will be able to maintain the site efficiently.

Test the Site and Obtain Client Approval

As a site is being uploaded and prepared for launch, an ongoing set of tests needs to be performed to ensure that the launch will be error-free. At a minimum, there should be a general check of the site, followed by six additional checks:

- Links
- Graphics
- Page access times
- Accessibility
- Usability
- Editorial content

Each check listed here has distinct purposes and procedures and must be performed systematically. The design team prepares a list of tasks to do on each page and then performs the tests on different browsers, not only different brands but also different versions, going back at least one or two versions (browsers render Web pages differently, so it is necessary to know what each browser will do to the design). The team performs the tests from the point of view of all identified users of the site and follows each of the scenarios associated with each profile, making notes of any problems.

GENERAL CHECK The purpose of the general check is to attempt to look at the site with new eyes, conducting a systematic walk-through, following each of the scenarios from the various points of view of the user profiles. The design team uses this check to catch as many potential problems as possible and resolves them before proceeding. The team attempts to perform actual tasks as though this is its first encounter with the screens. It is possible to catch inconsistencies and missing navigation or linking elements by simply walking through a sample visit, anticipating the various avenues users will follow, and carrying out a systematic process of following them to check for potential problems.

LINKS AND GRAPHICS CHECKS The team follows every link on every page to ensure that not a single broken link exists on the site. The team does the same for every graphic image on each page, checking to make sure an image shows and that it is the correct image. Missing graphics or broken links are noted.

One technical misstep sometimes results in missing graphics. If the HTML code specifies a path to a graphic on the designer's system rather than one on the Web server, an image will show from the designer's system but will not appear anywhere else. For example, before being uploaded, an image source of C://MyDocuments/lilypond.gif directs the browser to a file on the designer's hard drive. The image shows on the designer's system, but from any other system the image is missing because the path refers to directories on the designer's system and not to the structure of directories for the Web site. This problem is a subtle one to track down because the designer's system shows the site as functioning. Problems such as this can be detected earlier if the designer uploads portions of the project during Phase II. Uploading and testing small portions of a site can prevent linking problems from multiplying.

Testing links offers an opportunity to evaluate whether the navigational plan is intuitive. To do this requires following links to the end of a process. Thus, after testing the links on one page, the designer proceeds to test the links to the end of a task, evaluating whether the process is easy to understand, simple to use, and efficient. Designers also count the number of links required to accomplish a task. Although this issue should be addressed while designs for navigation are done during Phase II, test now to make sure no task has become unnecessarily complex. If more than three links are necessary to accomplish a task, there should be a good reason. Otherwise, the number of screens to reach and achieve the goal can and should be simplified. The designer identifies any revisions to the site's navigation process that might be necessary or helpful and, of course, repairs any broken links.

PAGE ACCESS TIME CHECK The purpose of the page access time check is to ensure that when entire pages, including all graphics, are loaded, they do not cause long download times. As stated in Chapter 4, downloads should be kept to less than 10 seconds even on a 56 Kbps modem. If there is good reason for a longer download delay, provide messages to that effect that will appear while visitors wait so they will know to expect a time lag.

Check downloads on a modem-based system and measure the time it takes for each page on a site to load, moving through all pages on the site. The question to be addressed is: "Do any pages load slowly?" Loading time is a function of cumulative file size, which means the total of all files to be downloaded for one page. Because a page might contain multiple images (or other elements) to be loaded, the total size of all files will be much greater than the base HTML file. This total load time is what must be considered in relation to the 10-second limitation.

Access times are influenced by the route a user has followed to specific pages. After an image file has been loaded as part of a page, it is retained in the **browser cache** of the user's system and will not be reloaded, but just reused when it appears as part of another page. Depending, then, on what sequence a user follows through the pages of the site, different combinations of images could be loading for the first time.

As the design team tests Web pages, the cache might already have some image files uploaded. As a result, the access times will be less than would be the case for the typical visitor. To test access times accurately, the team must clear its cache before loading each page in the sequence. This provides the full upload time as it will be experienced by someone who visits this page for the first time. To clear the cache, delete previously downloaded Internet files. Figure 7.4 shows the Internet Explorer dialog box where this is done. Clearing the cache forces the browser to bring all images in at the same time, thus providing a measure of the maximum time it will take for that full page to load. Although this method does not account for variations in download times caused by heavy Internet traffic, it does establish a more accurate estimate.

> **browser cache**
> An area of a computer's hard disk in which browsers store a copy of recently viewed pages and images. Saves time and bandwidth while browsing.

ACCESSIBILITY AND USABILITY CHECKS Each page for the site needs to be checked to determine the degree to which accessibility has been ensured and what needs

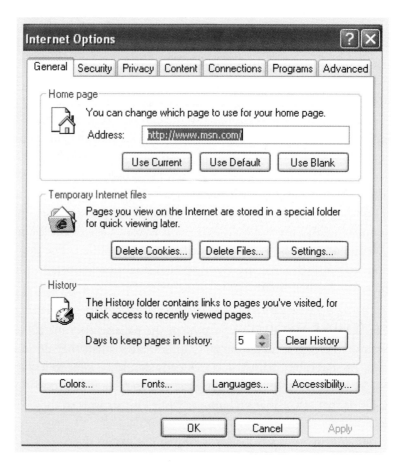

FIGURE 7.4 Clearing the Cache
To clear the cache in Internet Explorer, locate the Internet Options dialog box (under Tools).

to be changed if pages do not conform to the accessibility standards outlined in Chapter 4. As defined there, accessibility specifically involves making Web sites usable by individuals with physical or mental disabilities and individuals using wireless or other limited function modes of access. One way to check this is to use the accessibility testing utilities (such as Bobby) available on the W3C (World Wide Web Consortium) site to identify problems. (See Chapter 4 for a list of some more well-known utilities.)

Generally, usability refers to how easy a site is to use. The usability check is different from the accessibility check and determines the degree to which visitors targeted to use the site are able to do so. However glorious the rendering of the site, it is of little use to anyone unless visitors can figure out what to do with it and how. Evaluating usability involves making judgments about the ease of navigation, the legibility of text, the clarity of communication, and anything else that could be a source of confusion or frustration for users.

To perform a full-level usability check, bring in actual users and ask them to attempt to accomplish actual tasks using the site. One option is to use videotapes to capture the results. It is also a good idea to have these typical users speak as they move through the site, commenting on issues and questions they have as they attempt to accomplish the tasks.

When working with a user focus group, avoid talking or guiding the group. Instead, allow users to be led by the cues on the screen, making any errors or pursuing any dead ends they would have experienced without extra coaching. The users will not have the benefit of additional instruction, but will need to be able to follow along using only the navigational cues provided by the site. Make notes of difficulties, misconceptions, unproductive paths, and any other usability problems that need to be repaired.

EDITORIAL CHECK The primary purpose of the final editorial content check is to ensure that no grammatical errors or spelling mistakes appear on any page within the site. This procedure should be done to a preliminary degree throughout Phase II, but more formally during the testing period. A published site should be checked by an accomplished editor, or at a minimum, someone who is viewing the site through fresh eyes.

Errors damage the image of the site's sponsor. However careful its work, design teams should not assume a published site has no errors (although that would be a worthwhile achievement). A final edit is a necessary quality-assurance measure. An additional function of editing the site is to ensure that all meanings are clear and that the communication is effective. Judgments such as these sometimes change when the site has been uploaded and the material has been reviewed in the context of the complete site. Also, the fact that an uploaded site is public can heighten sensitivity to errors.

To perform this check, use a check sheet containing the title or file name of every page on the site. Visit each and every page of the site and check it off after visiting it. While visiting a page, read every word and mark only changes to be made, as needed. One technique that works well is to read the pages aloud. Some designers find that editing closely is best accomplished by printing out the pages, and then reading through them for flow. This provides a "new" view of the pages, enabling the eye to catch errors that might have been missed onscreen.

A thorough check of the editorial content should not focus exclusively on words, however. Irrelevant, outdated, incorrect, or even inappropriate text or images can become apparent. If dynamic content is being supplied from a database, careful proofreading of the data elements might reveal errors (items for purchase should show the correct price, for instance). Of course, if the data is coming from the client's database, a design team would, in most cases, need to communicate to the client any need for correction of the data.

OBTAIN CLIENT SIGN-OFF Finally, client approval is an essential step—both to ensure that the client is satisfied, and to mark the end of the project. One practice that clearly demonstrates and documents this approval is to obtain the signature of an authorized agent on printouts of each page of the completed site. In addition, at the point of sign-off, it is important to return to the original contract/plan to ensure that all deliverables have been accomplished, and that the project that was agreed upon has reached completion.

If the designer or design team needs to provide site maintenance and updates, a new contract must be negotiated. Even beyond this second type of contract, an additional contract might be necessary to revise and upgrade the site beyond routine maintenance and updates.

Promote the Site

After the site has been launched, checked, and approved, various tasks can be carried out to ensure that the targeted users of the site are able to locate it using the major directories, search engines, or some combination of the two. These tasks are initially carried out by the site design group. During Phase I of the design process, the team gathers information and learns the content area so it understands better how to design the site. Much of that information is useful for promoting the site. The vocabulary the design team learned is critical at this stage, because many of the key terms are placed within the meta tags at the head of HTML files for the site. But a broader understanding of the content area is also important. Broader understanding results in better use of the terms visitors are likely to use in searching out a site of interest to their particular needs.

Later in Phase III, after the site has been launched, checked, and approved, tasks associated with promoting the site are handled by the team designated for maintenance and updates. This team is responsible for evaluating whether the best methods for promoting the site have been used. Are the best search terms embedded in the HTML meta tags? Has the Web site description been written to appeal to the most likely users? Has the site been promoted in the best way to the editors of the directories the site should appear in?

The Yahoo! Site Registration Form

WEB DIRECTORIES For potential visitors to locate a newly launched site using Web directories such as Yahoo!, it is necessary to register the site with the directory, going directly to each directory site and completing the forms available there. Submitting registration information is no guarantee that a site will be listed, so design teams should treat this step as an important part of promoting the site. In essence, the team is "pitching" the site to editors who must choose the "best" Web sites to include in their directories. But one directory's idea of "best" can differ from another's. A directory that highlights Web sites of interest to business researchers (such as Northern Light at www.northernlight.com/) might not be the best place to pitch a site that sells craft supplies. Once submitted, however, registration information is reviewed by the staff for the directory site, and determinations are made as to whether the new site is worthy of inclusion in their collection and how it will be classified in its directory structure.

SEARCH ENGINES For targeted visitors to locate the newly launched site by conducting searches on major search engine sites such as Altavista.com and

Google.com, another kind of strategy is involved because the indexing of a new site for access via search engine sites is conducted through automated means. Search engines send out automated "spiders" (also called "robots" or "crawlers") that search a large portion of the vast number of Web pages in existence. Some pages are not visited by spiders. For instance, dynamically generated pages cannot be searched, because they cease to exist after a Web transaction has been completed. Also, pages that have few links leading to them might be ignored when spiders crawl the Web. In other words, there are some limitations to automated methods of cataloging Web pages, but the capability of spiders to automatically catalog Web pages without human intervention is amazing.

The elements of a Web page that are used by automated agents to catalog Web pages include:

- Title that appears between the <title> and </title> tags
- Information included in the meta tags for "keywords" and "description"
- Text that has been used to identify links
- Text that appears early in the page
- Text that appears frequently in the page
- Text that appears in headings
- Alt text that is provided along with graphic elements

Figure 7.5 illustrates why one site appears high on a search results list.

FIGURE 7.5

Analyzing a Search Result
When a search is done using the term "symphony," the Boston Symphony appears high on the list. Why? Notice how many times the word "symphony" appears in the meta tags for this site.

Web spiders are unable to index elements of the page that are solely graphic or, as mentioned before, that are produced on-the-fly as part of a dynamic page. Thus, as the entry pages for sites become more impressive (for example by using Flash movies), it becomes all the more important to design the home page of the site with the processes followed by Web spiders clearly in mind. Because Flash relies heavily on images, providing alt text for all graphics is an important way of assisting spiders to catalog a Flash site. Also, careful planning of the key words and description meta tags will help. Spiders also tend to have problems with frames-based sites because they are made up of a composite of pages. To assist spiders with frames-based sites, attend to meta tags in the frameset page as well as the target pages.

Preparing a site well for future access via search engines is a specialty that has developed and been refined over the past several years. This set of tasks can be outsourced to an expert if this is agreed to as part of the Site Development Plan and contract with the client. Using someone with this expertise to accomplish these tasks might be advisable and well worth the additional project costs.

The team should understand the level of service it will be getting from such a firm. Some services advertise the ability to list a site on 400–500 search engines. This type of "shotgun" listing service might not accomplish as much as selecting a smaller number of heavily used search engine sites and preparing the new site specifically to be accessible using the indexing approaches of these search engines. Smaller specialty search engines can be strategically important also, depending on the content area of the site. For example, a travel site offering users the ability to book transportation and lodging might want to focus considerable effort on getting listed on specialty search sites for travel or leisure activities.

After the site has been launched, the design team can proceed to test whether the site shows up in search engines. It can take some time (anywhere from two to four weeks or longer) for a site to show up on search engines. This is due to the fact that spider searches of the entire World Wide Web can take two to three weeks or longer. When testing to determine whether the site appears on search engine results, the design team tries to determine the degree to which strategies for promoting the site have been successful. Is it possible for the targeted users to find the site using the standard tools of a Web-wide search?

The procedure for carrying out this check is to follow a systematic process that replicates the targeted users' anticipated search strategies when attempting to locate sites of this type that will be of value to them. Using the same search tools that are available to these potential users and the kinds of combinations of terms and phrases these users are likely to enlist, conduct searches that should yield the site as part of the results list. Determine whether the site comes up as it should on these results lists. When the site appears on a results list, check the title and description information provided there. Does this descriptive information match the site's content? (It should, because the search engine is supposed to be making direct use of information the team has embedded in the site's HTML files.) Will this information seem useful to the visitor? If the description is a long one, does it still make sense when it is cut off, as it will be, to the fixed number of lines the search site allows for its results list? Last, enter the site using the links provided by the search. Determine the degree to which users will be able to navigate successfully from these various entry points, wherever they are located within the site structure. Will they be able to back up to the site's home page to benefit from the full content of the site?

activity

In this activity, do the following six tests on a posted Web site:

1. Links test
2. Graphics test
3. Page access time check
4. Accessibility check
5. Usability check
6. Editorial check

For this activity, select a site that contains numerous links and graphics, and fairly extensive text. Following is a list of sites that you can use. Your instructor might provide additional sites for this activity.

- American Symphony at www.symphony.org/
- Atlanta Symphony at www.atlantasymphony.org/
- Boston Symphony at www.bso.org/
- Chicago Symphony at www.cso.org/
- Dallas Symphony at www.dallassymphony.com/
- London Symphony at www.lso.co.uk/
- San Francisco Symphony at www.sfsymphony.org/
- Seattle Symphony at www.seattlesympony.org/

Figure 7.6 is an example of a checklist form that can be used to keep track of Web site testing. Document your findings on an expanded version of this form.

How did the site perform in your evaluation? Were there obvious shortcomings? Were there problems of a subtle nature? What does your evaluation say about the quality of the site's design? Share your results with others in your class.

URL: _____

Type of test	Notes
1. Links (Record any broken links.)	
2. Graphics (Record missing images and other problems.)	
3. Access time (Record download time after clearing cache.)	
4. Accessibility (two tests only) a. Tab order (Is it possible to tab through links or forms in an order that is logical or would make sense if text is being read by a screen reader?) b. Are access keys provided, allowing users to access parts of the page by issuing keyboard commands such as Alt + K?	
5. Usability (two tests only) a. Is the page clearly organized? b. Is the navigation easy to understand? (Do you think you would be able to use the navigational aids without having to spend time learning how?)	
6. Editorial check (Are there spelling or grammar mistakes? Is the language easy to understand?)	

FIGURE 7.6 Web Site Check Sheet

MAINTAIN, UPDATE, AND IMPROVE THE SITE

A Web site is like any other generative, live process: It is never completely finished. Once launched, the site needs to go through regular maintain-and-update cycles and also periodic review cycles. Routine maintenance involves regular updates and improvements; periodic review involves major updates and redesign plans. Each type of work requires a new contract with the client.

It is important to be clear about the levels of effort in implementing changes to a Web site. Routine maintenance, while requiring diligence, does not include the redesign of areas requiring major improvement. If major changes are conceptualized during routine maintenance, they are noted but not acted upon until the next periodic review. Periodic review of a site goes well beyond making small changes such as replacing older photographs with more recent ones. Still, at each point in either process, it becomes possible to see new potential for the site that might not have been conceivable earlier.

Maintain and Update

At the point when the Web site project shifts over to the maintain-and-update phase, the old contract, if performed to the client's satisfaction, is no longer in force. A new contract would cover different work, with a different focus and intent. This contract needs to be negotiated as its own entity, with clear statements of terms and conditions, such as:

- **Level of Effort** The number of contract hours to be spent.
- **Maintenance and Update Process** Frequency of site maintenance and updating activity, and how these reviews are to be carried out and documented.
- **Client-Designer Exchange Process** The procedure to be followed for making changes, including what types of changes will require further approval from the client, and other essential information about how the ongoing support of the site will be handled.
- **User Data Analysis Reports** If there are to be reports based on user data, what will those reports be, how will they be presented, to whom, and how often?
- **Recommendation Process** When recommendations are needed based on these reports and other feedback and observations, how are those to be handled?
- **Contact Plan** Who within the client enterprise will be the key contact for issues regarding the Web site from this point on?

Web site maintenance should occur on a regular basis and needs to be an anticipated and planned event. Maintenance can involve repairing problems as well as updating information to keep it current and interesting. The agreement with the client must be clear in terms of how often routine maintenance and updating will occur. Once every month? Once every three months? Once per semester? Twice per year? Whatever the frequency, this agreement becomes part of the maintain-and-update contract, with associated fees for services, and a clear client-designer interaction process. When these activities are to be carried out by internal staff, the same issues and process applies.

If the update schedule directs that the site be reviewed every three months, activities need to occur before that point, at that point, and after that point. Plans about these cycles should be worked out now, or it is unlikely that they will occur as needed, or expected. Highly satisfied clients can become dissatisfied quickly if their expectations about maintenance and updates are not met—and an expectation unvoiced is likely to become an expectation unmet.

The maintain-and-update contract might be carried out by a different designer or enterprise than the initial designer/developer of the site, or maintenance and updating might be handled by a person on the client's own staff. In either of these situations, the initial work on the site needs to be accomplished in a way that can be turned over readily. For this transfer of work to be accomplished, resources must be carefully organized early in the design process, and HTML and script code must be clearly blocked and well commented (so it can be easily interpreted and changed by a person other than the original creator). These objectives are critical to efficiency and success. Carefully organized resources make it easier for others without intimate knowledge of a project to know where to find what they need. But even when resources are carefully prepared and organized, difficulties can arise if those assigned to maintain and update the site do not have sufficient guidance on how HTML, scripts, and other code is organized.

To support effective transfer of site management, the care with which comments have been inserted into the HTML code and the visual formatting of the code for ease of review are critical. Comments serve a useful purpose, especially for long stretches of code in which it is easy to lose place or to forget what a particular piece of code does. Particularly when someone other than the writer of the commented code is making changes, comments and format are essential. Comments are placed within the code, beginning with <!--. The comment text does not appear on the Web page when it is viewed by a browser. Figure 7.7 shows a sample of well-commented code. Notice how sections of the code have been grouped, separated, and indented so that related bits of code are easy to locate.

When maintenance and update changes are being made to the site, they need to be made offline, not on the live version of the site. All changes should be tested before they are moved to the live site and replace functioning pages. Systematic version naming procedures need to be used to distinguish the various versions of each page that exist. This becomes critical if it becomes necessary at any point to back up to an earlier version. Archived versions of pages must be protected and backed up.

Many of the ideas about how a site could improve are provided and substantiated by users. Visitor usage data should be collected, compiled, and analyzed. This provides important feedback about how the site is performing, who is using it, and what dead ends or confusions users are encountering. Through analysis of visitor data, moderate changes might be needed immediately. Changes that are more ambitious should be noted as they become apparent; they will be used later to guide major plans when it is time for the site to be redesigned and upgraded.

Designers collect and respond to site data, looking at factors such as:

• What are the visitation levels for the site?

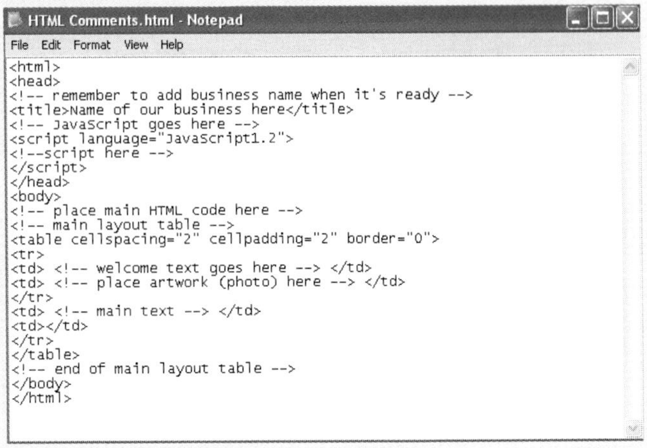

```
HTML Comments.html - Notepad
File Edit Format View Help
<html>
<head>
<!-- remember to add business name when it's ready -->
<title>Name of our business here</title>
<!-- JavaScript goes here -->
<script language="JavaScript1.2">
<!--script here -->
</script>
</head>
<body>
<!-- place main HTML code here -->
<!-- main layout table -->
<table cellspacing="2" cellpadding="2" border="0">
<tr>
<td> <!-- welcome text goes here --> </td>
<td> <!-- place artwork (photo) here --> </td>
</tr>
<td> <!-- main text --> </td>
<td></td>
</tr>
</table>
<!-- end of main layout table -->
</body>
</html>
```

FIGURE 7.7   HTML Comments
Comments can be used to indicate when missing content should be added.

- Are the correct visitors arriving at a site?
- Are these visitors successful in completing tasks?
- Do they return?
- Are all of the cross links available and are they being used?
- Are there particular pages that cause problems or become dead ends for users?

Visitor usage data can be obtained using various strategies, such as page counters, which show the number of visitors and monitor their usage of the pages of the site. When page counters are used, they are best kept invisible to the visitor, because a counter that shows a low number of visitors to the site might suggest to the user that the site is not worth visiting.

Another strategy is to use the **server log files**. These text files become voluminous quickly because they capture data about each click the user makes while on the site. For each page requested, the server log shows detailed information such as:
- The date and time of the request
- The size of the file transferred
- A code that communicates whether or not the Web page request was successful

The address of the computer that is accessing a Web page and the page on which the visitor was located when trying to access the new page also can appear in server log files. In other words, these logs contain play-by-play information that shows what users actually have looked at on the site and in what order.

These log files can contain important indicators of the problems a site might be having. By analyzing log files, the designer can estimate visitor behavior, such as which pages users read or do not read measured by how long they are on the page, and where they are moving in directions they do not consider to be useful, such as when they open a page and then immediately back out of it. This information is available from two server log files that typically are maintained by the host Web server: the file that logs access and the file that logs errors. The access log shows which pages are requested, and the error log contains a list of the error codes that correspond to errors that occurred during users' visits. Other logs that are used to provide information include referrer logs and agent logs. The referrer log shows from what other sites visitors arrived. The agent log provides routine information about the users such as what browsers they are using to access the site.

By analyzing the access log file and doing a comparison between times of requests, for example, it is possible to see how long a user might have been on a single page. The length of time users stay on different pages can indicate which pages are offering the most value to them. These pages are more important to users, but if these pages are buried deep in a navigational plan, the plan needs to be changed. This type of analysis might or might not warrant firm conclusions, however, because many users open multiple windows when they are on the Web, so a page that has been held on the screen for 20 minutes might simply be the page that was accessed last when that window was on top.

Software is available to automate the analysis of server log files and generate reports that make the voluminous raw data more useful. Several examples of such software include:
- Log Analyzer by WebTrends at www.netiq.com/
- SurfStats at surfstats.com/
- LogAnalyze at loganalyze.com/
- Happy Log at logfiles.virtualave.net/
- AWStats at awstats.sourceforge.net/

Reports that might be useful for determining what needs to be changed on the site include analyses of entry and exit points. From what page do users enter the site, and what page are they on when they exit? Also, while users are on the site, which pages do they use? On which pages do they stay for a long time? Are there other interesting patterns regarding time and date, such as increased use during special events; hours of the day; days of the week; days or weeks in the month; days, weeks or months in the year? Information gathered from log files might suggest better navigational plans or even result in marketing campaigns aimed at steering traffic to a site during a specific time.

Another possibility for analysis is the paths users take through the site and, in particular, whether or not they reach the critical pages that would provide closure to their experiences. This kind of information requires interpretation of entries in log files. For instance, if someone comes to a book-ordering Web site by using search terms "Web design" and "HTML," it would seem that this user wanted information about a book on designing Web pages using HTML, and possibly was interested in buying it. But if information in the log file suggests that the user left the book site without finding information on such a book or without purchasing, this would indicate that something prevented the user from getting that far in the site. If this appears to happen over and over to users making similar types of requests, this could mean that something about the site confuses or frustrates users.

Another issue that can be looked at is how many clicks are necessary to reach the goal. This information is obtained by counting the number of page hits between entrance to the site and exit from a page such as a purchase page or a download page. When the time comes for a major redesign of the site, this information helps guide changes to the navigation plan.

Information from the referrer log can be interesting and useful. Every site from which visitors arrive at the site is recorded in the target site's referrer log. This might show that sites expected to send the most visitors have not done so, that users are coming from an unexpected source, or that one source sends visitors that, after navigating their way through the target site, end up in the same exact spot, which could suggest a common reason these users are visiting the target site. When the referrer site is a search engine, analysis of the keywords used to reach the site can clarify how users are finding the site and what changes are needed for the "right" visitors to locate the site more easily.

Improve the Site

Analyzing user data is the basis for more ambitious plans that involve major revisions and upgrades to the site. These plans exist as ideas kept in a set of notes during the maintain-and-update period, but these ideas will provide guidance later when a proposal is developed to make major improvements that bring the site to its next level.

When major improvements to the design are considered, it is important that the site be viewed in terms of what has worked well and needs to be kept, and what has not worked, or could work better, and needs to be changed. One potential error in site redesign is to start over. Starting over might not necessarily result in improvements. If positive features of the earlier design are abandoned, the site might even move backward. To decide how to proceed with the redesign project, it is essential to know what has worked, and to keep that part of the design. Move beyond this to do something better, while retaining the positive aspects of the site. Starting over is dangerous because it assumes that nothing has been learned.

As improvements are planned, the process of evaluating the site identifies areas that can be considered for possible improvement, such as:

- Can the site be enriched in terms of content and links?
- Can communication be more effective?
- Would enhancements add to the visual impact?
- Would refinements make sense now in terms of user profiles and what users bring to the site as their expectations and needs?
- Would additional levels of interactivity improve the site from the standpoint of users?

These questions return us to the four parameters of Chapter 3: communications, visual appeal, utility, and engagement. By returning to these parameters, designers can now ask whether they can be met in improved ways. Is there a better means of offering the content in ways that are of value to the site's users? Enriching content and clarifying the purpose of links to external sites are other means of incorporating major improvements in the site's communicative quality. Enhancing visual impact during the redesign of the site is an opportunity to incorporate current technologies and a more up-to-date look and feel, thus making the site more appealing and interesting to new and returning visitors. Refinements based on user profiles and user data and feedback can help design higher levels of utility into the site so that users are able to use what the site has to offer in ways that are of value to them. An increase in the users' sense of engagement and participation can be accomplished by adding to the interactive features of the site.

As an example, a travel site or a home buyers site might add a virtual walk-through of a travel destination or a home available for purchase. A site for car enthusiasts might add a virtual walk-around of the restored classic cars that received trophies. A science museum, zoo, or aquarium site might add virtual exhibits that site visitors can experience online—the new butterfly exhibit, the baby bear cubs, the jellyfish exhibit lit with ultraviolet light so the luminescence glows.

Root Link www.hitl.washington.edu/
Direct Link www.hitl.washington.edu/research/exposure/
Why Go? To visit a site with an extensive collection of information about virtual reality projects. Read about how virtual-reality technology helped one woman lose her fear of spiders.

Generating ideas for redesigning an existing site in these and other examples should lead the site to a higher level of accomplishing its purpose. A site redesign is more than a set of cosmetic improvements. It has the potential of moving the site to the next

input*refresh*

VIRTUAL WORLDS: THE WEB IN 3-D

As changes in Web technologies converge with the increased sophistication of production tools, animations are becoming an integral part of many Web sites. The progression has moved ahead from the early use of image files that were constantly in motion, even annoying after awhile, toward the use of dynamics that increase interest, communicate concepts, and support themes. As technologies for Web-delivered animation continue to advance, full immersion "worlds" of 3-D will expand from the proving grounds of the gaming industry, into exciting advanced uses for communication, teaching, and learning.

EARLY ANIMATION TECHNIQUES In the days when images were all drawn by hand, artists created a full series of images based on the "flipbook" approach, with each image slightly different. When shown in quick succession (as with a flipbook, thumbing through the pages quickly), the sequence of images simulated motion. For the result to be fluid, it was necessary to create a sufficient number of drawings to support a playback rate of between 24 and 30 frames per second. As teams of artists worked on full animations, one technique was frame-based animation, also called cell animation. The process was to create the key frames—the main points in a sequence—and then to create all of the drawings for what came in between. Artists who created these in-between drawings were called "tweeners," and the process was called "tweening."

The early days of Web animation worked on the basis of a similar process, although the process was computerized. The primary tool computer animators used for early Web animation were animated GIF files, small files that could be created in any number of software packages. Within a single animated GIF file were stored a series of images to be "streamed" back as the file was downloaded, looping through the series for a fixed number of times, or indefinitely. When GIF files were more popular, it was not unusual to see Web pages that contained multiple moving images—dogs running across the screen, mailboxes opening and closing, and cartoon characters making faces. These could be amusing, at least for a while. But it was rare for them to integrate conceptually into the Web site and support its purpose.

ADVANCED 2-D ANIMATION Computer-generated animations offered additional possibilities. For frame-based animation, a special technique called morphing could be used to produce the in-between frames. Morphing involves one image gradually changing into another image, with the computer generating all of the transitional images.

Other possibilities supported by computer-generated animation included path-based animation, user-interactive motion, and program-based or script-based animation. For path-based animation, also called vector animation, a path is created along which the animated object moves. This path marks the beginning point, the direction, and the length of each motion. The path can be straight, curved, or jagged. With path-based animation, the artist creates the object and the path, and the computer manipulates the object along the path, drawing the sequence of frames needed to simulate the motion. A more powerful version of path-based animation is computational animation, in which the object moves based on computed x, y, and z coordinates.

Program-based or script-based animation employs Java applets, JavaScripts, or other small object-based programs, to provide logic that will control the sequence, movement, opacity, size, or frame that is shown. As the range of control increases, the possibilities for effects become more exciting and realistic. Java applets are computational and compiled in advance, so their effects can be delivered quickly via the Web because the processing actually is done on the user's own computer (the client). Flash animations also can be very small and powerful, allowing for many animation possibilities.

3-D ANIMATION When an animation is three-dimensional, this increases work for a designer and creative potential for the animation. The color, brightness, and texture of the third dimension are not elements to consider when working in two dimensions. However, with the addition of these elements, it is possible to immerse the viewer in what seems like an actual experience, with objects, landscapes, rooms and buildings, populated with virtual people and creatures controlled by other Internet users or sophisticated behavior algorithms.

The experience of navigating a 3-D space, with some suspension of disbelief, can evoke the sensation of traveling in another world. A skilled 3-D artist can create an exotic and impossible vista of waterfalls and twin moons rising over a castle, forbidding and dark, or perhaps a bright marketplace filled with tables of wares to examine. Creating these 3-D models of objects and buildings can be achieved by numerous means, from photographs and tracing, to careful measurements, or even total fabrication using the honing of primitive and algorithmic shapes (boxes, spheres, cones, blobs, curves). The results are impressive. How users, sitting at home, use this communal experience to communicate with others will reshape the ideas of place, geography, and distance as they create and explore these virtual worlds.

THE FUTURE As the power of home computers grows, users can expect to see a rapid approach toward an interactive realism that visually rivals television and film quality. The information age that brought telephone, fax, television, and the Web is poised to bring the vivid, interactive transmission of place, presence, objects, and motion. This enhancement extends the possible modes of communication, and will change the very ideas of location and setting. As just one example, imagine putting on a set of sophisticated display glasses or hood in an empty room and suddenly finding yourself sitting around a campfire, chatting face-to-face with friends who are actually a thousand miles away. One day, the location of the body might become secondary to the body's perceived virtual location.

generation. For any change that is presented for approval, the team should determine whether that change is necessary, or even constructive, for the purpose of the site and the image of the site's owner. Change, by its nature, is jarring—and expensive. There needs to be a "why?" to explain the need and the benefit of the change. Given that the existing Web site is the felt "presence" of the company that sponsors it, the responses to the changes that are expressed by the agents of that company are highly critical, as are the experiences of the site's users with old versus new versions of the site.

web 7.2 activity

WEB SITE SEARCH RESULTS

In this activity, evaluate a Web site's meta tags to devise a strategy by which the site can improve its placement on Web search results lists. Choose from the subject areas and search terms listed in Table 7.3, and enter the search terms in the appropriate places at a search engine of your choice. (Remember that search engines let you enter terms in different ways. The following terms can be entered as one phrase as written here, or, as on AltaVista's advanced search, you can split the search terms into different text fields clearly labeled. Also, be sure that you search the Web and not a directory that might be associated with the search engine you use.)

Be sure that your search produces many results (more than one page, preferably more than 20 results; the more the better). Go to the last page of results and look down the list of entries, but do not visit any of the sites yet. Depending on how many results appeared in response to your query, the last page could show entries that are clearly unrelated to the subject area of your search. If so, go back one page and view the results there to determine whether any entries are relevant to the subject area. If not, keep going back one page or two pages at a time until you see relevant results. When you do, select a site that is related to the subject matter but still seems low on the list of results.

Visit the site. Notice which page you have been taken to. Are you on the home page or on a page deeper in the folder structure for the site? Stay on the page you are on, and then view the source code for the page. Print out the code, locate the meta tag with the "keywords" attribute in it, and determine whether any terms there match the terms from your search. If not, inspect the rest of the page to determine where the matches occurred. Check other meta tags, the title tag, the main text within the body of the page, and any alt text in image tags.

After you have located the matches, ask why these matches did not produce a higher listing for the site. Were there too few matches? Were they buried deep down on the page? (To get a better sense of how the search engine you used produced higher-ranking results, you might visit one of the sites at the top of the results list and inspect that site's source code. You might also try the same search terms on a different search engine.)

Write a two- or three-page report indicating the changes you recommend making to the Web site so it places higher on the results list. Try to think beyond the additions you might recommend making to the meta tags. For instance, would you delete some words from the meta tags? Also, would you only recommend changes in the meta tags or alt text, or would your recommendations suggest a more far-reaching change to the site (reorganization, different navigational structure, and so on)?

TABLE 7.3 Possible Search Areas and Phrases

Subject Area	Search Phrase
free JavaScripts	free scripts
	free JavaScripts
	JavaScript tutorials
	JavaScript archives
wicker furniture	wicker
	wicker furniture
	outdoor furniture
ragtime music	ragtime
	ragtime music
Web design jobs	jobs AND Web design
	jobs AND Web designer
	jobs AND Web developer
online college degrees	college degrees AND online
	online colleges
	college AND online

PROFESSIONAL OBLIGATIONS

Designers' responsibilities go beyond building sites and maintaining good relationships with clients. The Web design process involves many ethical, professional, and legal issues associated with developing and launching Web sites. The Web was conceived as a tool by which information could be exchanged without the restrictions of paper documents and postal delivery. That goal has been achieved and surpassed, in ways not envisioned by the Web's founders and early pioneers. Despite these accomplishments, or perhaps in part because of them, the Web has lured some into believing that human behavior had been freed from constraints as well. Yet, as a publishing medium, the Web deals with publishing-related issues, including copyright; as a digital medium, the Web necessarily grapples with issues such as fair use of electronic resources such as bandwidth and software piracy.

If Web design is to be regarded as a profession, designers must take their responsibilities in this developing field seriously. They must learn not only what clients expect of them, but also what behaviors they must demand of clients. In addition, designers must remain aware of the expectations of professional organizations and legislative bodies. These expectations—some enforced by law, others established by public preference—are the standards by which Web designers balance accounts with their clients and the Web-using public at large. In assuring that their work and that of subcontractors demonstrates accountability, designers help build the Web design profession into a community committed to creating usable, accessible Web sites that promote worthwhile exchange among individuals and cultures.

Fair Use of Bandwidth

One very important responsibility designers have concerns the use of electronic resources—specifically, bandwidth. Web designers must make sure that a finished site does not make unfair use of the resources that are available on the Web. With bandwidth use, the critical concept is that every time a file is transmitted from a server, someone needs to pay. "Bandwidth theft" is a violation that occurs when one Web site designer makes use of a graphic (or other file) from another designer's Web site without first copying that file to their own system and then uploading the file to their own host. When one site uses an image that is stored on another site's host, every time the "borrower's" site accesses that image, the image's owner is charged for the bandwidth used for that transmission. If this bandwidth pilfering occurs frequently, charges for excessive use of bandwidth billed to the owner of the image can become prohibitively large. This is unfair and is considered a serious violation of the community consciousness and openness of the Web.

There are ways to link that would not constitute bandwidth theft. The concept of the Web relies on linking. Thus, providing a link that takes users to another Web site is considered permissible. But linking that appears to present some other Web site's work as the designer's own by directly uploading that work from another site is an example of bandwidth theft. Bandwidth theft uses a file on another server while giving the appearance that the file is part of the file structure on the designer's own server.

For example, consider a site (Site 1) that wants to provide audio content, say a recording of a speech by a well-known author. The audio file is a large file that is available on another site (Site 2). Without considering the consequences of what they are doing, Site 1's creators place a link to the audio file on Site 2. When the user activates the link on Site 1, the audio file plays, but from Site 2's server for which Site 2 will be charged for bandwidth use. The user has not left Site 1, but is using content stored on Site 2's server. This is bandwidth theft.

Bandwidth violations are easily detected by searching the Web using the full URL and file name for a sound or image. Web pages that use that sound or image can be located with such a search. If a designer suspects that other Web sites are using their files directly, the designer can type in the full URL of the original file (www.some_domain_name/some_image_name.extension [.gif, .jpg]). If the search results in a list of sites that use the file by directly linking to the image's source site, this identifies the violators. To further confirm which of these sites is practicing bandwidth theft, look at the source code for the sites that are using the image straight from the image owner's host server.

Another way to track down bandwidth theft is to use the data maintained and provided by the Web server's referrer logs. These logs are maintained automatically and show the sites from which another site was accessed. By using a Perl script to scan the referrer log for access patterns, the designer can create a report that clearly shows instances of access to a site's image files from pages outside that domain.

Sites that are victims of bandwidth theft have been known to employ strategies such as renaming (or even replacing) the graphics. This leads to missing images on the site that has attached itself improperly to the donor site. Other designers have solved the problem by refusing access to their site's JPEG, MIDI, or WAV files from anywhere off their own server. In other words, a user interested in viewing an image, for instance, must first be taken to the site that houses that image.

The consequences of bandwidth violations, and of other demonstrations of the absence of professional accountability, are damaging not only to the site that is being victimized, but also to the larger community of the Web. There have actually been cases in which the charges incurred at the hands of bandwidth "thieves" were so exorbitant that sites that had willingly provided royalty-free clip art and other resources have been forced to shut down to protect themselves, or at the very least, to discontinue their generous service of providing images for use by other designers. Thus, awareness of bandwidth theft can help design teams avoid linking directly to other sites, prevent others from doing so, as well as protect sites they have built themselves.

Software Piracy

Another serious issue is software piracy—the illegal use of software that has not been purchased. Again, the damage caused by this practice goes beyond the company whose software is being stolen. Violations in the use of their software leads publishers to tighten down the distribution of their products, and as a consequence, everyone suffers.

One notable consequence of software piracy is the move toward tighter registration processes for software, such as that used by Microsoft for its Windows XP product. In an effort to stop piracy of its software, Microsoft instituted a registration process that disabled the software within 30 days unless it was registered online as proof that it belongs to that person (or enterprise) to be used on that computer. This highly restrictive registration process caused numerous difficulties. But the underlying motivation for this process could be traced to the epidemic level of software piracy violations currently in practice.

Software piracy violations can easily be detected. Using Web technologies, companies can readily implement practices to track and monitor the use of their products and thereby identify those using software illegally. Methods for tracking software use are beyond the scope of this book, but for additional details, conduct a Web search using search strategies for terms such as "software piracy" AND "detection methods."

Respect for Copyright

The issue of software piracy is part of a larger set of points about copyright. Copyright law protects a wide range of created items: writings, photographs, drawings, or choreographed works. If it can be seen, read, or heard, it can be protected by copyright law. To be protected by copyright, the work must be in "tangible form," which means a copyrighted photograph, for instance, must exist in some physical way such as a print, slide, or digital form. An idea for a photograph cannot be copyrighted; the actual photograph can be.

There are exceptions to the inclusive sweep of material that can be copyrighted. Extremely short writings (other than poems), very simple line drawings, and materials that were created by artists and writers who have been dead for more than 50 years are some exceptions. Facts and ideas cannot be copyrighted, nor can titles, slogans, procedures, methods, processes, concepts, or principles (some of which can be protected by patents and trademarks). Any work that is made up entirely of information that is common property and contains no original authorship cannot be copyrighted. By no means is this an exhaustive list of works that cannot be covered by copyright; instead, it gives an idea of what types of works cannot have a claim of copyright attached to them.

Copyright law grants the creator of a resource exclusive rights to reproduce or distribute the work, to perform it or display it publicly, to prepare derivative works, or to grant those rights to others. In other words, copyright governs the ability to make copies of the work. In the United States, copyright applies with or without the display of a copyright symbol or registration of the copyright, although displaying the copyright symbol surely bolsters claims in U.S. courts of copyright in the work, as does registering the copyright (with the Library of Congress); in other countries, copyright symbols must be clearly displayed. Copyright infringement occurs whenever someone uses the work created by another as though it is his own. The line drawn here involves the value associated with the creative process. The person who creates it, owns it.

The Web contains many resources that are termed "royalty-free." Although these resources can be used without paying money, they can be used only when the owner's terms and conditions are strictly followed. If the owner prohibits alteration of the image, the image cannot be used in altered form. If the image's creator states that credit must be given, or a link must be provided back to the copyright owner's site, again these are requirements that must be followed to use the copyrighted work in compliance with the law. All of this applies even when the resource has been redeveloped. Making changes to someone else's original work does not change the fact that the original creator continues to own the work. Copyright law exists to protect the rights of the creator of the work.

A more subtle source of copyright violations can occur when a site designer uses royalty-free resources available on a Web site that has included resources not belonging to that site's creator, but without making it clear who the true owner is, and what terms and conditions the true owner requires of others who use his work. In terms of the law, any user of a resource is responsible for determining whether or not that use is allowed. Using resources from sites that are themselves violating copyright is still a violation.

An additional consideration concerns the use of frames on a Web site. When one of the frames of a site shows material from another site, it can appear that the "imported" material is an integral part of the current site. Because a screen made up of frames appears to be work produced by the owner of that site, it can be misleading if work created by others appears as a part of the borrower's work. Unless it is made clear who the creator actually is, this is a violation of the real owner's copyright.

It is sometimes possible to obtain permission from the owners and creators of resources and then use their work, giving proper credit. Obtaining such permissions involves communicating directly with the creator, describing the intended use, and obtaining written permission.

Protection of Confidentiality, Privacy, and Security

Web designers need to be both aware of and responsible for the protection of user confidentiality, privacy, and security. When confidential information is requested on the Web, security measures must be taken to ensure that information is not available to anyone other than the desired recipient.

One method for securing confidential data is to encrypt it. Encrypted data is scrambled according to a code that must be unlocked at the other end, using a "private key" in combination with a "public key" to convert the unreadable data back into readable form. When a secure transaction begins, most Web sites automatically switch to "secure mode" using Secure Sockets Layer (SSL) technology, a separate secure channel that travels on top of TCP/IP (Transmission Control Protocol/Internet Protocol). SSL controls assigning temporary private and public key pairs to encrypt and decrypt the data. After the transaction ends, these temporary keys are discarded. When a Web page is secure, an icon that looks like a padlock shows on the status bar.

Besides securing the information, the recipient of critical data needs to have a means of assurance that the source of the information sent was, in fact, the person the sender claimed to be. Given that anyone can pretend to be anyone else on the Web, the **authentication** process is used to verify the sender's identity. Security countermeasures also ensure that the contents of the transmitted critical data are tamper-proof and cannot be changed or deleted.

A **digital certificate** is a means for authenticating the identity of the user sending information, using an encrypted and password-protected file containing critical information, such as name, address, and e-mail address. The digital certificate functions like an ID card or driver's license. Outlook and Netscape mail provide the option of sending and receiving digital certificates to verify the identity of e-mail senders. Internet Explorer and Netscape browsers automatically receive and process digital certificates to verify that the Web site that looks like a familiar, trusted site, is, in fact, that Web site.

As part of a digital certificate, additional protections are embedded in the file, including a special key to unlock the certificate, an expiration date beyond which the certificate becomes invalid, and the verification of a certificate authority (CA). The main commercial CA is VeriSign, at verisign.com/.

A secure transaction might follow steps like these:

1. A customer requests an airline ticket. Before issuing the request, the customer's browser first obtains a digital certificate from the airline (or company selling the

---

Certificate General | Details | Certification Path

Certificate Information

This certificate is intended for the following purpose(s):
- Protects e-mail messages
- Ensures the identity of a remote computer
- 1.3.135.1.1.3

* Refer to the certification authority's statement for details.

Issued to: SIA Secure Client CA

Issued by: SIA Secure Client CA

Valid from 7/8/1999 **to** 7/8/2019

Issuer Statement

OK

A digital certificate is an electronic ID card to identify a data source.

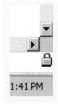

1:41 PM

A padlock icon, inserted by the SSL protocol, informs the user that a site is secure. This image, which appears below the browser's scroll bar, is placed automatically by the SSL protocol and is not coded in by HTML writers.

authentication
The process of confirming the source of data on a network or the Internet. Through strong authentication, users can verify the identity of both themselves to others and others to themselves. Entering a unique user name and password can verify the identity of a person who hopes to connect to services or Web pages on a distant computer.

VeriSign authenticates online businesses and encrypts sensitive data with an SSL certificate. Sites that enlist the services of VeriSign carry the globally recognized VeriSign Secure Site Seal (the orange logo on the screen).

ticket) to verify its validity. When this has been obtained, the customer's browser requests permission to purchase the ticket.

2. The airline's server requests a digital certificate that verifies the customer's identity.

3. The airline's server receives identification confirmation and sends order information to the customer. This information specifies that the public and private keys associated with the transaction can be used for just this one transaction.

4. The customer accepts the terms of the sale, and the airline's server completes the transaction after receiving confirmation from the customer's browser.

Another major security concern is the threat of computer viruses, transmitted via the Web. A computer virus is a program that has been specifically designed to transmit itself across the Internet, become active on each computer that it infects, and carry out the "payload" of the impact it was designed to produce. The impact of viruses varies according to the design. As an example, the W32.HLLO.Homer.C virus overwrites files in the Windows folder, replacing them with nonsense files. These corrupted files cannot be repaired. The impact is that Windows becomes unstable, does not function normally, and might not be able to start. When the virus is executed, a window appears with a message "You've been had by The Homer," with an image of a flying Homer Simpson, dodging bullets.

The primary way Web designers can take action against the spread of viruses is to make sure that none of the files on the server have been compromised by hackers. Hosting companies provide protection against such activity, but it is wise for those responsible for maintaining a site to check the files for any corruption.

One form of virus that spreads itself via e-mail attachment is known as a worm virus. A worm virus is activated when the recipient opens the e-mail attachment. After a machine is infected, these viruses automatically send themselves out to everyone in the address book for the infected machine, with a generic message designed to convince the recipients that the person with the infected machine is, in fact, the one who sent the message and attachment. Such messages can be spotted by their general tone. An example of a message that could have been sent by a worm virus might be: "Here's the picture I was telling you about" or "Take a look at this for a real chuckle." When these new recipients open the attachment, the virus infects their computers, and repeats the process of sending itself out to everyone in their e-mail directory. This is how a worm virus spreads—and spreads quickly.

The number of detected viruses reported by Symantec as of November 2002 was 62,320. Computer users, particularly those who use the Internet or are exposed to files from others who do, are highly advised to use virus protection software and to update it regularly.

There are other forms of intrusion from Internet criminals. When a computer is connected to the Internet it can be found by hackers, who use automated intrusion programs to locate connected PCs. Once found, a PC is open to the threat of the hacker locating and taking personal information. As protection from this type of threat, companies and individuals install **firewalls** that control all connections to and from the computer, blocking entry by unauthorized users and alerting the owner to any attempted intrusions. Firewall software provides additional protections, such as hiding the computer from Internet-intrusion programs, and guarding it against common hacking techniques. Both Symantec and McAfee offer personal firewall software to provide protection to individual Web users.

firewall
A software program designed to protect the data and resources of a private network from external users. Often runs on a computer designated as a "gateway server" through which all data traffic between in-network and external computers must travel. Data packets of disallowed types, sources, and destinations are blocked.

Accessibility Compliance

Taking responsibility for addressing the accessibility standards presented in Chapter 4 is an important part of the design process. Professional Web designers must be particularly aware of the standards agreed to by their professional community, represented by the W3C, and make every effort to meet them. Just as the AMA (American Medical Association) self-regulates medical practices that physicians are expected to follow, the W3C is the self-regulatory body of the Web design profession, and designers would be wise to heed its recommendations.

Accessibility standards might appear to be too difficult to achieve and to be applicable only to a small percentage of the Web-using population. But this segment of Web users cannot be ignored. No one should place requirements on the kinds of physical capabilities necessary to use a computer, but ignoring accessibility standards does just that. Beyond the social implications of restricting computer use to certain types of abilities, however, the issue of access devices must be considered.

As developing professionals, Web site designers need to demonstrate both the commitment and the capacity to adhere to these accessibility guidelines, and also encourage others to do likewise. It is constructive to begin early to think through what these standards mean in terms of the responsibilities of a professional designer. An important part of the learning process for Web designers is to develop strategies and methods whereby all sites they create will be in compliance with the accessibility guidelines, yet also demonstrate creativity and innovation.

Leadership Role

As responsible members of the profession, Web designers should become advocates—to other designers and to clients as well—of accountability and compliance. Well-informed designers should know the essential requirements and provide guidance to others. Although some earlier Web designers adopted a permissive attitude about Web design, those days are long gone. As Chapter 1 indicated, the Web is becoming increasingly essential to human exchange, so it is imperative to ensure that those who design for such an important medium uphold the standards and conventions of effective communication.

This sense of leadership extends beyond the work of the designer to a responsibility for protecting clients from becoming involved, however unintentionally, in illegal or unprincipled practices in terms of bandwidth, copyright, accessibility, and confidentiality. Because a Web site is an important "face" and impression of the company or institution, it is all the more critical that this image be within the professional bounds of compliance and accountability.

Web designers can play an influential and positive role as the Web continues to evolve. By accepting a leadership role they will become even more valuable and essential to the cyber community, and their contributions will ensure that the Web becomes a medium to interconnect all people of the world and to enable new levels of knowledge, collaboration, and participation.

Root Link www.webprofession.com/
Direct Link www.webprofession.com/legal/
Why Go? To visit a site complete with articles on Web culture, emerging technologies, and other issues. Links to education and training, too. Articles on legal issues cover a wide variety of topics.

---

web 7.3 activity

As a professional Web site designer, you will be expected to be fully aware of issues such as copyright, privacy and encryption, e-commerce issues, accessibility, and other requirements. Your knowledge of these areas must be current, and your practices must demonstrate compliance and professionalism.

The purpose of this activity is for you to start a process that needs to be repeated periodically throughout your career: that of gaining up-to-date information about issues to ensure that you—and through you, your clients and employers—have impeccable records in these regards.

To accomplish the goals of this Web Activity, complete these tasks:

1. Select one of these areas (or a similar area of your choice) about which you will gain updated information: 1) copyright, 2) encryption, or 3) e-commerce client protection. Do a search on your subject area, beginning on the W3C site at www.w3.org/Help/siteindex/. In addition to what you find on the W3C site, locate and review two additional credible and current sources from which to update your understanding about requirements. Determine the current requirements, practices, and issues, including their rationale.

2. Imagine that you are team leader for a major project for an important client. As you begin the project, you become aware that two of your team members have "casual" attitudes toward the set of requirements about which you have conducted your research update. Write a one-page directive, clearly presented and explained, to ensure that these team members come to understand the issues, why these issues are important, and how your project team wants to be perceived by the client in terms of them.

apply & practice

Online Quiz

As a review of the key concepts in this chapter, define the terms in the following list:

    authentication
    browser cache
    digital certificates
    firewall
    FTP
    server log files
    zip/unzip

After you are confident that you understand this chapter's content, go to this book's Internet Resource Center (IRC) at www.emcp.com/ and take the self-test online quiz for this chapter. Review any questions you answered incorrectly, and then study the related chapter material again. Retake the online quiz as many times as you need to reach full mastery (90–100%).

Topics Roundtable

1. What preparations would you make to ensure that a Web site launches smoothly?
2. Discuss dissenting views regarding copyright. Prepare for this discussion by conducting a Web search and reading several articles on the subject, or visit www.benedict.com/ and read descriptions of real copyright cases.
3. Present your views, pro and con, about those members of the Web culture who actively resist copyright strictures. What are the underlying issues in terms of what is right and fair, and how do you view them?
4. Investigate various methods (such as "watermarking") used by owners of copyrights to trace the use of their work. What issues are raised by these methodologies?
5. What areas of professional obligation are of interest to you? What steps will you take to see that you and those you work with abide by the best practices of the industry for those areas?

window to the web

META TAGS, WEB PAGE FINALIZATION, WEB HOSTS, AND FTP

➤ Understand meta tags.
➤ Finalize Web pages.
➤ Know what to look for in a Web host.
➤ Upload files using FTP.

technical walk-through

After your pages are complete, you are in a position to choose a description and keywords to describe their content. **Descriptions** are concise statements that communicate what the site contains. **Keywords** are words that you anticipate potential users of your site would be most likely to use when keying search terms in a search engine. The description and key words will be used in **meta tags** that are located between the start and end head tags. These two meta tags will help promote your Web pages by assisting search engines in cataloging your site. Other meta tags can be used to provide instructions to browsers, such as an instruction to move to another URL.

After the coding of your Web pages is complete, you are ready to finalize your pages. These tasks ensure that your pages are professional in appearance and function as intended. Spelling should be checked, and all links, both internal and external, should be tested to make sure they are working.

The next step is choosing a Web host. Many considerations are involved in choosing an appropriate Web host. Your requirements will vary depending on whether your Web site is private or commercial. The size of your Web site is also a factor. Develop a checklist that enables you to rate Web host services against your requirements.

After you have chosen a Web host, you will need to use a File Transfer Protocol (FTP) program to upload your Web pages to the host server. This can be accomplished using a browser-based FTP program or by using any one of the numerous FTP programs available as freeware or shareware on the Web.

Your work is not over after the Web site is up and running, however. To keep the site current, you must periodically update its contents. The performance of your Web host should also be reviewed to see that the host is holding up to its end of the bargain. You also must periodically check all links. Internal links can be inadvertently broken if you modify or edit your files, and external links might change due to circumstances beyond your control.

Description and Keywords Meta Tags

Meta tags are not paired, so the / is included as part of the open tag. A number of **meta tags** can be placed between the head open and close tags (<head></head>) on a Web page, but the two most important are the ones containing description and keyword attributes and values (see Figure 7.8). These meta tags were originally designed to assist search engines in cataloging Web pages. Search engines employ **spiders** to automatically crawl through Web pages and record information about their content. This information is used to organize and catalog Web pages, so that search engines can return results based on their relevance to keyword searches.

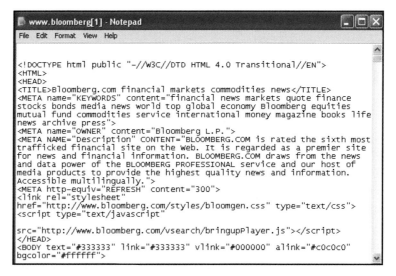

FIGURE 7.8

The description meta tag for the www.bloomberg.com/ financial news Web site contains a concise description of the page's contents. The keywords meta tag lists some of the keywords related to the page content.

Unfortunately, description and keywords meta tags were abused by some Web page developers, who packed keywords meta tags with repeated usage of the same word, or included keywords that were irrelevant to the actual page content to increase the chances that their site would appear at higher levels on search hit lists. This abuse led to some search engines attaching less importance to meta descriptions and keywords, or sometimes ignoring them altogether. Abusing meta tags in this way, or by other methods, can result in your pages not being listed, or in their being penalized so that their rankings are lower than they would be normally.

Before writing meta descriptions and keywords, conduct research on the meta tag policies for some of the most popular Web search engines (see Figure 7.9). Search engines have pages describing their policies, and this information is useful when you are formulating a meta description and keywords.

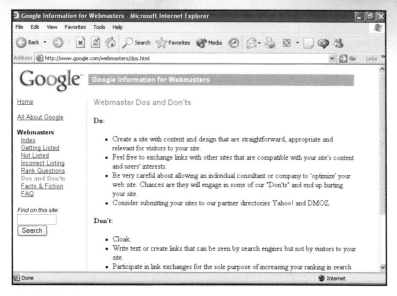

The Google search engine contains a Webmaster Dos and Don'ts page with information on how Google catalogs Web sites, and the best ways to get a page or site listed.

Do not rely solely on meta descriptions and keywords to promote your site. One of the best ways of promoting your site is to make sure that it actually contains the information you claim it does. If certain keywords legitimately occur throughout your pages, search engines will pick this up and rank your pages accordingly. Google, one of the most popular search engine sites, regards the number of links to a page as a "vote," and combines this data with the actual page content to arrive at a ranking. This means that your best strategy is to create pages that are truly relevant to their subject and that will be popular with users. More users will link to your pages, which increases your Google rating.

Because spiders "crawl" Web pages on a periodic basis, it might be some time before you notice the results of any changes in the way your pages are cataloged by a search engine due to changes you have made in the meta tags or in the page content. For example, Google states that its Web spiders visit sites on a monthly basis.

ADD DESCRIPTION AND KEYWORDS META TAGS

Add description and keywords meta tags to your Web pages. Use one of the pages you have created for your Window to the Web resource site for this step-by-step.

1. Review the Web page you have created and write a brief description of its contents.
2. Look at the Web page again and write down as many keywords or keyword phrases that appear on the page, or that could be used to describe the page contents. Try to put yourself in the shoes of someone searching for the information covered by your site. What search terms would you use? Write these down as keywords to be used in describing your site.

3. Use a text editor to open your Web page. Locate the cursor in a line between the head start and end tags, and key meta description and keywords tags. Use commas to separate keywords and keyword phrases.

```
<meta name="description" content="your description of your Web
page." />
<meta name="keywords" content="your keywords here" />
</head>
```

4. Save and close the file. Meta tag content is not visible on your browser.

The Refresh Meta Tag

The refresh meta tag (<meta http-equiv="refresh" content="time in seconds"; url="url" />) can be used to redirect visitors to another URL. The time that the redirect page is to be visible is specified (in seconds), as well as the URL for the new site. The refresh tag might not work with all browsers, so it is always a good idea to include a link on the page as well.

The refresh meta tag has three main uses: for sites that have moved, for splash pages, and for slide shows. When a site has moved to another location and therefore has a new URL, a single page with a refresh meta tag and some text can be maintained at the previous location to announce the change and redirect visitors to the new location. If you do not want to make any announcement, the time can be set to "0" so the redirect occurs instantly without visitors being aware they are being redirected.

Refresh meta tags are also used for "splash" pages. A splash page is an opening page with an announcement or graphic that appears for a few seconds before directing visitors to another page, usually a home page. The splash page is a technique used to attract the attention of visitors.

The third way that refresh meta tags can be used is to set up a slide show or tour. Each slide in the show contains a refresh meta tag specifying the number of seconds it is to be visible. The refresh meta tag contains the URL for the next slide in the series, which also contains a refresh meta tag. This continues until the last slide, which can contain a refresh meta tag directing viewers back to the sending or home page. Include some kind of warning or notice to visitors that clicking on a link will send them on a slide show in case they do not want to lose control of their browsers.

CREATE A REFRESH META TAG

Create a refresh meta tag directing visitors to one of your Web pages:
1. Use your text editor to open the **shell.html** file.
2. Save the shell.html file as **refresh_practice.html** using the Save As command.
3. Key a refresh meta tag, code, and text:

```
<head>
<title>This Is My Refresh Meta Tag Practice Page</title>
<meta http-equiv="refresh"
content="10;URL=links_practice_1.html" />
</head>
<body>
```

```
<p>
<font size="5">
My Web site has changed locations. It is now located at <a
href="links_practice_1.html">links_practice_1</a>. You will be
sent to the new location automatically after 10 seconds. If
nothing happens, please click on the above link. Please remember
to update your bookmarks.
</font>
</p>
</body>
```

4. Save the file and use your browser to open it. You should see the message you keyed for about 10 seconds, after which time the browser should open the links_practice_1.html page (see Figure 7.10).

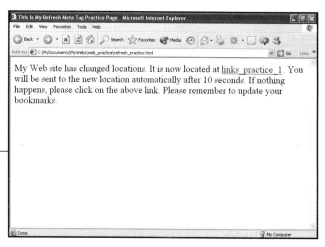

FIGURE 7.10

A refresh meta tag can be used to automatically redirect a browser to another URL after a specified amount of time.

Web Page Finalization

You should validate (check for errors) the code on your pages to be sure that it is correct and that it will work with different browsers. To assist you with this process, free HTML validating programs such as *Tidy* are available for download and use on your own computer. Another option is to use one of the free HTML validating services available on the Web. When using a Web-based service, you have two options for checking the code. If your pages are already online, you can enter their URLs in the appropriate box on the Web page of the HTML validating service, and the HTML Validator finds the page and checks it. If your pages are not yet online, you can use the Web page to upload files for checking (see Figure 7.11).

HTML validators will not find broken links, so you must check links yourself. Broken links are one of the biggest disappointments for visitors, and might cause them to go elsewhere. Few Web events are more frustrating than to think you have located something you are looking for only to discover that the link is not working.

During the course of creating your Web pages, it is possible that you keyed an anchor tag and path incorrectly. It is also easy to move pages between subdirectories without remembering to change the path in any anchor tags linking to those pages.

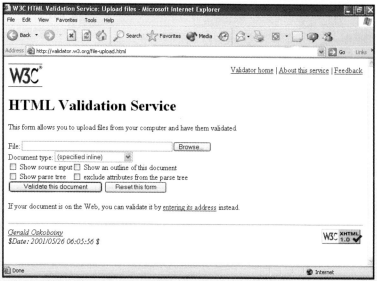

FIGURE 7.11

A Web-based HTML Validator can be used to check that the code on your pages complies with the HTML version information indicated in the page.

External links might not work if their location has changed or if they have been removed. It is important that you verify that every link on the Web pages functions correctly. Even if a link works, you need to verify that the link is correct. For example, a "Home" button link might work, but it might send visitors to a page other than the Home page if an incorrect URL has been entered in the anchor tag path.

Doing a complete spell check is another must. Even if you are an excellent speller, it is easy to miss spelling mistakes. Many HTML editors have a spell-checking program to check spelling. Text editors like Notepad generally do not include a spell-checking function. However, a shortcut around this problem is to copy code and content from the text editor and paste it into a word-processing program such as Microsoft Word. You can then use the spell-checking function in that program to check your spelling. After your spell check is complete, copy the material and paste it back in the Web page file. Some HTML validating programs or services offer spell checking as well.

When performing a spell check, you must be careful that you do not change the spelling of any paths or URLs or they will not work. Be sure to check that the page and all links still function after the spell check is complete.

Finally, try to check your Web pages by viewing them in as many different browsers (and browser versions) and platforms as possible. Not everyone uses the same browser or computer platform. By checking in multiple browsers, you will know if there are any problems that need correcting to ensure that most viewers can view your pages in the way that you intend.

Choosing a Web Host

After your Web pages are finalized, you are ready to choose a Web host for your site. From the research you have already conducted, you know that the features and capabilities offered by Web hosting providers vary considerably. The first choice you need to make is whether you want to use a free Web hosting provider or a professional fee-based service.

The most important difference between free Web hosting providers and professional fee-based hosts is that free hosts generally require that you accept advertising on your page, chiefly in the form of advertising banners. You will have no control over the content or number of these advertising banners, and most viewers find these ads annoying. Also, ads slow page loading speeds, which can reduce the appeal of viewing your pages. After taking this factor into consideration and comparing the features offered by free Web hosting services with fee-based Web hosting services, you may find it worthwhile to use a fee-based service. Fees have dropped considerably over the years, and a small site can be hosted for less than 10 dollars a month in many cases.

If your Web site is personal or noncommercial, a free Web hosting provider is probably the best option for you. Your Internet Service Provider (ISP) might offer free Web hosting as part of your subscription. A number of Web sites offer comparisons of free Web hosting providers (see Figure 7.12), making it easier for you to choose.

FIGURE 7.12

A Web search for "Free Web Hosting" will turn up a number of Web sites that feature information about free Web hosting providers. This site offers assistance, advice, feature comparisons, and more.

If you choose to use a free Web hosting provider, the best strategy is to decide which features you need, and then look for a free Web hosting provider matching your requirements. Some of the key criteria to choose from when selecting a free Web hosting provider include:

- **Space Allowance** You are allowed a certain amount of space on the Web host's server, measured in megabytes (MB). Unless your site contains a lot of graphics, you are unlikely to exceed the maximum allowance. A space allowance of 5 MB is more than enough for a personal Web site with a few graphics and under 100 pages. Allowances do vary considerably, so all other things being equal, you might want to choose a provider offering a generous space allowance.

- **Data Transfer Allowance** Your data transfer allowance (measured in MB) affects how many people can visit your site per month. If the number of visitors to your site exceeds this allowance, some visitors might be prevented from accessing your site, or you may be assessed additional fees. You can arrive at a rough estimate of your bandwidth needs by taking the size of a page and its images measured in bytes, and multiplying that figure by the number of views you expect for that page in a month. For example, if the total size of a page and its images is 35 kilobytes, and you estimate 50,000 people will view that page each month, the bandwidth need for that page would be 1.75 gigabytes ($35 \times 50,000 = 1,750,000$ KB or 1.75 gigabytes). By calculating this value for each of the pages on your site and then determining the site's total, you will have an estimate of your total bandwidth requirement. Bandwidth allowances vary considerably, so it is a good idea to shop around.

- **Domain Name (Address)** Some free Web hosting providers offer a sub-domain for your use, while others require users to purchase their own domain name. Still others allow you to use a domain name you have already purchased. Having your own domain name is nice, but you might decide that it is something you can live without. The prices for registering a domain name have now fallen to as little as $10 per year, down considerably from their peak when the Internet was in its infancy.

- **Uploading** Some free Web hosting providers only allow you to create and edit your pages on their Web site. This is slow and difficult. Other sites offer their own Web-based FTP service, which is slower than regular FTP. Look for sites that allow you to use an FTP program for uploading.
- **CGI** If you are going to incorporate forms into your Web pages, your Web host will need to provide CGI (Common Gateway Interface) support.
- **Advertisements (Banner Ads)** This is the way that most free Web hosting providers support their free service. As a condition for free hosting, many require that you accept advertising banners on your pages. Many people find these annoying, so you will have to consider whether or not the visitors to your site will find them disturbing.
- **Web Site Type** Some free Web hosting providers only host personal noncommercial pages, while others host personal as well as business pages.
- **E-Mail Service** Many free Web hosting providers offer free e-mail accounts. You need to decide whether this is important to you, and whether you want a regular e-mail account (POP3) or a Web-based account.

Browser-Based FTP

FTP is a utility (a program that performs a specific task) used to upload Web files to a server. The process of uploading Web files from your computer (the local or client computer) to a server (the remote or host computer) is often referred to as publishing. After your Web files are all located on the host server, the Web site is "live" and can be viewed by anyone with access to the Web.

Most recent browser versions can be used to transfer files using FTP. Netscape users can publish their Web pages using Netscape Composer. Dedicated FTP programs are also available, many of which are freeware or shareware. Dedicated FTP programs such as WS_FTP offer more functions and control compared to browsers. Some free Web hosting providers have their own Web-based FTP capability, but this is usually very slow compared to a regular FTP program. Older FTP programs demanded that users indicate whether a file to be uploaded was an ASCII (text) or binary (formatted material) file, but newer programs, including browser-based FTP programs, detect this automatically.

Three pieces of information will be provided by your Web host that are necessary before you can upload any files:
- **Upload Address** This is your Web host's FTP address. This is the address you will key in the address window of your browser or FTP utility.
- **User Name** This is the user name you selected when registering with the Web host.
- **Password** This is the password you chose when registering with the Web host.

After the registration process is complete, your Web host will either send an e-mail or return a new Web page to you containing the necessary information. You should print this information and store it in a safe place. If you lose it, you might find it very difficult to access your directory on the Web host's server.

Before beginning the upload process, read the Web host's instructions. This information is usually contained in the e-mail or Web page that informed you of your successful registration. Web hosts often provide a FAQ (frequently asked questions) document containing answers to the questions most often asked by beginners.

Use Internet Explorer to upload your Web page files:

1. Open Internet Explorer.
2. Key the FTP address supplied by your Web host in the address box located near the top of the browser.
3. A Log On dialog box appears (see Figure 7.13). Internet Explorer attempts to log in anonymously so the box will contain a message to the effect that the server does not allow anonymous logins. Ignore that and key the user name and password supplied by your Web host. Do not click the Log on anonymously box. You can check the Save Password box, but be aware that this could allow unauthorized parties access to your Web pages on the Web host server if they use your computer. Click Log On when you are finished keying the required information.
4. After your password is accepted, you will be logged on to your directory on the Web host's server (see Figure 7.14). The site might appear blank, or there might already be an index.html page and/or a directory located on the site. You should be able to upload your entire root directory folder to the site. If you upload a new index.html file, it will overwrite the index.html file already on the site, since there cannot be two files of the same name in the same directory. Procedures vary, so follow your host's instructions to learn how to arrange your Web site's file structure on the host server.
5. Minimize your browser by clicking on the minimize icon located in the upper-right portion of your browser.
6. Open your file management program (such as Windows Explorer) and locate and select the Web file, files or folder of files you want to upload. You can select more than one file at the same time by holding down the Ctrl key as you click on the files. Right-click when you are finished. Select Copy from the menu that appears.
7. Minimize the file-management program and restore the browser to its full size. Right-click to paste your files into the directory on the host server. A box appears that lets you know the progress of your upload (see Figure 7.15).

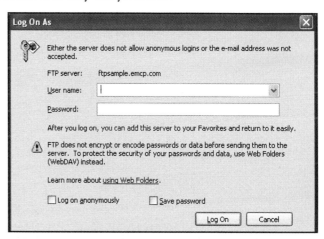

FIGURE 7.13

A Log On As dialog box prompts users to enter a user name and password after entering an FTP address in the Internet Explorer address box.

FIGURE 7.14

After you have successfully logged on to the FTP site, you will be in the directory location allocated to you by the Web host.

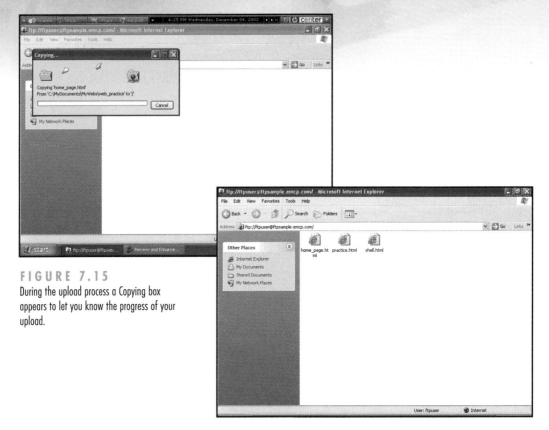

FIGURE 7.15
During the upload process a Copying box appears to let you know the progress of your upload.

FIGURE 7.16
After the uploading process is complete, the uploaded files and directories are visible on the FTP screen.

8. After the upload is complete, you should see your files and/or directories on the FTP screen (see Figure 7.16). Your Web site is now live and available to Web users around the world.
9. Verify that your Web pages are now online by entering the URL for your pages in the address box of your browser and pressing Enter.

You also can drag and drop files and directories between the file management program and the browser.

USE DRAG AND DROP TO UPLOAD FILES AND DIRECTORIES

Upload files to a server using drag and drop:
1. Use Internet Explorer to log on to your Web host's FTP site.
2. Click the restore icon in the upper-right portion of the browser screen to reduce it to about half its size. You can further reduce its size by clicking on an edge or corner of the program window and moving the black arrow that appears inward
3. Open Windows Explorer and reduce it to about half-size. You should now be able to view both the Windows Explorer window and your browser at the same time.

4. Locate the files and/or directories you want to upload. Click and hold your cursor over the files or directories you have selected. Drag them to your browser's screen (see Figure 7.17). Release the mouse button to begin the upload process.

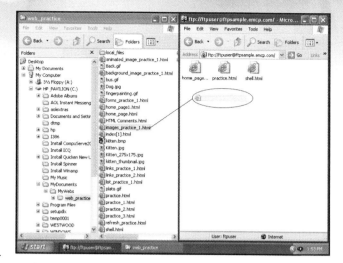

Files and directories can be "dragged and dropped" between Windows Explorer and the Internet Explorer FTP screen.

You can use Internet Explorer FTP to create a new folder (directory) if the host server allows it.

CREATE A NEW DIRECTORY

Create a new directory:
1. Make sure your browser is logged on to the FTP site.
2. Select File from the menu bar, point to New from the drop-down menu, and then click Folder.
3. If the host allows you to create a directory, you will see a folder image with New Folder highlighted in blue (see Figure 7.18). You can key a new name for the folder. If the host does not allow you to create directories, you will see a message box stating that this function is not allowed.

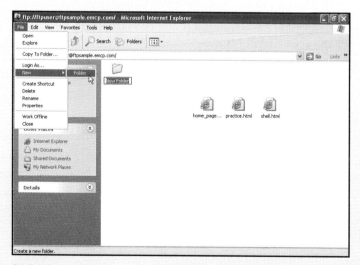

You can create a new folder (directory) on the host server if the host permits it.

Internet Explorer can be used to delete files and directories as well. Your ability to do this is controlled by the host server.

Delete a file or directory on the host server:
1. Right-click on the file or directory to be deleted.
2. Select Delete.
3. A box appears asking you to confirm that you want to delete the file or directory. Click Yes.
4. The file or directory is deleted and disappears from the FTP screen.

The most recent version of Netscape (version 7.0) allows users to publish their Web pages by using Netscape Composer, the HTML editing program that comes with the Netscape Navigator package. The FTP functionality of Composer is limited compared to Internet Explorer because users cannot create or delete files or directories.

design project

1. Use a search engine to research how different search engines catalog Web pages and treat meta tags. Create a table comparing the different methods and place this table on one of your existing Web pages, or create a new page for the table.
2. Key in meta descriptions and keywords for all your pages. Review your pages carefully so that their descriptions carefully summarize the page content. Try to select keywords or keyword combinations that are likely to be used by searchers looking for the type of information contained in your Web pages. Keep search engine requirements in mind as you are doing this.
3. Finalize your pages by checking that all links function as intended. Check the spelling and code. Try to view your pages in as many different browsers, browser versions, and platforms as possible to detect any problems.
4. When you are sure that your Web site is ready to launch, upload your files to the Web host you have chosen.
5. Log on to your site to view your Web site and to see how it performs. Pass your home page URL on to others and ask for their opinions and suggestions.

References

Chapter 1

BBN, "Internet Starts to Shrink," <http://news.bbc.co.uk/1/hi/sci/tech/1738496.stm> (January 2, 2002).

Berners-Lee, T. "Information Management: A Proposal." CERN. <www.w3.org/History/1989/proposal.html> (1989).

Berners-Lee, T. *Weaving the Web.* New York: HarperCollins, 1999.

Dertouzos, M. L., foreword to *Weaving the Web* by T. Berners-Lee (New York: HarperCollins, 1999).

Gilbert, Steven W. "A New Vision Worth Working Toward: Connected Education and Collaborative Change," <http://www.tltgroup.org/gilbert/NewVwwt200--2-14-00.htm> (2000).

Gillies, J., and R. Cailliau. *How the Web Was Born.* New York: Oxford University Press, 2000.

International Telework Association and Council, "Telework in the United States: Telework America Survey 2001," <www.telecommute.org> (2001).

Mesenbourg, T. L. *Measuring Electronic Business.* Maryland: U.S. Bureau of the Census, August 2001.

Netcraft, "October 2002 Survey," <http://www.netcraft.com/survey> (October 2002).

Rayasam, R. "E-Commerce Busts Early Projections," *Ziff Davis Smart Business for the New Economy,* <http://cma.zdnet.com> (January 2001).

Ross, F. "Make the Most of Web Marketing" *Smart Business,* (April 2001).

Seltzer, R., "The Internet and the Human Spirit,"<www.samizdat.com/spirit.html> (1995).

Steinberg, D. "The Smart Business 50," *Smart Business.* (September 2001).

Officetec.com, "Reworked Workplace of the Future," *The Telecommuter,* <www.officetec.com/newsletter1_1.html> (2000).

U.S. Census Bureau, "Measuring the Electronic Economy," <www.census.gov/eos/www/ebusiness614.htm> (2001).

U.S. Department of Commerce, "E-Stats," <www.census.gov/estats> (March 2001).

U.S. Department of Commerce, "Retail E-Commerce Sales in Third Quarter 2001 were $7.5 Billion, Up 8.3% from Third Quarter 2000," News, <www.census.gov/mrts/www/current.html> (November, 2001).

U.S. Department of Labor, "Telework and the New Workplace of the 21st Century," <www.dol.gov/asp/telework/execsum.htm> (2001).

Wendin, C. G. "Slash Purchasing Costs," *Smart Business.* <http://cma.zdnet.com> (April 2001).

Personal Computing Services, "World Wide Web User Statistics", <www.why-not.com/company/stats2.htm> (March 1999).

Chapter 2

Fruhlinger, Joshua A. "Usage Models That Work Together," *WebTechniques,* <www.newarchitectmag.com/archives/2001/12/fruhlinger/> (December 2001).

Holzschlag, Molly E. "How Specialization Limited the Web," *WebTechniques,* <www.newarchitectmag.com/archives/2001/09/desi/> (September 2001).

Howle, Amber. "Evolving the Team: How Companies Are Juggling Resources and Learning from Past Experiences," *WebTechniques,* < www.newarchitectmag.com/archives/2002/01/howle/> (January 2002).

Chapter 3

Abate, C., L. Anderson, M. Atanasov, D. deMyer, R. Rayasam, D. Steinberg. "The Smart Business 50," *Ziff Davis Smart Business*, <http"//cma.zdnet.com> (August 2001)

Davis, Jack and Susan Merritt. *Web Design WOW! Book: Showcasing the Best of On-Screen Communication*. Berkeley, Calif.: Peachpit Press, 1998.

Krug, Steve. *Don't Make Me Think*. Indianapolis: New Riders, 2000.

Siegel, David. *Creating Killer Web Sites: The Art of Third-Generation Site Design*. 2d ed. Indianapolis: Hayden Books, 1997.

Williams, Robin and John Tollett. *Web Design Workshop*. Berkeley, Calif.: Peachpit Press, 2000.

Williams, Robin and John Tollett. *The Non-designers Web Book: An Easy Guide to Creating, Designing, and Posting Your Own Web Site*. Berkeley, Calif.: Peachpit Press, 1998.

Chapter 4

Stephanidis, C., and A. Savidis. 2001. "Universal Access in the Information Society: Methods, Tools and Interaction Technologies," *Universal Access in the Information Society*. 1: 40–55.

European Commission Directorate, First Outline Proposal for a European Thematic Research Initiative Concerning "eAccessability for All." "General Information Society Technologies: Systems and Services for the Citizen, Applications relating to the disabled and the elderly," Brussels: (March 13, 2001).

Nielsen, Jakob and Donald Norman. "Usability on the Web Isn't a Luxury." *Information Week*, <http://www.informationweek.com/773/web.htm> (January 2000).

Paciello, Michael. *Web Accessibility for People with Disabilities*. Gilroy, CA: CMP Books, 2000.

Rayasam, R. "Telecommuting." *Ziff Davis Smart Business for the New Economy*, <http://cma.zdnet.com> (February 2001).

U.S. Department of Labor. "Telework and the New Workplace of the 21st Century: Executive Summary." <www.dol.gov/aspteleword/execsum.html> (2001).

Chapter 5

Coorough, C. *Multimedia and the Web: Creating Digital Excitement*. New York: Harcourt College Publishers, 2001.

Gillies, J. and R. Cailliau. *How the Web Was Born*. New York: Oxford University Press, 2000.

Modahl,, M. *Now or Never: How Companies Must Change Today to Win the Battle for Internet Consumers*. New York: Harper Collins, 2000.

Null, C. "Inside Line: Michael Schrage/MIT Media Lab" *Smart Business*. (December 2001/January 2002): 34.

Powell, T. A. *Web Design: The Complete Reference*. New York: McGraw-Hill, 2000.

Index

link styles and page usability,
176–177
lists
    bulleted, 203–204
    nested, 205
    numbered, 205
LI tag, 203–204
log file analysis programs, 364
LookSmart, 21

M

Macromedia Dreamweaver, 289–290,
    353
Macromedia Flash MX, 312–313
MacZip, 353
maintenance phase
    contracting for, 362–363
    improvements and revisions,
        365–368
    site data analysis, 364–365
marketing
    co-branding, 7
    competitive research, 230–231
    cross-linking, 231, 305–306
    site promotion, 357–360
    understanding target markets, 230
markup languages, 287
menus, drop-down, 217
metaphor, defined, 111
meta-search engines, 24
META tag, 380–381
Microsoft FrontPage, 289
MILNET, 14
modem access, and download time,
    115
monitor size, 170
monospaced text, 89
Mosaic, 19
mouseover effects, 286
multimedia
    alternatives for accessibility, 193
    defined, 74
    preparing files, 314

N

named anchor, 331
navigation
    accessibility guidelines, 197
    navigation system design, 57–58,
        304–305
    placement of aids, 177–178
    and Web site utility, 114–116
NCI (National Cancer Institute)
    usability guidelines, 162–163
needs analysis
    client's needs, 233–236
    defined, 233
    purposes of Web sites, 72–80
    user's needs, 237–241
netiquette, defined, 78

newsgroups, defined, 77
normative technique, 236
Northern Light, 21
NSFNET, 14–15
numbered (ordered) lists, 205

O

OCR (optical character recognition),
    249, 309
ODBC-compliant databases, 286
OL tag, 205
ordered lists, 205
organizing content files, 315–317

P

P tag, 46
packet switching, 14
page layouts
    composites, 318–320
    usability guidelines, 170–176
    using tables, 152, 153, 273, 323
PageScreamer, 200
paradigm shift, 29–30
parameters, Web site evaluation, 104
path, in URLs, 60
Perl (Practical Extraction and
    Reporting Language), 288
personal interconnection Web sites,
    77–78
physical structure of Web sites
    catalog, 301, 303
    grid, 297–298
    linear, 297–298, 299
    mesh, 301
    pyramid/hierarchical, 298–300
    star/cluster, 300–301
    tutorial, 301, 302
Pirouz, Raymond, 158–159
pixel, defined, 168
PKZip, 353
platforms, 37
PNG (Portable Network Graphics)
    format, 252, 263
pre-formatted text, 89
pre-launch testing, 354–357
preparation and planning phase
    competitive research, 230–231
    content area research, 226–228
    information about site sponsor,
        229–230
    needs analysis, 233–242
    Project Management Plan,
        256–259
    project plan creation, 244–259
    Site Specifications and Standards,
        244–256
    target market research, 230
PRE tag, 89
principles, Web page design, 104
printable pages, 177

print-to-text technology, 309
privacy concerns, 27, 373
programming knowledge, 64
programming languages, 288
Project Management Plan document
    roles and collaboration process, 258
    scope of work, 256–257
    time lines and checkpoints,
        258–259
    work process, tasks and subtasks,
        257–258
project phases, 225. *See also* Web site
    projects
Project Plan document
    Project Management Plan,
        256–259
    Site Specifications and Standards,
        244–256
protocols, in URLs, 60
prototypes
    client review and approval, 322
    composites, 318–320
    defined, 164
    storyboards, 320–321
purposes of Web sites
    decision support and problem solv-
        ing, 74–76
    entertainment and recreation,
        79–80
    information, 73–74
    personal interconnections, 77–78
    task assistance, 76–77

Q

quality control
    accessibility evaluation, 199–200,
        355–356
    editorial check, 357
    overview, 59
    page load time check, 355
    pre-launch checks, 354–357
    usability evaluation, 178–179
QuickTime movies, 314

R

radio buttons, 216
rapport, 119
readability, 107–108
real-time information, 9
recreation-oriented Web sites, 79–80
recruitment, 7
referrer logs, 365, 370
refresh meta tag, 382
relative links, 329
relative URLs, 327–328
reset button, 219
rights issues, 250, 371–372
rollover effects, 286
root directory, 38
ROWSPAN attribute, 141–142

S

sales knowledge, 65
sans serif fonts, 175
satellite Internet connection, 115
scanning print documents, 309, 310
scenarios, 246–249
scope of work, documenting, 256–257
screen resolution, 168–169
screen size, 170
scripting languages, 287
search engines
    how they work, 20–22, 24
    and META tags, 380–381
    and site promotion strategies, 358–360
    within sites, 178
    and TITLE tags, 44, 166
    use of, 23–24
secure data sending, 251, 373
security concerns, 27, 251, 373–374
Semantic Web initiative, 29
serif fonts, 175
server log files, 364
server-side strategies, 315
shareware, 351
Shockwave animations, 253
Siegel, David, 102–103
SimpleText, 37
site maps, 302–303
site promotion, 357–360
Site Specifications and Standards document
    clarified expectations, 256
    content requirements and sources, 249–250
    goal statements, 245
    technical requirements, 251–253
    URL selection, 253–255
    user profiles and scenarios, 246–249
site sponsor
    competitive research, 230–231
    content area research, 226–228
    information about site sponsor, 229–230
    pre-launch sign-off, 357
    prototype review and approval, 322
    research and study, 229–230
SIZE attribute
    changing font size, 96
    form input fields, 213
skills assessment worksheet, 69
software piracy, 371
source code, viewing, 41–42
space characters
    in HTML documents, 45
    non-breaking, code for, 145
special characters, 90–91
splash pages, 297, 382

SRC attribute, 264–265
SSL (Secure Sockets Layer), 373
start tags, 36
storyboards, 320–321
structures, Web site
    catalog, 301, 303
    grid, 297–298
    linear, 297–298, 299
    mesh, 301
    pyramid/hierarchical, 298–300
    star/cluster, 300–301
    tutorial, 301, 302
Stuffit Expander, 353
style (Web site look and feel), 110–111
styles
    of bullets in unordered lists, 203–204
    of numbers in ordered lists, 205
    of text, controlling, 93, 95–96
style sheets
    adaptability guidelines, 194, 196–197
    efficient use of, 323
    function of, 35–36
sublists, 209
submit button, 219
subordinate relations, 294
superordinate relations, 294
SVG (Scalable Vector Graphics) format, 311

T

tabbing order, adaptability guidelines for, 195
tab characters, in HTML documents, 45
tables
    accessibility guidelines, 193–194
    alignment, 141
    background color, 151
    borders, 138, 154
    cells spanning columns/rows, 141–142
    collapsed cells, 145
    column width, 139
    formatting with FONT, 150
    images in, 273
    for layout control, 152, 153, 273, 323
    lists in, 210
    nested, 153
    seamless, 154
    spacing and padding, 146–147
    stacked, 152
    width, 139
TABLE tag
    ALIGN attribute, 141
    BGCOLOR attribute, 151
    BORDER attribute, 138
    CELLPADDING attribute, 146

    CELLSPACING attribute, 147
    function of, 136–137
    HEIGHT attribute, 139–140
    WIDTH attribute, 139
tags
    defined, 36
    nesting of, 93
target market, studying, 230
task-oriented Web sites, 76–77
TCP/IP (Transmission Control Protocol/Internet Protocol), 14
TD element, 148
TD tag
    ALIGN attribute, 149
    BGCOLOR attribute, 151
    COLSPAN attribute, 141–142
    function of, 137
    ROWSPAN attribute, 141–142
    WIDTH attribute, 139
telecommuting, 7
templates, HTML, 43–44
templates, page, 323
Teoma, 21
testing
    accessibility, 199–200, 355–356
    overview, 59
    page load times, 355
    pre-launch, 354–357
    usability, 178–179
text
    alignment, 46, 87
    changing color of, 98
    changing font of, 95
    changing size of, 96
    changing style of, 93
    converting print to digital, 308–309
    paragraph alignment, 46
TEXTAREA tag
    COLS attribute, 218–219
    ROWS attribute, 219
text editors, 37
3G wireless technology, 33
TH tag, 150
thumbnail images, 335
time lines, 258–259
Times New Roman, 175
TITLE tag, 36, 44
Tollett, John, 346–347
Tomlinson, Ray, 14
tools, choosing, 286–288
transformative technologies, 5–6
"transitional" HTML, 35
Transmission Control Protocol. *See* TCP/IP
transparent GIF images, 262
TR tag, 137
TYPE attribute
    bullet style of unordered lists, 203–204
    numbering style of ordered lists, 205